Lecture Notes in Computer Science   9619

Commenced Publication in 1973
Founding and Former Series Editors:
Gerhard Goos, Juris Hartmanis, and Jan van Leeuwen

More information about this series at http://www.springer.com/series/7408

Maya Daneva · Oscar Pastor (Eds.)

Requirements Engineering: Foundation for Software Quality

22nd International Working Conference, REFSQ 2016
Gothenburg, Sweden, March 14–17, 2016
Proceedings

 Springer

Editors
Maya Daneva
University of Twente
Enschede
The Netherlands

Oscar Pastor
Universidad Politècnica de Valencia
Valencia
Spain

ISSN 0302-9743 ISSN 1611-3349 (electronic)
Lecture Notes in Computer Science
ISBN 978-3-319-30281-2 ISBN 978-3-319-30282-9 (eBook)
DOI 10.1007/978-3-319-30282-9

Library of Congress Control Number: 2016931187

LNCS Sublibrary: SL2 – Programming and Software Engineering

This Springer imprint is published by SpringerNature
The registered company is Springer International Publishing AG Switzerland

Preface

Welcome to the proceedings of the 22nd edition of REFSQ: the International Working Conference on Requirements Engineering – Foundation for Software Quality!

Requirements engineering (RE) has been recognized as a critical factor that impacts the quality of software, systems, and services. Since the term "requirements engineering" was coined, the community of practitioners and researchers has been working tirelessly on the identification, characterization, and evaluation of the multifaceted relationships between aspects of requirements processes, artifacts, and methods and aspects of software quality. The REFSQ working conference series has been well established as Europe's premier meeting place in RE and as one of the leading international forums dedicated to the conversation on RE and its many relationships to quality.

The first REFSQ was celebrated in 1994, in Utrecht, The Netherlands. Since then, the REFSQ community has been steadily growing and in 2010 REFSQ became a stand-alone conference. The five REFSQ editions in the period of 2010–2015 were hosted in Essen, Germany, and were organized by the Software Systems Engineering Team, under the leadership of Klaus Pohl, of the Ruhr Institute for Software Technology at the University of Duisburg-Essen, Germany. During March 14–17, 2016, we welcomed participants to REFSQ 2016, which was celebrated in Gothenburg, Sweden. The 22nd edition of REFSQ built upon the REFSQ editions hosted until 2015. It was a further step toward establishing an inclusive forum in which experienced researchers, PhD candidates, practitioners, and students can inform each other, learn about, discuss, and advance the state-of-the-art research and practice in the discipline of RE. We chose "Understanding an Ever-Changing World Through the Right Requirements" as the REFSQ 2016 special theme, in order to encourage submissions that highlight the utilization of RE for solving our society's great problems. Our theme invited an inclusive conversation covering various perspectives, such as systems engineering, economics, and management. A particular aspect of our 2016 theme is its strong focus on software ecosystems and inter-organizational collaboration, for example, between established companies and start-ups, in order to increase innovation capabilities, reduce time to market, and support development for and in software ecosystems.

We are pleased to present this volume comprising the REFSQ 2016 proceedings. It features 21 papers included in the technical program of REFSQ 2016 and presented during the conference. These papers were selected by an international committee of leading experts in RE who are affiliated with companies, universities, and academic institutions. The committee evaluated the papers via a thorough peer-review process. This year, 80 abstracts were initially submitted from 28 countries. Eleven abstracts were not followed up by papers and five abstracts were withdrawn. The review process included 64 papers. Each paper was reviewed by three members of the REFSQ 2016 Program Committee. An extensive online discussion among the Program Committee members enriched the reviews during the evaluation of the possible decision-making outcomes for each paper. During a face-to-face Program Committee meeting that took place on December 4, 2015, in Gothenburg, Sweden, the papers were discussed and selected for inclusion in the conference proceedings. Selected authors of rejected papers were encouraged to submit their papers to the REFSQ 2016 workshops.

The REFSQ 2016 conference was organized as a three-day symposium. Two conference days were devoted to presentation and discussion of scientific papers. These two days were connected to the conference theme with a keynote, an invited talk, and poster presentations. The keynote speaker was Magne Jørgenssen from Simula, Norway. The invited talk was delivered by Roel Wieringa from the University of Twente, The Netherlands. One conference day was devoted to presentation and discussion of RE research methodology and industry experiences. On that day, two tracks ran in parallel: the Industry Track, organized by Ivica Crnkovic, and the Research Methodology Track, organized by Barbara Paech and Oscar Dieste. In a joint plenary session, researchers met with practitioners from industry to discuss how to manage requirements in ecosystems.

REFSQ 2016 would not have been possible without the engagement and support of many individuals who contributed in many different ways. As program co-chairs, we would like to thank the REFSQ Steering Committee members, in particular Klaus Pohl, Bjorn Regnell, and Xavier Franch for their availability and for the excellent guidance they provided. We are indebted to Kurt Schneider and Samuel Fricker, the REFSQ 2015 co-chairs, for their extremely helpful advice. We are grateful to all the members of the Program Committee for their timely and thorough reviews of the submissions and for their time dedicated to the online discussion and the face-to-face meeting. In particular, we thank those Program Committee members who volunteered to serve in the role of mentor, shepherd, or gatekeeper to authors of conditionally accepted papers. We would like to thank Eric Knauss, leading the Local Organization at Calmers University, for his ongoing support and determination to make sure all operational processes ran smoothly at all times. We are grateful to the chairs, who organized the various events included in REFSQ 2016:

- Barbara Paech and Oscar Dieste, chairs of the Research Methodology Track
- Ivica Crnkovic, the REFSQ 2016 Industry Track chair
- Andrea Herrmann and Andreas Opdahl, the REFSQ 2016 workshop chairs
- Xavier Franch and Jennifer Horkoff, chairs of the Doctoral Symposium
- Sergio España and Kai Petersen, chairs of the Poster and Tools Session

Finally, we would like to thank Tobias Kauffmann and Vanessa Stricker for their excellent work in coordinating the background organization processes, and Anna Kramer for her support in preparing this volume.

All the research papers from the REFSQ 2016 main conference track and the Research Methodology Track can be found in the present proceedings. The papers included in the satellite events can be found in the REFSQ 2016 workshop proceedings published with CEUR.

We hope this volume provides an informative perspective on the conversations that shape the REFSQ 2016 conference. We hope you will find research results and truly new ideas that help us to better understand our changing world through the right requirements!

January 2016

Maya Daneva
Oscar Pastor

Organization

Program Committee

Joao Araujo	Universidade Nova de Lisboa, Portugal
Travis Breaux	Software engineering Institute, USA
Dan Berry	University of Waterloo, Canada
Nelly Bencomo	Aston University, UK
Sjaak Brinkkemper	Utrecht University, The Netherlands
David Callele	University of Saskatchewan, Canada
Eya Ben Charrada	University of Zürich, Switzerland
Nelly Condori Fernandez	Free University of Amsterdam, The Netherlands
Oscar Dieste	Universidad Politécnica de Madrid, Spain
Jörg Dörr	Fraunhofer IESE, Germany
Sergio España	Utrecht University, The Netherlands
Xavier Franch	Universitat Politècnica de Catalunya, Spain
Samuel Fricker	Blekinge Institute of Technology, Sweden
Vincenzo Gervasi	University of Pisa, Italy
Smita Ghaisas	Tata Consulting Services R&D, India
Giovanni Giachetti	Universidad Andrés Bello, Chile
Martin Glinz	University of Zürich, Switzerland
Tony Gorschek	Blekinge Institute of Technology, Sweden
Olly Gotel	Independent Researcher, USA
Paul Gruenbacher	Johannes Kepler Universität Linz, Austria
Renata Guizzardi	UFES, Brazil
Andrea Herrmann	Herrmann & Ehrlich, Germany
Jennifer Horkoff	City University, UK
Frank Houdek	Daimler, Germany
Erik Kamsties	University of Applied Sciences, Dortmund, Germany
Hermann Kaindl	TU Wien, Austria
Mohamad Kassab	Penn State University, USA
Marjo Kauppinen	Aalto University, Finland
Eric Knauss	Chalmers University of Gothenburg, Sweden
Anne Koziolek	Karlsruhe Institute of Technology, Germany
Kim Lauenroth	Adesso, Germany
Pericles Loucopoulos	University of Manchester, UK
Nazim Madhavji	University of Western Ontario, Canada
Patrick Mäder	Technical University Ilmenau, Germany
Andrey Maglyas	Lappeenranta University of Technology, Finland
Sabrina Marczak	PUCRS, Brazil

Fabio Massacci	University of Trento, Italy
Raimundas Matulevicius	University of Tartu, Estonia
Daniel Mendez	Technical University of Munich, Germany
John Mylopoulos	University of Trento, Italy
Cornelius Ncube	Bournemouth University, UK
Andreas Opdahl	University of Bergen, Norway
Olga Ormandjieva	Concordia University, Canada
Barbara Paech	University of Heidelberg, Germany
Anna Perini	Fondazione Bruno Kessler, Italy
Anne Persson	University of Skövde, Sweden
Kai Petersen	Blekinge Institute of Technology, Sweden
Klaus Pohl	University of Duisburg-Essen, Germany
Birgit Penzenstädler	University of California Long Beach, USA
Rosilawati Razali	Universiti Kebangsaan, Malaysia
Björn Regnell	University of Lund, Sweden
Camille Salinesi	Université Paris 1 – Sorbonne, France
Peter Sawyer	Lancaster University, UK
Kurt Schneider	University of Hannover, Germany
Norbert Seyff	University of Zürich, Switzerland
Guttorm Sindre	NTNU, Norway
Monique Snoeck	KU Leuven, Belgium
Thorsten Weyer	University of Duisburg-Essen, Germany
Roel Wieringa	University of Twente, The Netherlands
Krzysztof Wnuk	Blekinge Institute of Technology, Sweden
Didar Zowghi	University of Technology Sydney, Australia

Additional Reviewers

Klaas Sikkel	University of Twente, The Netherlands
Zornitza Bakalova	Deutsche Post, Germany

Sponsors

Platinum Level Sponsors

Gold Level Sponsors

Silver Level Sponsors

INFORMATION AND COMMUNICATION
TECHNOLOGY   A CHALMERS
AREA OF ADVANCE

Partners

UNIVERSITY OF TWENTE.

Contents

Requirements Engineering in the Automotive Domain

Empirical Studies in Requirements Engineering

Requirements Engineering Foundations

Human Factors in Requirements Engineering

Research Methodology in Requirements Engineering

Decision Making in Requirements Engineering

Risk-Aware Multi-stakeholder Next Release Planning Using Multi-objective Optimization

Antonio Mauricio Pitangueira[1]([⊠]), Paolo Tonella[2], Angelo Susi[2],
Rita Suzana Maciel[1], and Marcio Barros[3]

[1] Computer Science Department, Federal University of Bahia, Bahia, Brazil
antonio.mauricio@ifba.edu.br, ritasuzana@dcc.ufba.br
[2] Software Engineering Research Unit, Fondazione Bruno Kessler, Trento, Italy
{tonella,susi}@fbk.eu
[3] Post-graduate Information Systems Program-Unirio, Rio de Janeiro, Brazil
marcio.barros@uniriotec.br

Abstract. [**Context and motivation**]: Software requirements selection
is an essential task in the software development process. It consists of
finding the best requirement set for each software release, considering several requirements characteristics, such as precedences and multiple conflicting objectives, such as stakeholders' perceived value, cost and risk.
[**Question/Problem**]: However, in this scenario, important information
about the variability involved in the requirements values estimation are
discarded and might expose the company to a risk when selecting a solution. [**Principal ideas/results**]: We propose a novel approach to the risk-
aware multi-objective next release problem and implemented our approach
by means of a satisfiability modulo theory solver. We aim at improving
the decision quality by reducing the risk associated with the stakeholder
dissatisfaction as related to the variability of the value estimation made
by these stakeholders. [**Contribution**]: Results show that Pareto-optimal
solutions exist where a major risk reduction can be achieved at the price
of a minor penalty in the value-cost trade-off.

Keywords: Risk-aware decision making · Next release problem ·
Multi-stakeholder

1 Introduction

Software requirements selection for the next software release has an important
role, but is also a quite difficult task, in software development. In fact, the
identification of an optimal subset of candidate requirements for the next release
involves a complex trade-off among attributes of the requirements, such as their
value, cost and risk, which are usually perceived quite differently by different
stakeholders (e.g., users vs. developers vs. salesmen vs. managers) [31]. The
optimization process for the selection of a set of requirements from a whole set
of candidate requirements for the next version of the software is called the Next

© Springer International Publishing Switzerland 2016
M. Daneva and O. Pastor (Eds.): REFSQ 2016, LNCS 9619, pp. 3–18, 2016.
DOI: 10.1007/978-3-319-30282-9_1

Release Problem (NRP) [2]. When it involves multiple objectives, the problem is named Multiple-Objective Next Release Problem (MONRP) [31].

In real world situations, selecting the requirements for the next software release is a complex decision-making process because the solution space is combinatorial, with a huge number of combinations due to multiple objectives and different stakeholders. Because of such issues, the research on NRP/MONRP has resorted to single/multi-objective optimization algorithms and in particular to Search-Based Software Engineering (SBSE) approaches [4,9,14]. Among them, the most widely used techniques include genetic and other meta-heuristic algorithms, integer linear programming and hybrid methods [14,23,30].

To make the problem treatable, existing approaches simplify the real world scenario and model the different opinions of the stakeholders as their (weighted) average value estimates. However, such approximation discards important information about the variability involved in the value estimates and ignores the risk of selecting a solution that, although optimal in terms of average cost-value trade-off, might expose the company to a major risk associated with a high range of revenue values perceived by/delivered to different stakeholders. For instance, two candidate solutions might be identified as approximately equivalent in terms of average value and cost, but one might deliver all the value to a single customer; the other might deliver it uniformly across all customers. The risk of delivering a software release that is extremely satisfactory for a subgroup of stakeholders, while being at the same time largely unsatisfactory for another subgroup is not taken into account at all by existing approaches. We call such risk the *stakeholder dissatisfaction risk*. It is strictly related to stakeholder variability and to different perspectives of the stakeholders estimates, and it manifests itself with the occurrence of major fluctuations in the value assigned to a requirement.

In this paper, we re-formulate MONRP so as to explicitly include the risk associated with the presence of multiple stakeholders. We consider the *stakeholder dissatisfaction risk*, measured by the variance in the values assigned by different stakeholders to each requirement. We have implemented a solution to the problem based on Satisfiability Modulo Theory (SMT), which has been successfully used in other fields, such as schedule planning, graph problems and software/hardware verification [8,24]. We mapped our Risk-Aware formulation of MONRP (RA-MONRP) to an SMT problem, where requirements selection is modelled as a set of Boolean variables and logical constraints translate the multiple objectives to be optimized. The results obtained on two real world case studies indicate that an SMT solver can scale to the typical size of RA-MONRP instances and that the stakeholder dissatisfaction risk can be minimized with minimum impact on the other objectives being optimized. For instance, in one of our datasets we have identified solutions in which risk can be decreased up to 7.6 % by accepting a 0.15 % increase in cost and a 2.6 % loss in value.

The paper is structured as follows: in Sect. 2 we present the related work. Section 3 describes the background for our work and Sect. 4 details the RA-MONRP formulation of the problem considered in our work. In Sect. 5 we present the proposed approach, while Sect. 6 describes the implementation. Section 7 discusses the experimental data obtained from two real world case studies. Conclusions and future work are presented in Sect. 8.

2   Related Work

Albeit meta-heuristic algorithms have been extensively applied to NRP/ MONRP, only a few studies have considered risk and uncertainty as objectives. A comprehensive overview on search-based techniques tackling NRP/MONRP is provided by Pitangueira et al. [23].

Ruhe and Gree [26] developed quantitative studies in software release planning under risk and resource constraints. In this work, a risk factor is estimated for each requirement and a maximum risk reference value is calculated for each release. Each risk may refer to any event that potentially might affect the schedule with negative consequences on the final project results. The authors created the tool EVOLVE+, implementing various forms of genetic algorithms, which were used in a sample project with small instances based on artificial data.

Colares et al. [6] elaborated a multi-objective formulation for release planning taking into account the maximization of (average) stakeholders' satisfaction and the minimization of project risks, while respecting the available resources and requirements interdependencies. A risk value varying from 0 (lowest) to 5 (highest) is associated with each requirement. The multi-objective genetic algorithm NSGA-II was used to find the solution set and a comparison with a manually defined solution was carried out, showing that the approach proposed by the authors outperforms the human-based solution.

A MONRP formulation was proposed by Brasil et al. [3] taking into account stakeholders' satisfaction, business value and risk management, with the objective of implementing the requirements with high risks as early as possible. For the empirical validation, artificial data have been used and the problem was solved using two meta-heuristic techniques, NSGA-II and MOCell, the latter exhibiting better spread in all instances and faster execution time.

A Robust Next Release Problem was formulated by Li et al. [16], considering the maximization of revenue, the minimization of cost and the reduction of the uncertainty size, which measures the uncertainty related to the MONRP solutions. In this paper, the authors simulated uncertainty by means of stochastic variables. To solve the problem, a variation of Monte-Carlo simulation was developed and applied to a real world data set.

The key difference between our approach to risk modelling and the existing works is that we consider an intrinsic risk factor, associated with the presence of multiple stakeholders, i.e. the stakeholder dissatisfaction risk, while previous research assume that risk factors are additional, externally provided objectives to be optimized [3,6,26] or that risk is associated with uncertainty, i.e. stochastic fluctuations around the nominal values of revenue and cost [16]. We are the first to address the risk associated with the multiple viewpoints and opinions of different stakeholders.

3   Background on Next Release Problem

The original formulation of NRP by Bagnall et al. [2] is a constrained maximization problem: maximize the stakeholders' satisfaction without exceeding the total budget available. In this formulation, there is a set of n possible software requirements $R = \{R_1, \ldots, R_n\}$ which are offered to the set $S = \{S_1, \ldots, S_m\}$ of stakeholders. Each requirement R_i has an associated cost, forming a cost vector $cost = [cost_1, \ldots, cost_n]$. Each stakeholder has a degree of importance for the company, expressed as a set of relative weights $W = \{w_1, \ldots, w_m\}$ associated respectively with each stakeholder in S.

The importance of a requirement may differ from stakeholder to stakeholder [9]. Thus, the importance that a requirement R_i has for stakeholder j is modelled as $value(R_i, S_j)$, where a value greater than 0 indicates that stakeholder S_j needs the requirement R_i, while 0 indicates s/he does not [14]. Under these assumptions, the overall stakeholder satisfaction for a given requirement is measured as a weighted average of importance values for all the stakeholders: $avgvalue_i = \sum_{j=1}^{m} w_j \cdot value(R_i, S_j)$, with $\sum_{j=1}^{m} w_j = 1$.

A solution to NRP is a vector $x = [x_1, x_2, \ldots, x_n]$ representing a subset of R, where $x_i \in \{1, 0\}$, depending on whether R_i is included or not in the next release. In addition, precedence constraints and technological dependencies must often be enforced, hence restricting the admissible solution space. A precedence (resp. dependency) between R_i and R_j (resp. R_j and R_i) may be understood as a pair of requirements $\langle R_i, R_j \rangle$ interpreted as follows: if R_j is included in the next release, R_i must be included as well. In other words, the implication $x_j \Rightarrow x_i$ must hold. Let $D = \{\langle R_i, R_j \rangle, \ldots\}$ be the set of precedences/dependencies. Thus, the constrained single objective NRP can be formalized as in Eq. (1), where B is the budget designated by the company for the next release.

$$\text{Max} \sum_{i=1}^{n} x_i \cdot avgvalue_i \qquad \begin{aligned} &\text{subject to } \sum_{i=1}^{n} cost_i \cdot x_i \leq B \\ &\text{and } \bigwedge_{\langle R_i, R_j \rangle \in D} (x_j \Rightarrow x_i) \end{aligned} \qquad (1)$$

Starting from this formulation, Zhang et al. [31] elaborated the Multi-Objective Next Release Problem (MONRP), considering the maximization of the value for the company and minimization of the total cost required to implement the selected requirements. This formulation is presented in Eq. (2). The MONRP is not limited to two-objectives and multiple conflicting objectives, such as cost, value, utility, uncertainty and risk, can be added to the formulation [3,4,20].

$$\begin{cases} \text{Min} \sum_{i=1}^{n} cost_i \cdot x_i \\ \text{Max} \sum_{i=1}^{n} avgval_i \cdot x_i \end{cases} \qquad \text{subject to } \bigwedge_{\langle R_i, R_j \rangle \in D} (x_j \Rightarrow x_i). \qquad (2)$$

4 Managing Multiple Stakeholders and Risk

The problem of software requirements selection involves unstructured or loosely structured decision making characterized by a diversity of factors, such as complexity, risk, uncertainty, and multiple stakeholders participating in the decision process [26]. In the presence of multiple stakeholders, selecting a subset of requirement is a challenging task because stakeholders may have different perceptions and opinions. Consequently, their preferences may be conflicting [21] and their value assessments may vary a lot, because of the different viewpoints [28]. Moreover, requirements dependencies and technological constraints must be taken into account as well. In such an environment, the decision becomes very complex [9,14] and prone to the stakeholder dissatisfaction risk. The inherent uncertainty associated with such decision making process can be mitigated only if risk is explicitly taken into account and minimized [13,26].

According to Lamsweerde [27], a *risk* is an uncertainty factor whose occurrence may result in a loss of satisfaction of a corresponding objective and it can be said to have a negative impact on such objective. A risk has a likelihood of occurrence and one or several undesirable consequences associated with it, and each consequence has a severity in terms of degree of loss of satisfaction of the corresponding objective [27]. Risk analysis is frequently used in software development to identify events or situations that may have a negative impact on a software project [1,11,12].

Risks may be assessed in a qualitative or quantitative way. For instance, the probability of occurrence of a risk may be measured in an ordinal scale from 'very unlikely' to 'very likely', and its impact from 'negligible' to 'catastrophic', according to the severity of its consequences [27]. On the quantitative side, probability values, probability intervals, numerical scales, and standard deviation are used to measure risk [3,11,19,25,27].

The risk considered in this work is associated with multiple stakeholders involved in the decision making process and more specifically with the variability of their estimates of value. A high variability in the estimates indicates that there is a high probability of dissatisfaction of one or more stakeholders. The impact of such dissatisfaction depends on the value loss faced by the affected stakeholders. Hence, including a requirement with highly variable value estimates in the next release exposes the software company to the risk of stakeholder dissatisfaction and to the associated negative impact of loosing their support to the project. On the contrary, including a requirement with value estimates that are consistent among the stakeholders ensures that the value added by this requirement is delivered uniformly to all stakeholders, with a minimal risk of dissatisfaction.

Hence, we measure the intrinsic risk factor associated with the stakeholder variability and possibility of dissatisfaction as the weighted standard deviation of the value estimates [17,22]: $risk_i = \sum_j w_j \cdot (value(R_i, S_j) - avgval_i)^2 / n$. Correspondingly, the RA-MONRP can be formalized as follows:

$$
\begin{cases}
\text{Min } \sum_{i=1}^{n} cost_i \cdot x_i \\
\text{Max } \sum_{i=1}^{n} avgval_i \cdot x_i \qquad \text{subject to} \quad \bigwedge_{\langle R_i, R_j \rangle \in D} (x_j \Rightarrow x_i) \qquad (3) \\
\text{Min } \sum_{i=1}^{n} risk_i \cdot x_i
\end{cases}
$$

A Pareto-optimal solution is a triple $\langle total\ cost,\ total\ avgval,\ total\ risk \rangle$, as well as the associated subset of requirements assigned to the next release (those for which the solution returns $x_i = 1$). Additional constraints can be enforced, such as maximum cost budget (see Sect. 3), minimum delivered value, maximum acceptable risk or region of interest, specifying a lower bound and an upper bound for each objective. If the variability associated with the cost estimates is also a risk factor, RA-MONRP can be easily extended from three to four objectives, the fourth one measuring the weighted standard deviation of the developers' cost estimates. In our experience, stakeholders variability is typically much more important than the developers variability, but of course this might change from context to context.

5   Approach

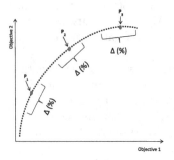

Figure 1 shows an overview and the main elements in our approach. The first step of the optimization process is to generate the Pareto front for the two objectives *cost* and *avgval*. Then, the stakeholders choose some Pareto solutions (i.e. points P_n) based on the acceptability of their value-cost trade-off; for example P_1, P_2 and P_3 in the figure. Once these points are selected, the stakeholders decide a tolerance margin for the risk-aware solutions to be analyzed, i.e., a neighbourhood is chosen and expressed in terms of an acceptable percentage variation (Δ) of cost and value. For instance, 5 % for cost and 4 % for avgval. These bounds are included in the three objective formulation (cost, avgval and risk) of RA-MONRP as constraints to the problem. Finally, an SMT solver is executed on the RA-MONRP formulation (see Sect. 4) and the solutions (triples $\langle cost,\ avgval,\ risk\rangle$) are presented for each region of interest to the stakeholders, who then can start an informed decision making process to plan for the next software release. The advantage of using an SMT solver instead of a meta-heuristic algorithm is that it gives the exact solution to the problem (i.e. the exact Pareto front). When the problem size increases, making the SMT solver inapplicable, meta-heuristic algorithms are resorted to, in order to obtain anyway an approximate, sub-optimal solution. In our experiments on two real world case studies, the SMT solver was able to handle all requirements and to produce the exact Pareto fronts for them.

Fig. 1. Regions of interest for the solutions P1, P2, P3

6   Implementation

We have implemented our approach using two quite popular and widely used SMT solvers to MONRP and RA-MONRP: Yices [10] and Z3 [7]. We have implemented our approach twice to see if there is any advantage associated with the use of one particular SMT solver as compared to another one. The pseudo code implementation for MONRP using Yices is shown in Algorithm 1.

Algorithm 1. Yices implementation

 1: Input: cost and avgval for each requirement
 2: Output: exact Pareto front
 3: Initialize lastcost and lastavgval with the minimum possible cost and avgval
 4: **while** lastcost $\leq$ totalcost **do**
 5:     InvokeYices ();
 6:     **if** yicesresult == SAT **then**
 7:         Update the Pareto solution set;
 8:         Let lastavgval = lastavgval + 1;
 9:     **else**
10:         Let lastcost = lastcost + 1;
11:     **end if**
12: **end while**

The Yices implementation searches the solution space by fixing the minimum cost (*lastcost*) and increasing the value (*lastavgvalue*) to find the maximum value for such minimum cost. If the MONRP formulation is satisfiable (SAT) according to Yices (invoked at line 5), the solution set and variables are updated. Otherwise, it means that there does not exist any solution that satisfies the current conditions (Yices returns UNSAT). When SAT is returned, our implementation increases *avgval*, so as to try to find a solution with the same cost and higher value. When UNSAT is returned, the cost is increased and the search is performed again to find solutions with higher cost and higher value. The loop stops when the total cost (for instance, the company budget available) is reached. Each solution found by Yices consists of the cost, the value and the requirements selected by the solution.

The other SMT solver used to implement our approach is Z3 [7]. We encoded the objective functions (max value and min cost) directly inside a Z3 template. In the Z3 template, each requirement is a Boolean variable, which has an associated cost and value. The relations between the requirements, such as precedence and dependency, are expressed as a logical implications. The following expression is used to associate a non zero cost to the selected requirements: (assert (and $(= \text{cost}_i$ (ite R_i costR_i 0)) $(\leq 0 \text{ cost}_i$) $(\leq \text{cost}_i \text{ costR}_i)$)). If requirement R_i is selected (ite = if-then-else), cost_i is equal to costR_i; otherwise it is zero. Similar expressions are used to associate a non zero value to the selected requirements. The Z3 template can be easily extended with variations, such as including more objectives, specifying a region of interest in the search space and adding further constraints.

7   Experimental Results

7.1   Case Study

The proposed approach was evaluated on two real data sets [15]. The first one (dataset-1) is based on the word processor Microsoft Word and it comes with 50 requirements and 4 stakeholders. The second (dataset-2) has 25 requirements

and 9 stakeholders and it is related to *ReleasePlanner*[TM], a proprietary decision support system used for the generation of strategic and operational release
planning[1]. We used these two datasets because they are from real world projects
and because they include detailed information and requirements description. It
is generally quite difficult to find real datasets with the information needed to
conduct our study: requirements cost estimates, direct precedence and dependencies between requirements and stakeholders information about the expected rev-
enue/value. The two chosen datasets include all such information. Moreover, we
are interested in the risk associated with the value perceived by different stakeholders. The two chosen datasets include multiple stakeholders who assigned
different levels of importance/revenue to each requirement, highlighting their
different wishes, sometimes in disagreement among each other.

7.2   Research Questions

The experiments we conducted aim at answering the following research questions:

– **RQ1 (Impact of Risk Reduction).** *Is it possible to reduce the stakeholder
  dissatisfaction risk with minimum impact on cost and value?*

   In order to answer this question, we focused on specific regions of interest
identified in the Pareto front. Each region was obtained by considering various
budget scenarios (small, medium or large budget available for the next release)
and by setting a lower bound and an upper bound percentage variation respectively for value and cost. To analyze the risk impact on cost and value, each
solution produced by the SMT solver (applied to RA-MONRP) is presented in
a histogram with the respective percentage distance to the closest, risk-unaware
solution. The objective is to provide the stakeholders with a way to compare the
RA-MONRP solutions and to support their decision making process, taking into
account risk reduction in addition to cost and value optimization.

– **RQ2 (Scalability).** *What is the scalability of the approach when using an
  SMT solver for MONRP/RA-MONRP optimization?*

   To test the scalability of our approach, we investigated the execution time
required to obtain the exact Pareto fronts using Yices and Z3. We also performed
initial comparisons with an approximate meta-heuristic algorithm, NSGA-II,
which might be required to scale to larger case studies than the two real ones
considered in our experiments. We have performed the experiments on a Red
Hat Enterprise Linux Workstation, core(TM) i7 CPU@ 2.80 GHz, 4 GB RAM.

7.3   Results

Tables 1 and 2 show the results for the first step of our approach, i.e. the total
time to obtain the solutions and the quantity of Pareto optimal solutions found

---

[1] https://www.releaseplanner.com.

for the bi-objective formulation (MONRP). Figures 2 and 3 show the Pareto fronts for each dataset. It can be noticed that Yices produced more solutions than Z3, in both cases. The reason is that Yices included weak Pareto solutions, where one objective is not different among some solutions, while the other objectives are not worse [5]. On the contrary, Z3 produced only strong Pareto solutions. If restricted to the strong Pareto front, the two outcomes become identical.

Table 1. Results for dataset-1

Solver	Time(s)	Solutions
Yices	538658	385
Z3	195051	285

Table 2. Results for dataset-2

Solver	Time(s)	Solutions
Yices	2939	146
Z3	56.21	143

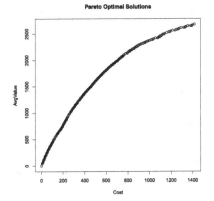

Fig. 2. Pareto front for dataset-1   **Fig. 3.** Pareto front for dataset-2

We artificially increased the number of objectives and requirements, to further compare the scalability of Yices vs. Z3. Results (not shown due to lack of space) indicate that Yices exhibits a dramatic drop in performance, taking days to find the solutions and sometimes never terminating [24,29], because of the time spent to prove the infeasibility of some instances [18]. The performance degradation of Z3 was instead much smoother. Due to these observations, we decided to focus our experiments on the Z3 SMT solver.

Table 3. Results by regions of interest for dataset-1

	Cost	avgval	Region	Δ	Solutions	Time(s)
P1	202	790	ROI 1	5 %	32	29.53
P2	958	2331	ROI 2	2 %	53	26.63
P3	1335	2629	ROI 3	3 %	40	0.60

Table 4. Results by regions of interest for dataset-2

	Cost	avgval	Region	Δ	Solutions	Time(s)
P1	9150	493	ROI 1	5 %	21	1.96
P2	18415	775	ROI 2	5 %	42	12.92
P3	32910	1033	ROI 3	5 %	36	0.24

We manually identified three Regions Of Interest (ROI) in each Pareto front, associated respectively with a small, medium or large budget available for the next release. Z3 was then executed to get solutions in each region of interest within the percentage variations allowed for cost and value. The results are summarized in Tables 3 and 4. The tables show the cost and average value (avgval) of the identified solutions (points P1, P2, P3) belonging to the three different ROI. They also report the required tolerance margin for cost and value percentage variation (Δ) and the number of solutions found around solutions P1, P2, and P3 in the required tolerance. The time for the calculation of these solutions is also reported.

For each ROI in each dataset, we generated three different views of the solutions: (1) a table and a histogram showing the triples ⟨cost, value, risk⟩ for each solution; (2) a table and a histogram showing the percentage variations of cost, value and risk for each solution, as compared to the closest risk-unaware (MONRP) solution; and (3) a tendency plot showing the same percentage variations through connected line segments. In our experience, the histogram with the percentage variations is the most useful view to explore the alternative scenarios of variation and to support the final decision. The tendency plot, on the other hand, clearly depicts the spread of value loss/gain against the risk reduction/increase. With no loss of generality, due to lack of space, one sample of views (2) and (3) is presented for each dataset.

Figure 4 shows the data for P3 in dataset-2 (see Table 4; $\Delta = 5\%$). The diagram shows the percentage variations for 21 of the 36 solutions around Solution 23 that is the initial MONRP solution, chosen in ROI 3. Solution 23 correspondingly has no percentage variation for any objective (all values equal to

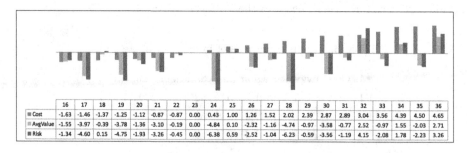

	16	17	18	19	20	21	22	23	24	25	26	27	28	29	30	31	32	33	34	35	36
▪ Cost	-1.63	-1.46	-1.37	-1.25	-1.12	-0.87	-0.87	0.00	0.43	1.00	1.26	1.52	2.02	2.39	2.87	2.89	3.04	3.56	4.39	4.50	4.65
▪ AvgValue	-1.55	-3.97	-0.39	-3.78	-1.36	-3.10	-0.19	0.00	-4.84	0.10	-2.32	-1.16	-4.74	-0.97	-3.58	-0.77	2.52	-0.97	1.55	-2.03	2.71
▪ Risk	-1.34	-4.60	0.15	-4.75	-1.93	-3.26	-0.45	0.00	-6.38	0.59	-2.52	-1.04	-6.23	-0.59	-3.56	-1.19	4.15	-2.08	1.78	-2.23	3.26

Fig. 4. Histogram of percentage variation for ROI 3 (dataset-2)

zero). All the other solutions produced for ROI 3 exhibit some (positive or negative) variation for each objective. A negative variation on risk indicates that the
solution has lower risk than the initial MONRP solution. Similarly for cost and
value: negative/positive variations indicate lower/higher cost/value as compared
to the initial MONRP solution. Figure 5 shows the tendency plot for dataset-
2 (ROI 3). Variation histogram and tendency plot for dataset-1 (ROI 3) are
shown in Figs. 6 and 7. Each tendency plot presents all the solutions found while
the histograms (due to lack of space) show the solutions nearby the reference
point P_n.

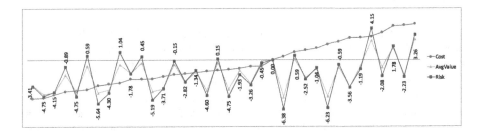

Fig. 5. Variation tendency for ROI 3 (dataset-2)

7.4   Discussion

From the plots reported in the previous section, it is quite apparent that interesting solutions, characterized by major dissatisfaction risk reduction at the
expense of minor cost increase and value decrease, do exist. Histograms (see
Figs. 4 and 6) and tendency plots (see Figs. 5 and 7) show scenarios with multiple possibilities that may be used to make a decision. In both datasets, there are
several solutions with slightly increased cost, lower risk and an impact on value
less than 2 %. Especially on dataset-2, higher risk reduction requires also higher
value decrease (see tendency plots).

For instance, for dataset-1 (see Fig. 6) a risk reduction as high as 7.69 %
(see Solution 31) can be achieved at the expense of just 0.15 % increased cost
and 2.66 % decreased value. For dataset-2 (see Fig. 4), a 6.38 % risk reduction
(see Solution 24) is achieved at minimal cost increase (0.43 %) but this time
with a not so negligible value decrease (4.84 %). In general, in dataset-2 we can
notice that risk reduction is paid in terms of value reduction much more than in
dataset-1 (compare the tendency plots in Figs. 5 and 7).

For what concerns the performance of the SMT solvers, Z3 is generally faster
than Yices. In the case of dataset-1 (which has twice the number of requirements
of dataset-2 and is hardly constrained by more than 60 precedence relations),
Yices' performance decreases severely, while Z3 remains relatively fast.

We conducted a preliminary comparison with NSGA-II. For the smallest dataset (dataset-2), using population size $= 100$, max evaluations $= 250000$

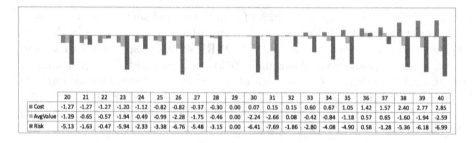

	20	21	22	23	24	25	26	27	28	29	30	31	32	33	34	35	36	37	38	39	40
■ Cost	-1.27	-1.27	-1.27	-1.20	-1.12	-0.82	-0.82	-0.37	-0.30	0.00	0.07	0.15	0.15	0.60	0.67	1.05	1.42	1.57	2.40	2.77	2.85
■ AvgValue	-1.29	-0.65	-0.57	-1.94	-0.49	-0.99	-2.28	-1.75	-0.46	0.00	-2.24	-2.66	0.08	-0.42	-0.84	-1.18	0.57	0.65	-1.60	-1.94	-2.59
■ Risk	-5.13	-1.63	-0.47	-5.94	-2.33	-3.38	-6.76	-5.48	-3.15	0.00	-6.41	-7.69	-1.86	-2.80	-4.08	-4.90	0.58	-1.28	-5.36	-6.18	-6.99

Fig. 6. Histogram of percentage variation for ROI 3 (dataset-1)

and 10 executions, the average execution time of NSGA-II was 5.19 s. For dataset-1 (50 requirements), NSGA-II with population size $= 300$, max evaluations $= 250000$ and 10 executions required an average execution time of 14.18 s. So, as expected NSGA-II is faster than the SMT solvers, but its solution is suboptimal (we indeed checked such suboptimality and found that several optimal solutions found by the SMT solver are missed by NSGA-II). SMT solvers are ensured to produce the exact Pareto front, so if they terminate within the given time limits, they should be preferred over NSGA-II.

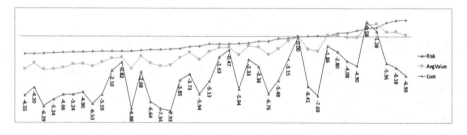

Fig. 7. Variation tendency for ROI 3 (dataset-1)

In summary, we can answer research questions RQ1 and RQ2 as follows:

RQ1: *The solutions produced by Z3 for RA-MONRP indicate that substantial stakeholder dissatisfaction risk reduction can be achieved with negligible impact on cost. The impact on value is generally small, but it depends on the specific dataset.*

RQ2: *Z3 was able to efficiently find the exact solutions to MONRP/RA-MONRP at acceptable computation time for both data sets.*

Our approach can be improved in several ways. Iterative, human-driven refinement of the solutions could be included in the process. After analyzing the solutions for a ROI, the stakeholders may decide to change the limits of a region by increasing/decreasing the bounds for the objectives. For instance, they may increase the limits for the loss of value, so as to explore more solutions, or they may want to start from a different two-objective solution. It is perfectly possible to put the human-in-the-loop to capture her/his preferences iteratively by successive refinements.

Overall, our approach showed the possibility to generate exact solutions for three objectives (cost, value, risk) in just a few seconds, once the regions of interest are identified by the stakeholders, even when the number of requirements is as high as 50 (dataset-1) and is hardly constrained.

8   Conclusions and Future Work

In this paper, we have proposed an approach to address the risk-aware multi-objective next release problem. The aim is to reduce the risk factor associated with different perceptions of value associated with different stakeholders and with different revenues delivered to different subgroups of stakeholders (stakeholder dissatisfaction risk). Our approach provides such risk reduction at the expense of a minimum impact on cost and value.

We conducted experiments on two real datasets of software requirements and results show that our approach can effectively find interesting solutions, even in a hard constrained scenario with several requirements and multiple stakeholders. In our future work, we plan to investigate scalability, by measuring how execution time varies in relation to the number of requirements and constraints of the problem. For this, we intend to create different scenarios in which the number of requirements and interdependencies is grown artificially, so as to test the execution time of SMT solvers and meta-heuristic algorithms like NSGA-II. Regarding the visualisation of the results, cluster analysis is a possibility that will be experimented, aiming at a better support for the interpretation of solutions, grouped into subsets by similarity.

In addition, we plan to conduct empirical studies involving human subjects to assess the acceptability and usability of our approach. We want to extend our approach so as to include the human-in-the-loop and capture the human preferences, for instance, for the selection of the tolerance margins in a ROI. We also plan to conduct a thorough comparison between SMT solvers and meta-heuristic algorithms applied to RA-MONRP, extending the preliminary evaluation reported in this paper.

Acknowledgments. We would like to thank Fitsum Meshesha Kifetew for his support to the implementation of the approach.

References

1. Asnar, Y., Giorgini, P., Mylopoulos, J.: Goal-driven risk assessment in requirements engineering. Requirements Eng. **16**, 101–116 (2011)
2. Bagnall, A., Rayward-Smith, V., Whittley, I.: The next release problem. Inf. Softw. Technol. **43**(14), 883–890 (2001)
3. Brasil, M.M.A., da Silva, T.G.N., de Freitas, F.G., de Souza, J.T., Cortés, M.I.: A multiobjective optimization approach to the software release planning with undefined number of releases and interdependent requirements. In: Zhang, R., Zhang, J., Zhang, Z., Filipe, J., Cordeiro, J. (eds.) ICEIS 2011. LNBIP, vol. 102, pp. 300–314. Springer, Heidelberg (2012)
4. Cai, X., Wei, O.: A hybrid of decomposition and domination based evolutionary algorithm for multi-objective software next release problem. In: 2013 10th IEEE International Conference on Control and Automation (ICCA), pp. 412–417, June 2013
5. Coello, C.C., Lamont, G., van Veldhuizen, D.: Evolutionary Algorithms for Solving Multi-Objective Problems. Genetic and Evolutionary Computation, 2nd edn. Springer, New York (2007)
6. Colares, F., Souza, J., Carmo, R., Pádua, C., Mateus, G.R.: A new approach to the software release planning. In: 2009 XXIII Brazilian Symposium on Software Engineering, pp. 207–215, October 2009
7. de Moura, L., Bjørner, N.S.: Z3: an efficient SMT solver. In: Ramakrishnan, C.R., Rehof, J. (eds.) TACAS 2008. LNCS, vol. 4963, pp. 337–340. Springer, Heidelberg (2008)
8. de Moura, L., Dutertre, B., Shankar, N.: A tutorial on satisfiability modulo theories. In: Damm, W., Hermanns, H. (eds.) CAV 2007. LNCS, vol. 4590, pp. 20–36. Springer, Heidelberg (2007)
9. Del Sagrado, J., Del Águila, I.M., Orellana, F.J., Túnez, S.: Requirements selection: Knowledge based optimization techniques for solving the next release problem. In: 6th Workshop on Knowledge Engineering and Software Engineering (KESE, 2010) (2010)
10. Dutertre, B., de Moura, L.: The Yices SMT solver. Technical report, SRI International (2006)
11. Feather, M.S., Cornford, S.L.: Quantitative risk-based requirements reasoning. Requirements Eng. **8**, 248–265 (2003)
12. Franch, X., Susi, A., Annosi, M.C., Ayala, C.P., Glott, R., Gross, D., Kenett, R.S., Mancinelli, F., Ramsamy, P., Thomas, C., Ameller, D., Bannier, S., Bergida, N., Blumenfeld, Y., Bouzereau, O., Costal, D., Dominguez, M., Haaland, K., López, L., Morandini, M., Siena, A.: Managing risk in open source software adoption. In: ICSOFT 2013 - Proceedings of the 8th International Joint Conference on Software Technologies, Reykjavík, Iceland, 29–31 July 2013, pp. 258–264 (2013)
13. Gueorguiev, S., Harman, M., Antoniol, G.: Software project planning for robustness and completion time in the presence of uncertainty using multi objective search based software engineering. In: Proceedings of the 11th Annual Conference on Genetic and Evolutionary Computation, GECCO 2009, pp. 1673–1680. ACM, New York (2009)

14. Harman, M., McMinn, P., de Souza, J.T., Yoo, S.: Search based software engineering: techniques, taxonomy, tutorial. In: Meyer, B., Nordio, M. (eds.) Empirical Software Engineering and Verification. LNCS, vol. 7007, pp. 1–59. Springer, Heidelberg (2012)

15. Karim, M.R., Ruhe, G.: Bi-objective genetic search for release planning in support of themes. In: Le Goues, C., Yoo, S. (eds.) SSBSE 2014. LNCS, vol. 8636, pp. 123–137. Springer, Heidelberg (2014)

16. Li, L., Harman, M., Letier, E.: Robust next release problem: handling uncertainty during optimization. In: Proceedings of 14th Annual Conference on Genetic and Evolutionary Computation - GECCO 2014, July 12–16 2014, Vancouver, pp. 1247–1254 (2014)

17. McNeil, A.J., Frey, R., Embrechts, P.: Quantitative Risk Management: Concepts, Techniques and Tools. Princeton Series in Finance. Princeton University Press, Princeton (2005)

18. Memik, S., Fallah, F.: Accelerated sat-based scheduling of control/data flow graphs. In: 2002 IEEE International Conference on Computer Design: VLSI in Computers and Processors, 2002 Proceedings, pp. 395–400 (2002)

19. Moores, T., Champion, R.: A methodology for measuring the risk associated with a software requirements specification. Australas. J. Inf. Syst. 4(1) (1996)

20. Ngo-The, A., Ruhe, G.: A systematic approach for solving the wicked problem of software release planning. Soft Comput. 12(1), 95–108 (2008)

21. Ortega, F., Bobadilla, J., Hernando, A., Gutiérrez, A.: Incorporating group recommendations to recommender systems: alternatives and performance. Inf. Process. Manage. 49(4), 895–901 (2013)

22. Peter Goos, D.M.: Statistics with JMP: Graphs, Descriptive Statistics and Probability, 1st edn. Wiley, Hoboken (2015)

23. Pitangueira, A.M., Maciel, R.S.P., Barros, M.: Software requirements selection and prioritization using SBSE approaches: a systematic review and mapping of the literature. J. Syst. Softw. 103, 267–280 (2015)

24. Regnell, B., Kuchcinski, K.: Exploring software product management decision problems with constraint solving - opportunities for prioritization and release planning. In: 2011 Fifth International Workshop on Software Product Management (IWSPM), pp. 47–56, August 2011

25. Rong, J., Hongzhi, L., Jiankun, Y., Yafei, S., Junlin, L., Lihua, C.: An approach to measuring software development risk based on information entropy. In: International Conference on Computational Intelligence and Natural Computing, 2009 (CINC, 2009), vol. 2, pp. 296–298, June 2009

26. Ruhe, G., Tn, A.B., Greer, D.: Quantitative studies in software release planning under risk and resource constraints University of Calgary. In: Empirical Software Engineering, pp. 1–10 (2003)

27. van Lamsweerde, A.: Requirements Engineering - From System Goals to UML Models to Software Specifications. Wiley, Hoboken (2009)

28. Veerappa, V., Letier, E.: Clustering stakeholders for requirements decision making. In: Berry, D. (ed.) REFSQ 2011. LNCS, vol. 6606, pp. 202–208. Springer, Heidelberg (2011)

29. Yuan, M., Gu, Z., He, X., Liu, X., Jiang, L.: Hardware/software partitioning and pipelined scheduling on runtime reconfigurable fpgas. ACM Trans. Des. Autom. Electron. Syst. 15(2), 13:1–13:41 (2010)

30. Zhang, Y.-Y., Finkelstein, A., Harman, M.: Search based requirements optimisation: existing work and challenges. In: Rolland, C. (ed.) REFSQ 2008. LNCS, vol. 5025, pp. 88–94. Springer, Heidelberg (2008)
31. Zhang, Y., Harman, M., Mansouri, S.A.: The multi-objective next release problem. In: Proceedings of the 9th Annual Conference on Genetic and Evolutionary Computation - GECCO 2007, p. 1129 (2007)

Goal-Based Decision Making

Using Goal-Oriented Problem Structuring and Evaluation Visualization for Multi Criteria Decision Analysis

Qin Ma[1]($^{(\boxtimes)}$) and Sybren de Kinderen[2]

[1] University of Luxembourg, Luxembourg City, Luxembourg
qin.ma@uni.lu
[2] University of Duisburg-Essen, Essen, Germany
sybren.dekinderen@uni-due.de

Abstract. [**Context and motivation**]: Goal-Oriented Requirements Engineering (GORE) and Multi Criteria Decision Analysis (MCDA) are two fields that naturally complement each other for providing decision support. Particularly, GORE techniques complement MCDA in terms of problem structuration and visualization of alternative evaluation, and MCDA techniques complement GORE in terms of alternative elimination and selection. Yet currently, these two fields are only connected in an ad-hoc manner. [**Question/Problem**]: We aim to establish a clearcut link between GORE and MCDA. [**Principal ideas/results**]: We propose the Goal-based Decision Making (GDM) framework for establishing a clearcut link between GORE and MCDA. We provide computational support for the GDM framework by means of tool chaining, and illustrate GDM with an insurance case. [**Contribution**]: With GDM, we contribute (1) The GDM reference model, whereby we relate MCDA concepts and GORE concepts; and (2) The GDM procedural model, whereby we provide a decision making process that integrates GORE modeling and analysis techniques and MCDA methods.

1 Introduction

Multi Criteria Decision Analysis (MCDA) concerns itself with decision aid for problems with multiple alternatives based on multiple criteria [2,14]. However, MCDA techniques, tools, and frameworks often start from a well specified decision making problem [6]. By themselves, they provide little aid to structure a decision making problem, e.g. in terms of the alternatives to be considered, the actors involved, and the actor goals. As a response an increasing number of problem structuring methods are used in conjunction with MCDA, see also Sect. 2. In addition, to support decision analysis it is deemed useful to have visualization of a decision making problem by means of software tool support [5,22]. Such tool support has the potential to foster visual interaction with decision makers,

---

Both authors are members of the EE-Network research and training network (www.ee-network.eu).

© Springer International Publishing Switzerland 2016
M. Daneva and O. Pastor (Eds.): REFSQ 2016, LNCS 9619, pp. 19–35, 2016.
DOI: 10.1007/978-3-319-30282-9_2

and/or to facilitate simulation of proposed decision making techniques, which, for example, can *dynamically* visualize the impact of alternative selection on the constituent parts of a decision making problem.

In this paper, we propose to leverage modeling and analysis techniques from Goal-Oriented Requirements Engineering (GORE) for decision problem structuring and evaluation visualization in the context of MCDA. More specifically, we use goal models to capture decision making problems including actors, objectives, alternatives and criteria, and use GORE analysis techniques and associated tool support to visualize the impact of alternative selection on actors' objectives.

Indeed, GORE modeling and analysis techniques have been increasingly used for decision support, e.g., in [1,11,21]. To make GORE techniques fit decision making they (loosely) borrow ideas from MCDA literature. For example, [21] provides quantitative (i.e., relying on quantifiable information) decision support for task plan selection in line with enterprise goals. To this end, it first relies on a part of the well established Analytic Hierarchy Process (AHP) [27] to determine the relative priorities of preferences. Subsequently, it follows the Weighted Additive decision making strategy to select the most preferred plan. Another example is [11], which provides a qualitative GORE decision technique (instead of relying on numeric data). It relies on pairwise comparison of alternative outcomes, called consequences, to reason about the satisfaction of goals.

While individual GORE-based decision making approaches often make a valuable contribution, each is a "one-off" approach. This means that they follow a specific selection of decision making strategies and suit one particular decision making situation. However, from decision making literature we know that decision making strategies are adaptive [13,24,28]: as one may intuit, rather than having a one-size-fits-all decision making strategy, different situations call for different combinations of strategies.

Furthermore, we observe that the mix of ideas from decision making literature and ideas from goal modeling is usually opaque. For example: [21] foregoes a large part of the decision making technique AHP, picking only a small part to determine importance weights by means of AHP's pairwise comparison. Why only a small part is used, or if alternatives such as ANP (a generalization of AHP) were considered, is left implicit.

As a response to the above, we argue for a clearcut relation between GORE and MCDA. Prominently, such a link would establish a structured connection between two fields that naturally complement to each other, yet are still connected in an ad-hoc way. Furthermore, for the GORE field, this relation would foster flexibility in selecting decision making strategies, as opposed to the "one-off" approaches currently in use.

This paper introduces the Goal-based Decision Making (GDM) framework, to establish this relation. The novelty of GDM is two-fold: (1) The GDM reference model, whereby we elucidate the relation between concepts used in decision making literature, and the concepts used in goal-oriented requirements engineering literature; (2) The GDM procedural model, whereby we provide a decision making process that integrates GORE modeling and analysis techniques and decision making techniques. We provide computational support for the GDM framework by chaining an example GORE modeling and analysis tool with Microsoft Excel, whereby the latter is used to simulate decision making strategies. Moreover, we apply the GDM framework to an illustrative enterprise architecture case.

Note that as a pilot study to systematically relate GORE and MCDA, this paper only considers a subset of basic decision making strategies (such as the Weighted Additive strategy, or the conjunctive/disjunctive decision rule) in the current version of the GDM framework. The purpose is more to explore their many touching points, rather than to claim complete coverage of the diverse and complex field of MCDA.

The rest of this paper is structured as follows. Section 2 discusses related work. In Sect. 3, we present the GDM framework and elaborate on its key ingredients. In Sect. 4, we apply the GDM framework to an illustrative case in the enterprise architecture domain. Finally Sect. 5 provides a conclusion and outlook.

2   Related Work

Several efforts have been made to complement MCDA with problem structuring theories such as the value-focused framework [20], a way of thinking for uncovering desired (end-) values of a decision problem; the Soft Systems Methodology (SSM) [23], an intervention for problem space exploration that consists of guidelines, processes and basic models of means-ends networks; and the use of formal problem structuring methods such as causal (or cognitive) maps [9]. The value-focused framework and SSM are more geared to providing a way of thinking, guidelines (such as SSM's CATWOE), and problem exploration processes. Similar to many techniques from the GORE domain, formal problem structuring methods use models (e.g., causal maps) as the main artifact across the whole process. However, as pointed out by [22], causal maps are not integrated with multi-attribute decision making techniques.

As an answer to this, the authors of [22] proposed an enhanced version of causal maps with integrated support for both problem structuring and evaluation, called reasoning maps. Reasoning maps consist of a network of means-ends concepts and relations between them, plus a specification of relationship strengths [22]. Similar to Gutman's means-ends chains for uncovering customer motivations [17], reasoning maps perform problem structuring by relating detailed attributes (e.g., "fluoride" for toothpaste) to high-level values (e.g., "being healthy") via intermediary consequences (e.g. "avoiding cavities in teeth"). For evaluation, then, reasoning maps can propagate the satisfaction of detailed attributes to the satisfaction of high level values via strengths of relations.

Reasoning maps enable a smooth and seamless transition from decision problem structuring to evaluation, by using a unified modeling notation for both the two phases. However, the modeling power of reasoning maps is limited: (1) only positive/negative contribution links from means to ends are provided; richer relations such as logical (X)OR/AND decomposition from ends to means are not supported; and (2) only qualitative assessments are supported, while quantitative and mixed modes are left out. Such extra expressiveness will enable additional perspectives from which the problem space can be explored. More importantly, reasoning maps have little visualization tool support: the visualization of decision analysis outcomes is done manually and provides only a single static view. Indeed, software tool support for automated, dynamic, and multi-perspective visualization of decision analysis outputs is regarded as an important future research direction for reasoning maps by [5,22].

Having discussed problem structuration and visualization from the perspective of MCDA, we now turn to our core contribution: GDM, which systematically links GORE to MCDA.

3   The GDM Framework

The main idea behind the GDM framework is to elucidate the connection between MCDA literature (e.g., as found in business discourse) and GORE literature, so as to provide an *integrated* approach towards problem structuring and multi criteria evaluation. To accomplish this connection, the GDM framework consists of four key parts, as depicted in Fig. 1.

Fig. 1. The Goal-based decision making (GDM) framework

(1) *Goal-Oriented Modeling and Analysis*, borrowed from GORE literature. On the one hand, the conceptual modeling techniques allow for expressing the decision making problem of interest. Here, conceptual models refer to visual artifacts that provide an abstraction of the situation under investigation, expressed in terms of concepts whose understanding is shared by the involved modeling stakeholders [7,29]. On the other hand, the goal-oriented analysis techniques allow for analyzing a particular alternative and visualizing the impact of choosing this alternative; (2) *Decision Making Techniques*, borrowed from MCDA literature. These decision making techniques consist of decision making strategies, both exhaustive ones (acting under full information, no time constraints, etc.) as well as heuristic ones (allowing one to select alternatives that are "good enough", using limited decision making effort). In addition, we exploit guidelines on selecting decision making strategies (extracted from decision making literature); (3) *The GDM Reference Model* represents the static aspect of the GDM framework. It incorporates key concepts (and their relationships) from GORE literature and MCDA literature, and makes explicit the bridge between the two domains; (4) *The GDM Procedural Model* represents the dynamic aspect of the GDM framework. Whereas the GDM reference model underpins conceptually the GDM framework and captures the relevant concepts, the GDM procedural model defines a process to guide decision makers to perform a decision making activity according to the GDM framework. During the process, we use the aforementioned goal-oriented modeling techniques, analysis techniques and decision making techniques, and operationalize the concepts captured in the GDM reference model.

The GDM framework is generic with respect to application domains. This is partially the result of the two domain independent streams of literature that we base ourselves on, namely GORE and MCDA literature. On the one hand, GORE techniques have been applied to a variety of domains, such as enterprise architecture [1], regulatory compliance [15], and business-IT alignment [12], to name a few. On the other hand, decision making techniques are applied similarly across domains [16] e.g., the legal, business, and medical domain. Moreover, we assume the design of the GDM reference model and GDM procedural model that bridge between GORE and MCDA can also be kept generic. This is exemplified by the application of the GDM framework in an insurance case study discussed in detail in Sect. 4.

In addition, the GDM framework can support quantitative, qualitative and hybrid reasoning techniques. For example, the insurance case study reported in Sect. 4 works with hybrid data on the GORE side and employs quantitative analysis on the MCDA side.

3.1   Goal-Oriented Modeling and Analysis

GDM uses GORE modeling techniques, such as GRL [18], TROPOS [8] and i* [30], to structure decision making problems in terms of goal models. The prominent intentional concept "goal" is used to capture actor purposes. Other intentional concepts such as "resources" and "tasks" can be used to indicate alternative means for achieving these goals. Furthermore various relationship types can be used for specifying relations between intentional elements. For example, a means-ends relation (e.g., a contribution relation or a decomposition relation) can be used to specify that the goal "Rabbit be fed" is fully satisfied by executing the task "Give three carrots to the rabbit".

In terms of individual alternative analysis, GDM uses (semi-)automated GORE analysis techniques to compute quantitatively and/or qualitatively the impact of selecting an alternative on actor goals. Such analysis techniques rely on a goal model's intentional elements and their relations to propagate, throughout the goal model, an initial set of populated values. For example: by satisfying the task "Give three carrots to the rabbit" for $1/3$ (i.e., to give one carrot), via the means-ends relation the goal "Rabbit be fed" is also satisfied by $1/3$.

Finally, the concept "soft goal" is used to distinguish amongst alternatives that satisfy equally a goal. For example, the soft goal "Healthier rabbit" can be used to distinguish between the resource "Biological carrot" and the resource "Non-biological carrot".

3.2   Multi Criteria Decision Analysis

In GDM, Multi Criteria Decision Analysis (MCDA) refers to various decision making strategies to select among alternatives, and guidelines about which strategies to use in which circumstances. In line with [13,24,28], we distinguish between two strategy types: compensatory and non compensatory. By employing *compensatory* strategies, one evaluates alternatives on a complete set of attributes, and, as implied by name, one allows a low score on one (or more) attributes to be compensated for by scores on other attributes. Typical examples of a compensatory strategy are Weighted Additive and Unweighted Additive decision strategies. By employing *non compensatory strategies*, one relies on heuristics to select amongst alternatives. Thereby, one eliminates alternatives that fail to meet a (small set of) minimal attribute and selecting an alternative that is "good enough". A typical example of a non compensatory strategy is the disjunctive rule, whereby an alternative is discarded if it fails to meet a minimum cutoff for one attribute, regardless of the score on remaining attributes.

To select strategies suitable for a particular decision making scenario, we rely on guidelines established in the decision making literature. For example in the context of consumer buying decision making, [28] identifies categories of decision making scenarios, e.g., lightweight investment such as buying a pack of salt, and heavy investment such as selecting a mortgage offer, and provides guidance on when to apply a complex but comprehensive decision making strategy such as AHP, and when to use a simple heuristic, such as the disjunctive rule. Furthermore, [16] argues that under time pressure non compensatory decision strategies such as the disjunctive rule outperform compensatory strategies, and that non compensatory strategies perform well for uncertain decision problems (i.e., when acting under incomplete information, or when the impact of a decision on future decision is hard to predict and control).

3.3   The GDM Reference Model

The GDM reference model as depicted in Fig. 2 integrates concepts from both GORE and MCDA literature and identifies relations among these concepts to establish the bridge between them. It is specified in terms of a metamodel, and provides a formal underpinning of the GDM framework.

Regarding the GORE concepts, a core subset of the Goal-oriented Requirements Language (GRL) [18] metamodel is used. This subset covers the main concepts that are shared with other often-used goal modeling languages, such as TROPOS [8] and i* [30]. However, we take GRL as the baseline because it is standardized by the Telecommunication Standardization Sector (ITU-T) and has a mature tool support in terms of jUCMNav[1].

Regarding MCDA, a core set of concepts common to the area is extracted and formalized into a metamodel. Note here that while there exist a diverse amount of multi criteria decision making techniques, underlying them is often an unchanging limited amount of core concepts [25], such as "alternatives", "attributes", and "cutoff values". This eases the formal conceptualization of concepts from MCDA literature, for example allowing us to add new decision strategies without having to change the core concepts that we rely upon.

Note that our reference model (Fig. 2) includes only a subset of basic decision making strategies from MCDA, focusing on multi attribute theory for the compensatory part and decision rules for the non compensatory part. This is because the current paper is meant as a first step to clarify the relation between

---

[1] http://jucmnav.softwareengineering.ca/ucm/bin/view/ProjetSEG/WebHome.

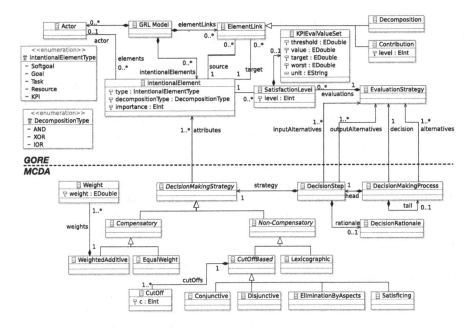

Fig. 2. The GDM reference model

MCDA and GORE, rather than to aim at an exhaustive coverage of all MCDA methods. In later iterations, we would also like to include other categories of decision making strategies such as outranking methods, the Analytic Hierarchy Process, or strategies that can deal with decision making under uncertainty [14].

For bridging GORE and MCDA, we establish a set of relations to enable the goal-based definition of key concepts in decision making, i.e., decision making problems, decision making activities, alternatives and attributes.

Decision making problems are captured in terms of goal models, wherein the high-level goals are the purposes to achieve and the low-level intentional elements, such as tasks and resources, are the means to achieve these purposes. Different sets of low-level intentional elements can be proposed as alternative ways to achieve the purposes. In line with [3], such an alternative is marked by an EvaluationStrategy (cf. Fig. 2). An evaluation strategy defines for each intentional element in the alternative an initial SatisfactionLevel. Furthermore, it shows the impact of selecting this alternative by propagating these values to compute satisfaction levels of the high-level goals through contribution and decomposition links.

Decision making activities are characterized by the notion of a DecisionMakingProcess (cf. the metamodel in Fig. 2), which takes a set of alternatives as input and decides upon one as output. A decision making process goes through several sequential steps, represented by the concept DecisionStep. Each DecisionStep makes an intermediate evaluation of current remaining alternatives and eliminate some of them by following one particular decision making strategy (cf.

the one-to-one correspondence between DecisionStep and DecisionMakingStrategy
in the metamodel). The concatenation of multiple steps into a DecisionMaking-
Process then continues until one alternative remains. This unique alternative is
the final decision. Note that decision making strategies can themselves vary from
a simple one-stage heuristic, such as the conjunctive rule, to a complex multi-
stage strategy, such as AHP. The notion of a DecisionStep is not to be confused
with the internal stages of a decision making strategy. More specifically, in case
a multi-stage strategy is applied within a DecisionStep, the execution of the step
involves several stages. But these internal stages are all encapsulated in one step
and are not visible to the DecisinMakingProcess.

For each DecisionStep, we advise the decision maker to follow guidelines established in the decision making literature to select an appropriate strategy (cf.
Sect. 3.2). Information about the decision making task faced by a DecisionStep,
e.g., to reduce the size of the alternative set to a great extent within a short time
interval, or to compare comprehensively limited number of alternatives, can be
documented in a DecisionRationale connected to the DecisionStep, together with
the relevant guidelines applicable in tackling such a task.

Finally, our reference model anchors attributes (used by MCDA strategies
to select alternatives) also in GORE literature. This is because how well an
alternative serves the purpose should be judged by how well the intended goals
are achieved by the alternative. More specifically, we allow the following three
intentional elements: Goal, Softgoal, and key performance indicator (KPI), to act
as attributes for assessing alternatives in the GDM framework. This is formalized
by an OCL constraint (omitted due to lack of space). Each individual alternative
is assessed by GORE analysis techniques, and the results of all alternatives are
synthesized by MCDA strategies to make a final decision.

3.4   The GDM Procedural Model

The GDM procedural model as depicted in Fig. 3 guides decision makers to reach
a decision within the GDM framework. It consists of three main steps and is
iterative between Step 2 and 3. More specifically, the procedure starts with Step 1
which entails framing the decision making problem in terms of a goal model
and identifying alternatives and selection criteria in the goal model in terms of
tasks, resources and soft goals. Then the procedure continues with executing a
DecisionMakingProcess (cf. the GDM reference model in Fig. 2) in terms of a loop
between Step 2 and 3. One iteration of Step 2 and Step 3 corresponds to the
execution of one DecisionStep by applying one decision making strategy (strategy
selection in Step 2 and execution in Step 3) to eliminate alternatives. As such,
repetition of Step 2 and 3 gradually narrows down the set of alternatives until
there is only one alternative left — the final decision.

1. Specify decision making problem in a goal model. The decision maker
needs to first specify the objectives and the context of the decision making
problem. This is done by goal modeling whereby he identifies key actors and
their goals, and refine goals into subgoals. Next, alternative ways to achieve

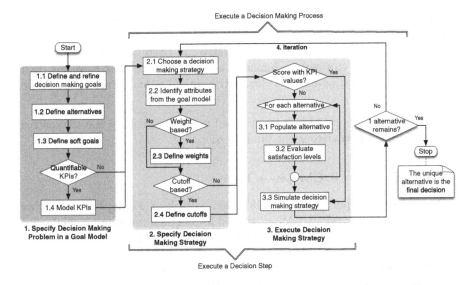

Fig. 3. The GDM procedural model

goals are identified and an additional set of soft goals is specified. If external quantitative data sources exist to measure the satisfaction of (soft) goals on a per alternative basis, they can be models as key performance indicators (KPIs).

2. Specify decision making strategy. Using the goal model as input, the decision maker then proceeds with the first round of alternative elimination (realized by this and the next step). It starts by selecting a decision making strategy and uses the information from the goal model to populate the strategy. More specifically, a set of goals, soft goals, and/or KPIs is identified as attributes to be used as criteria in the selected decision making strategy. Moreover, in case the strategy involves weights and/or cutoffs, these parameters are also specified. Note that the conversion of goal related intentional elements (i.e., goals, soft goals and KPIs) to attributes (used by MCDA strategies as criteria) is enabled by the cross domain relations defined in the reference model.

3. Execute decision making strategy. In this step, the decision maker first needs to score each individual attribute for each alternative. These scores can come from two sources. Either the measured values for KPIs can be used directly, or the satisfaction levels of the attributes (which are goals, soft goals, and/or KPIs in the goal model) will be calculated in the goal model and used. The latter case is achieved by Step 3.1 and 3.2. In Step 3.1, the decision maker populates an alternative in the goal model by assigning initial satisfaction levels to the intentional elements constituting the alternative in terms of a EvaluationStrategy. Because any goals, soft goals, and KPIs in the goal model can act as attributes (see Fig. 2), these initial satisfaction levels need to be propagated throughout the entire goal model. This is done in Step 3.2, by executing the evaluation strategy following GORE analysis algorithms. The satisfaction levels of the intentional elements that act as the attributes are then used as attribute scores for this alternative.

After scoring attributes for each alternative, in Step 3.3, the semantics of the decision making strategy is simulated to calculate a global score for each alternative by aggregating its individual attribute scores and to select/eliminate alternatives.

4. Iteration. Step 2 and Step 3 are iterated until there is only one alternative left. This unique alternative is the final decision.

3.5 Tool Support: jUCMNav + Excel

We provide tool support for the GDM framework by chaining the jUCMNav tool with Microsoft Excel. JUCMNav is used for decision problem modeling and attribute scores evaluation for individual alternatives. The macro environment of Excel is used to implement the semantics of decision making strategies for alternative selection/elimination. These two tools are used together by gathering data from jUCMNav and importing these data into Excel.

4 Applying GDM to Decision Making in the Insurance Domain

The GDM framework is domain independent. In this paper, we demonstrate how it can be applied to a case from the insurance domain. This case is inspired by a paper on the economic functions of insurance brokers [10], as well as the insurance case documented in an Open Group whitepaper [19]. In the remainder of this section, we illustrate the realization of this case by following the GDM procedural model (Fig. 3) whereby we focus on one particular decision problem in the case: choosing an IT solution for registering customer profiles. Note that the example is illustrated with hybrid (quantitative and qualitative) data on the GORE side and employs quantitative analysis techniques on the MCDA side.

1. Specify decision making problem in a goal model. ArchiSurance, a large insurance company, aims to reduce the adverse selection of risk profiles of its customers. Adverse selection refers to incomplete or faulty risk profiles [10], which leads an insurance company to sell insurance packages at an inappropriate premium, or worse still, to wrongfully offer insurances to customers.

The ArchiSurance board starts with domain modeling in GRL (Step 1.1 in Fig. 3) to explore how to reduce adverse selection. The goal model on the left side of Fig. 4 captures such an exploration. (A brief summary of the GRL notation is given on the right side of Fig. 4.) Here we see that ArchiSurance's approach to the adverse selection problem (modeled by G1) is to focus on the root cause of the problem, namely the quality of customer profiles in terms of both completeness and accuracy (modeled by G2).

The board identifies two measures to improve customer profile quality: to strengthen internal check of customer data (modeled by G4), or to outsource the

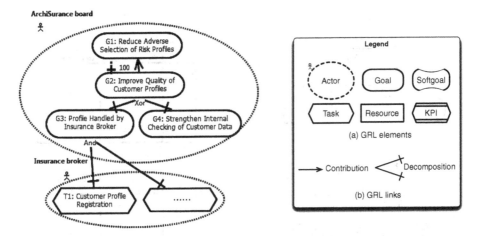

Fig. 4. Problem space exploration for ArchiSurance with GRL (left); Basic GRL notation (right)

customer profiles management function to insurance brokers (modeled by G3). Because the broker based model enjoys the advantage of having immediate access to qualified insurance agents with profile collection being an important part of their core competency [10], ArchiSurance first investigates the implementation of this measure.

As shown in Fig. 4, the broker based model entails a set of new tasks to be performed by the broker. For illustration purposes, we elaborate on the task of registering customer profiles (T1) and one decision making problem associated with it: choosing an IT solution for supporting T1.

The ArchiSurance IT department proposes three IT solutions as alternatives for supporting task T1 (Step 1.2 following Fig. 3): "IS1: COTS Application A", "IS2: COTS Application B", and "IS3: Upgraded Inhouse Application". These IT solutions, and their contributions to achieving T1, are depicted in Fig. 5.

Each of the three alternatives can by itself fully support the realization of T1 (depicted by the XOR decomposition from T1 to IS1, IS2, and IS3), which together with other tasks contributes to the full achievement of goal G3, and the subsequent achievement of G2 and G1. Figure 5 visualizes the satisfaction of goals and tasks in case of choosing alternative IS1. This visualization is automatically rendered by the goal modeling software tool jUCMNav for GRL (see Sect. 3.5). jUCMNav can handle both quantitative and qualitative data. More specifically, for specifying contribution links and satisfaction levels, both ways are supported: a quantitative value, ranging from −100 to 100, and a predefined qualitative value (with a predefined icon for representation). Moreover, for visualizing satisfaction levels of intentional elements, a color coding is also implemented, i.e., green for satisfied, yellow for none or neutral, red for denied, and a lot of shades for values in between. The right side of Fig. 5 summarizes these

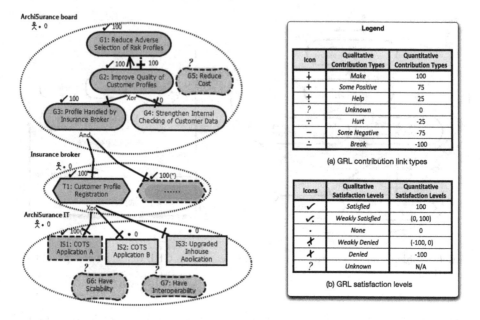

Fig. 5. Alternative IT solutions to support Task T1, and subsequent satisfaction of high level goals, illustrated for alternative IS1

values and the default mapping to convert between quantitative and qualitative values.

In case IS1 is selected, the satisfaction level of IS1 is set to 100 and the satisfaction levels of IS2 and IS3 remain 0 (not selected). Note that satisfaction levels that are set initially are shown with a suffix "(*)".

The satisfaction level of IS1 is propagated to T1 as a result of the XOR decomposition link between T1 and IS1-3. Subsequently, the satisfaction level of T1 is further propagated to higher-level goals, (1) via the AND decomposition link between T1-Tn and G3, which states that full satisfaction of all tasks T1-Tn implies satisfaction of G3 (whereby we assume full satisfaction of all Tn, n > 1, to fulfill the AND), (2) via the XOR decomposition link between G3-G4 and G2, which states that exactly one of the two measures should be implemented and this suffices to achieve G2, and finally (3) via the contribute link between G2 and G1, which states that satisfaction of G2 contributes 100 % to satisfaction of G1.

To distinguish the three alternatives and make a decision, the ArchiSurance also identifies three soft goals capturing their preferences. More specifically, the board prefers a solution that is cost efficient (specified by G5 in Fig. 5), while from an IT perspective, the interoperability with other information systems (G7) and the scalability (G6) are also relevant factors to consider. As a consequence, the final decision depends on how well the three alternatives satisfy these preferred requirements.

KPIs for IS1	T	Th	W	V
K2: # of Intermediaries IS1	2500	500	50	2000
K3: Buying Price of IS1	3.000 €	10.000 €	15.000 €	8.000 €
K4: # Supported Interfaces IS1	5	2	1	5
K5: Training Cost IS1	2.000 €	5.000 €	8.000 €	4.000 €
K1: Cost (=K3+K5)	5.000 €	15.000 €	23.000 €	12.000 €

KPIs for IS2	T	Th	W	V
K6: # of Intermediaries IS2	2500	500	50	2500
K8: Buying Price of IS2	3.000 €	10.000 €	15.000 €	12.000 €
K7: # Supported Interfaces IS2	5	2	1	5
K9: Training Cost IS2	2.000 €	5.000 €	8.000 €	4.000 €
K1: Cost (=K8+K9)	5.000 €	15.000 €	23.000 €	16.000 €

KPIs for IS3	T	Th	W	V
K10: # of Intermediaries IS3	2500	500	50	2000
K11: # Supported Interfaces IS3	5	2	1	5
K12: Development Hours IS3	50 h	150 h	230 h	90 h
K1: Cost (=K12x100€/hour)	5.000 €	15.000 €	23.000 €	9.000 €

T: Target Value; Th: Threshold Value; W: Worst Value; V: Measured Value

Fig. 6. KPIs for alternatives IS1-3

To this end, for each alternative a set of KPIs is defined (in Fig. 6) that provides measurements to enable assessment of the alternatives. More specifically, for each KPI, one needs to specify the *target value*, the *threshold value*, the *worst value*, and the current *measured value*. This enables one to calculate a satisfaction level, depending on where the measured value is in the scale marked by the other three values. Briefly, the closer the measured value is to the target value, the higher the satisfaction level.

Relations among KPIs and their contribution to soft goals are depicted by contribution links in the goal model. Figure 8 illustrates the case of IS1 (left) and IS3 (right). More specifically, ArchiSurance introduces the KPI "K1:Cost" to measure the cost of an alternative (depicted by the contribution link from K1 to G5). In case of purchasing a COTS application such as IS1, the cost involves both the buying price (K3) and the training costs (K5). In case of in-house development such as IS3, the cost comes from the amount of labor that is required for the development task (K12). In addition, we measure the number of supported interfaces (K4 for IS1 and K11 for IS3) as an indicator for interoperability (G7) and the number of intermediaries (K2 for IS1 and K10 for IS3) as an indicator for scalability (G6).

2. Specify decision making strategy. The ArchiSurance board sets an upper limit (15000€) for the application cost. Any alternative exceeding this threshold will be discarded directly. This corresponds to the disjunctive decision making rule. According to the reference model (Fig. 2), a disjunctive strategy is cutoff based. Therefore, for the specification of this strategy following the procedural model (see Fig. 3), we need to specify the evaluated attribute(s) (Step 2.2) and the cutoff(s) (Step 2.4). The cost attribute is represented by the KPI "K1: Cost" in the goal model, and the given upper limit (i.e., 15000€) denotes the cutoff.

3. Execute decision making strategy. This step entails executing the disjunctive rule and rejecting any alternatives whose cost exceeds the cutoff. Because the cutoff is expressed in terms of absolute amount of money (15000€), it is more intuitive and direct to use the measured values of K1 for the scores. These values, together with the cutoff, are then imported into Excel as shown in Fig. 7, left hand side. The disjunctive rule is implemented in terms of an Excel macro. The result of simulating this rule is shown in the first column: IS1 and IS3 are selected, IS2 is eliminated because its cost exceeds the cutoff value.

4. Iteration. Because there are still multiple alternatives left after applying the disjunctive rule, we repeat Step 2 and Step 3.

• **Repetition of Step 2.** In this iteration, the ArchiSurance board wants to make a *comprehensive* comparison between IS1 and IS3 with respect to all the

Disjunctive			
Decision	Alternatives	Attribute	K1: Cost
		CutOff	€ 15,000
✓	IS1: COTS Application A	KPIValue	€ 12,000
	IS2: COTS Application B	KPIValue	€ 16,000
✓	IS3: Upgrade Inhouse App	KPIValue	€ 9,000

Weigthed additive				
Decision	Alternatives	Attribute	G6	G5	G7
		Weight	0,61	0,28	0,11
✓	IS1	Satisfaction level	75	30	100
		Global score	65		
	IS3	Satisfaction level	25	60	33
		Global score	36		

Fig. 7. Simulate decision making strategies in Excel

three preferences namely cost (G5), scalability (G6), and interoperability (G7). We therefore apply the Weighted Additive strategy. To decide the weights of the three attributes (G5, G6 and G7), we ask the ArchiSurance board to provide us with a relative ranking of importance. We then use the Rank Order Centriod (ROC) formula [4] from the decision making literature to convert the relative importance ranking into the quantitative weights.

• **Repetition of Step 3.** The respective satisfaction levels of the soft goals G5, G6 and G7, in case of selecting IS1 or IS3, will be used as the respective scores of the three attributes. To arrive at these scores, we repeat Step 3.1 (populating an alternative) and Step 3.2 (evaluating satisfaction levels) for IS1 and IS3 individually, by using the goal-oriented satisfaction analysis technique in jUCMNav. Figure 8 visualizes the results in jUCMNav.

More specifically, part (a) of Fig. 8 illustrates the assessment of IS1 against the three attributes. In line with Step 3.1, to populate alternative IS1, initial satisfaction levels ([−100, 100]) are provided in jUCMNav to the intentional elements belong to IS1 namely the task "IS1:COTS Application A", and the KPIs K2, K3, K4 and K5.

In line with Step 3.2, the satisfaction levels of other intentional elements in the goal model are calculated, by propagating the initial values following the

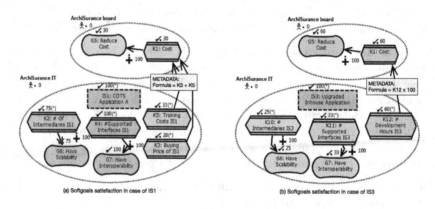

Fig. 8. Assessing soft goals satisfaction based on KPI measurements

contribution and decomposition links in jUCMNav. Following another repetition of Step 3.1 and 3.2, IS3 is similarly scored and visualized in part (b) of Fig. 8.

The visualization offered by jUCMNav shows, per alternative, what impact an alternative selection will have on the high level and low level goals of actors. This allows for a visual comparison across alternatives. For ArchiSurance, one can intuitively tell on which aspects IS1 outperform IS3, and vice versa: purchasing a COTS application (IS1) is more costly than inhouse development (IS3); however, IS1 offers better support for scalability and interoperability.

However, visualization itself can not make a comprehensive trade-off. Therefore, recall that for this iteration, the Weighted Additive strategy was chosen to make a comprehensive comparison between IS1 and IS3. Following Step 3.3, the weights and the satisfaction levels are then imported into Excel for simulation as shown in Fig. 7, right-hand side. Similar to the disjunctive rule, the semantics of the Weighted Additive strategy is implemented in an Excel macro. The result of simulating the strategy on the two alternatives is shown in the first column. Here IS1 is the final decision and IS3 is eliminated, because IS1 has a higher global score (65) than IS3 (36).

5   Conclusion

We have presented the GDM framework for goal based decision support, thus elucidating the relation between two streams of literature that naturally complement each other: GORE and MCDA. Particularly, we presented (1) the GDM reference model to bridge GORE concepts to MCDA concepts, and (2) the GDM procedural model to show how GORE and MCDA can be used together dynamically. Furthermore we have shown how to provide computational support for GDM by means of a tool chain. Finally, with an insurance use case we illustrated the dynamic visualization capabilities brought about by introducing GORE software tool support into MCDA.

For future research, we plan to do further practical validation of the GDM framework. This concerns the confrontation of GDM with experts from the GORE, and respectively the MCDA, domain. Informal discussions with people with GORE background already provides encouraging feedback, but this needs more rigor to support claims regarding GDM's usefulness. In addition, in-depth case studies are also on our research agenda, where the usability and effectiveness of the GDM framework will be validated in the presence of real-life data and with the involvement of actual stakeholders.

In this paper we explicitly focused on a limited set of basic decision making strategies from MCDA (see Fig. 2). To explore further the relation between GORE and MCDA we intend to include more decision making techniques into GDM, such as AHP, outranking methods, qualitative methods, and approaches that support decision making under uncertainty. Furthermore, with the expansion of supported MCDA strategies in GDM, a new challenge emerges when it comes to the correct understanding and proper selection of these strategies. In this paper, as a starting point, we advised the decision makers to follow established guidelines, which roughly explain under what conditions a decision making strategy is appropriate. In future work, we plan to conduct a systematic literature review on this aspect of MCDA and propose a taxonomy of MCDA methods. This taxonomy will complement the GDM framework in helping decision makers in deciding which MCDA strategies are most adequate for a particular selection scenario.

Acknowledgments. The authors would like to thank Sepideh Ghanavati for her valuable feedback on the usefulness of the GDM framework. Furthermore, the authors thank Sepideh Ghanavati and Daniel Amyot for their guidance on using the jUCMNav tool. This work has been sponsored by the *Fonds National de la Recherche Luxembourg* (www.fnr.lu), via the PEARL programme.

References

1. Akhigbe, O., Amyot, D., Richards, G.: A framework for a business intelligence-enabled adaptive enterprise architecture. In: Yu, E., Dobbie, G., Jarke, M., Purao, S. (eds.) ER 2014. LNCS, vol. 8824, pp. 393–406. Springer, Heidelberg (2014)
2. Al-Shemmeri, T., Al-Kloub, B., Pearman, A.: Model choice in multicriteria decision aid. Eur. J. Oper. Res. **97**(3), 550–560 (1997)
3. Amyot, D., Shamsaei, A., Kealey, J., Tremblay, E., Miga, A., Mussbacher, G., Alhaj, M., Tawhid, R., Braun, E., Cartwright, N.: Towards advanced goal model analysis with jUCMNav. In: Castano, S., Vassiliadis, P., Lakshmanan, L.V.S., Lee, M.L. (eds.) ER 2012 Workshops 2012. LNCS, vol. 7518, pp. 201–210. Springer, Heidelberg (2012)
4. Barron, F.H., Barrett, B.E.: Decision quality using ranked attribute weights. Manage. Sci. **42**(11), 1515–1523 (1996)
5. Belton, V., Montibeller, G.: Qualitative operators for reasoning maps. Eur. J. Oper. Res. **195**(3), 829–840 (2009)
6. Belton, V., Stewart, T.: Problem structuring and multiple criteria decision analysis. In: Ehrgott, M., Figueira, J.R., Greco, S. (eds.) Trends in Multiple Criteria Decision Analysis, pp. 209–239. Springer, Berlin (2010)
7. Bjeković, M., Proper, H.A., Sottet, J.-S.: Embracing pragmatics. In: Yu, E., Dobbie, G., Jarke, M., Purao, S. (eds.) ER 2014. LNCS, vol. 8824, pp. 431–444. Springer, Heidelberg (2014)
8. Bresciani, P., Perini, A., Giorgini, P., Giunchiglia, F., Mylopoulos, J.: Tropos: an agent-oriented software development methodology. Auton. Agents Multi-Agent Syst. **8**(3), 203–236 (2004)
9. e Costa, C.A.B., Ensslin, L., Cornêa, É.C., Vansnick, J.C.: Decision support systems in action: integrated application in a multicriteria decisionaid process. Eur. J. Oper. Res. **113**(2), 315–335 (1999)
10. Cummins, J.D., Doherty, N.A.: The economics of insurance intermediaries. J. Risk Insur. **73**(3), 359–396 (2006)
11. Elahi, G., Yu, E.: Comparing alternatives for analyzing requirements trade-offs-in the absence of numerical data. Inf. Softw. Technol. **54**(6), 517–530 (2012)
12. Ellis-Braithwaite, R., Lock, R., Dawson, R.: Towards an approach for analysing the strategic alignment of software requirements using quantified goal graphs. J. Adv. Softw. **6**(1), 119–130 (2013)

13. Elrod, T., Johnson, R.D., White, J.: A new integrated model of noncompensatory and compensatory decision strategies. Organ. Behav. Hum. Decis. Process. **95**(1), 1–19 (2004)
14. Figueira, J., Greco, S., Ehrgott, M.: Multiple Criteria Decision Analysis: State of the Art Surveys, vol. 78. Springer Science & Business Media, Berlin (2005)
15. Ghanavati, S., Rifaut, A., Dubois, E., Amyot, D.: Goal-oriented compliance with multiple regulations. In: The Proceedings of RE 2014, pp. 73–82 (2014)
16. Gigerenzer, G., Gaissmaier, W.: Heuristic decision making. Ann. Rev. Psychol. **62**, 451–482 (2011)
17. Gutman, J.: Means-end chains as goal hierarchies. Psychol. Mark. **14**(6), 545–560 (1997)
18. ITU-T: User requirements notation (URN)–language definition, November 2008. http://www.itu.int/rec/T-REC-Z.151/en
19. Jonkers, H., Band, I., Quartel, D.: The archisurance case study. White paper, The Open Group (2012)
20. Keeney, R.L.: Value-focused thinking: identifying decision opportunities and creating alternatives. Eur. J. Oper. Res. **92**(3), 537–549 (1996)
21. Liaskos, S., McIlraith, S.A., Sohrabi, S., Mylopoulos, J.: Representing and reasoning about preferences in requirements engineering. Requirements Eng. **16**(3), 227–249 (2011)
22. Montibeller, G., Belton, V., Ackermann, F., Ensslin, L.: Reasoning maps for decision aid: an integrated approach for problem-structuring and multi-criteria evaluation. J. Oper. Res. Soc. **59**(5), 575–589 (2008)
23. Neves, L., Dias, L.C., Antunes, C.H., Martins, A.G.: Structuring an MCDA model using SSM: a case study in energy efficiency. Eur. J. Oper. Res. **199**(3), 834–845 (2009)
24. Payne, J.W., Bettman, J.R., Johnson, E.J.: Adaptive strategy selection in decision making. J. Exp. Psychol. Learn. Mem. Cogn. **14**(3), 534 (1988)
25. Payne, J.W., Bettman, J.R., Johnson, E.J.: The Adaptive Decision Maker. Cambridge University Press, Cambridge (1993)
26. Pourshahid, A., Amyot, D., Peyton, L., Ghanavati, S., Chen, P., Weiss, M., Forster, A.J.: Business process management with the user requirements notation. Electron. Commer. Res. **9**(4), 269–316 (2009)
27. Saaty, T.L.: Decision making-the analytic hierarchy and network processes (AHP/ANP). J. Syst. Sci. Syst. Eng. **13**(1), 1–35 (2004)
28. Solomon, M.R.: Consumer Behavior: Buying, Having, and Being. Pearson, Upper Saddle River (2015)
29. Thalheim, B.: The theory of conceptual models, the theory of conceptual modelling and foundations of conceptual modelling. In: Embley, D.W., Thalheim, B. (eds.) Handbook of Conceptual Modeling, pp. 543–577. Springer, Berlin (2011)
30. Yu, E.: Towards modelling and reasoning support for early-phase requirements engineering. In: The Proceedings of RE 1997, pp. 226–235 (1997)

Optimizing the Incremental Delivery of Software Features Under Uncertainty

Olawole Oni and Emmanuel Letier[(✉)]

Department of Computer Science, University College London, London, UK
{olawole.oni.14,e.letier}@ucl.ac.uk

Abstract. **[Context]** Lean and agile software development processes encourage delivering software in small increments so as to generate early business value, be able to adapt to changes, and reduce risks. Deciding what to build in each iteration is an important requirements engineering activity. The Incremental Funding Method (IFM) partly supports such decisions by identifying sequences of features delivery that optimize Net Present Value (NPV). **[Problem]** The IFM, however, does not deal explicitly with uncertainty and considers the maximization of NPV as the only objective, without explicit consideration for other objectives such as minimizing upfront investment costs and maximizing learning so as to reduce uncertainty and risk for future iterations. **[Ideas]** This short paper presents our ongoing research to address these limitations by extending IFM with Bayesian decision analysis to reason about uncertainty and with Pareto-based optimization to support decisions with respect multiple conflicting objectives. **[Contributions]** The paper presents the current version of our tool-supported extension of the IFM, illustrate it on a small example, and outlines our research agenda.

Keywords: Software engineering decision analysis · Requirements engineering · Agile software development

1 Introduction

Delivering software in small increments is widely regarded as an appropriate approach to deal with requirements uncertainty, manage software development risks, and generate early business value [1]. An important requirements engineering activity in this context is to decide the sequence in which software features will be developed and delivered [2, 3]. The Incremental Funding Method (IFM) is a financially informed approach to support such decisions by analyzing the cash flows and Net Present Value (NPV) of alternative feature delivery sequences [4, 5]. These financial concerns are critical to requirements engineering decisions; they can turn a project that is not financially viable into one that becomes viable through an appropriate sequencing of feature delivery that brings in early value and funds to the project.

The IFM, however, has limitations. A first limitation is that while clients and software developers have inevitable uncertainty about the value and cost of individual features, the IFM does not represent and analyze such uncertainty explicitly. Extending the method to reason about such uncertainty would help requirements engineers analyze the uncertainty

© Springer International Publishing Switzerland 2016
M. Daneva and O. Pastor (Eds.): REFSQ 2016, LNCS 9619, pp. 36–41, 2016.
DOI: 10.1007/978-3-319-30282-9_3

and risks associated with alternative delivery sequences. A second limitation of IFM is that while clients and software developers generally have multiple conflicting goals, the IFM optimization algorithm considers the maximization of NPV as the sole objective. Extending the IFM to deal with multiple objectives would allow requirements engineers to systematically explore tradeoffs between, for example, maximizing NPV, minimizing upfront investment cost, and other non-financial goals.

This paper presents our initial work to address these limitations. Our approach consists in extending IFM with Bayesian decision analysis to reason about uncertainty [6, 7] and with Pareto-based optimization to support decisions with respect multiple conflicting objectives [8]. We give a brief overview of the current version of our tool-supported extension of the IFM, illustrate it on a small example, and present an agenda for future research.

2 Background

The IFM considers software systems to be composed of Minimum Marketable Features (MMF) and Architectural Elements (AE). A MMF is a small self-contained unit of functionality that provides value to the client. An AE is an element that does not provide client value in itself but is a prerequisite to the delivery of other AEs and MMFs. MMFs and AEs are collectively referred to as elements. An element X depends on an element Y means that X cannot be delivered before Y, because of constraints in the development process or application domain. To illustrate the IFM and our extension, we use the hypothetical example of the development of a web banking application first introduced in the IFM book [4]. Figure 1 shows the MMFs, AEs, and dependency relations for this application.

Once a system has been broken down into MMFs and AEs, we must analyze the projected cost and revenue of each element over a number of business periods. In our web banking application, the analysis will be over 4 years split into 16 trimesters. Projected costs and revenues are typically elicited from software architects, clients and marketing. The result of such analysis is recorded in a cash flow projection table, such as Table 1, that shows for each MMF and AE, one or more periods of initial investment during which the cash flow is negative followed by periods of revenues during which the cash flow is positive or zero. For example, in Table 1, AE 1 takes one period to deliver at a cost of $200,000, and MMF B takes two periods to deliver, each period requiring an investment of $200,000, followed by periods of increasing revenue starting at $90,000 and rising to $225,000 6 periods after delivery.

Once the cash flow projections are known, the IFM automatically analyzes possible delivery sequences and suggests a delivery sequence that maximizes NPV —a standard financial metric measuring the difference between revenues and costs (i.e. positive and negative cash flows) taking into account the time value of money at a fixed discount rate. In our example, we use a discount rate of 1 % per period.

When a system is composed of only a few AEs and MMFs, it is possible to compute the NPV of all possible delivery sequences and identify one that maximizes NPV. When such an exhaustive analysis is not possible, IFM uses a heuristic to find a near optimal solution. In our running example, assuming a single MMF or AE can be worked on during each period, IFM computes that the optimal delivery sequence consists in developing AE 1 first, followed by MMFs A, B, and C.

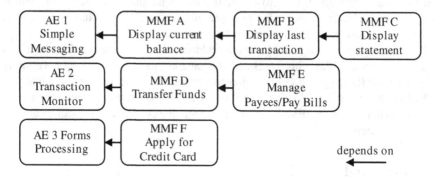

Fig. 1. IFM precedence graph for a hypothetical web banking system [1]

Table 1. Cash flow projections for the web banking MMFs and AEs [1]

	1	2	3	4	5	6	7	8	9	10	11	12	13	14	15	16
AE 1	-200	0	0	0	0	0	0	0	0	0	0	0	0	0	0	0
MMF A	-200	90	90	81	72	63	54	45	36	27	18	9	0	0	0	0
MMF B	-200	-200	90	117	144	171	198	225	225	225	225	225	225	225	225	225
MMF C	-200	-200	80	112	144	176	208	240	272	304	320	320	320	320	320	320
AE 2	-400	0	0	0	0	0	0	0	0	0	0	0	0	0	0	0
MMF D	-250	-250	45	72	90	108	126	144	162	180	180	180	180	180	180	180
MMF E	-350	-350	35	70	105	140	175	210	245	245	245	245	245	245	245	245
AE 3	-200	0	0	0	0	0	0	0	0	0	0	0	0	0	0	0
MMF F	-100	-100	90	90	135	135	135	135	135	135	135	135	135	135	135	135

In practice, the suggested optimal or near optimal delivery sequence provides a baseline that decision makers can adapt to take into consideration additional objectives and constraints not represented in the model. The IFM analysis is used to decide what to build in the first period and has to be repeated at the beginning of each new period, possibly with an updated list of MMFs, AEs and revised cash flow projections taking into account business changes and an increased understanding of the business needs and development technologies.

3   Related Work

Other software engineering decision methods take, like the IFM, a financial perspective to inform funding and design decisions [7, 9, 10]. These methods, however, support one-time upfront decisions only without considering how to deliver the system in small increments and optimize the delivery sequence. The IFM is also related to methods supporting release planning by reasoning about the priorities assigned by different group of stakeholders to different requirements [3]. Some release planning methods deal with uncertainty related to development effort [11, 12]. These methods aim to identify release plans that minimize cost and maximize value, where value is defined as a weighted sum of stakeholder's preferences rather than in financial terms.

Several extensions to the IFM have already been proposed: (i) to improve the IFM optimization algorithm [12], (ii) to extend IFM with uncertain cash flows and generate flexible investment policies in the form of decision trees [13], and (iii) to take into account the behavior of competitors using game theory [14]. In our approach, we model and analyze cash flow using probability distribution functions similarly to previous work [13] but differ from previous work by considering multiple optimization objectives and by aspiring to introduce concepts from Decision Analysis, such as the expected value of information [7], to guide decisions about which uncertainty to reduce in order to reduce risks and increase NPV.

4   Multi-objective IFM Under Uncertainty

In order to test the feasibility of extending IFM to deal with uncertainty and multiple objectives, we have developed a prototype tool (in R) and have applied it to a couple of small examples. Our tool has the following capabilities:

1. Uncertainty about MMF and AE cash flows are represented as triangular distributions. A triangular distribution is characterized by three parameters specifying the lowest, most likely, and highest value for a variable. We have chosen this distribution because it is easily understood and used in IT portfolio management tools [10]. We envision, however, extending our tool to additional probability distributions [15].
2. Our tool uses Monte-Carlo simulation to compute the impact of MMF and AE cash flow uncertainty on the NPV of alternative delivery sequences. For each delivery sequence, our tool then computes a series of statistics including its expected NPV (the mean NPV over all simulations), expected investment cost (the mean of the total cost to be invested in the project before it has a positive cash flow), and its investment risk (the ratio between its NPV standard deviation and its expected NPV [10]).
3. The statistics about the NPV simulations are then used to select the Pareto-optimal set of delivery sequences that maximize expected NPV, minimize expected investment cost, and minimize investment risks. We have chosen these objectives because they are used in IT project portfolio management tools [10]. Decision makers can, however, select alternative set of optimization objectives that suits their context.

Returning to our running example, we have extended the cash flow table of Table 1 with uncertainty by assuming that cost items were underestimated with an uncertain cost overruns having a triangular distributions with parameters $(0, 0.2c, 0.45c)$ where c is the initial cost prediction, and by assuming that revenue items tended to be overestimated and have a triangular distributions with parameters $(0, r, 1.2\ r)$ where r is the initial revenue prediction. Given these uncertainties, Fig. 2 shows a plot of the expected NPV and investment cost for all possible delivery sequences with the sequences identified as Pareto-optimal marked with a cross. Our tool also allows visualizing the cash flow uncertainty of any delivery sequence, as shown in Fig. 3 for one of the Pareto-optimal delivery sequences. The main black line represents the mean cash flow and the shaded area its standard deviation.

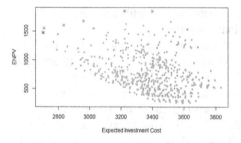
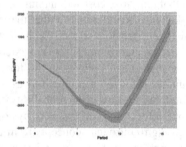

Fig. 2. Expected NPV and investment cost for the web banking application. Pareto-optimal sequences are marked with a cross.

Fig. 3. Uncertain cash flow for one of the Pareto-optimal delivery sequence

Our current implementation has a couple of limitations: (i) like the standard IFM algorithm, it assumes a single MMF or AE can be worked on during each period, and (ii) it uses an exhaustive search to identify Pareto-optimal delivery sequences which limits its scalability to problems involving no more than a dozen MMF and AEs. We intend to address these limitations by removing the assumption from our model and by using search-based evolutionary algorithms instead to improve scalability.

5   Future Work

Our end goal is to develop a sound and practical method to reason about uncertainty and take into account multiple goals during incremental software development projects. This paper presents our first steps towards that goal. Future work needed to achieve our goal include: (i) facilitating the elicitation of accurate cash flow uncertainty, notably by relying on methods used in other domains [15]; (ii) enriching the IFM decision model by integrating it with other requirements and architecture models, for example with quantitative goal models [16] and software value maps [17]; (iii) enriching the IFM so as to take into account learning objectives aimed at reducing uncertainty about the cost and value of future development activities, for example through using information value analysis [7]; (iv) helping decision makers interpret and act on the method's output, i.e. the Pareto-optimal solutions and uncertain cash flows, notably through clustering of Pareto-optimal delivery sequences [18]; and (v) evaluating the method scientifically through simulations and real case studies.

6   Conclusion

Requirements engineering decisions are inherently multi-objective and confronted with uncertainty. Developing and delivering software features in small increments helps managing uncertainty but raises the question of what to develop in each iteration. Today, such decisions are largely guided by intuition. We believe that a more scientific and evidence-based decision method could lead to better decisions and result in significantly reducing the cost and increasing the value of software projects. We have outlined our initial work and roadmap to develop such a method by extending the IFM with Bayesian decision analysis and Pareto-based optimization methods.

Acknowledgment. Olawole Oni's research is funded by the Tertiary Education Trust Fund (TETFund) in Nigeria.

References

1. Larman, G., Basili, V.R.: Iterative and incremental development: a brief history. IEEE Comput. **6**, 47–56 (2003)
2. Leffingwell, D.: Agile Software Requirements: Lean Requirements Practices for Teams, Programs, and the Enterprise. Addison-Wesley Professional, Boston (2010)
3. Greer, D., Ruhe, G.: Software release planning: an evolutionary and iterative approach. Inf. Softw. Technol. **46**(4), 243–253 (2004)
4. Denne, M., Cleland-Huang, J.: Software by Numbers. Sun Microsystems Press, Upper Saddle River (2004)
5. Denne, M., Cleland-Huang, J.: The incremental funding method: data-driven software development. IEEE Softw. **21**(3), 39–47 (2004)
6. Winkler, R.L.: An Introduction to Bayesian Inference and Decision, 2nd edn. Probabilistic Publishing, Gainesville (2003)
7. Letier, E., Stefan, D., Barr, E.T.: Uncertainty, risk, and information value in software requirements and architecture. In: Proceedings of 36th International Conference on Software Engineering (2014)
8. Harman, M., Jones, B.F.: Search-based software engineering. Inf. Softw. Technol. **43**(14), 833–839 (2001)
9. Moore, M., Kaman, R., Klein, M., Asundi, J.: Quantifying the value of architecture design decisions: lessons from the field. In: Proceedings of 25th International Conference on Software Engineering (2003)
10. Cantor, M.: Calculating and improving ROI in software and system programs. Commun. ACM **54**(9) (2011) (Ruhe, G., Greer, D. Quantitative studies in software release planning under risk and resource constraints. In: Proceedings of ISESE (2003))
11. Logue, K., McDaid, K.: Agile release planning: dealing with uncertainty in development time and business value. In: Proceedings of ECBS (2008)
12. Alencar, A.J., et al.: A statistical approach for the maximization of the financial benefits yielded by a large set of MMFs and AEs. Comput. Inform. **32**(6), 1147–1169 (2013)
13. Barbosa, B.P., Schmitz, E.A., Alencar, A.J.: Generating software-project investment policies in an uncertain environment. In: Proceedings SIEDS (2008)
14. da Cunha Mattos, E.M., et al.: Applying game theory to the incremental funding method in software projects. J. Softw. **9**(6), 1435–1443 (2014)
15. O'Hagan, A., Buck, C., Daneshkhah, A., Eiser, J., Garthwaite, P., Jenkinson, D., Oakley, J., Rakow, T.: Uncertain Judgments: Eliciting Experts' Probabilities. Wiley, Hoboken (2006)
16. Heaven, W., Letier, E.: Simulating and optimising design decisions in quantitative goal models. In: Proceedings of 9th International Conference on Requirements (2011)
17. Mahvish, K., Gorschek, T., Wilson, M.: The software value map—an exhaustive collection of value aspects for the development of software intensive products. J. Softw. Evol. Process **25**(7), 711–741 (2013)
18. Veerappa, V., Letier, E.: Understanding clusters of optimal solutions in multi-objective decision problems. In: Proceedings 19th International Conference on Requirements (2011)

Open Source in Requirements Engineering

Do Information Retrieval Algorithms for Automated Traceability Perform Effectively on Issue Tracking System Data?

Thorsten Merten[1(✉)], Daniel Krämer[1], Bastian Mager[1], Paul Schell[1], Simone Bürsner[1], and Barbara Paech[2]

[1] Department of Computer Science, Bonn-Rhein-Sieg University of Applied Sciences, Sankt Augustin, Germany
{thorsten.merten,simone.buersner}@h-brs.de,
{daniel.kraemer.2009w,bastian.mager.2010w,
paul.schell.2009w}@informatik.h-brs.de
[2] Institute of Computer Science, University of Heidelberg, Heidelberg, Germany
paech@informatik.uni-heidelberg.de

Abstract. [**Context and motivation**] Traces between issues in issue tracking systems connect bug reports to software features, they connect competing implementation ideas for a software feature or they identify duplicate issues. However, the trace quality is usually very low. To improve the trace quality between requirements, features, and bugs, information retrieval algorithms for automated trace retrieval can be employed. Prevailing research focusses on structured and well-formed documents, such as natural language requirement descriptions. In contrast, the information in issue tracking systems is often poorly structured and contains digressing discussions or noise, such as code snippets, stack traces, and links. Since noise has a negative impact on algorithms for automated trace retrieval, this paper asks: [**Question/Problem**] Do information retrieval algorithms for automated traceability perform effectively on issue tracking system data? [**Results**] This paper presents an extensive evaluation of the performance of five information retrieval algorithms. Furthermore, it investigates different preprocessing stages (e.g. stemming or differentiating code snippets from natural language) and evaluates how to take advantage of an issue's structure (e.g. title, description, and comments) to improve the results. The results show that algorithms perform poorly without considering the nature of issue tracking data, but can be improved by project-specific preprocessing and term weighting. [**Contribution**] Our results show how automated trace retrieval on issue tracking system data can be improved. Our manually created gold standard and an open-source implementation based on the OpenTrace platform can be used by other researchers to further pursue this topic.

Keywords: Issue tracking systems · Empirical study · Traceability · Open-source

© Springer International Publishing Switzerland 2016
M. Daneva and O. Pastor (Eds.): REFSQ 2016, LNCS 9619, pp. 45–62, 2016.
DOI: 10.1007/978-3-319-30282-9_4

1 Introduction

A considerable amount of requirements engineering (RE) research focusses on the automation of requirements traceability [10] by analyzing natural language (NL) of requirements artifacts (RA), e.g. [4,5,8]. These approaches report promising recall and accuracy. At the same time, RE research and best practices emphasize that high quality RAs should be written correctly, consistently, unambiguously, and organized[1]. In the context of automated trace retrieval, the performance of information retrieval (IR) algorithms benefits from documents that satisfy these criteria. However, the criteria are not satisfied by the data in issue tracking systems (ITS) [19]. Hence, the investigation and experiments in this paper are guided by the following main question:

Do information retrieval algorithms for automated traceability
perform effectively on issue tracking system data?

To answer this question, a study with the data of the ITSs of four open-source projects is conducted. For each project a gold standard traceability matrix is created and the optimal results out of five IR algorithms with and without text preprocessing efforts, such as stemming and stop word removal, as well as the impact of term weights on different issue parts, are calculated and reported. The results show that algorithms perform poorly without considering the nature of ITS data, but can be improved by ITS-specific preprocessing and especially by term weighting. Furthermore, they show that VSM and LSI algorithms perform better than different versions of BM25 with ITS data.

The next section gives background information on ITSs and IR algorithms in the context of automated trace retrieval. It explains how traces are used and represented in ITSs exemplified by excerpts of our data and it gives a brief overview of related work in the field. Afterwards, Sect. 3 gives a brief overview of related work in the field. Section 4 states our research questions which are derived from the main question above. Section 5 explains the experiment setup including data acquisition, the employed tools, and algorithm evaluation. The, often counterintuitive, results are discussed in Sect. 6 for every RQ and it includes an overall discussion. Section 7 discusses how we mitigated threats to validity and finally, Sect. 8 concludes the paper and reflects on how future work can tackle the problem of ITS traceability.

2 Background

This Section briefly explains the employed IR algorithms (Sect. 2.1) and how IR results are measured (Sect. 2.2). Then, it introduces ITSs (Sect. 2.3) and how data is handled in ITS. Finally, it bridges the gap between the nature of IR methods and the nature of ITS data (Sect. 2.4).

---

[1] Among other criteria as defined in ISO/IEC/IEEE 29148:2011 [14].

2.1   Information Retrieval Background

IR algorithms are designed "to retrieve all the documents that are relevant to a user query while retrieving as few non-relevant documents as possible [2, p. 4]". This definition can be applied to the problem of traceability: If I is the set of all issues, a relevance ranking of two issues i and $i' \in I$ can be computed by a function $similarity: I \times I \rightarrow R$, with $R = \{r \in \mathbb{R} | 0 \leq r \leq 1\}$. Because a trace has only two states (it is either present or not), a threshold t is applied so that $trace_t : I \times I \rightarrow \{true, false\}$ with

$$trace_t(i, i') = \begin{cases} true & : similarity(i, i') \geq t \\ false & : similarity(i, i') < t \end{cases} \quad (1)$$

computes whether a trace between issue i and i' exists. A trace matrix of size $|I| \times |I|$ with elements $a_{i,j} = trace_t(i, j)$ can now be created.

The following IR algorithms were used to calculate the *similarity* function in our experiments: The vector space model (VSM) [27] using term frequency, inverse document frequency (TF-IDF), latent semantic indexing (LSI) [7] using the cosine measure, the Okapi best match 25 (BM25) [25] as well as its variants BM25L [16], and BM25+ [15]. The following paragraph gives a brief overview of the basics and differences of these algorithms. We refer the reader to IR literature for further information and details, e.g. [2,17].

VSM maps the terms of an issue to vectors. By using a distance metric such as TF-IDF, the similarity (S) of two issues can be computed. One of the main problems in VSM is exactly this dependency on each term and each term's spelling. Furthermore, the terms may have multiple meanings. Therefore, the VSM approach may compute a high similarity between issues with equal terms which may have different meanings due to context. LSI copes with this problem. Instead of computing S between terms, LSI computes S between concepts of the issues. Concepts are an abstraction of multiple terms and represent the "topics" of an issue. LSI creates those concepts using singular value decomposition [2, p. 101] which also reduces the search space. In contrast to the above, BM25 is a probabilistic approach to calculate S. It relies on the assumption that there is an ideal set of issues that are related to i and computes the probability of each issue to be in this set. BM25L and BM25+ both try to compensate problematic behavior of BM25 on long issues [16].

It is important to note that all of the approaches depend on the following properties of an issue i in the issue set I: (a) the actual terms of i compared to another issue i', (b) the number of terms (term frequency) in i, and (c) the number of terms in i that are also in I (inverse document frequency). These properties can be influenced by text preprocessing. The most widely used preprocessing techniques are removing stop words (e.g. articles, prepositions, and conjunctions) and stemming (e.g. removing affixes; for example *connect* is the stem for connected, connecting, connection, ...)[2]. Due to these influences, it cannot be said

---

[2] More preprocessing techniques are available. As an example [9] consider only nouns, adjectives, adverbs, and verbs for further processing.

which algorithm performs best with a certain data set without experimenting, although BM25 is often used as a baseline to evaluate the performance of new algorithms for classic IR applications such as search engines [2, p. 107].

2.2 Measuring IR Algorithm Performance for Trace Retrieval

IR algorithms for trace retrieval are typically evaluated using the recall (R) and precision (P) metrics with respect to a reference trace matrix. R measures the retrieved relevant links and P the correctly retrieved links:

$$R = \frac{Correct Links \cap Retrieved Links}{Correct Links}, \qquad P = \frac{Correct Links \cap Retrieved Links}{Retrieved Links} \tag{2}$$

Since P and R are contradicting metrics (R can be maximized by retrieving all links, which results in low precision; P can be maximised by retrieving only one correct link, which results in low recall) the F_β-Measure as their harmonic mean is often employed in the area of traceability. In our experiments, we computed results for the F_1 measure, which balances P and R, as well as F_2, which emphasizes recall:

$$F_\beta = \frac{(1 + \beta^2) \times Precision \times Recall}{(\beta^2 \times Precision) + Recall} \tag{3}$$

Huffman Hayes et al. [13] define *acceptable*, *good* and *excellent* P and R ranges. Table 3 extends their definition with according F_1 and F_2 ranges. The results section refers to these ranges.

2.3 Issue Tracking System Data Background

At some point in the software engineering (SE) life cycle, requirements are communicated to multiple roles, like project managers, software developers and, testers. Many software projects utilize an ITS to support this communication and to keep track of the corresponding tasks and changes [28]. Hence, requirement descriptions, development tasks, bug fixing, or refactoring tasks are collected in ITSs. This implies that the data in such systems is often uncategorized and comprises manifold topics [19].

The NL data in a single issue is usually divided in at least two fields: A title (or summary) and a description. Additionally, almost every ITS supports commenting on an issue. Title, description, and comments will be referred to as *ITS data fields* in the remainder of this paper. Issues usually describe new software requirements, bugs, or other development or test related tasks. Figure 1[3] shows an excerpt of the title and description data fields of two issues, that both request a new software feature for the Redmine project. It can be inferred from the text, that both issues refer to the same feature and give different solution proposals.

---

[3] Figure 1 intentionally omits other meta-data such as authoring information, date- and time-stamps, or the issue status, since it is not relevant for the remainder of this paper.

ITS data field	Issue #1910	Issue #12700
Title	Delete/close created forum entry	Let messages have a "solved" flag
Description	I suggest a feature under the forums where the user can close or delete the topic he/she started. This way, other users will not get confused if the problem is already resolved.	It would be easier to go through the messages in the forums if there was a "solved" flag users could set to show that their questions have been answered. * A filter could then be used to only show "open" messages. [...]
Comments	[none]	[none]

Fig. 1. Excerpts of two example issues from the Redmine Project

Links between issues are usually established by a simple domain-specific language. E.g. #42 creates a trace to an issue with id 42. In some ITS the semantics of such traces can be specified (e.g. to distinguish duplicated from related issues). These semantically enriched links will be referred to as *trace types*. The issues in Fig. 1 are marked as *related* issues by the Redmine developers. However, issues are also traced because of other reasons, including but not limited to:

- To express that a bug is related to a certain feature issue.
- To divide a (larger) issue in child-issues (e.g. for organizational purposes).

In this paper, we report on the trace types *duplicate* and *generic*. A duplicate relation exists between two issues, if both issues describe exactly the same software feature and a *generic* relation exists, if two issues refer to the same software feature. This includes all the examples given above. Such a *generic* relation can for example be used to determine the total amount of time and money that was spent for a software feature, or to determine who was involved in developing, fixing, refactoring, and testing a feature.

Different semantics of an issue are subsequently referred to as *issue types*. ITS historically support the definition of one issue type per issue. Another approach is to tag issues with multiple descriptors[4]. In this paper we report on the issue types *bug* and *feature*, as well as the set of all issues that also includes uncategorized or untagged issues.

2.4 Impact of ITS Data on IR Algorithms

In previous research [19], we analyzed the content of NL in ITS data. We found that NL is often used imprecisely and contains flaws. Furthermore, NL is mixed with *noise* comprised of source code, stack traces, links, or repetitive information, like citations. Finally, the comments of an issue often drift from the original topic mentioned in the title and description towards something completely different (usually without being re-organized). Issues are seldom corrected and some issues

---

[4] The researched projects use the ITSs Redmine and GitHub. In Redmine the issue type needs to be specified, GitHub allows tagging.

or comments represent only hasty notes meant for a developer – often without forming a whole sentence. In contrast, RAs typically do not contain noise and NL is expected to be correct, consistent, and precise. Furthermore, structured RAs are subject to a specific quality assurance[5] and thus their structure and NL is much better than ITS data.

Since IR algorithms compute the text similarity between two documents, spelling errors and hastily written notes that leave out information, have a negative impact on the performance. In addition, the performance is influenced by source code which often contains the same terms repeatedly. Finally, stack traces often contain a considerable amount of the same terms (e.g. Java package names). Therefore, an algorithm might compute a high similarity between two issues that refer to different topics if they both contain a stack trace.

3   Related Work

Borg et al. conducted a systematic mapping of trace retrieval approaches [3]. Their paper shows that much work has been done in trace retrieval between RA, but only few studies use ITS data. Only one of the reviewed approaches in [3] uses the BM25 algorithm, but VSM and LSA are used extensively. This paper fills both gaps by comparing VSM, LSA, and three variants of BM25 on unstructured ITS data. [3] also reports on preprocessing methods saying that stop word removal and stemming are most often used. Our study focusses on the influence of ITS-specific preprocessing and ITS data field-specific term weighting beyond removing stop words and stemming. Gotel et al. [10] summarize the results of many approaches for automated trace retrieval in their roadmap paper. They recognize that results vary largely: "[some] methods retrieved almost all of the true links (in the 90 % range for recall) and yet also retrieved many false positives (with precision in the low 10–20 % range, with occasional exceptions)." We expect that the results in this paper will be worse, as we investigate in issues and not in structured RAs.

Due to space limitations, we cannot report on related work extensively and refer the reader to [3,10] for details. The experiments presented in this paper are restricted to standard IR text similarity methods. In the following, extended approaches are summarized that could also be applied to ITS data and/or combined with the contribution in this paper: Nguyen et al. [21] combine multiple properties, like the connection to a version control system to relate issues. Gervasi and Zowghi [8] use additional methods beyond text similarity with requirements and identify another affinity measure. Guo et al. [11] use an expert system to calculate traces automatically. The approach is very promising, but is not fully automated. Sultanov and Hayes [29] use reinforcement learning and improve the results compared to VSM. Niu and Mahmoud [22] use clustering to group links in high-quality and low-quality clusters respectively to improve accuracy. The low-quality clusters are filtered out. Comparing multiple techniques for trace retrieval, Oliveto et al. [23] found that no technique outperformed the others.

---

[5] Dag and Gervasi [20] surveyed automated approaches to improve the NL quality.

They also combined LDA with other techniques which improved the result in many cases. Heck and Zaidman [12] also performed experiments with ITS data for duplicate detection with good recall rates. In addition they found that extensive stop word removal can be counter-beneficial for ITS data.

4 Research Questions

We divided our main question into the following four research questions (RQ):

RQ$_1$: How do IR algorithms for automated traceability perform on ITS data in comparison to related work on structured RAs? *We expect (a) worse results to related work on RAs, due to little structure and much noise in ITS data, and (b) BM25 [+/L] variants to perform competitive for some projects.*
RQ$_2$: How do results vary, if ITS-specific preprocessing and weighting is applied? *We expect that removing noise improves results for all data sets as discussed in* Sect. 2.
RQ$_3$: How do results vary for different trace and issue types? *E.g.* [12,26,30] *used IR algorithms on bug report duplicates, only. Since duplicates usually have a high similarity, we expect good results for duplicates.*
RQ$_4$: How do results vary between different projects? *Experiments are run with the data of four projects with distinct properties (see* Sect. 5.1*). We expect a wide range of results due to these differences.*

5 Experiment Setup

The experiment setup has three important steps: (1) The extraction and preparation of the data, (2) the manual creation of a gold standard traceability matrix to evaluate the experiment results, and (3) the automated trace retrieval by different algorithms, different preprocessing techniques, and different term weighting.

5.1 Data Preparation

Generally, 100 consecutive issues per project (in total 400 issues) were extracted from the respective ITS APIs. We focused on consecutive issues, since it is more likely that issues in such a set are related (e.g. because they refer to the same software features) [24]. Thus, the possibility to find meaningful traces is higher in a consecutive set of issues than in randomly selected samples.

The selection includes features, bugs, and uncategorized issues. The projects that rely on the Redmine ITS categorize more issues than the ones using the GitHub ITS[6] (see Table 1 for details). In addition, the extraction process followed existing links to other issues in a breadth-first search manner to make sure that the extracted dataset includes traces. Existing links were automatically parsed and collected into a traceability matrix (referred to as Developer Trace Matrix, DTM). Beside the NL data fields and the existing traces, meta-data such as authors, date- and time-stamps, the issue status, or issue IDs were extracted.

---

[6] This is discussed in depth in [19].

Table 1. Project characteristics

	c:geo	Lighttpd	Radiant	Redmine
Software Type	Android app	HTTP server	content mgmt. system	ITS
Audience	consumer	technician	consumer / developer	hoster / developer
Main programming lang.	Java	C	Ruby	Ruby
ITS	GitHub	Redmine	GitHub	Redmine
ITS Usage	ad-hoc	structured	ad-hoc	very structured
ITS size (in # of issues)	~ 3850	~ 2900	~ 320	~ 19.000
Open issues	~ 450	~ 500	~ 50	~ 4500
Closed issues	~ 3400	~ 2400	~ 270	~ 14.500
Sample size	$100 \approx 3\%$	$100 \approx 3\%$	$100 \approx 30\%$	$100 < 1\%$
Sampled issues with link	$\sim 50\%$	$\sim 20\%$	$\sim 12\%$	$\sim 70\%$
Issues labeled explicitly as Feature or **Bug** in sample	25F/26B	30F/70B	0F/0B	31F/61B
Project size (in LOC)	$\sim 130,000$	$\sim 41,000$	$\sim 33,000$	$\sim 150,000$

Researched Projects and Project Selection. The data used for the experiments in this paper was taken from the following four projects:

- *c:geo*, an Android application to play a real world treasure hunting game.
- *Lighttpd*, a lightweight web server application.
- *Radiant*, a modular content management system.
- *Redmine*, an ITS.

The projects show different characteristics with respect to the software type, intended audience, programming languages, and ITS. Details of these characteristics are shown in Table 1. c:geo and Radiant use the GitHub ITS and Redmine and Lighttpd the Redmine ITS. Therefore, the issues of the first two projects are categorized by tagging, whereas every issue of the other projects is marked as a feature or a bug (see Table 1). c:geo was chosen because it is an Android application and the ITS contains more consumer requests than the other projects. Lighttpd was chosen because it is a lightweight web server and the ITS contains more code snippets and noise than the other projects. Radiant was chosen because its issues are not categorized as feature or bug at all and it contains fewer issues than the other projects. Finally, Redmine was chosen because it is a very mature project and ITS usage is very structured compared to the other projects. Some of the researchers were already familiar with these projects, since we reported on ITS NL contents earlier [19].

Gold Standard Trace Matrices. The first, third, and fourth author created the gold standard trace matrices (GSTM). For this task, the title, description, and comments of each issue was manually compared to every other issue. Since 100 issues per project were extracted, this implies $\frac{100 * 100}{2} - 50 = 4950$ manual comparisons. To have semantically similar gold standards for each project, a code of conduct was developed that prescribed e.g. when a generic trace should be created (as defined in Sect. 2.3) or when an issue should be treated as duplicate (the description of both issues describes exactly the same bug or requirement).

Table 2. Extracted traces vs. gold standard

# of relations	Projects			
	c:geo	Lighttpd	Radiant	Redmine
DTM generic	59	11	8	60
GSTM generic	102	18	55	94
GSTM duplicates	2	3	-	5
Overlapping	30	9	5	45

Table 3. Evaluation measures adapted from [13]

Acceptable	Good	Excellent
$0.6 \leq r < 0.7$	$0.7 \leq r < 0.8$	$r \geq 0.8$
$0.2 \leq p < 0.3$	$0.3 \leq p < 0.4$	$p \geq 0.4$
$0.2 \leq F_1 < 0.42$	$0.42 \leq F_1 < 0.53$	$F_1 \geq 0.53$
$0.43 \leq F_2 < 0.55$	$0.55 \leq F_2 < 0.66$	$F_2 \geq 0.66$

Since concentration quickly declines in such monotonous tasks, the comparisons were aided by a tool especially created for this purpose. It supports defining related and unrelated issues by simple keyboard shortcuts as well as saving and resuming the work. At large, a GSTM for one project was created in two and a half business days.

In general the GSTMs contain more traces than the DTMs (see Table 2). A manual analysis revealed that developers often missed (or simply did not want to create) traces or created relations between issues that are actually not related. The following examples indicate why GSTMs and DTMs differ: (1) Eight out of the 100 issues in the c:geo dataset were created automatically by a bot that manages translations for internationalization. Although these issues are related, they were not automatically marked as related. There is also a comment on how internationalization should be handled in issue (#4950). (2) Some traces in the Redmine based projects do not follow the correct syntax and are therefore missed by a parser. (3) Links are often vague and unconfirmed in developer traces. E.g. c:geo #5063 says that the issue "could be related to #4978 [...] but I couldn't find a clear scenario to reproduce this". We also could not find evidence to mark these issues as related in the gold standard but a link was already placed by the developers. (4) Issue #5035 in c:geo contains a reference to #3550 to say that a bug occurred before the other bug was reported (the trace semantics in this case is: "occurred likely before"). There is, however, no semantics relation between the bugs, therefore we did not mark these issues as related in the gold standard. (5) The Radiant project simply did not employ many manual traces.

5.2   Tools

The experiments are implemented using the OpenTrace (OT) [1] framework. OT retrieves traces between NL RAs and includes means to evaluate results with respect to a reference matrix.

OT utilizes IR implementations from Apache Lucene[7] and it is implemented as an extension to the General Architecture for Text Engineering (GATE) framework [6]. GATE's features are used for basic text processing and pre-processing functionality in OT, e.g. to split text into tokens or for stemming. To make both frameworks deal with ITS data, some changes and enhancements were made to

---

[7] https://lucene.apache.org.

Table 4. Data fields weights (l), algorithms and preprocessing settings (r)

Weight				Rationale / Hypothesis		Algorithm	Settings
Title	Description	Comments	Code			BM25	Pure, +, L
1	1	1	1	Unaltered algorithm		VSM	TF-IDF
1	1	1	0	– without considering code		LSI	*cos* measure
1	1	0	0	– also without comments			
2	1	1	1	Title more important		Preprocessing	Settings
2	1	1	0	– without considering code		*Standard*	
1	2	1	1	Description more important		Stemming	on/off
1	1	1	2	Code more important		Stop Word Removal	on/off
8	4	2	1	Most important information first		*ITS-specific*	
4	2	1	0	– without considering code		Noise Removal	on/off
2	1	0	0	– also without comments		Code Extraction	on/off

OT: (1) refactoring to make it compatible with the current GATE version (8.1), (2) enhancement to make it process ITS data fields with different term weights, and (3) development of a framework to configure OT automatically and to run experiments for multiple configurations. The changed source code is publicly available for download[8].

5.3   Algorithms and Settings

For the experiment, multiple term weighting schemes for the ITS data fields and different preprocessing methods are combined with the IR algorithms VSM, LSI, BM25, BM25+, BM25L. Beside stop word removal and stemming, which we will refer to as *standard preprocessing*, we employ *ITS-specific preprocessing*. For the ITS-specific preprocessing, noise (as defined in Sect. 2) was removed and the regions marked as code were extracted and separated from the NL. Therefore, term weights can be applied to each ITS data field and the code. Table 4 gives an overview of all preprocessing methods (right) and term weights as well as rationales for the chosen weighting schemes (left).

6   Results

We compute $trace_t$ with different thresholds t in order to maximize precision, recall, F_1 and F_2 measure. Results are presented as F_2 and F_1 measure in general. However, maximising recall is often desirable in practice, because it is simpler to remove wrong links manually than to find correct links manually. Therefore, R with corresponding precision is also discussed in many cases.

As stated in Sect. 5.1, a comparison with the GSTM results in more authentic and accurate measurements than a comparison with the DTM. It also yields better results: F_1 and F_2 both increase about 9 % in average computed on the

---

[8] http://www2.inf.h-brs.de/~tmerte2m – In addition to the source code, gold standards, extracted issues, and experiment results are also available for download.

unprocessed data sets. A manual inspection revealed that this increase material-izes due to the flaws in the DTM, especially because of missing traces. Therefore, the results in this paper are reported in comparison with the GSTM.

6.1 IR Algorithm Performance on ITS Data

Figure 2 shows an evaluation of all algorithms with respect to the GSTMs for all projects with and without *standard preprocessing*. The differences per project are significant with 30 % for F_1 and 27 % for F_2. It can be seen that standard preprocessing does not have a clear positive impact on the results. Although, if only slightly, a negative impact on some of the project/algorithm combinations is noticeable. On a side note, our experiment supports the claim of [12], that removing stop-words is not always beneficial on ITS data: We experimented with different stop word lists and found that a small list that essentially removes only pronouns works best.

In terms of algorithms, to our surprise, no variant of BM25 competed for the best results. The best F_2 measures of all BM25 variants varied from 0.09 to 0.19 over all projects, independently of standard preprocessing. When maximizing R to 1, P does not cross a 2 % barrier for any algorithm. Even for $R \geq 0.9$, P is still < 0.05. All in all, the results are not good according to Table 3, indepen-dently of standard preprocessing, and they cannot compete with related work on structured RAs.

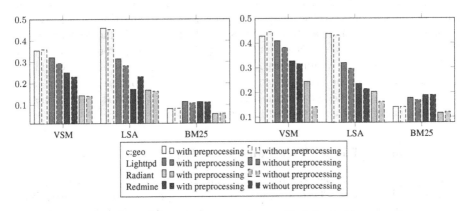

Fig. 2. Best F_1 (left) and F_2 (right) scores for every algorithm

Although results decrease slightly in a few cases, the negative impact is negli-gible. Therefore, the remaining measurements are reported with the standard preprocessing techniques enabled[9].

---

[9] In addition, removing stop words and stemming is considered IR best practices, e.g. [2,17].

6.2   Influence of ITS-specific Preprocessing and Weighting

This *RQ* investigates in the influence of *ITS-specific preprocessing*[10] and *ITS data field-specific term weighting* in contrast to *standard preprocessing*.

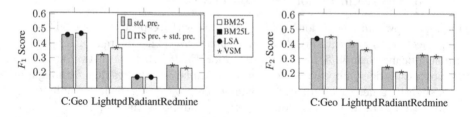

Fig. 3. Best results with and without removing noise

Contrary to our expectations, ITS-specific preprocessing impacts only c:geo clearly positively as shown in Fig. 3. For the other projects, a positive impact is achieved in terms of F_1 measure only. Since preprocessing always removes data, it can have a negative impact on recall. This is what we notice as a slight decrease of the F_2 measure for three of the projects (4 % for Lighttpd, 2 % for Radiant, and 1 % for Redmine). Overall however, precision improves with ITS-specific preprocessing.

Figure 4 shows the influence of different term weights in each of the projects. For a better comparison, the results are shown with *standard* and *ITS-specific preprocessing* enabled. The left axis represents the term weight factors for: *Title - Description - Comments - Code*. In contrast to ITS-specific preprocessing, Fig. 4 shows that some term weights clearly performed best. In general, the weighting schemes that stress the title yielded better results. In addition, the figure also shows that code should not be considered by IR algorithms for trace retrieval: Term weights of 0 for code yielded the best results.

6.3   Influence of Trace Types and Issue Types

Issue Types. Table 5 shows the best achievable results for F_1, F_2 and R on fully preprocessed datasets. The best results per issue type are printed in bold font. Since the Radiant dataset does not provide information on issue types, it is excluded in Table 5.

Trace retrieval from feature to bug issues worked best for the Lighttpd dataset. For Redmine retrieval between features worked best and for c:geo retrieval between bugs worked best; here, however, retrieval for other cases is much lower. Interestingly, there was no issue type, that worked best or worst for all projects.

---

[10] Removing code snippets and other noise can be achieved automatically, e.g. [18].

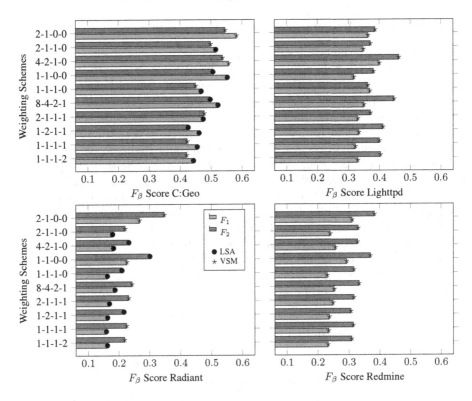

Fig. 4. Influence of term weighting

Trace Types. Table 6 compares the best achievable results for $trace_t : I \times I$ and $trace_t^{duplicate} : I \times I$. We restricted the comparison to generic relations and duplicates, since other annotated trace types in the GSTM[11] left too much room for interpretation by the annotators. E.g. it is hard to define when exactly an issue "blocks" another issue, without detailed knowledge of the project.

Table 6 shows that duplicate issues are detected competitively for c:geo and Redmine and rather poorly for Lighttpd. The latter contradicts our expectations for this *RQ*. However, a manual inspection of the data showed that duplicated issues often use different words to express the same matter, similar to the example given in Fig. 1. This can only be resolved by domain knowledge and/or knowledge of domain-dependant synonyms. Both of which cannot be handled by standard IR algorithms without additional effort. Note, that we cannot report on the Radiant dataset, since the GSTM does not contain any duplicates as shown in Table 2.

---

[11] We also allowed the annotation of the following trace types: I_1 precedes, is parent of, blocks, clones I_2.

6.4   Results per Project and Overall Discussion

Table 7 summarizes the best results per project for $F_{1/2}$ and R with (P) as well as the necessary settings to achieve these results. A baseline is represented by the best performing algorithm with *standard preprocessing* but without *ITS-specific preprocessing* and without *ITS data field-specific term weighting*. Although all results exceed this baseline, the positive impact of the ITS-specific efforts is only significant for c:geo and Radiant datasets ($F_{1,2}$ increase between 10 and 12 %) and it has only a small impact on the Lighttpd and Redmine datasets ($F_{1,2}$ increase between 5 and 8 %). This correlates with the ITSs that the projects employ. We hypothesize that data cleanup and weighting have a higher influence on the Github based projects, since the NL data looks a bit *untidy* in comparison to the Redmine based projects. With an improvement of 11 % for F_2 the best values were achieved for c:geo and Radiant. We think that this is because both ITSs contain the least technical discussions and terms. On the contrary, the next best results are measured for Lighttpd and the project's ITS contains much technical data as well as talk. All in all, combinations of weighting and ITS-specific preprocessing were responsible for the best obtainable results.

Table 5. Best results for different issue types

		$trace_t : I_{feature} \times I_{feature}$			$trace_t : I_{feature} \times I_{bug}$			$trace_t : I_{bug} \times I_{bug}$		
		Results	Alg.	Weights	Results	Alg.	Weights	Results	Alg.	Weights
c:geo	F_1	0.4	BM25	2,1,0,0	0.46	VSM	8,4,2,1	**0.64**	VSM	1,1,1,0
	F_2	0.53	VSM	4,2,1,0	0.41	VSM	8,4,2,1	**0.67**	VSM	1,1,1,0
	$R(P)$	1 (0.6)	BM25	1,1,0,0	1 (0.03)	BM25	1,1,0,0	1 (0.04)	VSM	1,1,0,0
Lightt.	F_1	**0.67**	VSM	1,1,0,0	**0.67**	VSM	1,1,1,0	0.33	LSA	8,4,2,1
	F_2	0.56	VSM	1,1,0,0	**0.71**	VSM	1,1,1,0	0.43	VSM	8,4,2,1
	$R(P)$	1 (0.02)	BM25	1,1,0,0	1 (0.8)	BM25	1,1,0,0	1 (0.01)	BM25	4,2,1,0
Redm.	F_1	**0.49**	VSM	2,1,0,0	0.29	VSM	4,2,1,0	0.29	VSM	4,2,1,0
	F_2	**0.55**	VSM	2,1,0,0	0.30	VSM	1,1,0,0	0.38	VSM	4,2,1,0
	$R(P)$	1 (0.07)	BM25	1,1,0,0	1 (0.03)	BM25	1,1,1,0	0.04 (1)	VSM	1,1,1,0

Table 6. Best results for different trace types

		$trace_t : I \times I$			$trace_t^{duplicate} : I \times I$		
		Results	Alg.	Weights	Results	Alg.	Weights
c:geo	F_1	0.58	VSM	2,1,0,0	**0.67**	LSA	1,1,0,0
	F_2	0.55	VSM	2,1,0,0	**0.56**	LSA	1,1,0,0
	$R(P)$	0.1 (0.03)	BM25+	1,1,1,1	1 (0.11)	BM25	1,1,0,0
Lightt.	F_1	**0.4**	VSM	4,2,1,0	0.18	LSA	1,1,0,0
	F_2	**0.46**	VSM	4,2,1,0	0.36	VSM	2,1,0,0
	$R(P)$	0.97 (0.04)	BM25	1,1,1,1	0.97 (0.3)	BM25	1,1,0,0
Redm.	F_1	**0.31**	VSM	1,1,0,0	**0.31**	LSA	1,2,1,1
	F_2	**0.38**	VSM	2,1,0,0	0.36	LSA	1,2,1,1
	$R(P)$	0.99 (0.03)	VSM	1,1,1,1	1 (0.01)	LSA	1,1,0,0

Table 7. Best results per project (trace and issue type not distinguished)

		Best Results $trace_t : I \times I$				Baseline
		Results Alg.	Weights	Std. Pre.	ITS-specific Pre.	Std. Pre. only no weighting
c:geo	F_1	0.58 VSM	2,1,0,0	true	true	0.46 LSA
	F_2	0.55 VSM	2,1,0,0	true	true	0.44 LSA
	$R(P)$	1 (0.03) BM25+	1,1,1,1	false	true	0.99 (0.03) BM25+
Lightt.	F_1	0.4 VSM	4,2,1,0	true	true	0.32 VSM
	F_2	0.46 VSM	4,2,1,0	true	true	0.41 VSM
	$R(P)$	0.97 (0.04) BM25	1,1,1,1	false	false	0.94 (0.03) VSM
Radiant	F_1	0.27 VSM	2,1,0,0	true	true	0.17 LSA
	F_2	0.35 VSM	2,1,0,0	true	true	0.24 VSM
	$R(P)$	1 (0.02) BM25	2,1,0,0	false	false	1 (0.02) BM25
Redm.	F_1	0.31 VSM	2,1,0,0	true	true	0.25 VSM
	F_2	0.38 VSM	2,1,0,0	true	true	0.33 VSM
	$R(P)$	0.99 (0.3) VSM	1,1,1,1	stopword only	false	0.99 (0.03) VSM

As discussed in RQ_3, not considering the code and emphasizing the title worked best for each project.

In addition, we compared the values of the fully preprocessed datasets from Table 5 to the same baseline as in Table 7 (only standard preprocessing). This comparison revealed that the preprocessed dataset performs better for different trace and issue types as well. We noticed improvements in every case. Most significantly, improvements in both, F_1 and F_2, of over 36 % are achieved for $trace_t : I_{bug} \times I_{bug}$ in c:geo and over 10 % for $trace_t : I_{feature} \times I_{bug}$ in c:geo. On average, F_1 increased by 19.5 % and F_2 by 13.33 % for all trace projects and trace types.

Since no BM25 variants performed best, we calculated the improvements in comparison to the baseline from Fig. 2. BM25 still performs worse than VSM and LSI. However, the F_2 scores for BM25[+,L] improved by 23 % for c:geo, 3 % for Lighttpd, 3 % for Radiant, and 6 % for Redmine.

Overall, the results show that there is neither the best algorithm, nor the best preprocessing for all projects. However, removing code snippets and stack traces (see the term weights for n-n-n-0 in Table 7) can be considered a good advice. It generally improves the results, especially precision, and has a negative impact of $< 4\%$ on the F_2 measure for Lighttpd in our experiments, only. Also, up-weighting title and down-weighting comments has an overall positive impact. Noticeably, the best measures in Table 7 are computed with the "simplest" algorithm: VSM. Since VSM considers every term of the text that was not removed by preprocessing, we hypothesize that this property is an important factor on ITS data.

7 Threats to Validity

Each GSTM was created by one person only. We tried to minimize this threat by (a) creating and discussing guidelines on how the gold standard should be made and when issues should be seen as related, and (b) peer reviewing the created gold standards by random samples. Although the authors knew the projects or took time to become acquainted with the projects, some traces were hard to decide on. In case of doubt, no trace was inserted in the GSTM. Even though we created rather large GSTMs of 100 × 100 traces, the GSTMs comprise only small parts of the projects ITSs. Therefore, a generalization from these results cannot be made, although we included about a third of the issues of the Radiant project which is a rather large sample. It gives, however, an indication of the importance of preprocessing and term weighting and shows that ITS data cannot be handled in the same way as structured RAs. In addition to the facts discussed in Sect. 6.3, due to the low number of duplicates in our datasets (see Table 2) the low results for duplicates might have occurred by chance. It is important to note that the definitions of *related and* duplicate issues have a major influence on the results. Different definitions would certainly lead to different results since trace matrices are always use-case-dependent.

Finally, OpenTrace creates queries in Apache Lucene to calculate *similarity* : $I \times I$. This involves data transformations from and to the GATE and OT frameworks. We inspected and enhanced the code very carefully to minimize implementation problems and publish the source code and all data along with this paper.

8 Conclusion and Future Work

In this paper, we presented an evaluation of five IR algorithms for the problem of automated trace retrieval on ITS data. To properly perform this evaluation, four gold standards for 100 × 100 issues were created. The evaluation considered four open source projects with distinct properties in terms of project size, audience, and so forth. Since the nature of feature descriptions in ITSs is not comparable to requirement artifacts, our results show that algorithms that perform quite well with RAs perform significantly weaker with ITS data. A combination of ITS-specific preprocessing as well as ITS data field-specific term weighting can positively influence the results.

To further improve trace retrieval in ITS, specific NL content needs to be better understood. Our experiment shows that standard IR preprocessing as well as ITS-specific efforts do generally have a positive impact on the results. However, results vary due to the entirely different nature of NL data in different projects. Our extended version of the OpenTrace framework can be used to find good preprocessing and weighting schemes automatically, if a gold standard is available, and it can be extended with other efforts from related work.

References

1. Angius, E., Witte, R.: OpenTrace: an open source workbench for automatic software traceability link recovery. In: 2012 19th Working Conference on Reverse Engineering, pp. 507–508 (2012)
2. Baeza-Yates, R., Ribeiro-Neto, B.: Modern Information Retrieval: The Concepts and Technology Behind Search. Addison-Wesley Professional, Boston (2011)
3. Borg, M., Runeson, P., Ardö, A.: Recovering from a decade: a systematic mapping of information retrieval approaches to software traceability. Empirical Softw. Eng. **19**(6), 1565–1616 (2014)
4. Chen, X., Hosking, J., Grundy, J.: A combination approach for enhancing automated traceability. In: Proceedings of the 33rd International Conference on Software Engineering, Waikiki, Honolulu, HI, USA, pp. 912–915. ACM (2011)
5. Cleland-Huang, J., Settimi, R., Romanova, E., Berenbach, B., Clark, S.: Best practices for automated traceability. Computer **40**(6), 27–35 (2007)
6. Cunningham, H., Maynard, D., Bontcheva, K.: Text Processing with GATE (Version 6). University of Sheffield Department of Computer Science (2011)
7. Furnas, G.W., Deerwester, S., Dumais, S.T., Landauer, T.K.: Harshman, R.A., Streeter, L.A., Lochbaum, K.E.: Information retrieval using a singular value decomposition model of latent semantic structure. In: Proceedings of the 11th International ACM SIGIR Conference on R&D in Information Retrieval - SIGIR 1988, pp. 465–480. ACM Press, New York (1988)
8. Gervasi, V., Zowghi, D.: Mining requirements links. In: Berry, D., Franch, X. (eds.) REFSQ 2011. LNCS, vol. 6606, pp. 196–201. Springer, Heidelberg (2011)
9. Gervasi, V., Zowghi, D.: Supporting traceability through affinity mining. In: IEEE 22nd International Requirements Engineering Conference, pp. 143–152. IEEE (2014)
10. Gotel, O., Cleland-Huang, J., Hayes, J.H., Zisman, A., Egyed, A., Grunbacher, P., Antoniol, G.: The quest for Ubiquity: a roadmap for software and systems traceability research. In: 20th IEEE International Requirements Engineering Conference, pp. 71–80. IEEE (2012)
11. Guo, J., Cleland-Huang, J., Berenbach, B.: Foundations for an expert system in domain-specific traceability. In: 21st IEEE International Requirements Engineering Conference (RE), pp. 42–51, no. 978. IEEE (2013)
12. Heck, P., Zaidman, A.: Horizontal traceability for just-in-time requirements: the case for open source feature requests. J. Softw. Evol. Process **26**(12), 1280–1296 (2014)
13. Huffman Hayes, J., Dekhtyar, A., Sundaram, S.K.: Advancing candidate link generation for requirements tracing: the study of methods. IEEE Trans. Softw. Eng. **32**(1), 4–19 (2006)
14. ISO/IEC/IEEE: Intl. STANDARD ISO/IEC/IEEE 29148: 2011 (2011)
15. Lv, Y.: Lower-bounding term frequency normalization. In: ACM Conference on Information and Knowledge Management, pp. 7–16 (2011)
16. Lv, Y., Zhai, C.: When documents are very long, BM25 fails! In: Proceedings of the 34th International ACM SIGIR Conference on R&D in Information Retrieval - SIGIR 2011, p. 1103, no. I. ACM, New York (2011)
17. Manning, C.D., Raghavan, P., Schütze, H.: Introduction to Information Retrieval, 1st edn. Cambridge University Press, New York (2008)

18. Merten, T., Mager, B., Bürsner, S., Paech, B.: Classifying unstructured data into natural language text and technical information. In: Proceedings of the 11th Working Conference on Mining Software Repositories - MSR 2014, pp. 300–303. ACM, New York (2014)

19. Merten, T., Mager, B., Hübner, P., Quirchmayr, T., Bürsner, S., Paech, B.: Requirements communication in issue tracking systems in four open-source projects. In: 6th International Workshop on Requirements Prioritization and Communication (RePriCo), pp. 114–125. CEUR Workshop Proceedings (2015)

20. Natt och Dag, J., Gervasi, V.: Managing large repositories of naturallanguage requirements. In: Aurum, A., Wohlin, S. (eds.) Engineering and Managing Software Requirements, pp. 219–244. Springer, Heidelberg (2005)

21. Nguyen, A.T., Nguyen, T.T., Nguyen, H.A., Nguyen, T.N.: Multi-layered approach for recovering links between bug reports and fixes. In: Proceedings of the ACM SIGSOFT 20th International Symposium on the Foundations of Software Engineering - FSE 2012, p. 1 (2012)

22. Niu, N., Mahmoud, A.: Enhancing candidate link generation for requirements tracing: the cluster hypothesis revisited. In: 20th IEEE International Requirements Engineering Conference, pp. 81–90. IEEE (2012)

23. Oliveto, R., Gethers, M., Poshyvanyk, D., De Lucia, A.: On the equivalence of information retrieval methods for automated traceability link recovery. In: 2010 IEEE 18th International Conference on Program Comprehension, pp. 68–71, June 2010

24. Paech, B., Hubner, P., Merten, T.: What are the features of this software? In: ICSEA 2014, The Ninth International Conference on Software Engineering Advances, pp. 97–106. IARIA XPS Press (2014)

25. Robertson, S.E., Walker, S., Hancock-Beaulieu, M., Gull, A., Lau, M.: Okapi at TREC. In: Proceedings of The First Text REtrieval Conference, TREC 1992, National Institute of Standards and Technology (NIST). Special Publication, pp. 21–30 (1992)

26. Runeson, P., Alexandersson, M., Nyholm, O.: Detection of duplicate defect reports using natural language processing. In: International Conference on SE, pp. 499–508 (2007)

27. Salton, G., Wong, A., Yang, C.S.: A vector space model for automatic indexing. Commun. ACM **18**(11), 613–620 (1975)

28. Skerrett, I.:The Eclipse Foundation: The Eclipse Community Survey (2011)

29. Sultanov, H., Hayes, J.H.: Application of reinforcement learning to requirements engineering: requirements tracing. In: 21st IEEE International Requirements Engineering Conference, pp. 52–61. IEEE (2013)

30. Wang, X., Zhang, L., Xie, T., Anvik, J., Sun, J.: An approach to detecting duplicate bug reports using natural language and execution information. In: 2008 ACM/IEEE 30th International Conference on Software Engineering, pp. 461–470 (2008)

How Firms Adapt and Interact in Open Source Ecosystems: Analyzing Stakeholder Influence and Collaboration Patterns

Johan Linåker[1]([✉]), Patrick Rempel[2], Björn Regnell[1], and Patrick Mäder[2]

[1] Lund University, Lund, Sweden
{johan.linaker,bjorn.regnell}@cs.lth.se
[2] Technische Universität Ilmenau, Ilmenau, Germany
{patrick.rempel,patrick.maeder}@tu-ilmenau.de

Abstract. [**Context and motivation**] Ecosystems developed as Open Source Software (OSS) are considered to be highly innovative and reactive to new market trends due to their openness and wide-ranging contributor base. Participation in OSS often implies opening up of the software development process and exposure towards new stakeholders. [**Question/Problem**] Firms considering to engage in such an environment should carefully consider potential opportunities and challenges upfront. The openness may lead to higher innovation potential but also to frictional losses for engaged firms. Further, as an ecosystem progresses, power structures and influence on feature selection may fluctuate accordingly. [**Principal ideas/results**] We analyze the Apache Hadoop ecosystem in a quantitative longitudinal case study to investigate changing stakeholder influence and collaboration patterns. Further, we investigate how its innovation and time-to-market evolve at the same time. [**Contribution**] Findings show collaborations between and influence shifting among rivaling and non-competing firms. Network analysis proves valuable on how an awareness of past, present and emerging stakeholders, in regards to power structure and collaborations may be created. Furthermore, the ecosystem's innovation and time-to-market show strong variations among the release history. Indications were also found that these characteristics are influenced by the way how stakeholders collaborate with each other.

Keywords: Requirements engineering · Stakeholder collaboration · Stakeholder influence · Open source · Software ecosystem · Inter-organizational collaboration · Open innovation · Co-opetition

1 Introduction

The paradigm of Open Innovation (OI) encourages firms to look outside for ideas and resources that may further advance their internal innovation capital [1]. Conversely, a firm may also find more profitable incentives to open up an intellectual property right (IPR) rather than keeping it closed. For software-intensive firms

© Springer International Publishing Switzerland 2016
M. Daneva and O. Pastor (Eds.): REFSQ 2016, LNCS 9619, pp. 63–81, 2016.
DOI: 10.1007/978-3-319-30282-9_5

a common example of such a context is constituted by Open Source Software (OSS) ecosystems [2,3].

The openness implied by OI and an OSS ecosystem makes a firm's formerly closed borders permeable for interaction and influence from new stakeholders, many of which may be unknown to a newly opened-up firm. Entering such an ecosystem affects the way how Requirements Engineering (RE) processes are structured [4]. Traditionally these are centralized, and limited to a defined set of stakeholders. However, in this new open context, RE has moved to become more decentralized and collaborative with an evolving set of stakeholders. This may lead to an increased innovation potential for a firm's technology and product offerings, but also imply frictional losses [5]. Conflicting interests and strategies may arise, which may diminish a firms own impact in regards to feature selection and control of product planning [6]. Further, as an ecosystem evolves, power structures and influence among stakeholders may fluctuate accordingly. This creates a need for firms already engaged or thinking of entering an OSS ecosystem to have an awareness of past and present ecosystem governance constellation in order to be able to adapt their strategies and product planning to upcoming directions of the ecosystem [7].

Given this problematization, we were interested in studying how stakeholders' influence and collaboration fluctuate over time in OSS ecosystems. Researchers argue that collaboration is core to increase innovation and reduce time-to-market [8]. Hence, another goal was to study the evolution of OSS ecosystems' innovation and time-to-market over time. We hypothesize that this could be used as input to firms' planning of contribution and product strategies, which led us to formulate the following research questions:

RQ1. How are stakeholder influence and collaboration evolving over time?
RQ2. How are innovation and time-to-market evolving over the same time?

To address these questions, we launched an exploratory and quantitative longitudinal case study of the Apache Hadoop ecosystem, a widely adopted OSS framework for distribution and process parallelization of large data.

The rest of the paper is structured as follows: Sect. 2 presents related work. Section 3 describes the case study design and methodology used, limitations and threats to validity are also accounted for. Section 4 presents the analysis and results, which are further discussed in Sect. 5. Finally, Sect. 6 concludes the paper.

2   Related Work

Here we present related work to software ecosystems and how its actors (stakeholders) may be analyzed. Further, the fields of stakeholder identification and analysis in RE are presented from an ecosystem and social network perspective.

2.1 Software Ecosystems

Multiple definitions of a software ecosystem exists [9], while we refer to the one by Jansen et al. [3] - *"A software ecosystem is a set of actors functioning as a unit and interacting with a shared market for software and services, together with relationships among them. These relationships are frequently underpinned by a common technological platform or market and operates through the exchange of information, resources and artifacts."*. The definition may incorporate numerous types of ecosystems in regards to openness [10], ranging from proprietary to OSS ecosystems [9], which in turn contains multiple facets. In this study we will focus on the latter with the Apache Hadoop ecosystem as our case, where the Apache Hadoop project constitutes the technological platform underpinning the relationships between the actors of the Apache Hadoop ecosystem.

An ecosystem may further be seen from three scope levels, as proposed by Jansen et al. [7]. Scope level 1 takes an upper perspective, on the relationships and interactions between ecosystems, for example between the Apache Hadoop and the Apache Spark ecosystems, where the latter's project may be built on top of the former. On scope level 2, one looks inside of the ecosystem, its actors and the relationships between them, which is the focus of this paper when analyzing the Apache Hadoop ecosystem. Lastly, scope level 3 takes the perspective from a single actor and its specific relationships.

Jansen et al. [7] further distinguished between three types of actors: dominators, keystone players, and niche players. Dominators expand and assimilate, often on the expense of other actors. Keystone players are well connected, often with a central role in hubs of actors. They create and contribute value, often beneficial to its surrounding actors. Platform suppliers are typically keystone players. Niche players thrive on the keystone players and strive to distinguish themselves from other niche players. Although other classifications exist [9,10], we will stick to those defined above.

In the context of OSS ecosystems, a further type of distinction can be made in regards to the Onion model as proposed by Nakakoji et al. [11]. They distinguished between eight roles ranging the passive user in the outer layer, to the project leader located in the center of the model. For each layer towards the center, influence in the ecosystem increases. Advancement is correlated to increase of contributions and engagement of the user, relating to the concept of meritocracy.

2.2 Stakeholder Networks and Interaction in Requirements Engineering

To know the requirements and constraints of a software, one needs to know who the stakeholders are, hence highlighting the importance of stakeholder identification and analysis in RE [12]. Knowing which stakeholders are present is however not limited to purposes of requirements elicitation. For firms engaged in OSS ecosystems [3,9], this is important input to their product planning and contribution strategies. Disclosure of differentiating features to competitors, un-synced release cycles, extra patch-work and missed out collaboration opportunities are some possible consequences if the identification and analysis of the ecosystem's stakeholders is not done properly [2,5,6]. Most identification methods however refer to the context of traditional software development and lack empirical validation in the context of OSS ecosystems [13].

In recent years, the research focus within the field has shifted more towards stakeholder characterization through the use of, e.g., Social Network Analysis (SNA) [13]. It has also become a popular tool in empirical studies of OSS ecosystems, hence highlighting potential application within stakeholder identification.

In regards to traditional software development, Damian et al. [14] used SNA to investigate collaboration patterns and the awareness between stakeholders of co-developed requirements in the context of global software development. Lim et al. [15] constructed a system based on referrals, where identified stakeholders may recommend others. Concerning RE processes within software ecosystems in general, research is rather limited [16] with some exceptions [17]. Fricker [16] proposed that stakeholder relations in software ecosystems may be modeled as requirement value chains " ... *where requirements emerge from and propagate with inter-stakeholder collaboration*". Knauss et al. [17] investigated the IBM CLM ecosystem to find RE challenges and practices used in open-commercial software ecosystems. Distinction is made between a strategic and an emergent requirements flow, where the former regard high level requirements, and how business goals affect the release planning. The latter considers requirements created on an operational level, in a Just-In-Time (JIT) fashion, commonly observed in OSS ecosystems [18].

In OSS ecosystems specifically, RE practices such as elicitation, prioritization, and selection are usually managed through open forums such as issue trackers or mailinglists. These are also referred to as informalisms as they are used to specify and manage the requirements in an informal manner [19], usually as a part of a conversation between stakeholders. These informalisms constitute an important source to identify relevant stakeholders. Earlier work includes Duc et al. [20] who applied SNA to map stakeholders in groups of reporters, assignees, and commentators to issues with the goal to investigate the impact of stakeholder collaboration on the resolution time of OSS issues. Crowsten et al. [21] performed SNA on 120 OSS projects to investigate communication patterns in regards to interactions in projects' issue trackers.

Many studies focused on a developer and user level, though some exceptions exist. For example, Martinez-Romeo et al. [22] investigated how a community and a firm collaborates through the development process. Orucevic-Alagic et al. [23] investigated the influence of stakeholders on each other in the Android project. Texiera et al. [24] explored collaboration between firms in the Openstack ecosystem from a co-opetition perspective showing how firms, despite being competitors, may still collaborate within an ecosystem.

This paper contributes to OSS RE literature by addressing the area of stakeholder identification and analysis in OSS ecosystems by investigating a case on a functional level [24]. Further it adds to the software ecosystem literature and its shallow research of RE [16,17] and strategic perspectives [9] in general.

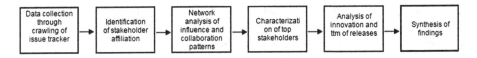

Fig. 1. Overview of the case study process

3 Research Design

We chose the Apache Hadoop project for an embedded case study [25] due to its systematically organized contribution process and its ecosystem composition. Most of the contributors have a corporate affiliation.

To create a longitudinal perspective, issues of the Apache Hadoop's issue tracking and project management tool were analyzed in sets reflecting the release cycles. The analysis was narrowed down to sub releases, spanning from 2.2.0 (released 15/Oct/13) to 2.7.1 (06/Jul/15), thus constituting the units of analysis through the study. Third level releases were aggregated into their parent upper level release.

Issues were furthermore chosen as the main data source as these can tie stakeholders' socio-technical interaction together [14,20], as well as being connected to a specific release. To determine who collaborated with whom through an issue, patches submitted by each stakeholder were analyzed, a methodology similar to those used in previous studies [22,23]. Users who contribute to an issue package their code into a patch and then attach it to the issue in question. After passing a two-step approval process comprising automated tests and manual code reviews, an authorized committer eventually commits the patch to the project's source configuration management (SCM) system. The overall process of this case study is illustrated in Fig. 1 and further elaborated on below.

3.1 Data Collection

The Apache Hadoop project manages its issue data with the issue tracker JIRA. A crawler was implemented to automatically collect, parse, and index the data into a relational database.

To determine the issue contributors' organizational affiliation, the domain of their email addresses was analyzed. If the affiliation could not be determined directly (e.g., for @apache.org), secondary sources were used such as LinkedIn and Google. The issue contributors' full name functioned as keyword.

3.2 Analysis Approach and Metrics

Below we present the methodology and metrics used in the analysis of this paper. Further discussion of metrics in relation to threats to validity is available in Sect. 3.3.

Network Analysis. Patches attached to issues were used as input to the SNA process. Stakeholders were paired if they submitted a patch to the same issue. Based on stakeholders' affiliation, pairings were aggregated to the organizational level. A directed network was constructed, representing the stakeholders at the organizational level as vertices. Stakeholder collaboration relationships were represented as edges. As suggested by Orucevic-Alagic et al. [23], edge weights were calculated to describe the strength of the relationships. Since stakeholders created patches of different size, the relative size of a stakeholder's patch was used

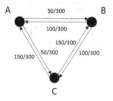

Fig. 2. Example of a weighted network with three stakeholders.

for the weighting. We quantified this size as changed lines of code (LOC) per patch. A simplified example of calculating network weights without organizational aggregation is shown in Fig. 2. Each of the stakeholders A, B, and C created a patch that was attached to the same issue. A's patch contains 50 LOC. B's patch contains 100 LOC, while C's patch contains 150 LOC. In total, 300 LOC were contributed to the issue. Resulting in the following edge weights: A→B = 50/300, A→C = 50/300, B→C = 100/300, B→A = 100/300, C→B = 150/300, and C→A = 150/300.

The following network metrics were used to measure the influence of stakeholders and the strength of the collaboration relationships among the stakeholders.

- *Out-degree Centrality* is the sum of a all outgoing edges' weights of a stakeholder vertex. Since it calculates the number of collaborations where the stakeholder has contributed, a higher index indicates a higher influence of a stakeholder on its collaborators. It also quantifies the degree of contributions relative to the stakeholder's collaborators.
- *Betweeness Centrality* counts how often a stakeholder is on a stakeholder collaboration path. A higher index indicates that the stakeholder has a more central position compared to other stakeholders among these collaboration paths.
- *Closeness Centrality* measures the average relative distance to all other stakeholders in the network based on the shortest paths. A higher index indicates that a stakeholder is well connected and has better possibilities in spreading information in the network, hence a higher influence.
- *Average Clustering Coefficient* quantifies the degree to which stakeholders tend to form clusters (connected groups). A higher coefficient indicates a higher clustering, e.g., a more densely connected group of stakeholders with a higher degree of collaborations.
- *Graph Density* is the actual number of stakeholder relationships divided by the possible number of stakeholder relationships. A higher value indicates a better completeness of stakeholder relationships (collaborations) within the network, where 1 is complete and 0 means that no relationships exist.

Innovation and Time-to-Market Analysis. Innovation can be measured through input, output, or process measures [26]. In this study, input and output measures are used to quantify innovation per release. Time-to-market was measured through the release cycle time [27].

- *Issues* counts the total number of implemented JIRA tickets per release and comprises the JIRA issue types *feature*, *improvement*, and *bug*. It quantifies the innovation input to the development process.
- *Change size* counts the net value of changed lines of code. It quantifies the innovation output of the development process.
- *Release cycle time* is the amount of time between the start of a release and the end of a release. It indicates the length of a release cycle.

Stakeholder Characterization. To complement our quantitative analysis and add further context, we did an qualitative analysis of electronic data available to characterize identified corporate stakeholders. This analysis primarily included their respective websites, press releases, news articles, and blog posts.

3.3 Threats to Validity

Four aspects of validity in regards to a case study are *construct, internal* and *external validity*, and *reliability* [25].

In regards to *construct validity*, one concern may be definition and interpretation of network metrics. The use of weights to better represent a stakeholder's influence, as suggested by Orucevic-Alagic et al. [23] was used with the adoption to consider the net of added LOC to further consider the relative size of contributions. A higher number of LOC however does not have to imply increased complexity. We chose to see it as a simplified metric of investment with each LOC representing a cost from stakeholder. Other options could include consideration software metrics such as cyclomatic complexity. Further network metrics, e.g. the eigenvector centrality and the clustering coefficient could offer further facets but was excluded as a design choice.

Furthermore, we focused on input (number of issues) and output (implementation change size) related metrics [26] for operationalizing the innovation per release. Issues is one of many concepts in how requirements may be framed and communicated in OSS RE, hence the term requirement is not always used explicitly [19]. Types of issues varies between OSS ecosystem and type of issue tracker (e.g., JIRA, BugZilla) [18]. In the Apache Hadoop ecosystem we have chosen the types feature, improvement and bug to represent the degree of innovation. We hypothesize that stakeholders engaged in bug fixing, are also involved in the innovation process, even if a new feature and an improvement probably includes a higher degree of novelty in the innovation. Even bugs may actually include requirements-related information not found elsewhere, and also relate to previously defined features with missing information. In future work, weights could be introduced to consider different degrees of innovation in the different issue types.

Release cycle times were used for quantifying the time-to-market as suggested by Griffin [27]. Since we solely analyzed releases from the time where the Apache Hadoop ecosystem was already well established, a drawback is that a long requirements analysis ramp up time may not be covered by this measure.

A threat to *internal validity* concerns the observed correlation of how the time-to-market and the innovativeness of a release is influenced by the way how stakeholders collaborate with each other. This needs further replication and validation in future work.

In regards to *external validity*, this is an exploratory single case study. Hence observations need validation and verification in upcoming studies in order for findings to be further generalized. Another limitation concerns that only patches of issues were analyzed, though it has been considered a valid approach in earlier studies [22,23]. In future work, consideration should also be taken into account, for example, as this may also be an indicator of influence and collaboration. Further, number of releases in this study was limited due to a complicated release history in the Apache Hadoop project, but also a design choice to give a further qualitative view of each release in a relative fine-grained time-perspective. Future studies should strive to analyze longer periods of time.

Finally, in regards to *reliability* one concern may be the identification of stakeholder affiliation. A contributor could have used the same e-mail but from different roles, e.g., as an individual or for the firm. Further, sources such as LinkedIn may be out of date.

4 Analysis

In this section, we present our results of the quantitative analysis of the Apache Hadoop ecosystem across the six releases R2.2-R2.7.

4.1 Stakeholders' Characteristics

Prior to quantitatively analyzing the stakeholder network, we qualitatively analyzed stakeholders' characteristics to gain a better understanding of our studied case. First, we analyzed how each stakeholder uses the Apache Hadoop platform to support its own business model. We identified the following five user categories:

- **Infrastructure provider**: sells infrastructure that is based on Apache Hadoop.
- **Platform user**: uses Apache Hadoop to store and process data.
- **Product provider**: sells packaged Apache Hadoop solutions.
- **Product supporter**: Provides Apache Hadoop support without being a product provider.
- **Service provider**: Sells Apache Hadoop related services.

Second, we analyzed stakeholders' firm history and strategic business goals to gain a better understanding of their motivation for engaging in the Hadoop ecosystem. We summarize the results of this analysis in the following list:

- **Wandisco** [Infrastructure provider] entered the Apache Hadoop ecosystem by acquiring AltoStar in 2012. It develops a platform to distribute data over multiple Apache Hadoop clusters.
- **Baidu** [Platform user] is a web service company and was founded in 2000. It uses Apache Hadoop for data storage and processing of data.

- **eBay** [Platform user] is an E-commerce firm and was founded in 1995. It uses Hadoop for data storage and processing of data.
- **Twitter** [Platform user] offers online social networking services and was founded in 2006. It uses Apache Hadoop for data storage and processing of data.
- **Xiaomi** [Platform user] is focused on smartphone development. It uses Apache Hadoop for data storage and processing of data.
- **Yahoo** [Platform user] is a search engine provider who initiated the Apache Hadoop project in 2005. It uses Apache Hadoop for data storage and processing of data. It spun off Hortonworks in 2011.
- **Cloudera** [Product provider] was founded in 2008. It develops its own Apache Hadoop based product *Cloudera Distribution Including Apache Hadoop* (CDH).
- **Hortonworks** [Product provider] was spun off by Yahoo in 2011. It develops its own Apache Hadoop based product *Hortonworks Data Platform* (HDP). It collaborates with Microsoft since 2011 to develop *HDP for Windows*. Other partnerships include Redhat, SAP, and Terradata.
- **Huawei** [Product provider] offers the Enterprise platform *FusionInsight* based on Apache Hadoop. FusionInsight was first released in 2013.
- **Intel** [Product supporter] maintained its own Apache Hadoop distribution that was optimized to their own hardware. It dropped the development in 2014 to support Cloudera by becoming its biggest shareholder and focusing on contributing its features to Cloudera's distribution.
- **Altiscale** [Service provider] was founded in 2012. It runs its own infrastructure and offers Apache Hadoop as-a-service via their product *Altiscale Data Cloud*.
- **Microsoft** [Service provider] offers Apache Hadoop as a cloud service labeled *HDInsight* through its cloud platform Azure. It maintains a partnership with Hortonworks who develops *HDP for Windows*.
- **NTT Data** [Service provider] is a partner with Cloudera and provides support and consulting services for their Apache Hadoop distribution.

Firms that belong to the same user category apply similar business models. Hence, we can identify competing firms based on their categorization.

4.2   Stakeholder Collaboration

Figure 3 shows all stakeholder networks that were generated for the releases R2.2 to R2.7. The size of a stakeholder vertex indicates its relative ranking in regards to the outdegree centrality. Table 1 summarizes the number of stakeholders and stakeholder relationships per release. It illustrates that the number of stakeholders and collaboration relationships varies over time. Except for the major

Table 1. Number of stakeholder (vertices) and collaboration relationships (edges) per release

	R2.2	R2.3	R2.4	R2.5	R2.6	R2.7
Stakeholders	9	35	25	34	38	44
Collaboration relationships	21	97	81	108	96	122

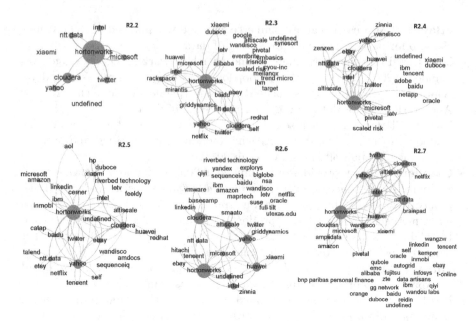

Fig. 3. Network distribution of releases R2.2-R2.7

increase from R2.2 to R2.3, the network maintains a relatively consistent size, though the number of collaborations are in the interval between 81 to 122 for R2.4 to R2.7.

A general observation among the different releases is the existence of one main cluster where a core of stakeholders is present, whilst the remaining stakeholders make temporary appearances. Many stakeholders are not part of these clusters implying that they do not collaborate with other stakeholders at all. The number of those stakeholders shows strong variation among the releases. This could imply that stakeholders implement their own issues, which is further supported by the fact that 65 % of the patches are contributed by the issue reporters themselves.

The visual observation from the networks being weakly connected in general is supported by the Graph Density (GD) as its values are relatively low among all releases (see Table 2). The values describe that stakeholders had a low number of collaborations in relation to the possible number of collaborations. The Average Clustering Coefficient (ACC) values among all releases (see Table 2) further indicate that the stakeholders are weakly connected to their direct neighbors in the releases R2.2 - R2.6. This correlates with the observation that there are many unconnected stakeholders and only a few core stakeholders collaborating

Table 2. Average Clustering Coefficient (ACC) and Graph Density (GD) per release.

	R2.2	R2.3	R2.4	R2.5	R2.6	R2.7
ACC	0	0.207	0.303	0.198	0.237	0.552
GD	0.292	0.082	0.135	0.096	0.068	0.064

Table 3. Stakeholder collaborations among the different user categories.

	Infrastructure provider	Platform user	Product provider	Product supporter	Service provider
Infrastructure provider	0	2	4	1	0
Platform user	2	24	73	6	14
Product provider	4	73	124	23	50
Product supporter	1	6	23	0	3
Service provider	0	14	50	3	10

with each other. The ACC value however indicates a significantly higher number of collaborations for release R2.7.

Table 3 summarizes stakeholder collaborations among the different user categories. It shows that collaborations took place among all user categories, except between infrastructure providers and service providers. The product providers were the most active and had the highest number of collaborations with other product providers. They also have the highest amount of collaborations with other user categories. These results show that stakeholders with competing (same user category) and non-competing (different user category) business models collaborate within the Apache Hadoop ecosystem.

4.3 Stakeholder Influence

To analyze the evolving stakeholder influence over time, we leveraged the three network centrality metrics: outdegree centrality, betweeness centrality, and closeness centrality.

The left graph in Fig. 4 shows the outdegree centrality evolution for the ten stakeholders with the highest outdegree centrality values. These stakeholders are most influential among all Apache Hadoop stakeholders in regards to weighted

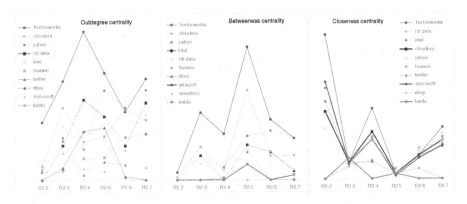

Fig. 4. Evolution of stakeholders' outdegree, betweeness, and closeness centrality across the releases R2.2-R2.7

issue contributions. The graph also shows that the relative outdegree centrality varies over time. To further investigate this evolution, we created a stakeholder ranking per release using the relative outdegree centrality as ranking criteria. This analysis revealed that Hortonworks was most influential in terms of issue contributions. It was five times ranked first and once ranked third (average ranking: 1.3). The other top ranked stakeholders were Cloudera (average ranking: 3.3) and Yahoo (average ranking: 3.3). The stakeholders NTT Data (avg ranking = 4.7) and Intel (average ranking: 4.8) can be considered as intermediate influencing among the top ten outdegree centrality stakeholders. The stakeholders Huawei (average ranking: 8.2), Twitter (average ranking: 8.5), eBay (average ranking: 9.0), Microsoft (average ranking: 9.5), and Baidu (average ranking: 10.2) had the least relative outdegree centrality among the ten stakeholders.

The center graph in Fig. 4 shows the betweeness centrality evolution of the ten stakeholders with the highest accumulated values. As the metric is based on the number of shortest paths passing through a stakeholder vertex, it indicates a stakeholder's centrality with regards to the possible number of collaborations. The resulting top ten stakeholder list is very similar to the list of stakeholders with the highest outdegree centrality. The top stakeholders are Hortonworks (average ranking: 1), Cloudera (average ranking: 2.7), and Yahoo (average ranking: 3.0). Intel (average ranking: 4.2), NTT Data (average ranking: 4.7), and Huawei (average ranking: 5.3) are influencing among the top ten beweeness centrality stakeholders. eBay (average ranking: 6.7), Amazon (average ranking: 6.7), WANdisco (average ranking: 7.0), and Baidu (average ranking: 7.2), the group of stakeholders with the least betweeness centrality among the top ten stakeholders differs compared to the group of stakeholders with the least outdegree centrality. The stakeholders Twitter and Microsoft were replaced by Amazon and WANdisco.

The right graph in Fig. 4 shows closeness centrality evolution of the ten stakeholders with the highest accumulated values. A higher degree of closeness centrality indicates higher influence, because of closer collaboration relationships to other stakeholders. The resulting top ten closeness centrality stakeholder list differs compared to the outdegree and betweeness centrality list. Our analysis results do not show a single top stakeholder with the highest closeness centrality. The stakeholders Hortonworks (avgerage ranking: 3.2), NTT Data (average ranking: 4.0), Intel (average ranking: 4.3), Cloudera (average ranking: 4.8), and Yahoo (average ranking: 5.5) had relatively similar closeness rankings among the releases. This is also reflected in Fig. 4 by very similar curve shapes among the stakeholders. Also the remaining stakeholders with lower closeness centrality values had very similar average rankings: Huawei (average ranking: 7.7), Twitter (average ranking: 8.0), Microsoft (average ranking: 8.3), eBay (average ranking: 9.2), Baidu (average ranking: 9.3).

The results of our analysis also show that the stakeholders with the highest outdegree centrality, betweeness centrality, and closeness centrality were distributed among different stakeholder user categories: 4 platform user, 3 product provider, 2 service provider, and 1 product supporter. However, it is notable

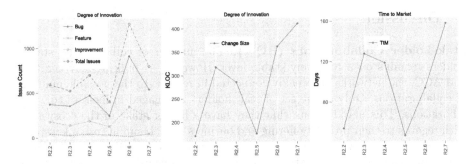

Fig. 5. Evolution of the degree of innovation over time with respect to implemented JIRA issues and changed lines of code and time to market.

that the average ranking differs among these user categories. Product providers had the highest average influence ranking. Platform users and service providers had lower influence ranking. This implies that product providers are the most driving forces of the Apache Hadoop ecosystem.

4.4 Innovation and Time-to-Market Over Time

The evolution of the degree of innovation and time-to-market from release R2.2 to R2.7 is summarized in Fig. 5 by three consecutive graphs. The first graph in Fig. 5 shows the number of issues that were implemented per release. The illustrated number of issues is broken down into the issue types: bug, improvement, and feature. The number of implemented features (avg: 33.5, med: 37, std: 9.88) remains steady across all analyzed releases. This is reflected by a relatively low standard deviation. Similarly, the number of implemented improvements (avg: 198.3; med: 183; std: 71.62) remains relatively steady across the releases with one exception. In release R2.6, the double amount of improvement issues was implemented compared to the average of the remaining releases. The number of implemented bugs (avg: 482.5; med: 423; std: 212.52) features stronger variation among the releases.

The second graph in Fig. 5 shows the number of changed lines of code per release. The total number of changed lines of code per release (avg: 287,883.33; med: 302,257; std: 89,334.57) strongly varies across the analyzed releases. Each of the analyzed releases comprises code changes of significant complexity. Even the two releases R2.2 and R2.5, with the lowest change complexity (R2.2: 171 KLOC; R2.5: 176 KLOC), comprised more than 170 KLOC. The remaining releases comprised change complexities of more than 250 KLOC. Further, the graph indicates that the change complexity scatters randomly among the studied releases. A steady trend cannot be determined.

The third graph in Fig. 5 depicts the time between the start and the end (time-to-market) of each analyzed release. Analogous to the evolution of the changed lines of code, the time-to-market scatters randomly among the analyzed releases.

5 Discussion

Stakeholder Collaborations (RQ-1). The number of collaborating stakeholders remains on a relatively stable level. However, as indicated by the GD and ACC, the networks are weakly connected in regards to the possible number of collaborations. Only a core set of stakeholders is engaged in most of the collaborations. This may indicate that they have a higher stake in the ecosystem with regards to their product offering and business model, and in turn a keystone behaviour [7]. From a requirements value chain perspective, collaborations translate into partnerships and relationships. This may prove valuable in negotiations about requirements prioritization and how these should be treated when planning releases and road maps [16]. The results also show that many stakeholders do not collaborate at all. This is supported by the fact that 65 % of the reported issues are implemented by reporters themselves without any collaboration. This indicates that a lot of independent work was performed in the ecosystem. Reasons for this could be that issues are only of interest for the reporter. It also indicates that the ecosystem is relatively open [10] in the sense that it is easy for stakeholders to get their own elicited requirements implemented and prioritized, but with the cost of own development efforts.

Another aspect of the collaborations can be inferred from the different user categories. Firms with competing business models collaborate as openly as non-rivaling firms do, as presented in Table 3 and reported in earlier studies [24]. Some of the collaborations may be characterized through the partnerships established between the different stakeholders, as presented in our qualitative analysis of stakeholder characteristics. One of Hortonworks many partnerships include that with Microsoft through the development of their Windows-friendly Apache Hadoop distribution. Cloudera's partnerships include both Intel and NTT Data. None of these partnerships, or among the others identified in this study, occurs within the same user category. Yet still, a substantial part of the ecosystem collaboration occurs outside these special business relationships.

Independent of business model, all firms work together towards the common goal of advancing the shared platform, much resembling an external joint R&D pool [2]. As defined through the concept of co-opetition, one motivation could be a joint effort to increase the market share by helping out to create value, and then later diverge and capture value when differentiating in the competition about the customers [28]. Collaboration could further be limited to commodity parts whereas differentiating parts are kept internal, e.g. leveraged through selective revealing [29].

Stakeholder Influence (RQ-1). Although the distribution of stakeholders' influence fluctuated among the releases, we identified that the group of most influential stakeholders remained very stable. Even the influence ranking within this group did not show high variations. It can be concluded that the development is mainly driven by the stakeholders Hortonworks, Cloudera, NTT Data, Yahoo, and Intel, which may also be referred to as keystone players, and in some cases also niche players relative to each other [7]. Due to this stable evolution, it can be expected that these stakeholders will also be very influential firms in the future. The stakeholder distribution represents multiple user categories, although the product providers Hortonworks and Cloudera tend to be in the top. This may relate to their products being tightly knit with the Apache Hadoop project. In turn, service-providers may use the product-providers' distributions as a basis for their offerings.

Tracking that influence may be useful to identify groups and peers with key positions in order to create traction on certain focus areas for the road map, or to prioritize certain requirements for implementation and release planning [16]. Further, it may help to identify emerging stakeholders increasing their contributions and level of engagement [11], which may also be reflected in the commercial market. Huawei's increase in outdegree centrality, for example, correlates with the release of their product FusionInsight, which was launched in the beginning of 2013.

The fact that the network metrics used revealed different top stakeholders, indicates the need of multiple views when analysing the influence. For example, the betweeness centrality Xiaomi, Baidu, and Microsoft in the top compared to the outdegree centrality. This observation indicates that they were involved in more collaboration but produced lower weighted (LOC) contributions relative to their collaborators.

Evolution of Ecosystem in Regards to Innovation and Time-to-Market (RQ-2). The analysis results indicate that the number of implemented features does not vary among the analyzed releases. A possible reason for this could be the ecosystem's history. From release R2.2 to R2.5, the project was dominated by one central stakeholder (Hortonworks). Although, additional stakeholders with more influence emerged in release R2.6 and R2.7, Hortonworks remained the dominating contributor, who presumable continued definition and implementation of feature issues. Another potential reason for the lack of variance among features could be the fact that our analysis aggregated all data of third level minor releases to the upper second level releases.

However, our results indicate that the number of implemented improvements show variations among the releases. From release R2.2 to R2.5, the number of implemented improvements per release remained at a steady level. For release R2.6 and R2.7, the number of implemented improvements increased (double the amount). A possible reason for the observed effect could be the fact that other stakeholders with business models get involved in the project to improve the existing ecosystem with respect to their own strategic goals that helps to optimally exploit for their own purpose. The number of implemented bugs varies among all analyzed releases. The high variance of the number of defects could be a side effect of the increased number of improvement issues that potentially imply increase in overall complexity within the ecosystem. Further, the more stakeholders get actively involved in the project to optimize their own business model the more often the ecosystem is potentially used, which may increase the probability to reveal previously undetected defects.

The analysis results with respect to the evolution of the change size indicate a strong variance among all analyzed releases. Similarly to the change size, the time-to-market measure showed great variance among the analyzed releases. Covariances of stakeholder collaboration, degree of innovation, and time-to-market measure among the analyzed releases may indicate relationship between these variables. However, to draw this conclusion a detailed regression analysis of multiple ecosystems is required.

Implications for Practitioners. Even though an ecosystem may have a high population, its governance and project management may still be centered around a small group of stakeholders [11], which may further be classified as keystone and in some cases, niche players. Understanding their evolving composition and the influence of these stakeholders may indicate current and possible future directions of the ecosystem [7]. Corporate stakeholders could use this information to better align their open source engagement strategies to their own business goals [24]. It could further provide insights for firms, to what stakeholders' strategic partnerships should be established to improve their strategic influence on the ecosystem regarding, e.g., requirement elicitation, prioritization and release planning [16]. Here it is of importance to know how the requirements are communicated throughout the ecosystem, both on a strategic and operational level for a stakeholder to be able to perform the RE processes along with maximized use of its influence [17]. Potential collaborators may, for example, be characterized with regards to their commitment, area of interest, resource investment and impact [30].

The same reasoning also applies for analysis of competitors. Due to the increased openness and decreased distance to competitors implied by joining an ecosystem [7], it becomes more important and interesting to track what the competitors do [5]. Knowing about their existing collaborations, contributions, and interests in specific features offer valuable information about the competitors' strategies and tactics [24]. The methodology used in this study offers an option to such an analysis but needs further research.

Knowledge about stakeholder influence and collaboration patterns may provide important input to stakeholders' strategies. For example, stakeholders may develop strategies on if or when to join an OSS ecosystem, if and how they should adapt their RE processes internally, and how to act together with other stakeholders in an ecosystem using existing practices in OSS RE (e.g., [18,19]). This regards both on the strategic and operational level, as requirements may be communicated differently depending on abstraction level, e.g., a focus area for a road map or a feature implementation for an upcoming release [17]. However, for the operational context in regards to how and when to contribute, further types of performance indicators may be needed. Understanding release cycles and included issues may give an indication of how time-to-market correlates to the complexity and innovativeness of a release. This in turn may help to synchronize a firm's release planning with the ecosystem's, minimizing extra patchwork and missed feature introductions [6]. Furthermore, it may help a firm planning their own ecosystem contributions and maximize chances for inclusion. In our analysis, we found indications that the time-to-market and the innovativeness of a release is influenced by the way how stakeholders collaborate with each other. Hence, the results could potentially be used as time-to-market and innovativeness predictors for future releases. This however also needs further attention and replication in future research.

6 Conclusions

The Apache Hadoop ecosystem is generally weakly connected in regards to collaborations. The network of stakeholders per release consists of a core that is continuously present. A large but fluctuating number of stakeholders work independently. This is emphasized by the fact that a majority of the issues are implemented by the issue reporters themselves. The analysis further shows that the network maintains an even size. One can see that the stakeholders' influence as well as collaborations fluctuate between and among the stakeholders, both competing and non-rivaling. This creates further input and questions to how direct and indirect competitors reason and practically work together, and what strategies are used when sharing knowledge and functionality with each other and the ecosystem.

In the analysis of stakeholders' influence, a previously proposed methodology was used and advanced to also consider relative size of contributions, and also interactions on an issue level. Further, the methodology demonstrates how an awareness of past, present and emerging stakeholders, in regards to power structure and collaborations may be created. Such an awareness may offer a valuable input to a firm's stakeholder management, and help them to adapt and maintain a sustainable position in an open source ecosystem's governance. Consequently, it may be seen as a pivotal part and enabler for a firm's software development and requirements engineering process, especially considering elicitation, prioritization and release planning for example.

Lastly, we found that innovation and time-to-market of the Apache Hadoop ecosystem strongly varies among the different releases. Indications were also found that these factors are influenced by the way how stakeholders collaborate with each other.

Future research will focus on what implications stakeholders' influence and collaboration patterns have in an ecosystem. How does it affect time-to-market and innovativeness of a release? How does it affect a stakeholder's impact on feature-selection? How should a firm engaged in an ecosystem adapt and interact in order to maximize its internal innovation process and technology advancement?

Acknowledgments. This work was partly funded by the SRC in the SYNERGIES project, Dnr 621-2012-5354, and BMBF grant 01IS14026B.

References

1. Chesbrough, H.W.: Open Innovation: The New Imperative for Creating and Profiting from Technology. Harvard Business Press, Boston (2006)
2. West, J., Gallagher, S.: Challenges of open innovation: the paradox of firm investment in open-source software. R&D Manage. **36**(3), 319–331 (2006)
3. Jansen, S., Finkelstein, A., Brinkkemper, S.: A sense of community: a research agenda for software ecosystems. In: 31st International Conference on Software Engineering, pp. 187–190. IEEE (2009)
4. Linåker, J., Regnell, B., Munir, H.: Requirements engineering in open innovation: a research agenda. In: Proceedings of the 2015 International Conference on Software and System Process, pp. 208–212. ACM (2015)
5. Dahlander, L., Magnusson, M.: How do firms make use of open source communities? Long Range Plan. **41**(6), 629–649 (2008)
6. Wnuk, K., Pfahl, D., Callele, D., Karlsson, E.-A.: How can open source software development help requirements management gain the potential of open innovation: an exploratory study. In: Proceedings of the ACM-IEEE International Symposium on Empirical Software Engineering and Measurement, pp. 271–280. ACM (2012)
7. Jansen, S., Brinkkemper, S., Finkelstein, A.: Business network management as a survival strategy: a tale of two software ecosystems. In: Proccedings of the 1st International Workshop on Software Ecosystems, pp. 34–48 (2009)
8. Enkel, E., Gassmann, O., Chesbrough, H.: Open R&D and open innovation: exploring the phenomenon. R&D Manage. **39**(4), 311–316 (2009)
9. Manikas, K., Hansen, K.M.: Software ecosystems-a systematic literature review. J. Syst. Softw. **86**(5), 1294–1306 (2013)
10. Jansen, S., Brinkkemper, S., Souer, J., Luinenburg, L.: Shades of gray: opening up a software producing organization with the open software enterprise model. J. Syst. Softw. **85**(7), 1495–1510 (2012)
11. Nakakoji, K., Yamamoto, Y., Nishinaka, Y., Kishida, K., Ye, Y.: Evolution patterns of open-source software systems and communities. In: Proceedings of the International Workshop on Principles of Software Evolution, pp. 76–85. ACM (2002)
12. Glinz, M., Wieringa, R.J.: Guest editors' introduction: stakeholders in requirements engineering. IEEE Softw. **24**(2), 18–20 (2007)
13. Pacheco, C., Garcia, I.: A systematic literature review of stakeholder identification methods in requirements elicitation. J. Syst. Softw. **85**(9), 2171–2181 (2012)
14. Damian, D., Marczak, S., Kwan, I.: Collaboration patterns and the impact of distance on awareness in requirements-centred social networks. In: 15th IEEE International Requirements Engineering Conference, pp. 59–68. IEEE (2007)
15. Lim, S.L., Quercia, D., Finkelstein, A.: Stakenet: using social networks to analyse the stakeholders of large-scale software projects. In: Proceedings of the 32nd ACM/IEEE International Conference on Software Engineering, pp. 295–304. ACM (2010)
16. Fricker, S.: Requirements value chains: stakeholder management and requirements engineering in software ecosystems. In: Wieringa, R., Persson, A. (eds.) REFSQ 2010. LNCS, vol. 6182, pp. 60–66. Springer, Heidelberg (2010)
17. Knauss, E., Damian, D., Knauss, A., Borici, A.: Openness and requirements: opportunities and tradeoffs in software ecosystems. In: IEEE 22nd International Requirements Engineering Conference (RE), pp. 213–222. IEEE (2014)
18. Ernst, N., Murphy, G.C.: Case studies in just-in-time requirements analysis. In: IEEE Second International Workshop on Empirical Requirements Engineering, pp. 25–32. IEEE (2012)

19. Scacchi, W.: Understanding the requirements for developing open source software systems. In: IEE Proceedings Software, vol. 149, pp. 24–39. IET (2002)
20. Nguyen Duc, A., Cruzes, D.S., Ayala, C., Conradi, R.: Impact of stakeholder type and collaboration on issue resolution time in OSS projects. In: Hissam, S.A., Russo, B., de Mendonça Neto, M.G., Kon, F. (eds.) OSS 2011. IFIP AICT, vol. 365, pp. 1–16. Springer, Heidelberg (2011)
21. Crowston, K., Howison, J.: The social structure of free and open source software development. First Monday, 10(2) (2005)
22. Martinez-Romo, J., Robles, G., Gonzalez-Barahona, J.M., Ortuño-Perez, M.: Using social network analysis techniques to study collaboration between a floss community and a company. In: Russo, B., Damiani, E., Hissam, S., Lundell, B., Succi, G. (eds.) Open Source Development, Communities and Quality. IFIP, vol. 275, pp. 171–186. Springer, Heidelberg (2008)
23. Orucevic-Alagic, A., Höst, M.: Network analysis of a large scale open source project. In: 40th EUROMICRO Conference on Software Engineering and Advanced Applications, pp. 25–29. IEEE, Verona, Italy (2014)
24. Teixeira, J., Robles, G., González-Barahona, J.M.: Lessons learned from applying social network analysis on an industrial free/libre/open source software ecosystem. J. Internet Serv. Appl. 6(1), 1–27 (2015)
25. Runeson, P., Höst, M.: Guidelines for conducting and reporting case study research in software engineering. Empirical Softw. Eng. 14(2), 131–164 (2009)
26. Knight, D., Randall, R.M., Muller, A., Välikangas, L., Merlyn, P.: Metrics for innovation: guidelines for developing a customized suite of innovation metrics. Strategy Leadersh. 33(1), 37–45 (2005)
27. Griffin, A.: Metrics for measuring product development cycle time. J. Prod. Innov. Manage. 10(2), 112–125 (1993)
28. Nalebuff, B.J., Brandenburger, A.M.: Co-opetition: competitive and cooperative business strategies for the digital economy. Strategy Leadersh. 25(6), 28–33 (1997)
29. Henkel, J., Schöberl, S., Alexy, O.: The emergence of openness: how and why firms adopt selective revealing in open innovation. Res. Policy 43(5), 879–890 (2014)
30. Gonzalez-Barahona, J.M., Izquierdo-Cortazar, D., Maffulli, S., Robles, G.: Understanding how companies interact with free software communities. IEEE Softw. 5, 38–45 (2013)

Natural Language

Evaluating the Interpretation of Natural Language Trace Queries

Sugandha Lohar[(✉)], Jane Cleland-Huang, and Alexander Rasin

School of Computing, DePaul University, Chicago, IL 60604, USA
{slohar,jhuang}@cs.depaul.edu, arasin@cdm.depaul.edu

Abstract. [**Context and Motivation:**] In current practice, existing traceability data is often underutilized due to lack of accessibility and difficulties users have in constructing the complex SQL queries needed to address realistic Software Engineering questions. In our prior work we therefore presented TiQi – a natural language (NL) interface for querying software projects. TiQi has been shown to transform a set of trace queries collected from IT experts at accuracy rates ranging from 47 % to 93 %. [**Question/problem:**] However, users need to quickly determine whether TiQi has correctly understood the NL query. [**Principal ideas/results:**] TiQi needs to communicate the transformed query back to the user and provide support for disambiguation and correction. In this paper we report on three studies we conducted to compare the effectiveness of four query representation techniques. [**Contribution:**] We show that simultaneously displaying a visual query representation, SQL, and a sample of the data results enabled users to most accurately evaluate the correctness of the transformed query.

Keywords: Traceability · Queries · Speech recognition · Natural language processing

1 Introduction

Traceability is prescribed across many software projects for purposes of certification, approval, and compliance [15]. It supports a diverse set of requirements engineering activities including safety-analysis, impact analysis, testing, and requirements coverage [2]. Unfortunately, despite the significant cost and effort that is expended to construct and maintain trace links, the traceability data is often underutilized in practice. In many projects, trace data is constructed immediately prior to certification, and is not used for any other purpose. Even when project stakeholders would like to utilize existing trace data, they are often hindered by the non-trivial challenge of generating Structured Query Language (SQL) or XML Path Language (XPath) queries to retrieve the needed data [8,13].

To address this problem, we previously developed *TiQi* - an interface which accepts spoken or written natural language (NL) queries, transforms them into SQL, executes the query, and then returns results [13,14]. While a variety of NL

© Springer International Publishing Switzerland 2016
M. Daneva and O. Pastor (Eds.): REFSQ 2016, LNCS 9619, pp. 85–101, 2016.
DOI: 10.1007/978-3-319-30282-9_6

approaches exist for issuing general database queries, it is widely accepted that effective interfaces must be customized for specific domains [11]. TiQi is therefore supported by a traceability domain model which understands trace query terminology and project-specific terms. Our long-term goal is to integrate TiQi into a variety of case tools including requirements management tools, Eclipse and Visual Studio IDEs, and across modeling tools such as Enterprise Architecture.

TiQi's current NL to SQL transformation process utilizes a set of heuristics which are designed to transform words and phrases in the query into tokens understandable by TiQi. For example, *question terms* such as "Show me" are mapped to SELECT, *join* terms such as "with" or "that have related" are mapped to SQL terms such as WHERE, and domain terms such as 'source code', 'created before', and 'on-board motor' are mapped onto specific artifact types (tables), attributes, and data values respectively. However, there are often multiple options for performing the mapping, and TiQi may fail to correctly interpret the users' intent of the query. In this case, the generated query and the returned data will be incorrect.

NL interface tools, such as TiQi, must interact with human users to communicate the translated query in a way that allows the user to quickly determine whether it is correct and to provide affordances for making corrections. Trace queries exhibit unique characteristics that differ from those of general database queries. For example, they tend to require multiple joins across multiple connected artifacts, to include frequent negations, and to use basic predicate constraints [13,14]. In contrast, more general database queries tend to relate fewer tables and to include more complex filter conditions. It is therefore important to evaluate query representations directly in the software domain.

The goal of this paper is to comparatively evaluate techniques for representing and visualizing trace queries. To this end, we present three user studies. The first study extends our prior work [9] which comparatively evaluated two query presentation techniques. We add two additional approaches – one of which has recently been used quite broadly in the Database community. We experimentally determine which approach allows the user to more quickly and accurately interpret the meaning of a trace query. The second study uses eye-tracking to explore how users integrate knowledge from different query representations in order to comprehend the meaning of the query. In particular we are interested in whether individuals use multiple sources of information, and whether different people favor different representations. Finally, based on observations made in the eye-tracking study, we designed simplified query representations and investigated how the reduced formats impacted speed and accuracy of user comprehension. Results from these studies have delivered foundational knowledge that can improve TiQi's ability to provide critical feedback to the user.

The remainder of this paper is laid out as follows. Section 2 provides a brief overview of TiQi. Section 3 describes various query representations including the four used in our study. Sections 4, 5, and 6 describe the three studies we conducted to evaluate query representations. Finally, Sects. 7, 8, and 9 discuss threats to validity, related work, and conclusions.

2   An Overview of TiQi

We first provide an overview of TiQi and the natural language transformation process including the *query elicitation* and *query transformation* process.

In order for a user to issue a trace query, they need to understand exactly what artifacts and attributes are available for tracing purposes. TiQi therefore *prompts* for a query by displaying a *Traceability Information Model* (TIM) as illustrated in Fig. 1 [8]. A TIM is similar to a database schema. Software artifact types, such as *regulatory-codes* and *requirements* are represented as classes and attributes. For example, we can see in Fig. 1 that *Hazards* have IDs, hazard descriptions, severity classifications, and probabilities. The TIM also depicts semantically typed links between artifact types such as the *causes* link between *faults* and *hazards*. Given a TIM, users can formulate natural language trace queries such as "which hazards are associated with recently failed test cases?" or "Are any environmental assumptions related to Fault ID F101?"

TiQi takes the natural language query through a series of transformation steps in order to produce an executable SQL query. These steps are described in detail in our previous papers [13] and are summarized here. First a pre-lexicon processor performs a series of tasks that include detecting known synonyms, recognizing commonly used terms for representing 'group-by', 'negation', and 'yes/no' terminology, removing stop words, preprocessing summation queries, and recognizing number and date identities etc. The pre-lexicon processor outputs a tokenized query structure. Next, the *disambiguator* maps each token onto a SQL keyword (e.g. WHERE), a table or attribute defined in the TIM (e.g. Hazard or Hazard classification), or to an underlying data value (e.g. a word found in the hazard description). When multiple mapping options exist, a sequence of disambiguators are applied to resolve the ambiguity. Finally a *post-lexicon* processor generates a query object from which SQL query can be directly generated. For example, a query such as *"Which requirements have assumptions related to fault tolerance?"* can have (at least) two possible interpretations. *Requirements* and *assumptions* are mapped directly to their relevant tables, but TiQi is uncertain whether to map the term *fault tolerance* to the table named *Fault* or to assumption records containing the terms *fault* and/or *tolerance*. While this example has only one ambiguity, in more complex queries, multiple mapping options can expand to many candidate SQL queries. For this reason, TiQi, and other NL interfaces, must present the **interpreted** query to the user and elicit corrections where necessary.

3   Query Representations

The goal of this paper is to investigate different techniques for communicating a TiQi query to the user so that the user can determine if it has been correctly interpreted. We limited our initial study to four approaches for representing queries in textual and visual forms.

Structured Textual Representation: The most common structured, textual representations are SQL and XPath. SQL is commonly used to construct, modify, and query a relational database. Trace Query Language (TQL) is designed

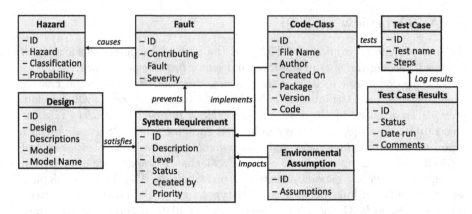

Fig. 1. Traceability Information Model (TIM) showing artifacts and traceability paths.

specifically for issuing trace queries against artifacts represented in XML format [10]. TQL specifies queries on the abstraction level of artifacts and links and hides low-level details of the underlying XPath query language through the use of extension functions. For the purposes of our study, we selected SQL as the representative structured approach, because more people are familiar with it and also because of our underlying relational database.

Visual Representation: Queries can also be presented visually. The *Visual Trace Modeling Language* (VTML) [8] represents trace queries as connected subsets of the artifacts and traceability paths defined in the TIM. The initial query scope ranges from a single artifact to the entire set of artifacts. Each artifact type is represented as the name of the artifact type, properties used in filter conditions or to specify return results, and functions used to compose and extract aggregated data from the class. Values to be returned by the query are annotated with a bar chart symbol. Similarly, properties used to filter results are annotated with a filter symbol augmented by a valid filter expression.

Reverse Snowflake Joins is a general-purpose database query visualization technique that represents a SQL statement as a graph. As shown in Fig. 2, a snowflake model depicts tables augmented with key parts of the underlying SQL query. For example, a table might be annotated to show ID=30, GROUP BY (Hazard), HAVING AVG(Probability) < 0.1. The notation accommodates Cartesian joins and loops.

Tools such as MS Access provide an *interactive query builder*, whose primary function is to help the user construct a query. However, the depicted information is very similar to that shown in the Snowflake approach and our initial evaluation suggested that the more graphical layout of Snowflake improved comprehension of the query over the tabular query builder.

Other graphical query languages have been proposed and commercially offered in the database domain. The PICASSO approach by Kim et al. [4] represents one of the earliest graphical query languages and was built on top of the universal relation database system System/U. Visual SQL by Jaakkola et al. [3]

translates all features of SQL into a graphical representation similar to entity relationship models and UML (Unified Modeling Language) class diagrams. Furthermore, a variety of commercial and open source tools provide graphical support for the specification of queries (e.g., Microsoft Visual Studio^{TM}, Microsoft Access^{TM}, Active Query Builder and Visual SQL Builder). For purposes of the study we selected *VTML*, which was designed specifically for tracing purposes, and also *Reverse Snowflake Joins* (SFJ) as a more general database representation with a high degree of expressiveness.

Query Output: In practice, people often issue a query, review the data returned, and then realize that the query needs further refinement. We therefore included *results* as the fourth presentation technique, and presented the first four rows of the returned data to the user. Throughout the remainder of the paper we refer to this as Query Output (QO).

4   Initial Study

The first study evaluated the effectiveness of four query representation techniques by addressing the following research questions: **(RQ1) Which query representation technique enables users to more accurately analyze the meaning of a query?** and to **(RQ2) more quickly perform the analysis?**

4.1   Experimental Design

Each study participant was presented with sixteen different queries divided equally between SQL, VTML, SFJ, and QO. Figure 2 shows a sample query, "Show all environmental-assumptions related to security requirements", expressed in each of the query representations. For each query we provided three candidate NL interpretations, as well as "none of the above" and "I don't know" options. The participants were tasked with determining which NL text (if any) matched the presented query. We collected participants' answers and also recorded the time it took them to answer the query. Questions were rendered in the same order to all participants; however, we used an interwoven experimental design to determine the way the query would be presented to each user. In this way, each of the sixteen individual queries was presented to a participant four to five times in each style.

We sent recruitment emails to graduate students in DePaul's Professional Master program and also to Software Engineering PhD students at other institutions. As a result we recruited 18 participants to the study. Of these, eight had 1–5 years of experience in the IT industry, seven had 6–10 years, two had more than 10 years, and one had no professional experience.

With respect to our participants' prior traceability experience, eight participants said they had never previously used traceability, five said they had created trace links in a trace matrix (e.g. in a spreadsheet), four said they had used links directly from the spreadsheet, and six said they had written customized scripts to retrieve traceability information. Only one participant had used traceability

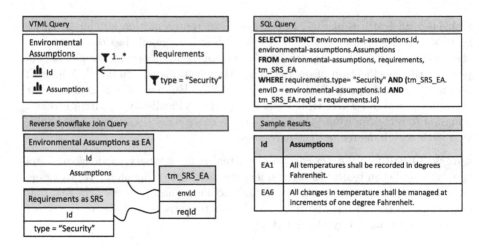

Fig. 2. Four query representations presented to participants.

features in a requirements management tool such as DOORS. For the participants who had previously used traceability, four had used it for testing, six for requirements coverage analysis, one for compliance verification, and two each for safety analysis and impact analysis. We also asked participants to report on their SQL experience. One person claimed expertise, ten claimed competency, and six said they understood SQL but were 'rusty'. All participants claimed at least an understanding of SQL. 86 % of the participants had taken a database course and all of them had taken an object-oriented analysis course in which they had been exposed to basic UML. From this meta-data we inferred that our participants are representative of people in the IT domain who utilize traceability data.

The survey was taken online. It included an initial explanation of the study with a basic introduction to traceability. Further, we provided brief tutorials on VTML and SFJ. Each tutorial included three pages (screens) which presented the core notation and concepts of each technique and provided a multiple-choice self-test. The tutorials were purposefully brief as our goal was to identify a presentation technique which is intuitive and which requires minimal training.

4.2   Results and Discussion

Results for each query were tallied across the different techniques and categorized as correct, not correct, or don't know. As each query did have a valid answer provided, we included responses for 'none of the above' in the incorrect responses. It is notable that while there were few 'none of the above' responses for VTML (1), SQL (2), or SFJ (3), there were 6 for QO. As depicted in Fig. 3, VTML had the highest number of correct responses (41), followed by SQL(36), SFJ (25), and QO (21). Unsurprisingly QO produced the highest number of incorrect results (38). VTML and SQL produced 27 and 24 incorrect results respectively. While SFJ produced only 24 incorrect results, it also produced 23 'don't know' answers. QO also produced a fairly high number of 'don't knows' (12).

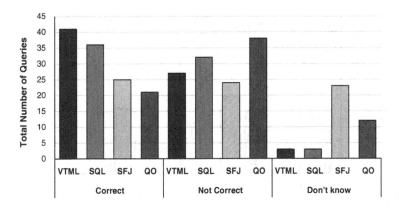

Fig. 3. Analysis of responses by query presentation type. VTML enabled users to identify errors slightly more effectively than SQL, but participants still failed to identify approximately 43 % of the errors (Color figure online).

It is important to note that none of the techniques resulted in high degrees of accuracy. VTML produced an overall accuracy rate of only 56.9 % followed by SQL at approximately 50 %. This means that for VTML in approximately 43.1 % of the cases the user would fail to recognize errors in the transformed query. Nevertheless, we can answer **RQ1** by observing that VTML produced the most accurate results followed by SQL. Despite observable differences in the VTML and SQL scores, a Wilcoxon Signed-rank test showed no significant difference between the two groups ($W = 26.5$, $Z = -0.5779$ $p < 0.05$). We can further observe that QO and SFJ are clearly insufficient for the task given, that QO had more incorrect than correct answers, and SFJ returned equal numbers of correct and incorrect results, but an unexpectedly high count of 'don't knows'.

To address **RQ2**, we assessed the time taken by each participant to evaluate queries using each technique. Results are reported in Fig. 4, and show results for all queries as well as correctly answered queries only. An analysis of the results shows that participants analyzed VTML representations more quickly than other types of queries. SQL and QO were approximately equal with participants spending slightly longer on SQL queries that they answered incorrectly, than those that they answered correctly. In the case of VTML, SFJ, and QO, participants gave correct answers more quickly than incorrect ones. Finally, it is quite evident from these results that participants took far longer to answer SFJ queries correctly, with an average time of approximately 2 min (120 s) versus 50–70 s for the other types of presentation. The Wilcoxon Signed-rank test showed a significant difference between the two groups ($W = 15$, $Z = -2.7406$ $p < 0.05$).

4.3 Exit Questions

At the end of each survey we asked participants to rate each technique according to the ease at which they could understand the query on a scale from 1 to 4, where 1 = easy to understand and 4 = difficult. Results are depicted as dots in Fig. 4 plotted against the y-axis on the right hand side of the graph.

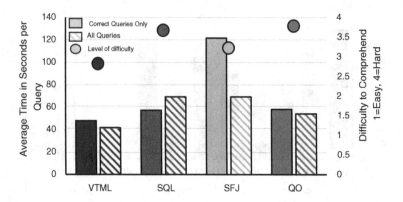

Fig. 4. Time taken by participants to analyze each query presentation type and participants' perception of the difficulty of comprehending queries (Color figure online)

Finally, we asked each participant which technique they preferred. Four preferred query output, six preferred VTML, eight preferred SQL, and nobody preferred SFJ. Some participants also provided exit comments. One person said "*The visual representation of VTML, once a person understand and gets used to (sic), will be faster and more convenient. Reading equivalent SQL query will take longer time and might be confusing. I found snowflake method ambiguous... Query output may also be ambiguous or have incomplete information.*" Another participant said "*Its easy to relate 'what is required' with 'what is the output' and identify if they satisfy each other.*" One of the participants who favored SQL, said "*Maybe because I use SQL in my day to day work (I am) more comfortable with it...*", whereas the one who favored VTML said, VTML "*is a lot easier to understand and follow.*" Finally, one person pointed out that even with visual representations there is a learning curve: "*Initially I found it difficult to learn and adapt to Visual representations but after few questions I think I understood how to use them.*"

In summary, we found VTML produced more accurate results than the other techniques (RQ1) at slightly faster analysis times (RQ2). These results confirm and extend findings from our earlier study which compared readability and writability of SQL and VTML [8]. Further, our results show that VTML outperformed the more general database solution in this context.

Given these results, we did not include Snowflake Joins in the subsequent studies reported in this paper. Even though query output produced inaccurate results on its own, we carried it forward with VTML and SQL into the eye-tracker study, as it provides orthogonal information and we were curious whether it might be helpful to users for interpreting a query.

5   Eye-Tracking Study

Eye-tracking has been used in a number of software engineering studies to determine how programmers parse source code and UML diagrams in order to comprehend the code for bug detection and summarization tasks [16,17]. The goal of our study is to determine *how* IT professionals utilize VTML, SQL, and query output to determine whether a query is correct or not. We were particularly interested in determining whether users integrated knowledge from multiple representations to analyze the query. With this goal in mind, we incorporated multiple representations as depicted in Fig. 5. Our study was designed to address the research question **RQ3: To what extent did individual users leverage information from each of the three displays in order to analyze a single query?**

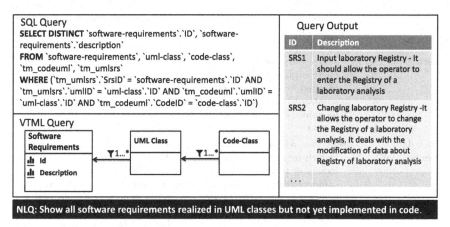

Fig. 5. A sample screen from the eye-tracking study.

5.1   Methodology

Each participant in the study was presented with nine queries in which the SQL, VTML, and QO represented an incorrect interpretation of the NL query. For example, the query depicted in Fig. 5 requests requirements realized in UML classes but **not** implemented in code, while the SQL, VTML, and QO representations show software requirements that are realized in UML **and** also implemented in code. The participant's task is to identify how the NL Query differs from the other representations. The errors applied to each of the nine queries were derived from commonly occurring ambiguities and subsequent interpretation errors observed through analyzing results from our prior study [13]. We identified common causes as inherent ambiguity of the query, awkwardly worded sentences which the machine (TiQi) has difficulty parsing, and logic errors in the underlying transformation algorithm. These observations are summarized in Table 1. In Table 2 we show the queries we selected for inclusion in our study, the modified form of the query (used by SQL, VTML, and QO), and the classes of error which they represent.

We used MyGaze Eye tracker to conduct the study in conjunction with Morae (usability software). The plugin provides capabilities to capture user's interaction with the screen and document the coordinates and timing of eye-gaze locations. Morae is non-intrusive but requires an initial calibration phase.

Table 1. Common query ambiguities which could lead to interpretation errors

Ambiguity	Resultant error
Which table? (T)	Projects may have artifacts with similar names and/or users may refer to the artifact using a synonym or abbreviated form. For example, it is unclear whether a user requesting "all failed tests", is referring to unit test cases or user acceptance tests. As a result, an incorrect artifact (table) may be referenced in the query. This type of error can result in the inclusion of an **additional** table which creates unnecessary joins or constraints or in the **erroneous replacement** of an intended table.
Which attribute? (A)	Different artifacts may have similar attribute names. For example *source code* and *requirements* may both have status fields, and a query containing the phrase "high status" could be erroneously mapped to the wrong artifact. Such ambiguities can cause *additional* tables or *erroneous table replacements* but may also introduce the problem of *returning unnecessary fields* in the query output
Which data value? (DV)	Users often add data-filters to their queries. For example in the query "which requirements are addressed by components controlling incubator temperatures?" the user intends to filter results by component functionality. However, the term *temperature* may occur across multiple artifacts such as requirements, source-code, and test-cases. If mapped to the incorrect attribute and/or table, a variety of problems could occur including *additional, missing*, and *erroneous* tables and columns, and *missing and/or incorrect constraints*
Incorrect JOIN types (J)	In the query "list all requirements with at least two associated classes" the phrase "with at least two" tells us something about the type of JOIN and cardinality constraints. There are a myriad of ways that users can express relations between tables and misinterpretations lead to *incorrect JOIN types* e.g. JOIN vs. LEFT OUTER JOIN, and/or incorrect *cardinality constraints*
Incorrect Definition Transformation (DT)	NL interfaces such as TiQi depend upon predefined definitions. For example, the phrase *in the past week* should be transformed to TODAY-7 days. Incorrect definitions could introduce *unexpected* or *incorrect column constraints*
Aggregation and negation errors (AN)	Aggregations may be applied to the wrong attribute due to parsing errors. For example for the query "How many HIPAA goals are related to safety requirements?" the aggregation should be applied to HIPAA goals and not to requirements. Aggregations may be missed if terms such as "add up" are not (yet) recognized by TiQi. Similar problems can occur with negations

Eleven participants were recruited. The distribution of demographics was similar to that of the initial survey with a few exceptions. Six of the eleven participants had no prior traceability experience - however, all had at least one year of industry experience, with six having over five years. Five of the participants had participated in the original study while six were entirely new.

Table 2. Queries used in the eye-tracking study

#	Original query	Modified query	Err
1	List any test cases which have **failed in the past week.**	List any test cases which have **failed in the past month.**	DT
2	List all requirements with **missing test cases.**	List all requirements which **have been tested**	AN, J
3	Are there any requirements implemented in **more than one class**?	Are there any requirements implemented in **at least one class**?	DT
4	Show all requirements related to operator login **which have not passed** their acceptance tests	Show all requirements related to operator login **which have passed** their acceptance tests.	AN
5	On changing **thermostat related requirements,** which code classes will be impacted?	List code classes and associated **requirements related to package "Thermostat"**	DV
6	Show all software requirements realized in UML classes but **yet to be implemented in** code.	Show all software requirements realized in UML classes **which have also been implemented** in code	AN, J
7	How many requirements will be **impacted if test case TC12 fails**?	How many requirements are **tested by test case "TC12"**	DT
8	Does package P2 have any **high severity hazards** associated with it?	Does package P2 have any **high severity faults** associated with it?	T
9	**How many HIPAA goals** are not related to safety requirements?	**How many safety requirements** are not related to hippa goals?	AN

Each participant was presented with each of the nine queries in turn; however, we systematically rotated the position in which each of the techniques was displayed in order to reduce location bias that might be introduced if one technique were always placed in a preferred position (e.g. top left). Participants were asked to determine whether the NL Query was correctly represented by examining any combination of the VTML, SQL, or QO representations. Secondly, they were asked to explain how the query representations differed from the original NL query. During this process, participants were directed to use the 'think-out-loud' protocol to articulate their thoughts. Thinking out loud provided insights into how useful each of the query representations was in supporting the user achieve their task [5].

The eye-tracker captures and logs the time and screen locations of the participants' eye gaze. From this we computed three metrics, all of which are commonly used in eye-tracking studies [17]. **Fixation time** measures the total number of milliseconds spent on a specific query display. **Fixation count** measures the number of screen locations viewed by a participant for at least 100 ms. We compute *fixation count* for each of the three query displays. Finally, **Regression count** measures the number of times a participant returned to a display type (e.g. VTML) after viewing a different one. Regression count serves as an indicator of the importance a specific feature has to a user.

To illustrate the use of Morae, Fig. 6 depicts two interactions for the same query. Morae depicts fixation time by the size of the circle, and maps the coordinates of the eye gaze onto the screen.

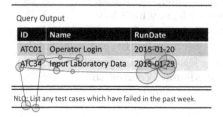

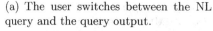

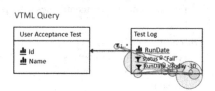

(a) The user switches between the NL query and the query output.

(b) The user focuses on the date and cardinality depicted in the VTML.

Fig. 6. Eye-tracking output showing gaze fixation points.

5.2   Eye-Tracking Results

The total gaze fixation time in milliseconds for each query type is depicted in Fig. 7(a). Participants spent significantly more time looking at SQL than either at VTML or QO with a mean time per query for SQL of approximately 200,000 ms, versus 140,000 for VTML and 40,000 for QO.

The total regression count for each of the three query representation types is depicted in Fig. 7(b) and shows that participants regressed (i.e. returned) to the VTML display slightly more frequently than to the SQL one. For each participant, we calculated the "usage bias" based on regression counts, in order to identify the dominant technique favored by him. For each query we identified the query representation which had the highest regression count. For example, for one of the participants, VTML was dominant in 5 queries, SQL in 3 queries, and QO in one query - therefore we deemed VTML to be the dominant type. Further, we considered the response to the exit question of *Which technique did you find easiest for analyzing the meaning of a query?* as the participant's preferred query representation.

We found a strong correlation between user preference and usage bias, but low correlation between the self-declared DB expertise of the user and the favored approach. For example, one of the participant declared herself to be rusty at SQL but then used it as the primary means of analysis across all experiments. On the other hand, several participants who claimed expertise or competency in SQL favored VTML in practice, explaining that it was 'simpler' and provides

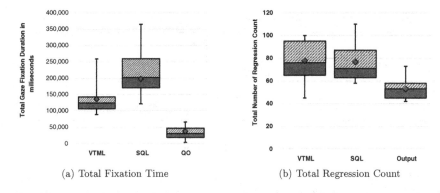

(a) Total Fixation Time   (b) Total Regression Count

Fig. 7. Fixation and regression counts per query display type

a 'cleaner organization of the flow of the query command.' These sentiments were echoed by non-experts. For example, one non-expert said that VTML was 'easier to grasp', and 'showed relevant information clearly'. On the other hand the people who preferred SQL claimed that they were 'familiar with SQL' or that it was what they were 'most used to'.

The survey results suggested that VTML tends to produce more correct results than SQL and takes less time to process; however, the eye-tracker results clearly demonstrated that when faced with multiple options, some of the users with strong SQL background favored it more.

In every case, users viewed at least two of the query representations, and in most cases they viewed all three. The "think-out-loud" protocol provided insights into the way they synthesized knowledge from multiple sources. In many cases, they focused on one particular query representation - but then sought confirmation from another. Out of the 11 users, there were only three users who almost exclusively favored one technique over any other. Two of these users favored SQL, and one favored VTML.

We are now in a position to answer **RQ3** and conclude that while most users favored either VTML or SQL, the majority of them leveraged information from multiple sources – including Query Output, during the query analysis process. This is an important finding because it suggests that trace query disambiguation techniques should incorporate multiple query representations.

6   Reduced Query Representation

One of the observations from the eye-tracking study was that users often spent a disproportionate amount of time looking at details which were not pertinent to the query at hand. We therefore designed a reduced version of the VTML and SQL format as shown in Fig. 8. In the case of VTML, intermediate classes occurring along the trace path which did not contribute attributes or predicates were hidden from view and replaced by a dotted line, while in the case of SQL, we removed references to the trace matrices from the query and used keyword "JOIN" to depict connection between the two artifacts.

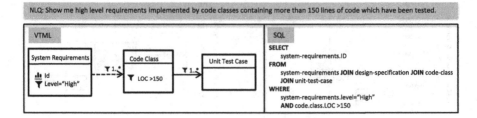

Fig. 8. Simplified versions of VTML and SQL query representations.

We then conducted a final study to address the research questions: **(RQ4) does the reduced representation format increase user query evaluation accuracy?** and **(RQ5) does it reduce evaluation time?**

This study included 10 experienced software engineers who had not participated in our previous study, and ten queries (nine of which were used in the eye-tracking study). We divided the 10 queries into two groups: *Matching* queries, in which the NL representation matched the SQL, VTML, and QO displays; and *Non-matching* queries, in which the NL representation did not match the other displays. Each query was prepared in *reduced* and *non-reduced* form. Participants were divided into two groups and each group was presented with a carefully interwoven mix of reduced vs.non-reduced and matching vs. non-matching queries, such that each query was presented five times in each format. Participants were tasked with determining whether the NL query matched the other representations or not. They were also allowed a "don't know" answer.

6.1 Results and Discussion

We computed the accuracy and mean speed achieved for each combination of matching/non-matching and reduced/non-reduced formats and report results in Fig. 9. The reduced display resulted in accuracy of 60 % compared to 48 % for the original displays. Users took an average of 51 s to analyze a query presented in reduced form compared to 68 s in non-reduced format. Notably, for the subset of queries which were *non-matching*, users took an average of only 31 s to identify the error using *reduced-form* displays and 63 s in the *non-reduced form*. However, the same speedup in analysis time was not observed in the case of *matching* queries. When errors were not-present users took an average of 72 s using *reduced-form* and 73 s using *non-reduced* form. Further analysis will be needed to fully understand this phenomenon. We can now address our research questions. Addressing **RQ4**, we observed that the reduced-form improved user accuracy; however answering **RQ5** is more complex. A statistical Wilcoxon signed rank test showed no significant difference between the analysis speed of reduced vs. non-reduced queries ($W = 19$, $Z = -0.8664$ p ¡$= 0.05$). While there were insufficient data points to perform a statistical analysis on the subset of *non-matching* queries, our results suggest that the reduced format allowed users to identify errors far more quickly than the original format does – achieving a critical goal of our work.

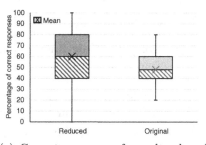
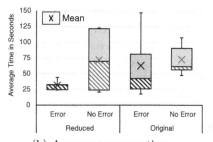

(a) Correct responses for reduced and original query representations.

(b) Average response time.

Fig. 9. Results using reduced formats for SQL and VTML

7 Threats to Validity

One threat to validity is introduced by the fact that logistical constraints limited us to evaluate four different query representations. It is plausible that better techniques exist for representing queries, which were not included in our study. Furthermore, due to the difficulty of recruiting people to our rather time-intensive study, we were only able to evaluate a limited number of queries. While these queries were taken from examples collected from software engineers, we cannot guarantee that they are fully representative of all likely trace queries. In our study, evaluating correctness was relatively straightforward, however the on-line nature of parts of our study meant that we could not guarantee that users did not take breaks during the query analysis process. We did not identify any extreme outliers however and so did not remove any data from the analysis. Finally, we mitigated systematic error in our user study by randomly assigning participants to groups, and then adopting an interleaving approach in which different groups were given query representations in different orders.

8 Related Work

Several researchers have used eye-tracking to evaluate how programmers read, review, and summarize source code. For example, Crosby et al. concluded that programmers alternate between comments and code, focusing on important sections [1]. Uwano found that programmers who took longer scanning the overall code were able to locate more bugs than those who fixated early on specific sections [20]. Sharif et al. showed a correlation between scan time and bug detection [17]. Finally Rodeghero et al. performed an eye-tracking study to identify parts of the code that helped programmers comprehend the intent of the code, and then used this to develop new code summarization techniques [16]. For purposes of our work, the eye-tracking study allowed us to identify which query representations were most useful to our users.

In addition to source-code analysis, other researchers have used eye-tracking to investigate the impact of visual layout on comprehension. For example,

Sharif et al. showed that UML layout impacted the comprehension of design pattern usage [18]. Given the importance of fast triaging of the TiQi query to determine first and foremost whether it is correct or not – these prior studies suggest that even small nuances in the presentation of the query can impact comprehension.

Apart from the work described in Sect. 3, relatively little research has focused on query disambiguation for natural language queries. However, many visualization techniques exist [19]. The NaLIX project [7] improved natural language XML queries by focusing on individual term disambiguation. A recently developed SeeDB [12] begins with an initial user-provided query and builds on it to provide "interesting" views by scoring additional similar queries that might detect useful data trends. Finally, Li and Jagadish developed the NaLIR tool [6] that converts NL queries into a tree structure, iteratively asking users to disambiguate each tree node as necessary (e.g. by "VLDB" did you mean "VLDB conference" or "VLDB Journal"?).

9   Conclusion

In this paper we performed three exploratory studies to investigate the efficacy of several trace query presentation techniques. As different users showed preferences for visual versus structured representations, our final solution presented SQL, VTML, and Query Output results. Furthermore, results from the eye-tracking study showed that users fixated on details. We therefore simplified both the VTML and the SQL solution to focus only on the artifacts and traceability paths which contributed fields or constraints. Other intermediate artifacts were hidden from view. The findings from this study have been implemented in the feedback mechanisms integrated into the current version of TiQi. We provide a live demo for a limited set of queries at[1]. In ongoing work we focus on interactive query disambiguation techniques.

Acknowledgment. The work in this paper was partially funded by the US National Science Foundation Grant CCF:1319680.

References

1. Crosby, M.E., Stelovsky, J.: How do we read algorithms? a case study. IEEE Comput. **23**(1), 24–35 (1990)
2. Gotel, O., et al.: Traceability fundamentals. In: Cleland-Huang, J., Gotel, O., Zisman, A. (eds.) Software and Systems Traceability, pp. 3–22. Springer, Heidelberg (2012). doi:10.1007/978-1-4471-2239-51
3. Jaakkola, H., Thalheim, B.: Visual SQL – high-quality ER-based query treatment. In: Jeusfeld, M.A., Pastor, Ó. (eds.) ER Workshops 2003. LNCS, vol. 2814, pp. 129–139. Springer, Heidelberg (2003). doi:10.1007/978-3-540-39597-3.

---

[1] http://tiqianalytics.com.

4. Kim, H.-J., Korth, H.F., Silberschatz, A.: Picasso: a graphical query language. IEEE Comput. **18**, 169–203 (1988)
5. Kuusela, H., Paul, P.: A comparison of concurrent and retrospective verbal protocol analysis. IEEE Comput. **113**(3), 387–404 (2000)
6. Li, F., Jagadish, H.: Constructing an interactive natural language interface for relational databases. IEEE Comput. **8**(1), 73–84 (2014)
7. Li, Y., Yang, H., Jagadish, H.V.: Term disambiguation in natural language query for XML. In: Larsen, H.L., Pasi, G., Ortiz-Arroyo, D., Andreasen, T., Christiansen, H. (eds.) FQAS 2006. LNCS (LNAI), vol. 4027, pp. 133–146. Springer, Heidelberg (2006)
8. Mäder, P., Cleland-Huang, J.: A visual traceability modeling language. In: Petriu, D.C., Rouquette, N., Haugen, Ø. (eds.) MODELS 2010, Part I. LNCS, vol. 6394, pp. 226–240. Springer, Heidelberg (2010)
9. Mäder, P., Cleland-Huang, J.: A visual language for modeling and executing traceability queries. IEEE Comput. **12**(3), 537–553 (2013)
10. Maletic, J.I., Collard, M.L.: TQL: A query language to support traceability. In: TEFSE 2009: Proceedings of the ICSE Workshop on Traceability in Emerging Forms of Software Engineering, pp. 16–20. IEEE Computer Society, USA (2009)
11. McFetridge, P., Groeneboer, C.: Novel terms and cooperation in a natural language interface. KBCS 1989. LNCS, vol. 444, pp. 331–340. Springer, Heidelberg (1990)
12. Parameswaran, A., Polyzotis, N., Garcia-Molina, H.: SeeDB: Visualizing database queries efficiently. Proc. VLDB Endowment **7**(4), 325–328 (2013)
13. Pruski, P., Lohar, S., Aquanette, R., Ott, G., Amornborvornwong, S., Rasin, A., Cleland-Huang, J.: TiQi: towards natural language trace queries. In: IEEE 22nd International Requirements Engineering Conference, RE, Karlskrona, Sweden, 25–29 August 2014, pp. 123–132 (2014)
14. Pruski, P., Lohar, S., Ott, G., Goss, W., Rasin, A., Cleland-Huang, J.: TiQi: answering unstructured natural language trace queries. Requir. Eng **20**(3), 215–232 (2015)
15. Rempel, P., Mäder, P., Kuschke, T., Cleland-Huang, J.: Mind the gap: assessing the conformance of software traceability to relevant guidelines. In: 36th International Conference on Software Engineering (ICSE) (2014)
16. Rodeghero, P., McMillan, C., McBurney, P.W., Bosch, N., D'Mello, S.K.: Improving automated source code summarization via an eye-tracking study of programmers. In: 36th International Conference on Software Engineering, ICSE 2014, Hyderabad, India, May 31–June 07, pp. 390–401 (2014)
17. Sharif, B., Falcone, M., Maletic, J.I.: An eye-tracking study on the role of scan time in finding source code defects. In: Proceedings of the Symposium on Eye-Tracking Research and Applications, ETRA 2012, Santa Barbara, CA, USA, 28–30 March 2012, pp. 381–384, (2012)
18. Sharif, B., Maletic, J.I.: An eye tracking study on the effects of layout in understanding the role of design patterns. In: 26th IEEE International Conference on Software Maintenance (ICSM), 12–18 September 2010, Timisoara, Romania, pp. 1–10 (2010)
19. Stolte, C., Tang, D., Hanrahan, P.: Polaris: a system for query, analysis, and visualization of multidimensional relational databases. IEEE Comput. **8**(1), 52–65 (2002)
20. Uwano, H., Nakamura, M., Monden, A., Matsumoto, K.: Analyzing individual performance of source code review using reviewers' eye movement. In: Proceedings of the Eye Tracking Research & Application Symposium, ETRA, San Diego, California, USA, 27–29 March 2006, pp. 133–140 (2006)

Indicators for Open Issues
in Business Process Models

Ralf Laue[1]([⊠]), Wilhelm Koop[2], and Volker Gruhn[2]

[1] Department of Computer Science, University of Applied Sciences of Zwickau,
Dr.-Friedrichs-Ring 2a, 08056 Zwickau, Germany
Ralf.Laue@fh-zwickau.de
[2] Paluno - The Ruhr Institute for Software Technology,
University of Duisburg-Essen, Gerlingstr. 16, 45127 Essen, Germany
{Wilhelm.Koop,Volker.Gruhn}@paluno.uni-due.de

Abstract. [**Context and motivation**] In the early phases of requirements engineering, often graphical models are used to communicate
requirements. In particular, business process models in graphical languages such as BPMN can help to explain the process that a software
system should support. These models can then be used to derive more
detailed requirements. [**Question/Problem**] Often, such models are
incomplete (showing only the most important cases) or contain labels
in natural language that are prone to ambiguities and missing information. The requirements engineer has to identify missing / ambiguous
information manually. The aim of this paper is to discuss certain classes
of such potential problems and how they can be found automatically.
[**Principal ideas/results**] First, we analyzed a collection of business
process models and found that they frequently contain typical types of
problems. Second, we described those potential problems in a formal way.
We present a catalogue of indicators for potential problems and suggest
questions to be asked by a requirements engineer for getting additional
information about the depicted process. We also developed a tool prototype that uses a combination of linguistic analysis and inspection of the
control flow. This tool prototype was applied to 2098 business process
models. [**Contribution**] The paper presents a catalogue of potential
problems in business process models. It also shows how these problems
can be identified automatically.

Keywords: Business Process Models · Natural language processing

1 Introduction

Business Process Models (BPM) are widely used for different purposes, in particular for documenting and improving business processes and for making them
accessible to stakeholders. In this paper, we will refer to imperative, control-
flow oriented BPM which are usually modelled using graphical notations, such
as BPMN or Event-Driven Process Chains (EPC). From the perspective of a

© Springer International Publishing Switzerland 2016
M. Daneva and O. Pastor (Eds.): REFSQ 2016, LNCS 9619, pp. 102–116, 2016.
DOI: 10.1007/978-3-319-30282-9_7

requirements engineer, these notations can be useful for making the processes more understandable, for communicating the goals of a system-to-be with many stakeholders and for deriving requirements from these models. Both Cardoso et al. [4] and de la Vara et al. [19] have found in case studies that business process modelling was helpful for clarifying the requirements.

However, in practice BPM are often not suitable for deriving a sound and complete set of requirements. For example, Miers [27] proposes to reduce the complexity of BPM by visualising only the most common process execution (the so-called "happy path") and omitting alternatives for infrequently occurring situations. If requirements should be derived from such a model, the information contained in the model is not sufficient.

In this paper we identify some classes of common BPM modelling issues in order to support the requirements engineer in the task of identifying problems (e.g., incomplete information) in a model. In addition, we suggest questions that should be asked in order to resolve the problems

The remainder of this paper is structured as follows: In Sect. 2, we repeat the most basic concepts of BPM notations and outline the idea of a combined analysis of the graph built by the BPM together with the natural language labels. In Sect. 3, we develop a formal notation for describing relations between natural language labels Sect. 3.1, present our catalogue of indicators for possible modelling problems Sect. 3.2 based on these relations, and describe a prototypical implementation Sect. 3.3 for finding the indicators as well as the results of applying it to a collection of models Sect. 3.4. In Sect. 4, we compare our approach to related work before concluding the paper with Sect. 5 which gives an outlook on future work.

2 Understanding the Intended Meaning of Business Process Models

The most common business process modelling languages in practice are BPMN and Event-Driven Process Chains (EPCs). Both languages share the basic concept that the tasks being conducted in a process are depicted as rectangles. Arrows between them show the order of execution. Connectors (called *gateways* in the BPMN terminology) are used to split and join the flow of control in three different ways: AND-connectors are used to mark start and end of parallel executions. XOR-connectors are used for modelling decisions (only one of several possible flows of control is selected), and OR-connectors allow the parallel execution of one or more alternative paths in parallel. For both XOR- and OR-connectors, the conditions that determine which path(s) should be taken have to be included in the model. For BPMN models, these conditions are modeled as guard conditions which are written on the arrows (see Fig. 1). In addition, events can be used to show the state of the process at a certain point of time. In EPCs, events (depicted as hexagons) are used both for expressing the conditions that determine the path of control and for showing the state of a process (see Fig. 2).

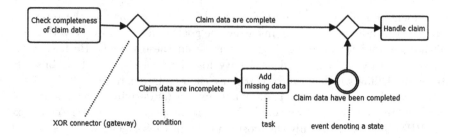

Fig. 1. BPMN model fragment

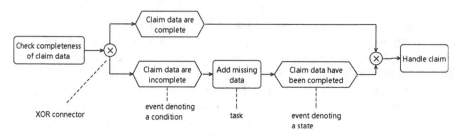

Fig. 2. EPC model fragment

For understanding the intended meaning of a BPM, two things need to be comprehended: First, the order of the graphical elements (usually expressed by boxes, arrows and other shapes) and second, the natural language labels that are attached to the graphical elements. Those labels - as each natural language text - are prone to ambiguities, missing information and redundancies. If a label allows more than one reasonable interpretation, the business process model can lead to misunderstandings. While modelling problems that result from the order of the graphical elements are well understood, there is much less work on modelling problems that can be detected by inspecting the textual labels of these graphical elements.

The analysis of BPM is different from the analysis of requirements given in full prose. First, BPM labels typically contain very short text fragments only (instead of complete sentences). This minimizes the risk of structural ambiguities (when a text can be given more than one grammatical structure). On the downside, it makes the automatic analysis by using natural language processing (NLP) tools more difficult, because tools such as parsers or POS taggers work best when applied to full sentences. Our suggestions to deal with this problem from the technical point of view of NLP tools can be found in [34]. For the purpose of this article, we identified problems that can be found automatically even if only short text fragments are available in the labels.

Second, the analysis of BPM needs to inspect the control flow (i.e. the symbols that define in which order the tasks have to be performed) in combination with the textual labels. As the meaning of a BPM is given as well by the control flow as by the natural language labels, both the symbols defining the control flow as the texts describing tasks, events and conditions have to be analysed in order to find potential modelling problems.

3   Indicators for Potential Modelling Deficits

3.1   Relations Between Words and Relations Between Labels

In Subsect. 3.2, we will present a catalogue of indicators for potential modelling problems. In order to find those indicators automatically, they need to be formalized. We do so by using relations on pairs of words. As BPM describe the process tasks which are expressed by verbs, relations between verbs are especially important to us (see [6,11]):

Synonymity: Two words (or groups of words) are synonyms if they have (roughly) the same meaning. For our purposes, we neglect subtle differences in the meaning. For example, we regard "accept", "grant" and "approve" as synonyms, because they all refer to a positive decision. This relation is symmetric, reflexive and transitive.

Antonymy: Two words or group of words are antonyms if one of them has the opposite meaning of the other one. For example, the verb "grant" is an antonym of the verb "deny". This relation is symmetric.

Happens-Before: Two verbs are in a happens-before relation if the activity denoted by the first verb has to happen before the activity denoted by the second verb when both verbs refer to the same object. For example, "produce" happens before "ship". This relation is transitive and asymmetric.

Hyponymy: Two words (or groups of words) are in a hyponymy relation (also known as "is-a" relation) if one is a special form of the other. For example the verb "to fax" is a special case of "to send". This relation is transitive and asymmetric.

   While hyponomy does not occur explicitly in the following definitions, our algorithm for finding indicators for modelling problems uses the hyponomy relation implicitly as follows: If a and b are antonyms and b^* is a special form of b than it is concluded that b^* is an antonym to a. Analogously, if a happens before b there can exist an a^* that is a special form of a or a b^* that is a special form of b. This means that a^* happens before b, a^* happens before b^* and a happens before b^*.

   Based on these relations between *words* (or *groups of words*), we can now define relations between *labels* in a business process model. Let A and B be two labels and a_i and b_i groups of one or more words contained in those labels. If for example label A is "print visa documents", we could split it into a_1 =PRINT, a_2 =VISA and a_3 =DOCUMENTS. Another possible way to split the label A would be to set a_1 =PRINT and a_2 =VISA DOCUMENTS. When we write $A = a_1 a_2 \ldots a_n$ in the following, the exact meaning is that A *can* be split into groups of one or more words $a_1, \ldots a_n$. While in the most cases each a_i will be exactly one word, this has not always to be the case. Now we define the relations between labels:

Synonymity (symbol: $A \equiv B$) holds iff: $A = a_1 a_2 \ldots a_n$ and $B = b_1 b_2 \ldots b_n$ and a_i is a synonym to b_i for each i.

For example "choose initial value" is a synonym to "select initial value" because "choose" and "select" are synonyms and the rest of the text is the same (and therefore synonymous) for both labels.

Antonymy (symbol: $A \mathbin{!} B$) holds iff: $A = a_1 a_2 \ldots a_n$ and $B = b_1 b_2 \ldots b_n$ and a_i is a synonym to b_i for each i with exception of exactly one $i = j$ for which a_j is an antonym to b_j.

For example, for $A =$INFORMATION ARRIVED IN TIME and $B =$INFO ARRIVED TOO LATE we have $A \mathbin{!} B$ because "information" is a synonym to "info", "arrived" is trivially a synonym of itself and "in time" is a antonym of "too late".

Happens-Before (symbol: $A \prec B$) holds iff: $A = a_1 a_2 \ldots a_n$ and $B = b_1 b_2 \ldots b_n$ and a_i is a synonym to b_i for each i with exception of exactly one $i = j$ for which a_j and b_j are in the relation "happens before". For example, we have $A \prec B$ for $A =$PRINT DOCUMENT and $B =$SIGN DOCUMENT.

In Sect. 3.2, we will make use of these relations for formally defining a list of indicators for modelling issues. When defining those indicators, we will mostly use the EPC terminology, i.e. we will refer to events when discussing the conditions that determine the flow of control. We expect that the description can easily be transferred to BPMN and other modelling languages such as UML activity diagrams. For those languages (see Fig. 1), the arrow labels have to be considered instead of the events.

3.2 Indicators

To identify common problems in BPM we manually inspected models from public repositories (in particular the BPM Academic Initiative repository at bpmai.org), textbooks, scientific papers, student papers and real-world projects. We identified several cases for incomplete modelling or modelling errors and compiled a list of indicators for such problems. This list will be presented in this section. The most prominent problem was that while a BPM contains some kind of test activity, the model does not have any information what happens if the test should fail (the "happy-path" problem mentioned before). When inspecting the first 250 models from the bpmai.org repository, we found 59 models for which this was the case at least once.

When building our catalogue of indicators for potential problems (see Tables 1, 2 and 3), we took the perspective of a requirement engineer. For a business process analyst, some of these cases do not impose a problem at all. It is typical that business analysts often deliberately omit information (such as exceptions or infrequently occurring cases) to make a model more readable. From the perspective of a requirements engineer, it is the aim to identify those points where it is necessary to ask additional questions in order to get a complete set of requirements. Therefore, the entries of the tables explaining the indicators contain four parts: *Indicator* (how the potential problem can be found), an *Example*, *Consequences* (what the existence of such a pattern means) and *Questions* (that the requirement engineer should ask when being confronted with such a model).

In addition to the manual analysis of a model repository, a second starting point for building the catalogue was the existing literature on ambiguities. Ambiguities have been studied and classified both for texts in general [8] and for requirement specifications [2,3]. However, during our analysis of BPM we also found several indicators that are specific to the process modelling domain.

We concentrated on such indicators that can be found automatically. We do not claim that our catalogue is complete or that our tool-based approach can replace a manual inspection of the models. We are, however, convinced that it can assist a requirements engineer to identify a considerable number of potential modelling problems and unclear situations very quickly.

3.3   Technical Realisation of a Tool Prototype

We built a prototype of a tool that can locate the indicators listed in Tables 1, 2 and 3. Currently, this tool supports models in the modelling language Event-Driven Process Chains with labels in German language. We think, however, that the main ideas can be applied both to other modelling languages as to labels in other natural languages.

As our method heavily relies on the synonymity, antonymy and happens-before relations between verbs, identification and stemming of verbs is a prerequisite for applying our pattern-based approach. Because the German language has a richer morphology than English, we were able to identify the verbs in a label and to obtain their infinitives with a few lines of Prolog code. In English, specialized part-of-speech tagging tools would have to be used to find out whether a word such as "plan" or "test" is a verb or a noun. In [34], we show how identification of verbs and objects can be achieved for English labels with a high accuracy. Therefore, we believe that the ideas presented in this paper can be transferred to models with English labels as well.

Also, we decided not to use an existing semantic database such as *WordNet* [11] (or its German version *GermaNet*) for reasoning about relations between words. The main reason for this decision was that we wanted to have full control about what we regard as synonyms, antonyms and hyponyms. Furthermore, building an own catalog of relations between words and word groups that frequently occur in business process models gave us the opportunity to include technical terms that cannot be found in a general-purpose semantic database.

Building our own list of relations between words and word groups was important in particular for the happens-before relation which is not included in the *WordNet* database. This relation has been introduced by the *VerbOcean* project [6]. However, in a test with models in English language, we realised that the happens-before pairs mined from an Internet text corpus in the *VerbOcean* project did not work well in the area of BPM analysis. For example, *VerbOcean* would conclude that "sell" should happen before "cash" while in a

Table 1. Problem indicators: missing information

Optionality	A task label contains an optional part
	Indicator: A task label contains a phrase such as "if needed", "can" or "optionally".
	Example: Task "Repeat inspection if necessary"
	Consequences: The decision that leads to inclusion or omission of the optional part needs to be made explicit
	Questions: How and by whom the decision is made whether the optional part should be included?
Or	"or" between verbs
	Indicator: A task label contains more than one main verb, separated by the word "or"
	Example: Task "Send or hand over documents"
	Consequences: If a function has a label "Doing A or B", the information about the decision process whether A or B should be done is missing.
	Questions: How and by whom the decision is be made whether A or B has to be executed? Are there cases where both tasks have to be processed?
Useless Test	For a task that indicates a test, only one possible outcome is modelled
	Indicator: A task label contains a verb that indicates a test (such as "check", "test", "verify"), but this task is not followed by an (exclusive or inclusive) OR split that would indicate that this test has more than one possible outcome.
	Example: Task "Test financial standing" is followed by task "Sell travel package"
	Consequences: This is an indicator that only the "normal" (or "happy") path has been modelled.
	Questions: What should be done in the case that the task does not has the "normal" outcome?
Missing Negative Case	Only the positive result of something is modelled
	Indicator: An event label L_1 contains a phrase such as "successfully", "without errors", "in time" etc. No preceding decision ((X)OR connector) which also leads to a task with a label L_2 with $L_1 ! L_2$, can be found in the model.
	Example: There is an event "Customer has been registered successfully", but no corresponding event describing the negative case.
	Consequences: If there is a chance of running into a failure (otherwise, there would be no need to stress the success), this case has not been modeled.
	Questions: Under which circumstances the execution could lead to a failure state and what are the consequences of such an unsuccessful execution?
Unclear Responsibility	For a task, no responsible organizational role is defined
	Indicator: No organizational unit is attached to a task (applies to EPC models only)
	Consequences: It is unclear by whom a task has to be done.
	Questions: Who is responsible / accountable for this task? Do other roles contribute or have to be informed about the results?
Forgotten Edge Case	Comparison between two values does not include the case "equality"
	Indicator: A split has exactly two outgoing arcs with condition labels L_1 and L_2 such that L_1 is "$x < y$" and L_2 is "$x > y$' (also in textual form such as "x is greater/smaller as y" or "x exceeds/underruns y").
	This is a special case of the more general problem to check condition labels for consistency and completeness as described in [30].
	Example: An XOR split is followed by exactly two events (in BPMN by exactly two outgoing sequence flows with the conditions) "more than 20 participants" and "less than 20 participants".
	Consequences: It is possible that the edge case, i.e. the case $x = y$ has been forgotten.
	Questions: Is the edge case possible? How to act in this case?

Table 2. Problem indicators: Possible modelling errors

Unseparated "Yes/No"	AND- or inclusive OR-Split after a yes/no-Question
	Indicator: A binary decision is followed by (a) a split with more than two outgoing arcs or (b) an AND- or inclusive OR-split which has two outgoing arcs.
	Labels indicating such a decision are ones ending with a question mark or containing phrases such as "check whether...".
	Example: Task "Does file exist?" is followed by an inclusive OR-split.
	Consequences: This is an indicator of a wrong model. An exclusive OR-split with exactly two outgoing arcs should be used instead.
	Questions: Case (a): Are the possible results of the decision described clearly enough? Do we miss another decision?; Case (b): Can it really be the case that both paths can be taken in parallel? If yes: How should the decision be rewritten?
Contradiction	Contradicting events can occur / contradicting tasks can be performed at the same time
	Indicator: An AND- or inclusive OR-split is (directly or indirectly) followed by two events or by two tasks which have the labels L_1 and L_2 such that (a) $L_1 \mathbin{!} L_2$ or (b) $L_1 \prec L_2$.
	Example: Tasks "Accept proposal" and "Deny proposal" both follow an inclusive OR-split
	Consequences: This is an indicator that the situation has been modeled wrongly, and an XOR-split should be used instead.
	Questions: Should the AND- or inclusive OR-split be replaced by an XOR-split? If not: What exactly does it mean that tasks that seem to be contradicting to each other can be performed at the same time? What will be the final result?
Double Activity	The same task can be performed twice in parallel
	Indicator: An AND- or inclusive OR-split gateway starts two paths that can be taken in parallel. On one path, there is a task with label L_1, on the other path there is task with label L_2, and we have $L_1 \equiv L_2$.
	Example: Having two potentially parallel task named "update account" could lead to a race condition (i.e. the final result may depend on the order in which the two instances of the task are completed).
	Consequences: It is questionable whether indeed one and the same task should be performed twice.
	Questions: Are both labels referring to exactly the same task? Should it really be done twice? If yes: Why? And what will be the (combined) result? Are different participants responsible for executing the task? Do they have to collaborate?
Missing Automation	Tasks that usually profit from automation are modelled as manual task
	Indicator: A task label use verbs referring to activities that are usually done automatically (such as "calculate", "sort").
	There is no information system object attached to this task (for EPC models) / the task is modelled as a manual task (for BPMN models)
	Example: manual task "Calculate fees"
	Consequences: Either the system in use for automating the task has been forgotten in the model or there is an option to improve the process by automation.
	Questions: Is this task supported by a system? If no: Could it be? How is the task performed manually now? Does the actor use any individual tools (such as spreadsheets) outside the "official" IT infrastructure of the organization?
Do / Undo	A task is directly followed by another tasks with the opposite effect
	Indicator: A task label contains verb A, and the task label of the subsequent task contains verb B such that $A \mathbin{!} B$
	Example: A task referring to receiving an object is directly followed by a task referring to forwarding the same object to someone else. Other activities (e.g., a decision to whom it should be forwarded or whether it is allowed to forward the object) are missing.
	Consequences: It is unclear what exactly is the purpose of the tasks.
	Questions: What exactly is done before the activity denoted by verb B?

Table 3. Problem indicators: Elements that can be understood in more than one way

And	"and" between verbs
	Indicator: A task label contains at least two main verbs V_1 and V_2, separated by the word "and", and there is not $V_1 \prec V_2$.
	Example: This indicator would apply for a task "update account and pay for the services", while a task "print and sign document" would not be affected because of the relation PRINT $\prec$ SIGN (here it is reasonable to assume that no misunderstandings about the order are possible).
	Consequences: The conjunction "and" can have several meanings. "Doing A and B" could imply a temporal order (first A, than B). Another possible meaning is that A and B can be done in parallel. This information should be made explicit in the process model.
	Questions: Do *A* and *B* have to be processed in a particular order? Can they be executed in parallel? Are there cases where only one of the tasks has to be processed?
Vague Verb	A verb in a task label does not explain exactly what to do in a task
	Indicator: The activity label contains a verb such as "support" or "manage"
	Example: Task "Ensure correct customer identification"
	Consequences: With such a label, it is not clear which activities have to be performed.
	Questions: What exactly are the activities described by "to support" etc.?
Vague Criteria	A label contains a decision based on vague or subjective criteria
	Indicator: The labels contains subjective or judgmental phrases such as "adequate", "enough", "normal", "similar" or "sufficient".
	Example: An event (or a guard condition in BPMN) is named "Solvency not sufficient"
	Consequences: The requirements engineer should ask for details about the decision
	Questions: What exactly is regarded to be "enough" etc.? For example, the event "A similar case has already been reported" should lead to the questions under which circumstances two cases are considered as being similar to each other

business process both orders (sell before cash or cash before sell) can be found. A happens-before relation in *VerbOcean* means that in the *majority* of mined sentences one action happens before another one. However, we did not want to constrain creative thinking in process design by alerting the modeler when actions are done in an innovative way which is different from the usual one. Therefore, our happens-before relation includes only such pairs of verbs where there is no reasonable doubt that the first has always to be done before the second (for example: READ ≺ DISCARD or CALCULATE ≺ RECALCULATE).

In addition to defining pairs of words or word groups that are in one of the relations introduced in Sect. 3.1, our program makes use of the transitivity properties of the hyponomy and happens-before relation. E.g., if we have stated that "produce" happens before "use" and "use" happens before "recycle", it is also concluded that "produce" happens before "recycle". Furthermore, negative prefixes (such as *non-*) are taken into account for identifying antonyms that are not explicitly included in our list of antonym pairs. In the same way, we conclude that word pairs such as "pre-*xxx*" and "post-*xxx*" are in the happens-before relation.

We realized that only a rather small number of verbs are actually used in BPM. Currently our tool is able to identify 841 verbs. 91.5 % of the 6286 labels in our repository used one of these verbs (where many of the remaining labels contained misspelled verbs or no verbs at all).

For locating the patterns, we used a Prolog-based approach. First, the BPM is transformed into Prolog facts. Queries on those facts can find occurrences of certain patterns. In previous papers, we explained this approach in detail and demonstrated how such a pattern-based method can be used for detecting syntactic errors [14], control-flow related problems [16], reducing the cognitive complexity of models [15] and also to find some modelling errors (from the perspective of a business analyst) related to the labels [17].

3.4   Results

We applied our tool prototype to a repository of 2098 German-language EPC models. It contains models from a variety of 186 sources (including 786 models from the BPM Academic Initiative repository at bpmai.org, 605 models from the SAP reference model, 78 models from the Keewee reference model at wi-wiki.de, 297 models from 14 real-world projects and models from various research papers, bachelor, diploma, master and PhD theses).

Only a small subset of these models contained symbols for organizational roles and information systems (which is quite common for EPC models). Therefore, we had to exclude the indicators that rely on these symbols ("unclear responsibility" and "missing automation") from our search.

The results of a search for the indicators discussed in this paper are shown in Fig. 3. Note that the diagram shows the number of models reported by an indicator. The actual number of reported potential issues is even higher, because often more than one instance of the same potential issue can be found in a model.

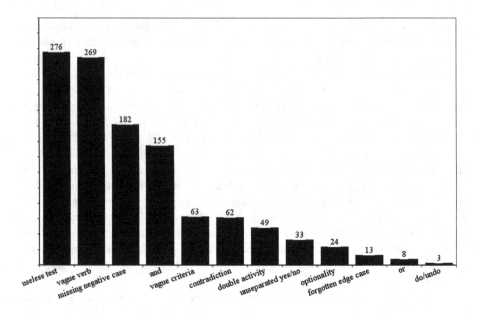

Fig. 3. Models for which the indicators have been detected (out of 2098 models)

The most frequently found issue is that a task which should have more than one possible result is followed by only one outcome. This reflects the results from our manual inspection mentioned in Sect. 3.2. The issue placed third in Fig. 3 is very similar: Here an event shows that something has been done "successfully"/"without error", etc. but there is no information about alternative outcomes. Both cases have in common that they refer to a model where only the normal (most likely) way of executing a process has been modelled. While this may perfectly fit the needs of a business analyst, a person who has to derive requirements from a BPM needs additional information. The same is true for the second- and fifth-ranked indicator. For the people who work in a process, it can be very clear what a task "support sales staff" (indicator "vague verb") or "Check whether enough spare parts are in stock" (indicator "vague criterion") actually means. For an requirement engineer, this is where the true work begins: He or she has to ask for the activities, decision rules and responsibilities behind the tasks. It is evident that models which have initially been created for other purposes than supporting requirements elicitation often do not include all the information that would be necessary for formulating the requirements.

4   Related Work

Automatic reviews of business process models have been the topic of a large number of scientific papers. The surveys in [1,7,12,13] give a comprehensive overview on the papers addressing quality of BPM and on methods for checking the compliance of BPM to given business rules or legal requirements. Only a minority of the scientific work on BPM quality discusses the labels in a BPM, and those papers that use natural language processing (NLP) techniques on BPM labels have mostly two objectives: enforcing naming conventions [24,25] and avoiding terminological inconsistency [18,31].

None of the papers discussing the quality of BPM took the perspective of the requirements engineer whose task it is to identify not only possible errors in the model but also possibly missing information about exceptions and less frequently processed branches.

Our contribution is motivated by approaches that use NLP for assessing the quality of requirements documents [10]. Such approaches are already used in a large number of academic and commercial tools [20].

For example, the tool *QuARS* [9] uses NLP techniques for finding indicators for ambiguities and incompleteness in natural language requirement specifications. Similar methods have been implemented in several other tools such as *Newspeak* [29], *RUBRIC*[9], *RESI* [21], the *Requirements Analysis Tool* [35] or the *Ambiguity Detector* [28]. More references to other tools can be found in [32].

Lami et al. [23] have shown in an empirical study that using an automatic tool for locating linguistic ambiguity can significantly improve the requirements analysis process.

Our approach combines the existing ideas that use NLP for improving requirements with the analysis of the graphical notation of a BPM (i.e. graph analysis). This way, we analyse both the semantics expressed by the symbols of the modelling language as the semantics expressed by the natural language labels.

5   Conclusions and Future Work

We believe that our tool for an automatic analysis of BPM can help requirement engineers to locate unclear situations in BPMs. Usually, such problems would have to be resolved together with the process experts. We have to stress that using the pattern-based method is no substitute for a manual model review. We think, however, that using automatic analysis can support such a review. Our Prolog-based search is fully integrated into the open-source modelling tool *bflow* toolbox* (www.bflow.org), and it is our intention to make our tool open source as well after adding some more technical improvements.

In our current research, we focused on the control flow depicted in a BPM. Although we observed that many BPM in practice are restricted to modelling the control flow, it would be useful to take other aspects (in particular, data flow and resources) into account as well. Also, further research is needed both for extending the catalogue of problem indicators as for extending our list of semantic relations between words. For this purpose, both approaches for mining such relations from model repositories [22,33] as the classification of verbs as described in [26] could be helpful.

Another direction for future research should be to analyse the actual nocuousness of the potential problems found by our approach. For this purpose, involving human judgment will be necessary to differentiate those situations where an model fragment located by our indicators actually causes understanding problems from those where the process model can easily be interpreted anyway (cf. [5] for ambiguities in requirements written in prose).

Acknowledgments. We thank the German Research Foundation (DFG) for funding the AUTEM project in which this research has been done (grant no. 599444).

References

1. Becker, J., Delfmann, P., Eggert, M., Schwittay, S.: Generalizability and applicability of model-based business process compliance-checking approaches a state-of-the-art analysis and research roadmap. BuR - Bus. Res. **5**(2), 221–247 (2012)
2. Berry, D.M., Kamsties, E., Krieger, M.M.: From Contract Drafting to Software Specification: Linguistic Sources of Ambiguity, A Handbook (2003). http://se. uwaterloo.ca/~dberry/handbook/ambiguityHandbook.pdf
3. Berry, D., Kamsties, E.: Ambiguity in requirements specification. In: do Prado Leite, J.C.S., Doorn, J.H. (eds.) Perspectives on Software Requirements. he Springer International Series in Engineering and Computer Science, vol. 753, pp. 7–44. Springer, Heidelberg (2004)
4. Cardoso, E., Almeida, J.P.A., Guizzardi, G.: Requirements engineering based on business process models: a case study. In: 13th Enterprise Distributed Object Computing Conference Workshops, pp. 320–327. IEEE (2009)
5. Chantree, F., Nuseibeh, B., Roeck, A.N.D., Willis, A.: Identifying nocuous ambiguities in natural language requirements. In: International Conference on Requirements Engineering 2006, pp. 56–65. IEEE Computer Society (2006)
6. Chklovski, T., Pantel, P.: VerbOcean: mining the web for fine-grained semantic verb relations. In: Proceedings of the 2004 Conference on Empirical Methods in Natural Language Processing, pp. 33–40. ACL (2004)
7. de Oca, I.M.M., Snoeck, M., Reijers, H.A., Rodriguez-Morffi, A.: A systematic literature review of studies on business process modeling quality. Information and Software Technology (2014). (accepted for publication)
8. Empson, W.: Seven types of ambiguity. Chatto & Windus, London (1956)
9. Fabbrini, F., Fusani, M., Gnesi, S., Lami, G.: An Automatic Quality Evaluation for Natural Language Requirements. In: Proceedings of the Seventh International Workshop on RE: Foundation for Software Quality (REFSQ 2001), vol. 1 (2001)
10. Fantechi, A., Gnesi, S., Lami, G., Maccari, A.: Application of linguistic techniques for use case analysis. In: Proceedings of the 10th Anniversary IEEE Joint International Conference on Requirements Engineering, pp. 157–164 (2002)
11. Fellbaum, C. (ed.): WordNet: An Electronic Lexical Database (Language, Speech, and Communication). The MIT Press, Cambridge (1998)
12. Fellmann, M., Zasada, A.: State-of-the-art of business process compliance approaches. In: 22 European Conference on Information Systems (2014)
13. Groefsema, H., Bucur, D.: A survey of formal business process verification: from soundness to variability. In: Proceedings of the Third International Symposium on Business Modeling and Software Design, pp. 198–203 (2013)

14. Gruhn, V., Laue, R.: Checking properties of business process models with logic programming. In: Proceedings of the 5th International Workshop on Modelling, Simulation, Verification and Validation of Enterprise Information Systems, pp. 84–93 (2007)
15. Gruhn, V., Laue, R.: Reducing the cognitive complexity of business process models. In: Proceedings of the 8th IEEE International Conference on Cognitive Informatics, pp. 339–345. IEEE Computer Society (2009)
16. Gruhn, V., Laue, R.: A heuristic method for detecting problems in business process models. Bus. Proc. Manag. J. **16**(5), 806–821 (2010)
17. Gruhn, V., Laue, R.: Detecting common errors in event-driven process chains by label analysis. Enterp. Modell. Inf. Sys. Architect. **6**(1), 3–15 (2011)
18. Havel, J., Steinhorst, M., Dietrich, H., Delfmann, P.: Supporting terminological standardization in conceptual models - a plugin for a meta-modelling tool. In: 22nd European Conference on Information Systems (2014)
19. de la Vara, J.L., Sánchez, J., Pastor, Ó.: Business process modelling and purpose analysis for requirements analysis of information systems. In: Bellahsène, Z., Léonard, M. (eds.) CAiSE 2008. LNCS, vol. 5074, pp. 213–227. Springer, Heidelberg (2008)
20. Kiyavitskaya, N., Zeni, N., Mich, L., Berry, D.M.: Requirements for tools for ambiguity fication and measurement in natural language requirements specifications. Requir. Eng. **13**(3), 207–239 (2008)
21. Körner, S.J., Brumm, T.: RESI - a natural language specification improver. In: IEEE International Conference on Semantic Computing, pp. 1–8 (2009)
22. Koschmider, A., Reijers, H.A.: Improving the process of process modelling by the use of domain process patterns. Enterp. Inf. Syst. **9**(1), 29–57 (2015)
23. Lami, G., Ferguson, R.W.: An empirical study on the impact of automation on the requirements analysis process. J. Comput. Sci. Technol. **22**(3), 338–347 (2007)
24. Leopold, H., Eid-Sabbagh, R., Mendling, J., Azevedo, L.G., Baião, F.A.: Detection of naming convention violations in process models for different languages. Decis. Support Syst. **56**, 310–325 (2013)
25. Leopold, H., Smirnov, S., Mendling, J.: On the refactoring of activity labels in business process models. Inf. Sys. **37**(5), 443–459 (2012)
26. Mendling, J., Recker, J., Reijers, H.A.: On the usage of labels and icons in business process modeling. IJISMD **1**(2), 40–58 (2010)
27. Miers, D.: Best practice BPM. ACM Queue **4**(2), 40–48 (2006)
28. Nigam, A., Arya, N., Nigam, B., Jain, D.: Tool for automatic discovery of ambiguity in requirements. IJCSI Int. J. Comput. Sci. **9**(5), 350–356 (2012)
29. Osborne, M., MacNish, C.: Processing natural language software requirement specifications. Int. Conf. Requirements Eng. **1996**, 229–237 (1996)
30. Pap, Z., Majzik, I., Pataricza, A., Szegi, A.: Methods of checking general safety criteria in UML statechart specifications. Reliab. Eng. Sys. Saf. **87**(1), 89–107 (2005)
31. Peters, N., Weidlich, M.: Using glossaries to enhance the label quality in business process models. In: Dienstleistungsmodellierung 2010 (2010)
32. Raffo, D., Ferguson, R., Setamanit, S., Sethanandha, B.: Evaluating the impact of requirements analysis tools using simulation. Softw. Process: Improv. Pract. **13**(1), 63–73 (2008)

33. Smirnov, S., Weidlich, M., Mendling, J., Weske, M.: Action patterns in business process model repositories. Comput. Ind. **63**(2), 98–111 (2012)
34. Storch, A., Laue, R., Gruhn, V.: Flexible evaluation of textual labels in conceptual models. In: Enterprise modelling and information systems architectures - EMISA 2015. (2015)
35. Verma, K., Kass, A., Vasquez, R.G.: Using syntactic and semantic analyses to improve the quality of requirements documentation. Semantic Web **5**(5), 405–419 (2014)

Compliance in Requirements Engineering

Automated Classification of Legal Cross References Based on Semantic Intent

Nicolas Sannier[(✉)], Morayo Adedjouma, Mehrdad Sabetzadeh,
and Lionel Briand

SnT Centre for Security, Reliability and Trust, University of Luxembourg,
Luxembourg City, Luxembourg
{nicolas.sannier,morayo.adedjouma,mehrdad.sabetzadeh,
lionel.briand}@uni.lu

Abstract. [**Context and motivation**] To elaborate legal compliance requirements, analysts need to read and interpret the relevant legal provisions. An important complexity while performing this task is that the information pertaining to a compliance requirement may be scattered across several provisions that are related via cross references. [**Question/Problem**] Prior research highlights the importance of determining and accounting for the semantics of cross references in legal texts during requirements elaboration, with taxonomies having been already proposed for this purpose. Little work nevertheless exists on automating the classification of cross references based on their semantic intent. Such automation is beneficial both for handling large and complex legal texts, and also for providing guidance to analysts. [**Principal ideas/results**] We develop an approach for automated classification of legal cross references based on their semantic intent. Our approach draws on a qualitative study indicating that, in most cases, the text segments appearing before and after a cross reference contain cues about the cross reference's intent. [**Contributions**] We report on the results of our qualitative study, which include an enhanced semantic taxonomy for cross references and a set of natural language patterns associated with the intent types in this taxonomy. Using the patterns, we build an automated classifier for cross references. We evaluate the accuracy of this classifier through case studies. Our results indicate that our classifier yields an average accuracy (F-measure) of $\approx 84\,\%$.

Keywords: Compliance requirements · Legal cross references · Semantic taxonomy · Automated classification

1 Introduction

In many domains such as public administration, healthcare and finance, software systems need to comply with laws and regulations. To identify and elaborate legal compliance requirements for these systems, requirements analysts typically need to read and interpret the relevant provisions in legal texts. This task is

© Springer International Publishing Switzerland 2016
M. Daneva and O. Pastor (Eds.): REFSQ 2016, LNCS 9619, pp. 119–134, 2016.
DOI: 10.1007/978-3-319-30282-9_8

often made difficult by the complexities of legal writing. An important source of complexity is that one cannot consider the legal provisions independently of one another, due to the provisions being inter-dependent. The dependencies between the provisions are captured using *legal cross references* (CR).

The semantic intent of a legal CR directly impacts the way the CR is handled during requirements elaboration [17]: For example, when a provision, say an article, A, cites a provision, B, to state that A does not apply in an exceptional situation described by B, it is best to create a new requirement for the exception. In contrast, when A cites B for a definition, it is more sensible to add the definition to the glossary, rather than creating a new requirement.

A number of useful taxonomies have already been developed to enable the classification of CRs according to their semantic intent [3,4,13,17,24]. These taxonomies nevertheless consider classification as a manual task, and thus do not provide automation for the task.

In this paper, we develop an automated approach for classifying CRs based on their semantic intent. Such automation has two main benefits: First, the number of CRs that need to be considered by analysts may be large, in the hundreds or thousands [1,3,20]. Automated classification helps both to reduce effort, and further to better organize requirements engineering activities, noting that automated classification provides a-priori knowledge about the intent of CRs. Second, research by Massey et al. [15] and Maxwell et al. [16] suggests that software engineers without adequate legal expertise find it difficult to determine the intent of CRs. Automation can provide useful guidance in such situations.

Research Questions (RQs). Our work is motivated by the following RQs:

- **RQ1: What are the possible intents of (legal) CRs?** RQ1 aims at developing a taxonomy of CR intents. This RQ is informed by the existing CR taxonomies, as we explain later.

- **RQ2: Are there natural language (NL) patterns in legal texts that suggest the intent of CRs?** RQ2 aims at investigating whether there are patterns in the text with a direct link to the intent of CRs. Such patterns would enable the automatic classification of CRs.

- **RQ3: How accurately can NL patterns predict CR intent?** Provided that the answer to RQ2 is positive, RQ3 aims at measuring how accurate (in terms of standard accuracy metrics) an automated classification approach based on NL patterns is.

Approach. Figure 1 outlines our approach. We address RQ1 and RQ2 based on a qualitative study of 1079 CRs from Luxembourg's legislative corpus. Our study is guided by the principles of Grounded Theory (GT) [6] – a systematic methodology for building a theory from data. However, GT normally starts without preconceived knowledge about the theory. In contrast, our study leverages existing CR taxonomies, notably those by Breaux [3], Hamdaqa et al. [13], and Maxwell et al. [17]. The qualitative study yields an enhanced taxonomy (Table 1), along with a collection of NL patterns observed in the text appearing

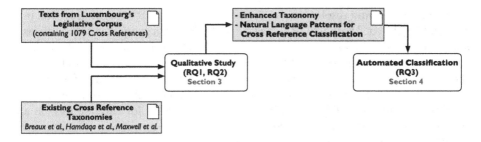

Fig. 1. Overview

in the vicinity of CRs of each intent type (partially shown in Table 2). We utilize the taxonomy and the identified NL patterns for developing an automated classification solution, and evaluate the accuracy of the solution through case studies.

Contributions and Key Remarks. Our proposed taxonomy brings together and extends existing taxonomies with the goal of automating CR classification. Our work on NL patterns presents the first systematic attempt we are aware of, where the collocation of CRs and adjacent phrases has been studied for the purpose of determining CR intent. We demonstrate that a rule-based classification approach based on NL patterns is effective. To this end, we report on two case studies. The first case study is over a random sample of pages from various Luxembourgish legislative texts, and the second – over the French editions of the Personal Health Information Protection Act (PHIPA) of Ontario, Canada and the 2014 compilation of the amendment provisions on Canadian consolidated laws [22]. The two case studies collectively include 2585 CRs. Our evaluation of automated classification shows F-measures of 87.57 % and 80.59 % for the first and second case studies, respectively, yielding an average F-measure of 84.48 %.

Our work exclusively considers legal texts in French. The consistency seen between our CR taxonomy and the ones developed previously over English legal corpora provides confidence about our taxonomy being generalizable. Adapting our approach to texts in other languages will nevertheless prompt a reinvestigation of RQ2 and RQ3. The observations that we expect to carry over from our work to such adaptations are: (1) There are indeed patterns in legal texts to suggest the intent of CRs; and (2) A reasonably-sized manual investigation of these patterns provides an accurate basis for automated classification.

Structure. The remainder of the paper is organized according to the flow of Fig. 1. Section 2 reviews related work. Sections 3 and 4 present our qualitative study and automated classification solution, respectively. Section 5 discusses practical considerations and threats to validity. Section 6 concludes the paper.

2   Related Work

Several papers address automated detection and resolution of CRs in legal texts. Detection refers to the ability to recognize the complete textual fragment that constitutes a CR, and resolution – to the ability to find a CR's target provision in the right legal text. Work on CR detection and resolution spans several countries and jurisdictions, including the Dutch, Italian, Japanese and Luxembourgish legislation, respectively [8, 20, 23, 24], as well as US regulations [4]. In contrast to the above work, in this paper, we focus on automatically extracting information about the semantics of CRs, once they have been detected. Automated detection (but not resolution) of CRs is a prerequisite to our work; for this, we rely on a tool from our previous research [20].

Work already exists on the semantic classification of CRs. Maxwell et al. [17] propose a CR taxonomy, where they distinguish definitions (the cited provision provides a definition needed by the citing one), constraints (the cited provision imposes additional conditions on the citing one), exceptions (the cited provision restricts the applicability of the citing one), general (generic citations such as to "applicable law"), unrelated (the cited provision is orthogonal to software requirements), incorrect (wrong provision cited), and prioritization (establishing a priority between the citing and the cited provisions).

Breaux and Antón [3, 4] distinguish refinements (the cited provision elaborates upon the citing one), exceptions (same as by Maxwell et al. [17]) and continuations (which, like refinements, elaborate on information in the citing provisions, but through subsequent sub-divisions). Breaux [3] further considers definitions and constraints, but in a more general context than CRs per se.

Hamdaqa et al. [13] classify CRs under definitions (same as above), specifications (the cited provision provides more information about the citing one), compliance (the cited provision complies with the citing one in some manner), and amendments. Amendments are further specialized into insertions (amending by adding a new provision), deletions (amending by repealing a provision), striking (amending by replacing the wording within a provision), and redesignation (amending by changing the name of the cited provision).

Our work builds on and is closely guided by the above three taxonomies. A detailed comparison between our taxonomy and these earlier ones is provided in Sect. 3. Broadly speaking, none of these earlier taxonomies alone provide a complete basis for automated CR classification.

Finally, we note that the general problem of automated classification in legal texts has been studied for a long time. Existing work on this topic mainly address the classification of deontic modalities, e.g., rights, obligations, permissions, and delegations. A number of techniques for this type of classification have been proposed based on machine learning [2], natural language processing [24], and the combination of the two [5]. In contrast to these strands of work, our focus is on automatic classification of CRs.

3   A Qualitative Study of CR Intent Types

We first describe the units of analysis and the analysis procedure in our qualitative study, outlined earlier in Fig. 1. We then address RQ1 and RQ2.

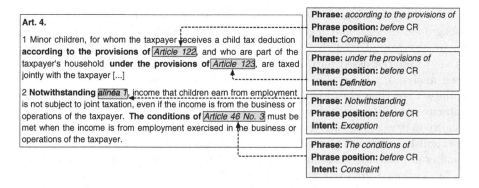

Fig. 2. Examples of recorded information for CRs during the qualitative study

3.1 Units of Analysis

We manually identified and analyzed CRs from two Luxembourgish legislative texts. These texts are: (1) the 2014 edition of Luxembourg's Income Tax Law [12] and (2) Chamber of Deputies' Draft Law No. 6457 [11]. Both texts are in French.

We chose the Income Tax Law based on advice from legal experts who deemed this law to be among the most complex in terms of CRs. This law, which has been regularly revised since it was first drafted in 1967, further offers a window into several decades of legal writing practices. The second text was chosen to address an a-priori-known limitation posed by the Income Tax Law for our study. In particular, the Income Tax Law is generally not meant to make amendments to other laws, and consequently contains a very small number of amendment CRs. The second text has several such CRs, thus providing more conclusive grounds for studying this class of CRs.

In total, we examined, using the procedure described next, 141 pages from the above legislative texts. These pages collectively contain 1079 CRs: 729 CRs come from the first seven chapters of the Income Tax Law (117 pages) and the remaining 350 CRs – from the first chapter of Draft Law No 6457 (24 pages).

3.2 Analysis Procedure

Using the judgment of the first two authors, we classified each CR according to the taxonomies by Breaux [3], Hamdaqa et al. [13], and Maxwell et al. [17]. If some CR was not classifiable using any of these taxonomies, we defined a new intent type. After classifying a CR, we considered exclusively the sentence in which the CR appeared and documented any phrase(s) that affected human judgment, along with whether the phrase(s) appeared before or after the CR. No phrase was derived if the judgment happened to rely on information other than the sentence in which the CR appeared (e.g., previous sentences), or if the sentence had no relevant phrase(s) in it. In Fig. 2, we illustrate the information maintained for four CRs from the Income Tax Law (translated from French).

The first two authors, both of whom are native French speakers and have background in legal and regulatory requirements, worked together throughout the procedure explained above. In each case, the intent and the identified phrases (if any) were discussed until an agreement was reached. Once all the CRs had been analyzed, the phrases obtained for each intent type were reviewed. The phrases were then clustered into groups of semantically-equivalent variations. Subsequently, NL patterns were developed to characterize each cluster. A technicality in developing the NL patterns is that some languages, including French, distinguish gender and plurality (and the combinations thereof). To minimize the number of patterns, we defined suitable abstractions over gender and plurality.

We excluded from our analysis an investigation of the content of the provision(s) being cited by a CR. This decision was motivated by two observations: First, the provision(s) cited by a CR seldom refer back to the context in which they are being cited. The provision(s) are therefore unlikely to provide useful information about the intent of the citation. Second, the cited provision(s) may constitute a large amount of text, e.g., several articles and chapters, or even entire laws. Given that potential benefits from considering the content of cited provision(s) is limited, processing this content is not justified in either the qualitative study, or the automated classification solution that builds on the study.

3.3   Results

Tables 1 and 2 present the main results from our qualitative study. Specifically, Table 1 lists the intent types of our proposed CR taxonomy and their definitions, along with a mapping of the types to those in the taxonomies of Breaux [3], Hamdaqa et al. [13] and Maxwell et al. [17]. The table further shows, for our qualitative study, the relative frequency of each intent type, the number of phrases retrieved per type, and the number of distinct patterns derived from the phrases.

Table 2 details, for each intent type, the most frequent patterns and the relative frequencies of these patterns. The table further provides illustrating examples for the most frequent patterns in our study. Although the analysis was performed over French texts, we provide (unofficial) English translations to facilitate readability. For each intent type, we provide the frequency of patterns with less than three occurrences, denoted *rare*. We use this notion later in our discussion of RQ2.

Taxonomy of Intent Types (RQ1). Our taxonomy (Table 1) distinguishes eleven intent types for CRs. Except for the *General Amendment* type, all types in our taxonomy have a corresponding type in the taxonomies of Breaux's, Hamdaqa et al.'s, and Maxwell et al.'s. Nevertheless, and as suggested by Table 1, none of the above three taxonomies alone provide, for the purpose of automated classification, adequate coverage of the intent types. At the same time, there are intent types in these three taxonomies that our taxonomy does not cover. Below, we discuss the main differences between our taxonomy and the other three:

Breaux's taxonomy is at a higher level of abstraction than ours. Our taxonomy is primarily an amalgamation of those by Hamdaqa et al. and Maxwell et al.

Table 1. Taxonomy of semantic intent types for CRs

Intent Type	Definition	Mapping			Frequency	# of phrases	# of distinct patterns
		Breaux [3]	Hamdaqa et al. [13]	Maxwell et al. [17]			
Compliance	The cited provision(s) apply along with the citing provision.	--	compliance	--	16,03%	173	24
Constraint	The cited provision(s) introduce additional constraints.	constraint	--	constraint	1,76%	19	4
Definition	The cited provision(s) provide a definition.	definition	definition	definition	30,95%	334	7
Delegation	The citing provision delegates authority to an (often) unspecific legal text for further elaboration.	--	--	general	10,47%	113	4
Exception	The citing provision introduces an exception to the cited provision(s).	exception	--	exception	6,12%	66	11
Refinement	The citing provision elaborates upon the cited provision(s).	refinement	specification	--	2,50%	27	8
General Amendment	The citing provision amends the cited provision(s) without precisely stating what the modification(s) are.	--	--	--	15,01%	162	3
Amendment by Addition	The citing provision adds new provision(s) to the (single) cited provision.	--	Amend. by Addition	--	4,08%	44	6
Amendment by Deletion	The cited provision is deleted.	--	Amend. by Deletion	--	3,52%	38	3
Amendment by Redesignation	The cited provision's title or number is changed as per described in the citing provision.	--	Amend. by Redesignation	--	1,48%	16	1
Amendment by Replacement	The cited provision's wording is changed as per described in the citing provision.	--	Amend. by Striking	--	7,41%	80	1
Unclassified					0,65%	7	
Total					**100%**	**1079**	**72**

In particular, our intent types for *Compliance, Refinement,* and the various notions of amendment are aligned with Hamdaqa et al.'s; whereas, the rest are aligned with Maxwell et al.'s. We note that our choice of names for some intent types differs from those in the above taxonomies. This is mainly to provide better overall contrast between the types in our taxonomy.

Our current taxonomy does not envisage a type for CRs whose intent is *Prioritization*, as proposed by Maxwell et al. We cannot rule out the existence of such CRs in the Luxembourgish legal corpus, but draw attention to an absence of observations in our qualitative study. The main implication of this lack of observations is that our automated classification solution (Sect. 4) cannot handle CRs whose intent is prioritization. Furthermore and on a different note, our taxonomy does not cover the notions of *Unrelated* and *Incorrect* in the work of Maxwell et al. Determining the relevance and correctness of CRs is outside the scope of our current work.

Finally, as shown in Table 1, we were unable to classify a small fraction (0,65 %) of the CRs in our study due to these CRs being too general or vague. The low incidence of manually-unclassifiable CRs makes it more likely that one can achieve good classification coverage through automation.

Table 2. NL patterns associated with intent types along with examples[a]

Intent Type	Most Frequent Patterns (% of all patterns for intent type)	(No.) Example excerpt from legal text
Compliance *(rare patterns: 36.68%)*	applicable (22.10%)	(1) Provisions of *alineas 2, 3 and 4 of article 386* **are applicable.**
	by virtue of (18.23%)	(2) [...] pensions for survivors who lived [...] with the insured [...] are complemented [...] up to the pension to which the deceased would be entitled **by virtue of** *Article 186.*
	conforming to / in accordance with (13.81%)	(3) Pensions calculated **in accordance with** *Article 225* are multiplied by [...]
Constraint *(rare patterns: 10.53%)*	within the conditions of (68.42%)	(4) **Within the conditions of** *the previous alinea*, the State shall [...]
	within the limits of (21.05%)	(5) Donations in cash or in kind [...] are deductible [...] as special expenses **within the limits of** *Articles 109 and 112 of the law of 4 December 1967*
Definition *(rare patterns: 4.18%)*	under (67.67%)	(6) The three-year reference period is extended if and to the extent that it overlaps with the periods **under** *Article 172* [...]
	within the meaning of (22.16%)	(7) [...] persons exercising a professional activity on behalf of their spouse or partner **within the meaning of** *article 2 of the law of 9 July 2004* shall [...]
	specified / defined (5.99%)	(8) [...] confiscation **as defined by** *Article 31* can be imposed as a principal penalty [...]
Delegation *(rare patterns: 5.31%)*	future tense (in French) (55.75%)	(9) A *grand ducal regulation* **will** establish the extent and what may be part of the net invested assets [...]
	infinitive form (in French) (26.55%)	(10) With regard to property acquired either free of charge or [...], by a date **to be provided by** *a grand-ducal regulation*, the purchase or cost price is replaced by [...]
	modals (may / can / will) (12.39%)	(11) *A grand-ducal regulation* **may** fix a minimum below which gifts will not be considered.
Exception *(rare patterns: 8.63%)*	negativeform (53.44%)	(12) Interests on debts of every kind **not under** *alineas 2, 3 or 4* and including loans, assets [...]
		(13) The following extraordinary incomes shall be considered as taxable incomes [...] provided they **do not fall** within the provisions of *paragraph 2*
	derogation (29.31%)	(14) **Notwithstanding** *alinea 1*, income that children earn from employment is not subject to [...]
Refinement *(rare patterns: 7.40%)*	applies to (66.67%)	(15) the provisions of *this subsection* **shall apply to** co-farmers of a collective enterprise, as if each farmer operated individually.
	for the application of (18.52%)	(16) **For the application of** *Article 114* concerning the deferral of losses, losses are considered as not compensated [...]
	also concerns (7.41%)	(17) The *previous provision* **also concerns** foreign personal income taxes [...]
General Amendment *(rare patterns:0%)*	modified (62.35%)	(18) In *paragraph 2, alinea 1* **is modified** as follows:
	Following [+addition] (37.65%)	(19) **Following** *Article 16a* **is inserted a new** *Article 16b* [...]
Amendment By Addition *(rare patterns:0%)*	is added (40.91%)	(20) A new *paragraph 8* **is added** with the following wording [...]
	is completed (36.36%)	(21) In *paragraph 2*, the list of functions **is completed** as follows: "-mediator in the Public Service"
	is inserted (22.71%)	(22) In *paragraph 2*, a new alinea **is inserted** with the following wording [...]
Amendment By Deletion *(rare patterns:0%)*	is deleted	(23) In *alinea 1*, the following words **are deleted**: "of Public Service and administrative reform"
Amendment By Redesignation *(rare patterns:0%)*	becomes the new	(24) The current *paragraph 3* **shall become** the new *paragraph 1*
Amendment By Replacement *(rare patterns:0%)*	is replaced by	(25) In *paragraph 2, alineas 2 and 3* **are replaced by** the following paragraphs: [...]

[a]In the examples (column 3), the CRs are *italicized* and the pattern occurrences are **bolded.**

NL Patterns for Semantic Classification (RQ2). One of the most interesting observations from our qualitative study is that, for more than 98 % of the CRs investigated, we could find a phrase located within the same sentence as a given CR to suggest what the intent of that CR is.

As stated in Sect. 3.2, these phrases are the basis for the NL patterns that we have developed for classification. The patterns are partially listed and exemplified in Table 2. We do not provide in this paper the complete list of the identified phrases and the patterns derived from them. See [19] for details.

To build confidence in the usefulness of our patterns, we need to consider two important factors: (1) whether our qualitative study has covered a reasonably large number of observations for each intent type, and (2) whether the usage frequency of the patterns is reasonably high. A large proportion of patterns with very few occurrences, which we earlier denoted as rare, may indicate a large degree of flexibility in legal writing practices and hence a negative impact on the automatability of CR classification. Below, we discuss these factors for the intent types in our taxonomy based on the information in Tables 1 and 2.

Definition is the most represented intent type constituting nearly 31 % of the entire set of CRs in our study. This intent type exhibits a relatively small number of patterns (7 patterns). The three most frequent patterns for this intent type cover more than 95 % of the cases, with just over 4 % of the patterns being rarely used. Similar observation can be made for the *Delegation* and *General Amendment* types; that is, the types are both well-represented and further have a dominant set of patterns that cover a large majority of cases.

The second most represented intent type is *Compliance*. In contrast to the ones discussed above, this intent type is associated with 24 distinct patterns, with a relatively high rate of rare patterns ($\approx$37 %).

The *Refinement* and *Constraint* types have a low representation in our qualitative study. At the same time, the number of rare patterns for these intent types is quite limited (7.53 % and 10.53 %, respectively).

Finally and with regard to amendment CRs, despite the limited representation of the individual intent types, the CRs are covered by a small number of dominant patterns. This could be either due to the lack of sufficient diversity in our units of analysis (mainly, the portion of Draft Law No. 6457 investigated in our study), or due to legal writing practices being stringent and systematic with regard to amendments.

Our analysis of the NL patterns further led to some technicalities that need to be taken into account for the development of an automated classification tool. First, the occurrences of the NL patterns may not be immediately before or after the CRs. In particular, some *auxiliary phrases*, e.g., "the provisions of", may appear between a pattern occurrence and a CR, e.g., in "[...] as **mentioned in** the provisions of *article 2*". In our qualitative study, we kept track of all the auxiliary phrases encountered, recording a total of 95 of them. Due to the potentially large set of possible auxiliary phrases, providing sufficient coverage of such phrases through patterns seems unlikely to be effective. Nevertheless, we observed that the length of the auxiliary phrases (in terms of tokens) is short.

More precisely, the average length of an auxiliary phrase in our study is 2.6 tokens, with the longest phrase observed being five tokens long.

To deal with auxiliary phrases without having to enumerate them all, one can implement a strategy to look back and ahead by a certain number of tokens from where a CR is located when searching for patterns. Based on our study, we recommend that a pattern occurrence as far away as 5 tokens from a given CR should be considered, as long as the occurrence is within the same sentence as the CR and the location of the occurrence matches the before/after property maintained for the underlying pattern (illustrated in Fig. 2). Since this look-back/look-ahead distance is short (≤ 5 tokens), the risk of the CR and the pattern occurrence being in different contexts (and thus, the risk of incorrectly associating the pattern to the CR) is low.

Second, different grammatical variants of the same phrase may imply different intent types and thus different patterns. For instance, the French phrase "prévu" ("under", in English) suggests a *Definition* (Example 6 in Table 2); whereas the negative form of the phrase, "non prévu" ("not under", in English), suggests an *Exception* (Example 12), and the infinitive form of the phrase, "à prévoir" ("to be provided by", in English), suggests a *Delegation* (Example 10). Similarly, the *Compliance* and *Refinement* intent types have similar associated patterns (Examples 1, 15, 16).

Given what we stated above, one cannot simply use the root forms of terms as the basis for defining patterns. In a similar vein, preprocessing techniques commonly used in Information Retrieval, particularly stemming [18] and similarity measures [14], may yield poor results if applied for CR intent classification.

4   Automated Classification of Cross References (RQ3)

We have developed an automated CR intent classifier based on the results of RQ1 and RQ2 in the previous section. The classifier, which is built as an application within the GATE NLP Workbench [7], works in two steps:

1. It runs our previously-developed CR detector [20] to identify and mark the CRs in a given corpus.
2. Using the NL patterns of RQ2, the classifier attempts to assign an intent type to each detected CR.

To deal with auxiliary phrases, our classifier applies the look-back/look-ahead strategy discussed previously. If multiple overlapping pattern matches are found for a CR, the longest match (in terms of the number of characters in the matching region) determines the CR type.

In the rest of this section, we report on two cases studies aimed at evaluating the accuracy of our classifier. We exclude a re-evaluation of our CR detection technique (the first step), for which we already provided empirical results in our previous work [20].

4.1   Case Study over Luxembourgish Legal Texts

Our first case study is over selected legislative texts from the Luxembourgish legal corpus. The texts cover a long time span –from 1808 to 2014– and several domains, including, among others, the civil code, social security, trade, and data protection. To avoid biasing the results, the two texts in our qualitative study of Sect. 3 were excluded from the selection. Overall, the selected texts have 1830 pages, excluding non-content pages such as prefaces, tables of contents, and indices. We ran our classifier over these pages. We then randomly picked 10 % of the pages (183 pages) for a manual inspection of the classification results.

The random page sample contains a total of 1396 (detected) CRs. The first author reviewed the classification results for all the CRs in the sample and computed, for every intent type X of Table 1, the following four counts:

(c1) *Correctly Classified*: The number of CRs of type X for which automated classification is correct.

(c2) *Incorrectly Classified, Type 1*: The number of CRs that were assigned type X by automated classification, but the correct type is in fact different.

(c3) *Incorrectly Classified, Type 2*: The number of CRs that are of type X, but were assigned a different type by automated classification.

(c4) *Unclassified*: The number of CRs of type X for which automated classification yields no intent type.

Using these counts, we compute the accuracy of automated classification through recall, precision, and F-measure. To do so, we note that c1 denotes *True Positives (TP)*, c2 denotes *False Positives (FP)*, whereas c3 and c4 denote *False Negatives (FN)*. Recall is computed as $R = TP/(TP + FN)$, precision as $P = TP/(TP + FP)$, and F-measure as $F = (2 * P * R)/(P + R)$.

The results of automated classification at the level of individual intent types and at an aggregate level are presented in Table 3. Overall, our classifier provided a correct classification for 1113 CRs (c1), an incorrect classification for 33 CRs (c2 and c3), and no classification for 250 CRs (c4). These counts are respectively given in columns 3–6 of the table. We note that c2 and c3 are redistributions of one another; nevertheless, both counts are important, as a false positive for one intent type implies a false negative for another. The classification accuracy metrics are given in columns 7–9. For this case study and at an aggregate level, our classifier has a recall of 79.73 % and a precision of 97.12 %, thus giving an F-measure of 87.57 %.

From the table, we observe that nearly half (16/33) of the incorrect classifications are *Refinement* CRs being erroneously classified as *Compliance* ones. These misclassified CRs are explained by the similarities between the patterns associated with the two intent types in question, as we discussed in Sect. 3 (under RQ2). A further six classification errors are *Delegation* CRs being classified as *Definition* ones. All these cases were due to an individual variant of an existing pattern for *Delegation* CRs being missing from our pattern catalog.

With regard to unclassified CRs (column 6), 153 cases were due to missing patterns. Our subsequent investigation of these cases resulted in the identification of 75 new patterns. Of these, 60 had less than three occurrences and would

Table 3. Classification results for Luxembourgish legal texts

Intent Type	Total CRs	Correctly Classified (TP)	Incorrectly Classified T1 (FP)	Incorrectly Classified T2 (FN)	Unclassified (FN)	Recall	Precision	F-Measure
Compliance	415	334	20	2	79	80,48%	94,35%	86,87%
Constraint	23	4	0	1	18	17,39%	100,00%	29,63%
Definition	548	511	9	3	34	93,25%	98,27%	95,69%
Delegation	93	85	2	6	2	91,40%	97,70%	94,44%
Exception	56	43	2	3	10	76,79%	95,56%	85,15%
Refinement	81	13	0	16	52	16,05%	100,00%	27,66%
General Amendment	61	48	0	1	12	78,69%	100,00%	88,07%
Amend. by Addition	33	28	0	0	5	84,85%	100,00%	91,80%
Amend. by deletion	8	6	0	0	2	75,00%	100,00%	85,71%
Amend. by redesignation	2	1	0	0	1	50,00%	100,00%	66,67%
Amend. by replacement	45	40	0	0	5	88,89%	100,00%	94,12%
Unclassifiable	31	0	0	1	30		NA	
total	1396	1113	33	33	250	79,73%	97,12%	87,57%

fall under rare patterns, as defined in Sect. 3. Another 27 unclassified CRs were explained by missing variants of already-known patterns. A further 47 cases where due to the patterns being located more than 5 token away from the CRs, i.e., outside the classifier's look-back/look-ahead range discussed earlier.

During our manual inspection, we encountered 31 CRs whose intent we could not determine due to vagueness. These cases are shown as *Unclassifiable* in Table 3. Our classifier left 30 of these CRs unclassified but matched one to an unrelated pattern (because of our 5-token look-back and look-ahead strategy). When calculating the overall accuracy of our classifier, we take a conservative approach for the unclassifiable cases. In particular, we treat all these cases as false negatives (FN), meaning that we assume a subject matter expert would have been able to determine what the intents of these CRs are.

Finally, we observe from Table 3 that recall is low for the *Constraint* and *Refinement* types. This provides evidence for our hypothesis from Sect. 3 about these two types lacking sufficient representation in our qualitative study.

4.2 Case Study over Canadian Legal Texts

Our second case study is a step towards assessing the generalizability of our approach in other countries where French is an official language of the law. Specifically, we run our classifier *as-is* (i.e., without extending our qualitative study of Sect. 3) to the French editions of two Canadian legal texts. These texts are: Ontario's Personal Health Information Protection Act (PHIPA) [21] and the 2014 compilation of the amendment provisions on Canadian consolidated laws [22]. PHIPA is a major legal text, which has been already studied in the RE community [9,10] due to its important implications on software requirements in healthcare systems. The second text is aimed at enabling the evaluation of amendments CRs, which are underrepresented in PHIPA.

We ran our classifier over these two texts, which collectively contain 87 content pages. The first two authors then inspected all the classification results. Our classifier detected a total of 1189 CRs in the texts, of which, it could infer types for 816, leaving the remaining 353 unclassified. We calculated the same

Table 4. Classification results for Canadian legal texts

Intent Type	Total CRs	Correctly Classified (TP)	Incorrectly Classified T1 (FP)	Incorrectly Classified T2 (FN)	Unclassified (FN)	Recall	Precision	F-Measure
Compliance	445	311	5	4	130	69,89%	98,42%	81,73%
Constraint	9	0	0	0	9	0,00%	0,00%	0,00%
Definition	306	225	0	0	81	73,53%	100,00%	84,75%
Delegation	44	43	12	0	1	97,73%	78,18%	86,87%
Exception	31	10	2	3	18	32,26%	83,33%	46,51%
Refinement	42	30	1	0	12	71,43%	96,77%	82,19%
General Amendment	5	4	0	0	1	80,00%	100,00%	88,89%
Amend. by Addition	4	0	0	0	4	0,00%	0,00%	0,00%
Amend. by deletion	8	5	0	0	3	62,50%	100,00%	76,92%
Amend. by redesignation	0	0	0	0	0	NA	NA	NA
Amend. by replacement	243	188	0	1	54	77,37%	100,00%	87,24%
Unclassifiable	44	0	0	4	40	NA		
Prioritization	8	0	0	8	0	NA		
total	1189	816	20	20	353	68,63%	97,61%	80,59%

counts (c1–c4) as in the previous case study (Sect. 4.1). The results are shown in Table 4. For this case study, the classifier has a recall of 68.63 % and a precision of 97.61 %, giving an F-measure of 80.59 %. We observe that the precision score for this case study is in the same range as that for the previous one; whereas the recall score is lower by ≈11 %. Some decrease in recall was to be expected due to the potentially-different legal drafting styles and thus the use of new patterns. In particular, the patterns required for the *Constraint* type were absent from our catalog, resulting in all CRs of this type to go unclassified.

A total of 20 CRs were misclassified. All these cases were caused by unrelated pattern being present in the vicinity of the CRs in question. Our inspection further revealed eight CRs of the *Prioritization* type [17]. As stated earlier, we had not encountered any such CRs in our qualitative study. Consequently, our patterns did not cover this particular type. All the *Prioritization* CRs seen in this case study used the same pattern, which we denote "prevails" (l'emporte), e.g., in "[...] this act and its regulations prevail unless [...]".

With regard to the *Compliance* and *Refinement* types, we observed that, unlike in the first case study, the patterns used for CRs of these types were sufficiently distinct. No misclassification occurred due to our classifier failing to tell apart CRs of these two types.

With regard to the CRs that our tool could not classify, the same observations as those in the previous case study hold, although the proportions differ. A noteworthy difference in the proportions is that we had more CRs not being classified because of long auxiliary phrases. The increase in the length of auxiliary phrases is mainly due to the bilingual context of the Canadian legal corpus, where one has to additionally differentiate between the French and English editions of the laws in the auxiliary phrases. One way to deal with longer auxiliary phrases would be to increase the acceptable distance between the patterns and the CRs (currently 5 tokens, as stated earlier). Doing so however necessitates further investigation because such an increase could lead to reductions in precision caused by the potential presence of unrelated patterns at farther distances.

Lastly, we note that the number of CRs that were deemed *Unclassifiable* by our manual inspection was proportionally larger in this case study than in the previous one (44/1189 versus 20/1396). We believe that this discrepancy is partly due to the more hierarchical nature of Canadian laws, where federal, provincial, and territorial laws co-exist, thus leaving room for more vague citations.

5 Discussion

Usefulness of Our Approach. The ultimate validation for our approach is whether practitioners who work with legal requirements would benefit from our automatic classification results. Such validation requires a user study which is not tackled in this paper. Nevertheless, the case studies of Sect. 4 provide some preliminary insights about usefulness. In particular, we observe that, over these case studies, our approach yields an average F-measure of 84.48 %, with an average recall and an average precision of 74.62 % and 97.33 %, respectively. The high precision indicates that users need to spend little effort on finding and correcting errors in the classification recommended by our approach. At the same time, the recall suggests that our approach is capable of classifying nearly three quarters of the CRs. This, in light of the high precision, is expected to lead to significant savings in manual effort.

Considering the limited size of our qualitative study (1079 CRs from two texts), the results are encouraging. We believe that recall can be further improved through additional case studies and iteratively expanding the NL patterns.

Threats to Validity. The most important aspects of validity for our work are internal and external validity. Below, we discuss threats to these forms of validity.

Internal Validity: The main threat to internal validity is related to the correctness of the taxonomy and the patterns derived from our qualitative study. To mitigate this threat, the first two authors (who are Francophone and further have legal requirements engineering background, as noted earlier), worked closely together throughout the qualitative study. An additional mitigation measure we applied was to build on and align with existing taxonomies as much as possible.

Another potential threat to internal validity is that we may have associated some NL patterns with the wrong intent types. This does not pose a major problem as one can move patterns from one intent type to another, without affecting overall classification accuracy. Finally, we note that the automated classification results in Sect. 4 were inspected by the authors. To avoid bias, we discussed and developed, based on our experience from the qualitative study, an inspection protocol prior to conducting the inspections.

External Validity: We distinguish two dimensions for external validity: (1) generalizability to texts which are written in French, but which come from different countries or jurisdictions than what we considered here, and (2) generalizability to texts written in languages other than French. With regard to (1), external validity mainly has to do with the completeness and relevance of our patterns outside the context in which they were observed. While more case studies are required, the good results from our second case study provide initial evidence for this type of generalizability. With regard to (2), qualitative studies over legal texts written in other languages such as English will be needed. Further investigation of bilingual texts, e.g., from the Canadian legal corpus, will provide an opportunity to study the generalization of our approach to other languages while at the same time establishing a connection to our current results in French.

6   Conclusion

We proposed an approach for the automated classification of cross references in legal texts according to the cross references' semantic intent. Our approach is motivated by providing requirements engineers with tools and support for more efficient and effective elaboration of legal compliance requirements. The basis for our approach is a qualitative study of selected Luxembourgish legislative texts. Through this study, we derived a taxonomy of semantic intent types for cross references along with natural language patterns that enable distinguishing these types in an automated manner. We conducted an empirical evaluation of our automated classification approach over Luxembourgish and Canadian legal texts, demonstrating that the approach yields good accuracy. The promising evaluation results for Canadian legal texts further provides evidence about the generalizability of our approach, noting that the observations in our qualitative study were based exclusively on the Luxembourgish legal corpus.

In the future, we would like to conduct a more thorough evaluation of our approach. In particular, we plan to more closely examine the completeness of our natural language patterns for classification by conducting a series of case studies in succession. This will enable us to have a feedback loop between the case studies and measure whether our catalog of patterns will saturate as it is iteratively extended. Another facet of investigation would be to study legal texts written in other languages, e.g., English, to validate the basic observations behind our approach. Finally, user studies will be necessary to more conclusively determine whether our approach brings about benefits in realistic settings.

Acknowledgments. Financial support for this work was provided by Luxembourg's National Centre for Information Technologies (CTIE) and National Research Fund (FNR) under grant number FNR/P10/03. We thank members of CTIE, particularly Ludwig Balmer and Marc Blau, for their valuable feedback.

References

1. Adedjouma, M., Sabetzadeh, M., Briand, L.: Automated detection, resolution of legal cross references: approach and a study of Luxembourg's legislation. In: RE 2014, pp. 63–72 (2014)
2. Biagioli, C., Francesconi, E., Passerini, A., Montemagni, S., Soria, C.: Automatic semantics extraction in law documents. In: ICAIL 2005, pp. 133–140 (2005)

3. Breaux, T.: Legal requirements acquisition for the specification of legally compliant information systems. Ph.D. thesis, North Carolina State University, Raleigh, North Carolina, USA (2009)
4. Breaux, T., Antón, A.: Analyzing regulatory rules for privacy and security requirements. IEEE TSE **34**(1), 5–20 (2008)
5. Brighi, R.: An ontology for linkups between norms. In: DEXA Workshops, pp. 122–126 (2004)
6. Corbin, J., Strauss, A.: Basics of Qualitative Research: Techniques and Procedures for Developing Grounded Theory, 3rd edn. SAGE Publications, Los Angeles (2008)
7. Cunningham, et al.: Developing Language Processing Components with GATE Version 7 (a User Guide)
8. de Maat, E., Winkels, R., van Engers, T.: Automated detection of reference structures in law. In: JURIX 2006, pp. 41–50 (2006)
9. Ghanavati, S., Amyot, D., Peyton, L.: Towards a framework for tracking legal compliance in healthcare. In: Krogstie, J., Opdahl, A.L., Sindre, G. (eds.) CAiSE 2007. LNCS, vol. 4495, pp. 218–232. Springer, Heidelberg (2007)
10. Ghanavati, S., Rifaut, A., Dubois, E., Amyot, D.: Goal-oriented compliance with multiple regulations. In: RE 2014, pp. 73–82 (2014)
11. Government of Luxembourg. Draft Law No 6457 of the Regular Session 2011–2012 of the Chamber of Deputies (2012)
12. Government of Luxembourg. Modified Law of December 4, 1967 on Income Taxes (2014)
13. Hamdaqa, M., Hamou-Lhadj, A.: An approach based on citation analysis to support effective handling of regulatory compliance. Future Gener. Comput. Syst. **27**(4), 395–410 (2011)
14. Manning, C., Raghavan, P., Schütze, H.: Introduction to Information Retrieval. Cambridge University Press, New York (2008)
15. Massey, A., Smith, B., Otto, P., Anton, A.: Assessing the accuracy of legal implementation readiness decisions. In: RE 2011, pp. 207–216 (2011)
16. Maxwell, J., Antón, A., Earp, J.: An empirical investigation of software engineers' ability to classify legal cross-references. In: RE 2013, pp. 24–31 (2013)
17. Maxwell, J., Antón, A., Swire, P., Riaz, M., McCraw, C.: A legal cross-references taxonomy for reasoning about compliance requirements. REJ **17**(2), 99–115 (2012)
18. Porter, M.: An algorithm for suffix stripping. Program **14**(3), 130137 (1980)
19. Sannier, N., Adedjouma, M., Sabetzadeh, M., Briand, L.: Supplementary Material for Automatic Classification of Legal Cross References Based on Semantic Intent (2015). http://people.svv.lu/sannier/CRSemantics/
20. Sannier, N., Adedjouma, M., Sabetzadeh, M., Briand, L.: An automated framework for detection and resolution of cross references in legal texts. Requirements Eng. (2015, in press)
21. The Ontario Ministry of Consumer and Business Services and the Ontario Ministry of Health and Long Term Care. Personal Health Information Protection Act (2004)
22. The Parliament of Canada. Canada Corrective Act (2014)
23. Tran, O., Bach, N., Nguyen, M., Shimazu, A.: Automated reference resolution in legal texts. Artif. Intell. Law **22**(1), 29–60 (2014)
24. Zeni, N., Kiyavitskaya, N., Mich, L., Cordy, J., Mylopoulos, J.: GaiusT: supporting the extraction of rights and obligations for regulatory compliance. REJ **20**(1), 1–22 (2015)

Deriving Metrics for Estimating the Effort Needed in Requirements Compliance Work

Md Rashed I. Nekvi[(✉)], Ibtehal Noorwali, and Nazim H. Madhavji

University of Western Ontario, London, Canada
{mnekvi, inoorwal}@uwo.ca, madhavji@gmail.com

Abstract. **[Context and motivation]** Making acceptable effort estimates of achieving regulatory compliance of requirements in large-scale systems engineering projects has eluded project management. **[Problem]** Traditional effort estimation tools working with LOC, function-point, and object point metrics do not consider requirements compliance work. Consequences include: poor estimates, project delays, cost overruns, quality problems, and customer dissatisfaction. **[Principal ideas/results]** In this short paper, we describe a novel methodological approach for deriving metrics for estimating the effort for conducting requirements compliance work. This method was created from analysing a number of impediments to achieving compliance in a large systems engineering project, along with their associated metrics. **[Contribution]** The methodological approach described is the key contribution. It lays a foundation for deriving metrics needed for creating an effort-estimation model for compliance work in the RE process.

Keywords: Metrics · Effort estimation · Regulatory compliance of requirements · Requirements engineering

1 Introduction

In large systems engineering projects, ascertaining regulatory compliance of requirements is not avoidable lest there are penalties for non-compliance, not to mention credibility at stake. Once all regulatory requirements have been elicited or identified, implementation can ensure that the system satisfies these requirements, hence guaranteeing compliance – in theory. In practice, however, such a process can be extremely difficult and arduous [9] because of: unbounded cross-references within and across documents, non-contiguity of regulatory requirements, abstractness of the requirements, multi-domain complexity, implicit regulatory requirements, and others. There is supporting evidence on some of the causes: e.g., cross-references in [4]; non-contiguity of regulatory requirements in the health act HIPAA [3] and across multiple jurisdictions [6]; and detection of relevant regulatory codes [5].

This situation raises several uncertainties, for example: whether all the regulatory requirements have been elicited or identified from complex documents; whether changes in regulations have been accounted for; and whether the effort estimation of requirements compliance work is realistic. A noteworthy complain from industry is that underestimation of effort is rampant, with consequences on cost overrun, project delay, quality problems, and customer dissatisfaction [12].

© Springer International Publishing Switzerland 2016
M. Daneva and O. Pastor (Eds.): REFSQ 2016, LNCS 9619, pp. 135–141, 2016.
DOI: 10.1007/978-3-319-30282-9_9

Literature abounds on approaches for effort estimation, example: COCOMO [2], neural networks [14], regression and decision trees [11], and analogies [10] – to cite a few. These are based on such metrics as Lines of Code, Function Points, and number of defects. These approaches are meant for general software development effort, not compliance-related effort.

In requirements engineering (RE), research on metrics has been conducted in two areas: (i) utilising requirements to estimate entire software development effort [13]; and (ii) approaches to estimate the RE effort only [7]. The latter is of concern here. Hoffman et al. mention average effort at 16 % of the overall project, while the most successful projects expend as high as 28 % [8]. Further, Seilevel's approach for estimating RE effort is based on three primary estimates: (i) 15 % of overall work effort estimation; (ii) 6:1 developer to Business Analysts (BA) ratio; and (iii) bottom-up estimation derived from breakdown of RE activities and their associated historical effort [1].

Compared to the cited related work on effort estimation, our work is fundamentally different. Since "compliance" work at RE-time, as described earlier, has particular characteristics (e.g., analysing a large set of legal documents) that are quite different from those of a "standard" elicitation process (e.g., interviews, focus groups, prototyping, etc.). Thus, any effort estimation method aimed at requirements compliance work needs to take this into account.

In this short paper, we describe a novel approach – the main contribution of this paper – for deriving key metrics for estimating the effort needed in requirements compliance work. These metrics are of fundamental importance for creating an effort estimation model; the model itself, however, is outside the scope of this paper. The proposed method is developed from the analysis of the impediments identified in conducting requirements compliance work [9] (i.e., those compliance-related RE activities that are considered challenging), where each impediment has its corresponding effort metric. We anticipate that this method can possibly be applied in some form to other projects for deriving their own metrics tailored to the specifics of the projects.

The rest of the paper is organised as follows: Sect. 2 sketches the background of the project we investigated. Section 3 describes our approach for deriving effort-estimation metrics, and finally, Sect. 4 wraps up the paper with discussion, future work, and conclusion.

2 Background

We describe the RE-part of a rail upgrade infrastructure project [9] from which we derived metrics for estimating the effort for carrying out requirements compliance work. The RE project had a 1000-page contract that describes approx. 12,000 requirements referred to as *contractual requirements*. Approx. 6 % of the contractual requirements refer to a variety of 'regulations and engineering standards' (i.e., *regulatory documents*) to which they need to comply. The total number of regulatory documents referenced from the contract is in excess of 300. The size of approx. 25 % of the documents is over 100 pages; a few amongst them are much larger (over 2000 pages).

The RE process had to identify regulatory requirements from the contract. Since the contractual requirements are specified at a high-level (i.e., are not testable), the requirements for the project had to be derived from the contract (and regulatory documents) and categorised (e.g., system, subsystem, component, and cross-cutting). Also, note that regulatory documents often contained requirements that are characterised by numerous cross-references, ambiguities, conflicts, domain-specific terms, etc. [9]. Further, the elicitation of regulatory requirements involved frequent aid from legal and domain experts. Once elicited, the regulatory requirements were logged in a requirements management tool and appropriate tracing links were generated.

However, time and effort spent on analysing these documents are typified by numerous impediments [9]. Thus, in such projects, there is a significant amount of uncertainty as to when the task of compliance analysis would actually be complete. This situation was a strong motivator to define appropriate metrics in order to reduce estimation variability and, hence, improve such project variables as resource allocation, time to completion and requirements (and hence system) quality.

3   A Method for Deriving Effort-Estimation Metrics

The method for deriving metrics for RE work on regulatory compliance is based on three investigative questions:

Q1. What are the effort-critical activities and artefacts in the RE work for regulatory compliance?

Effort-critical activities and artefacts are those that are considered to take an inordinate amount of person-hours to accomplish the goals of those activities and artefacts. Since our objective is to determine metrics to estimate the effort needed for compliance tasks, it is important to identify the activities that contribute significantly to this effort so that they are not ignored in the overall effort estimation.

Q2. Which characteristics of the activities and artefacts identified in Q1 are primarily responsible for making them effort-critical?

This question investigates characteristics of the artefacts and activities (Q1), which are root causes for imposing impediments in achieving compliance of requirements.

Q3. What are the metrics that can be used to measure the effort-criticality level of the characteristics identified in Q2?

This question probes into metrics that can correspond to the effort-criticality level of the characteristics (Q2) of the activities and artefacts.

Below, we treat each of the questions in turn.

3.1   Identification of Effort-Critical Activities and Artefacts (Q1)

In compliance work, the complexity of effort-critical activities typically originates from certain type of artefacts and associated activities. In our study [9], we obtained information about compliance work: (i) through a couple of workshops; (ii) by gathering and analysing project artefacts such as contract, regulatory documents, and system descriptions; and (iii) by interacting with project staff.

By analysing the gathered information, we determined a number of ad-hoc tasks carried out by the analysts that addressed compliance issues (e.g., implicit regulatory requirements, diverse regulatory references, and abstract requirements). It is this type of tasks that was not accounted for at the outset and thus was a factor in under estimation of the overall effort. Clearly, metrics (described in Sects. 3.2 and 3.3) need to be associated with this type of tasks for estimating compliance effort. We grouped the identified tasks into clusters of artefacts and activities (see column 1 in Table 1). These clusters represent project specific variables such as the contract, regulatory documents, and system structure.

Note, however, that RE activities and artefacts used can vary across projects. Thus, in the manner described in this section, one must consider project-specific variables.

Table 1. Derived effortful activities and associating characteristics

Activities and artefacts	Effortful characteristics (Impediments)	Effort-critical aspect
Obtaining relevant regulatory documents	Identification of applicable regulatory documents	It requires analysing an unbounded set of engineering standards and laws from diverse authorities for determining their relevance to system.
	Capturing regulatory codes in RE tools	Incorporation of regulatory codes as "objects" within RE tools is a manual and tedious.
Analysing contractual complexities	Non-contiguity of regulatory requirements in the contract	Regulatory requirements mixing in non-contiguous manner in the voluminous contract.
	Diverse regulatory references within one contractual requirement	All referenced documents (codes) must be analysed for resolving possible conflicts and to define concrete requirements.
	Abstractness of contractual requirements specifications	Those regulatory documents abstractly (without proper index) referenced need thorough analysis by domain experts from all the subsystems covered by the abstract requirements.
	Implicit reference to regulatory requirements	Eliciting implicit requirements from indirectly referenced documents need help of domain-experts.
Analysing complexities in regulatory documents	Large set of regulatory documents	Monitoring and managing legal changes made by external authorities (e.g., government officials) require dedicated role and technique.

(Continued)

Table 1. (*Continued*)

Activities and artefacts	Effortful characteristics (Impediments)	Effort-critical aspect
	Identification of the relevant sections	Separate domain experts are required to analyse regulatory documents from various domain.
	Frequent cross-referencing within the content	All cross-referenced segments needs to be followed and understood correctly by their semantics, possibly by the help of legal experts.
Analysing the aspects of large and complex system	Vertical and lateral communications of the teams	Inter subsystem/component team communication is required to resolve regulatory-related issues resulting from cross-cutting requirements.
	Non-aligned organisation of the contract with respect to component/subsystem specifications	Contractual requirements need restructuring in order to generate subsystem or component specifications to be delivered to third party developers responsible for subsystem or component delivery.
	Cross-cutting requirements	"40 % of the cross-cutting requirements are regulatory" [9] indicates substantive compliance effort.

3.2   Characteristics of Effort-Critical Activities and Artefacts (Q2)

In this step, we analysed each type of the artefacts and the associated activities in order to identify their underlying effort-critical characteristics (referred to as *impediments* in the RE process). It is important to identify these (effort-critical) characteristics because without knowing them it is not possible to determine the compliance workload which, in turn, is needed to estimate the compliance effort.

The criteria we used to identify the effort-critical characteristics include such aspects as: voluminous content, manual process, need for domain-expertise, and need for inter-team communication. Using these criteria, we derived the effort-critical characteristics (impediments) as listed in column two of Table 1. The column three of Table 1 gives rationale of why the impediments (Table 1- column 2) fit the effort-critical criteria mentioned above.

3.3 Deriving Metrics (Q3)

Below, we describe three analytical steps for deriving appropriate metrics for a given characteristic identified in Q2 (see column 2 in Table 1 and Sect. 3.2):

(i) *Identify the type of items that are affected by the given characteristic:* In this step, there is a need to identify the type of items to which the given characteristic (e.g., *cross-references*) belongs. Example item-types are: project requirements, contractual requirements, sections of a regulatory document, and system organisation.

(ii) *Metrics concerning the breadth of impact*: In this step, we assess the *extent* to which the given characteristic (e.g., *cross-references*) exists in the item-type identified in step (i) (e.g., *sections of a regulatory document*). Example metric is: *percentage of the sections of a regulatory document containing cross-references.*

(iii) *Metrics concerning the depth of impact*: In this step, we assess the *intensity* with which the characteristic (e.g., *cross-references*) has an impact on an individual item (e.g., *a section of a regulatory document*). Example metric is: *average number of cross-references per section of a regulatory document.*

Further, if we have the average value of the effort needed to process a single cross-reference (i.e., the coefficient value) then, in essence, the above analytical steps gives us a way to estimate the effort required to process the cross-references contained in the sections of a regulatory document. This method can be generalised to other characteristics in a given compliance project.

4 Discussion, Future Work and Conclusion

Compliance work on requirements can be difficult and arduous because of: unbounded cross-references within and across documents, ambiguity in the content, abstractness of the requirements, multi-domain complexity, levels of jurisdictions to contend with, and others [9]. This situation makes the task of estimating the effort needed for requirements compliance work particularly challenging. Traditional effort estimation techniques (see Sect. 1), normally used for estimating development effort, are not suited to estimating requirements compliance work that involves characteristics such as those described in Table 1.

Section 3 proposes a new method for deriving effort-estimation metrics for conducting requirements compliance work in a large systems engineering project. Although deriving metrics from only one case study has generalisability threats, there is indeed literature support for certain impediments (see Table 1, column 2) upon which our metrics are based. For example: "non-contiguity of regulatory requirements" [3, 6]; "cross-references" in regulatory documents [4]; and some others.

While the preliminary method described here is encouraging, much work still remains to be done; for example, solidifying the metrics described in [9] through empirical studies, constructing and validating the effort estimation model, and transferring the model for productive use in industry.

Acknowledgment. We sincerely thank the reviewers for their excellent comments, which have helped significantly in improving this paper.

References

1. Beatty, J.: Requirements estimation for business analysts. www.requirements.seilevel.com/requirements-estimation-for-business-analysts-free-estimation-tool-download
2. Boehm, B.: Software Engineering Economics. Prentice Hall, Englewood Cliffs (1983)
3. Breaux, T.D., Anton, A.I.: Analyzing regulatory rules for privacy and security requirements. IEEE Trans. Softw. Eng. **34**(1), 5–20 (2008)
4. Breaux, T.D., Gordon, D.G.: Regulatory requirements traceability and analysis using semi-formal specifications. In: 19th International Working Conference on REFSQ, pp. 141–157 (2013)
5. Cleland-Huang, J., Czauderna, A., Gibiec, M., Emenecker, J.: A machine learning approach for tracing regulatory codes to product specific requirements. In: 32nd ACM/IEEE International Conference on Software Engineering (ICSI), pp. 155–164 (2010)
6. Ghanavati, S., Rifaut, A., Dubois, E., Amyot, D.: Goal-oriented compliance with multiple regulations. In: IEEE 14th Requirements Engineering Conference, pp. 73–82 (2014)
7. Goldsmith, R.F.: Reliably estimating the software requirements effort. In: Tech Target, Software Quality (2010)
8. Hoffman, H.F., Lehner, F.: Requirements engineering as a success factor in software projects. IEEE Softw. **18**(4), 58–66 (2001)
9. Nekvi, M.R.I., Madhavji, N.H.: Impediments to regulatory compliance of requirements in contractual systems engineering projects: a case study. ACM Trans. Manag. Inf. Syst. **5**(3), 15:1–15:35 (2015)
10. Madhavji, N.H., Nekvi, M.R.I: Personal communication with personnel from industry, March 2012
11. Shepperd, M., Schofield, C.: Estimating software project effort using analogies. IEEE Trans. Softw. Eng. **23**(12), 736–743 (1997)
12. Srinivasan, K., Fisher, D.: Machine learning approaches to estimating development effort. IEEE Trans. Softw. Eng. **21**(2), 126–137 (1995)
13. Verlaine, B., Jureta, I.J., Faulkner, S.: A requirements-based model for effort estimation in service-oriented systems. In: Lomuscio, A.R., Nepal, S., Patrizi, F., Benatallah, B., Brandić, I. (eds.) ICSOC 2013. LNCS, vol. 8377, pp. 82–94. Springer, Heidelberg (2014)
14. Wittig, G.E., Finnie, G.R.: Using artificial neural networks and function points to estimate 4GL software development effort. Australas. J. Inf. Syst. **1**(2), 87–94 (1994)

Requirements Engineering
in the Automotive Domain

Requirements Defects over a Project Lifetime: An Empirical Analysis of Defect Data from a 5-Year Automotive Project at Bosch

Vincent Langenfeld[1,2(✉)], Amalinda Post[1], and Andreas Podelski[2]

[1] Robert Bosch GmbH, Automotive Electronics, Stuttgart, Germany
Vincent.Langenfeld@bosch.com
[2] University of Freiburg, Freiburg im Breisgau, Germany

Abstract. [**Context and motivation**] Requirements defects are notoriously costly. Analysing the defect data in a completed project may help to improve practice in follow up projects. [**Question/Problem**] The problem is to analyse the different kinds of requirements defects that may occur during the lifetime of an industrial project, and, for each kind of requirement defect, the respective number of occurrences and the cost incurred. [**Principal ideas/results**] In this paper, we present a post hoc analysis for an automotive project at Bosch. We have analysed 588 requirements defects reported during the elapsed project lifetime of 4.5 years. The analysis is based on a specific classification scheme for requirements defects which takes its eight attributes (incorrect, incomplete, etc.) from the IEEE 830 standard and refines them further by distinguishing nine possible defect sources (relating to parameters, wording, timing, etc.). The analysis yields that a large chunk of the requirements defects (61 %) stems from incorrectness or incompleteness. The requirements defects that are the most costly to fix are incompleteness and inconsistency. [**Contribution**] The insights gained from the analysis of the defects data allow us to review several design decisions for the requirements engineering process and to suggest new ones (such as to incorporate the classification of the requirements defects into the requirements review and into the defect reporting).

1 Introduction

Requirements defects are notoriously costly. In order to derive effective measures that help avoid common requirements defects, we need to know more about requirements defects as they occur during the lifetime of an industrial project. Typical questions are: What are the different kinds of requirements defects that occur? Which kind occurs relatively often? Which kind of requirements defect is relatively costly to fix?

In this paper, we present a post hoc analysis for an automotive project at Bosch. We have analysed the requirements defects reported during the elapsed project lifetime of 4.5 years.

© Springer International Publishing Switzerland 2016
M. Daneva and O. Pastor (Eds.): REFSQ 2016, LNCS 9619, pp. 145–160, 2016.
DOI: 10.1007/978-3-319-30282-9_10

The project in question is the development of a commercial DC-to-DC converter for a *mild hybrid* vehicle. The project had a runtime of approximately five years. During this runtime, six hardware samples were produced, together with 25 software versions with a total of 2500 changes (these changes include both, defect fixes and additional functionalities). The project has more than 10.000 requirements, including customer, system, software, hardware, mechanic and test requirements. The analysis presented in this paper is based on the 588 defects in system requirements (the set of system requirements changed during the runtime of the project; its size at the end of the project is around 2000). The development process in the project followed the V-model. A review was done after every development step. The review of the system requirements was done by the engineers in the respective domain, in the presence of a system tester (as a walkthrough or as an inspection, depending on the complexity of the change of requirements). The project team consisted of about 50 team members. The work of at least 30 out of the 50 team members depended directly on the system requirements (to develop the hardware, software, mechanic or derive test cases). Out of the 50, five team members were responsible for system requirements.

In the analysis, we have used a classification scheme which is based on the IEEE 830 standard and which we have further refined with the classification of the defective part of a requirement. Our results demonstrate the applicability of the defect classification scheme, and the insight into common requirements defects in the project, we gained thereof. The analysis yields that a large chunk of the requirements defects (61 %) relate to either *incorrectness* or *incompleteness*. The most costly requirements defects (most costly to fix) are *incompleteness* and *inconsistency*. In the remainder of the paper, we will present the analysis and its results based on the classification, as well as the conclusions we have drawn for improving the practice in follow up projects.

The paper is organised as follows. Section 2 describes the general approach followed by the analysis. Section 3 presents the results of the analysis. Section 4 presents the lessons learned and the conclusions we have drawn for improving the practice in follow up projects. Section 5 discusses potential threats to validity. Section 6 gives an overview of related work and puts the concepts used in this paper into a larger context. Section 7 presents concluding remarks.

2   The General Setup of the Analysis

2.1   Goals and Questions

The analysis is part of a larger research effort to investigate how the requirements engineering process can be changed in order to improve the quality of the system requirements specification. The idea is to exploit the wealth of information which is accumulated in the defect reports gathered during the lifetime of an industrial project. Concretely, we take the already mentioned DC-to-DC project at Bosch. Over the whole period of 4.5 years of the project lifetime, the requirements defects were documented in 588 defect reports. The defect reports were used to fix the defects.

The first step to extract information from this rather large number of defect reports is to choose a classification of the requirements defects. We base our classification on the IEEE 830 standard which lists attributes that determine the quality of requirements specifications in software projects. It is widely agreed that the attributes according to the IEEE 830 standard are useful to define the quality of a requirements specification because generally, the defect of a requirement results from a violation of one of the attributes. Thus we can classify the defect according to the attribute that is violated, whether the requirement is *incorrect, ambiguous, incomplete, inconsistent, not ranked, not verifiable, not modifiable*, or *not traceable*. Here the requirements defect may be named after the violation of the attribute that results directly or indirectly in the requirements defect (for example, *not traceable* is not a requirements defect per se but may result in one).

We will use the classification of the requirements defects according to the violation of the attributes of requirements in the IEEE 830 standard for the analysis. In particular we will analyse the following questions.

1. **What classes of requirements defects occur most often?** We analyse the requirements defects in these classes for common features that could help us to detect these requirements defects or even prevent them.

    With regards to the requirements engineering process, a good strategy may be to concentrate on requirements defects in these classes before others.

2. **What classes of requirements defects occur least often?** Requirements defects in these classes may fall into one of two cases, depending on whether they occur more rarely or whether they are just detected more rarely. We need to consider both cases and either find the reason why the DC-to-DC project does not suffer from those requirements defects, or improve the detection of those requirements defects.

    With regards to the requirements engineering process, the obvious consequence of the knowledge of the absence of requirements defects in one class is to re-allocate the corresponding effort to the detection of defects in other classes.

3. **What classes of requirements defects are most costly to fix?** The number of defects per class is not sufficient per se; we furthermore need to take into account that the amount of time needed to fix a requirements defect can vary considerably, especially if detected in a later development phase.

    With regards to the requirements engineering process, the most costly defect classes call for more involved detection and prevention methods.

4. **What classes of requirements defects are least costly to fix?** The later in the development phases the requirements defects in those classes are detected, the higher becomes the risk that they induces new defects.

    With regards to the requirements engineering process, the obvious consequence of the knowledge of such classes is thus to invest the comparatively little cost to fix the defects to prevent them from becoming costly later.

2.2   Collecting the Data of the Analysis

The 588 requirement defect reports that were issued over the lifetime of the DC-to-DC project stem from two different sources, namely the requirements specification reviews (data set 1) and the fault reporting system for later development phases of the project (data set 2); see Fig. 1.

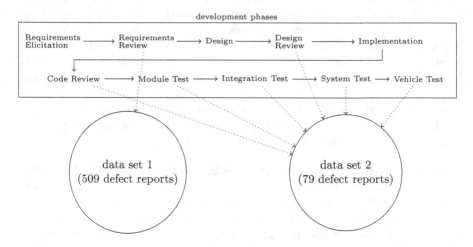

Fig. 1. The two data sets used for the analysis: data set 1 contains the requirements defects that were detected in the requirements review phase, data set 2 contains the requirements defects that were detected in later development phases. The dotted arrows depict the flow of defect reports.

The 509 requirements defect reports in data set 1 (i.e., those detected during the requirements reviews) each contain a rather brief explanation of the requirements defect and a proposed solution for its removal.

The 79 requirements defect reports in data set 2 (i.e., those detected in later development phases) contain detailed information on the defect, the development phase the defect has been injected in, the development phase the defect has been detected in, and the time effort (in man-hours) it took to fix the defect and its ramifications.

2.3   Performing the Analysis

The classification of the defect reports was conducted by two employees of the DC-to-DC project, each of them being responsible for one of the two data sets. The workload between the two employees was even. In fact, due to the free structure of the reports in data set 2, the analysis of a defect in a report in data set 2 was relatively involved and time consuming.

We spent considerable effort to ensure the objectivity of the classification of the requirements defects. Fortunately, a requirements engineer who had been employed in the DC-to-DC project from the very beginning, was constantly available for questions about hard cases. We have analysed the *stability* of the classification (stability meaning that the results of the classification are not dependent on the person who performs the analysis), using 16 randomly selected samples of the defect reports from both data sets. With 75 % agreement (Cohen's Kappa of $\kappa = .57, p < .001, n = 16$), we obtain that the result of the classification is *moderately stable*, in the terminology of [2].

During the course of the analysis, we found that the classification based on IEEE 830 (as described in Sect. 2.1 was too coarse to yield informative results with regard to our first research question. We have refined the classification further, based on nine possible *defect sources*, where we use *defect source* to refer to the specific part of a requirement which is the cause of the requirements defect. We list the nine *defect sources* below.

parameter. The defect lies in a parameter (for example, the value of the parameter is written directly in the text, or parameter has a wrong value, or the parameter has the wrong unit).

variant. The defect lies in the elements that are used to document or manage variants or versions (for example, the marker to indicate that a requirement is valid only for one version, is missing).

wording. The requirement is not written compliant to formulations, template phrases or the desired precision of requirements that were agreed upon in the project (for example, usage of words like 'would' or 'should').

timing. The defect is in a specified timing parameter (for example, timing is not correct or even possible).

state machine. The defect is related to the state machine that is modelling the system behaviour (for example, the guard of a state change is missing).

calculation. The defect is related to a calculation or comparison (for example, wrong sign, wrong comparison, use of wrong variable or function in a calculation).

figure. The defect is in a figure or related to a figure (for example, the depicted process is labelled with wrong numbers).

organisation. The structure of the requirements document is flawed (for example, missing/wrong links to resources, misplaced/duplicated requirements).

functionality. The requirements defect is related directly to a description of a functionality and none of the eight other defect sources applies (meaning, the requirement has a defect that cannot be fixed by removing one of the other defect sources).

The above list of defect sources is based on the ideas behind the defect classification schemes described by Chillarege *et al.* [1]. The *defect sources* are mutually orthogonal (no requirements defect can be assigned to two *defect sources*). The *defect sources* cover as many requirements defects as possible with only few classes. We have been able to successfully apply the above classification scheme for requirements defects in the DC-to-DC project; the investigation whether the classification scheme is generally applicable (for requirements defects in other projects) goes beyond the scope of this work.

Table 1. The result of the first step of the analysis which uses the classification based on the IEEE 830 standard.

	incorrect	ambiguous	incomplete	inconsistent	not ranked	not verifiable	not modifiable	not traceable	Σ
data set 1	175	41	135	22		29	72	35	509
data set 2	30	7	19	9	1		3	10	79
Σ	**205**	48	**154**	31	1	29	**75**	45	588

3   Results of the Analysis

The results of the classification of the 588 requirements defects in data sets 1 and 2 are presented in Tables 1 and 2. Table 1 refers to the classification of the requirement defects based on the IEEE 830 standard (as described in Sect. 2.1), and Table 2 to its refinement based on the defect source (as described in Sect. 2.3). Whereas the classification based on the IEEE 830 standard covers 100 % of the 588 requirements defects in data sets 1 and 2, the refined classification covers only 67 % (395 out of 588). The remaining third of requirements defects cannot be assigned to one of the nine defect sources used for the refined classification.

Next we use the classification in order to analyse the four questions which we have formulated in Sect. 2.1.

What Classes of Requirements Defects Occur Most Often? Table 1 shows that 61 % of the requirements defects (359 of 588) belong to two out of the eight possible classes, namely *incorrect* and *incomplete*. In order to analyse the requirements defects in more depth, we will use the classification according to the defect source; see Table 2.

parameter. As in programming, parameters are used to abstract away from concrete values. Concrete values used in requirements are not written directly into the requirement; instead, they are referenced by a parameter. The concrete value of the parameter is defined in a specific data base. For example, the variants of the DC-to-DC converter get defined only through the assignment of variant-specific values to the set of parameters (except for special cases; see below).

Out of the 86 requirements defects whose defect source can be assigned to *parameter*, 18 fall into the class *incomplete* (16 in data set 1 and 2 in data set 2). Here, simply the assignment of concrete values to parameters in the data base had been forgotten. Another 33 out of those 86 requirements defects fall into the class *incorrect* (26 in data set 1 and 7 in data set 2). We note that 7 cases out of the 33 (which happen to be among the 26 that belong

Table 2. IEEE-830 classification and defect source. Using the nine defect sources we managed to classify 395 defects (340 from data set 1 and 55 from data set 2).

Detail / Iso	data set 1									data set 2								
	incorrect	ambiguous	incomplete	inconsistent	not ranked	not verifiable	not modifiable	not traceable	Σ_1	incorrect	ambiguous	incomplete	inconsistent	not ranked	not verifiable	not modifiable	not traceable	Σ_2
parameter	26	1	16			1	8	22	74	7	2	2				1		12
variant	13	4	34	3			1	4	59								6	6
wording	35	12	9	2		14	13		85									
timing	4		4						8			2	2					4
state machine	15	1	3	2					21	5		7	2					14
calculation	15								15	7								7
figure	6	1	9	2			1	1	20									
organisation	7	3	9	1			7	8	35		1		1	1			2	5
functionality	11	4	1	2		2	3		23	3	1	2	1					7
no category	43	15	50	10		12	39		169	8	3	6	3			2	2	24
Σ	175	41	135	22		29	72	35	509	30	7	19	9	1		3	10	79

to data set 1) share a pattern. That is, the parameters had been assigned tentatively (to some seemingly plausible value) before the information on the hardware was available, just in order to be able to run a test, and then, once information on the hardware was available, the update to the correct value was forgotten.

variant. Out of the 65 requirements defects whose defect source can be assigned to *variant*, 34 of them fall into the class *incomplete* (all of them stem from data set 1, i.e., none is from data set 2). To give an example, a requirement defining the characteristics of the cooling fan, which obviously applies only to the variants of the DC-to-DC converter that actually have a fan, had not been marked as such.

All these 34 requirements defects have in common that they arise from forgetting the treatment of a special case. As explained above, the variants of the DC-to-DC converter were usually defined through the assignment of variant-specific values to the set of parameters. That is, a requirement that refers to only one variant (as in the example above) is a special case. Such variant restrictions had to be written as part of the requirement, which could easily be forgotten. Allocating a specific attribute in the database of system requirements to record the variants a requirements applies to might have helped with variant management but might have introduced other issues.

wording. The 85 requirements defects whose defect source can be assigned to *wording* all stem from data set 1, i.e., none are from data set 2. This means that, if a *wording* defect was detected then it was detected in the requirements review phase. The fact that none was detected in a later development phases means that either all of them were detected through the requirements reviews, or, at least, those that were not did not cause any follow-up defect, at least not one that was detected in later development phases.

We now consider 12 out of the 85 *wording* defects that fall into the class *ambiguous*. The particularity of the defects in this subset is that their follow-up defects can be hard to detect due to the subtle ways in which they exteriorise. To give an example, the wording `average` is ambiguous (for example, because the exact set of samples is not specified). Different interpretations of the term `average` may lead to results whose incorrectness is not immediately apparent.

The *wording* defects that belong to classes other than *ambiguous* are rather of cosmetic nature, i.e., with little or no potential to cause damage (because the user gives the requirement its intended, rather than its actual meaning). We give two examples to demonstrate this. The first example: `After the request to rise the target voltage, the PCU reaches [voltage]` belongs to the class *incorrect*; the correct wording is: `After the request to rise the target voltage, the output voltage U_HV reaches [voltage]` (it is not the DC-to-DC converter that reaches the voltage but the output voltage; PCU stands for Power Control Unit). The second example: `[...] has an output voltage level [...] before t_LV_CTRL has elapsed` belongs to the class *not verifiable*); the correct wording is: `[...] has an output voltage level [...] at the latest when t_LV_CTRL has elapsed`.

Our analysis determines that the high number of *wording* defects (belonging to classes other than *ambiguous*) stem from copying similar requirements that already had the defect.

state machine. Out of the 21 requirements defects whose defect source can be assigned to *state machine* (3 in data set 1 and 7 in data set 2), 10 fall into the class *incomplete*. To give an example, non-determinism was introduced by accident, e.g., by forgetting guards on outgoing transitions (where the transition to an *error state* should be chosen in any case, if possible).

calculation. All of the 22 requirements defects whose defect source can be assigned to *calculation* (15 in data set 1 and 7 in data set 2) fall into the class *incorrect*. To give an example from data set 1, the requirement: `The overshoot caused by the LV jump must not exceed U_HV_DUMP_OVERSHOOT` should have been: `The overshoot caused by the LV jump must not exceed U_HV_Target + U_HV_DUMP_OVERSHOOT`. In the 7 cases that belong to data set 2 (i.e., requirements defects detected not during the requirements review but in later development phases), the requirements defects were particularly costly to fix (8 man-hours per requirements defect, on average). All of these 7 cases in data set 2 correspond to the same kind of mistake, namely a wrong sign or the wrong comparative symbol (< instead of >, etc.).

figure. The 20 requirements defects whose defect source can be assigned to *figure* all stem from data set 1, i.e., none are from data set 2. In the DC-to-DC project figures are always backed by requirements (written as text), which information from figures could be validated with. The fact that none was detected in a later development phase means that either all of them were detected through the requirements reviews, or, at least, those that were not did not cause any follow-up defect, at least none that was detected in later development phases.

What Classes of Requirements Defects Occur Least Often? There are three classes of requirements defects that occur least often: *not verifiable* (29), *inconsistent* (31), and *not ranked* (1); see Table 1.

not verifiable. The fact that the number of requirements defects that fall into the class *not verifiable* is relatively low can be explained by the combination of two measures taken for the two processes of requirements elicitation and requirements review. For the process of requirements elicitation, the requirement engineers formulated the functional requirements while having in mind their translation into a restricted subset of natural language which itself maps directly to a formal language (a subset of temporal propositional logic; see [9]). For the process of requirements review, from the beginning of the project, a test engineer had to be present in every review meeting.

inconsistent. The relatively low number of requirements defects that fall into the class *inconsistency* may seem surprising at first, given that the project has more than 1600 system requirements. The explanation for the low number lies in the fact that the project is the development of a new product and that the set of requirements engineers did not change over the whole project lifetime (i.e., the risk of inconsistency between new and old requirements was relatively small).

As we will discuss further below, the cost for fixing can be relatively high for requirements defects that fall into the class *inconsistency* (29 h per requirements defect on average; 86 h in the worst case).

ranked. There is only one requirements defect that falls into the class *ranked* (which stands for *ranked for importance and stability*). Even though the project mostly adheres to the IEEE 830 standard for requirements specifications, an exception is made in this class and it was decided to omit the ranking of requirements. In the project, all system requirements are *equally important* since every single one of them gets implemented in the final product (customer requirements that need not to be implemented are not elicited as system requirements).

What Classes of Requirements Defects Are Most Costly to Fix? Table 3 shows that the most expensive requirements defects fall into the class *inconsistent* (29 man-hours per requirement), the class *incomplete* (17 h), and the class *incorrect* (12 h).

On single cases, the cost for fixing a requirements defect of the class *inconsistent* can be rather high: 86 h in the example of a requirements defect with the error source *state machine* which was detected during system testing. The reason that it was not detected in the requirements reviews lies in the fact

Table 3. The effort spent on fixing a requirements defect (in man-hours per requirements defect, on average, rounded to integers). By effort we mean the set of activities that were needed to fix the defect in the requirement and all of its ramifications, including reviewing, implementation, and testing. The columns refer to the IEEE 830 classification. The rows refer to the development phases. The requirements defects stem from data set 2, i.e., from development phases later than the requirements review phase. This applies also to the requirements defects in the first row marked reqs review*. These stem from work on the requirements that took place after the requirements review phase, for example when the requirement was refined (into software, hardware, or mechanic requirements), when another (closely related) requirement was added, or when formal analysis in the style of [7,8] was applied. The average is calculated on the basis of the corresponding set of requirements defects whose size is listed in the table on the right, under the heading "requirements defects".

detected by	average effort (in hours)									requirements defects								
	incorrect	ambiguous	incomplete	inconsistent	not ranked	not verifiable	not modifiable	not traceable	avg.	incorrect	ambiguous	incomplete	inconsistent	not ranked	not verifiable	not modifiable	not traceable	% per phase
reqs review*	3	1	5	6				3	3.4	2	1	5	4				2	18
design review	9	3	11	1			3		5.4	9	3	1	1			1		20
module test	5		28						16.5	1		1						3
system test	14	16	16	86	3		3	1	19.9	10	1	7	1	1		1	2	30
vehicle test	33	23	38	23			11	8	22.7	2	2	4	3			1	6	24
other	10		2						6.2	3		1						5
avg.	12	11	17	29	3		6	4		30	7	19	9	1		3	10	

that it involves 16 requirements from different requirements documents. The 16 requirements specify interacting conditions on error signals.

Regardless of the class into which a requirements defect falls, the later in development it is detected, the higher is the effort necessary to fix it. This general tendency is confirmed by the numbers in Table 3. The effort lies between 3 and 5 h for the early development phases (reqs review* and design review), whereas it rises to 23 h for the latest development phase (vehicle testing).

Table 3 refers to only 76 out of the 79 requirements defects in data set 2. For three requirements defects, two of class *incorrect* with the defect source *calculation*(33 h resp. 18 h), one of class *incorrect* with the defect source *parameter* (32 h), we were unable to determine the development phases in which they were detected.

We did not set up a table for the classification of requirements defects according to the defect source because the basis for calculating the average cost would become somewhat thin. We only mention that the most costly defect sources are *functionality* (14 man hours per requirements defect on average), *state machine* (14 h), and *parameter* (12 h).

What Classes of Requirements Defects Are Least Costly to Fix? Table 3 shows that the least expensive requirements defects fall into the class *not traceable* (4 man- hours per requirement on average) and the class *not modifiable* (6 h) (we do not take into account the class *not ranked* for the same reasons as explained above).

Among the development phases, the highest cost occurs with the requirement defects detected in the latest development phase, i.e., vehicle test (8 resp. 11 man-hours per requirement on average). We observe, however, the increase of cost with respect to the early development phases (requirements review* and design review, 3 man hours per requirement on average) is not as drastic for *not traceable* and *not ranked* as with the costly requirements defect classes which we have discussed above.

The maximal cost for fixing a single requirements defect of the class *not traceable* was 18 h. The maximal cost for fixing a single requirements defect of the class *not modifiable* was 6 h. This is still far away form the maximal cost of 86 h for fixing a single requirements defect of the class *inconsistent*.

4   Lessons Learned

In Sect. 3 we have presented a post hoc analysis of the data collected during a 5-year industrial project. In this section, we will present the conclusions which we have drawn and which may help to improve the practice in follow-up projects.

The results of the analysis seem to justify a number of decisions that have been made regarding the requirements engineering processat the beginning of the DC-to-DC project. We list these decisions below.

Include test engineers in the project from the beginning. In every requirements review session, a test engineer participated. As the analysis reveals, the effect of the decision is that *not verifiable* requirements were detected during the reviews and not later during testing.

Separate parameters in the requirements from their concrete values. The requirements are formulated using a parameter, i.e., a name for a value (instead of the value itself). The parameter is bound to a concrete value only in the parameter data base. The motivation behind this decision is to help the management of variants (since the set of parameter values can be defined individually for each variant and the set can be exchanged without modifying the requirements). The analysis reveals that this decision introduced a rather large number of requirements defects. However, these requirements defects are of the kind that can be detected automatically. Since the analysis also reveals that the number of modifiability defects linked to parameters and version management is small, the decision seems well justified. Another effect of the decision is to minimise the risk of incorrectness defects (due to forgotten updates of parameters values). Since the analysis also reveals that incorrectness defects are among the most costly to fix, the benefit is apparent.

Develop the requirements specification in a refinement process along the functional structure. Concretely, in the project, the functionality of the DC-to-DC converter was decomposed into sub functionalities with defined interaction and responsibility; this decomposition was iterated until the single parts could be described by few requirements. This means a lot of effort spent on the front-loading (with a detailed system concept, with respect to both, a functional and a component view, which was then used to organise and detail the system requirements). Since the analysis reveals that the number of inconsistency defects in the DC-to-DC converter project was rather low (considerably lower than, e.g., in the projects studied in [4,6,7]), the decision seems effective in decreasing the risk of inconsistency defects.

We next list a few recommendations for the requirements engineering process that seem justified in light of the analysis.

Apply automated tools to detect inconsistencies. Table 1 shows that 9 out of 31 requirements defects that fall into the class *inconsistent* were not detected during the requirements review phase. Table 3 shows that those 9 requirements defects have a rather high cost for fixing the defect of 29 man-hours per requirement on average (as we have described above, in one case, where the cost amounts to 86 h, the inconsistency involves 16 requirements which specify an intricate interaction between error signals). In the future, the systems that we develop will become even more complex, and the risk that a requirements defect escapes the manual review process will become even higher. This calls for the use of automated tools that use model checking techniques to detect even elaborate forms of inconsistencies between requirements (and even between timing constraints); see, e.g., [7–9]. The use of automated tools involves an initial extra effort which is needed for formulating requirements in a machine-readable format. Our analysis suggests that the investment of such an effort might pay off.

Include the type of the requirements defect in the defect report. In our analysis, we specified the type of a requirements defect by the class (in the classification based on the IEEE 830 standard) and/or by the defect source (the defect part of the requirement). The person who writes the defect report will know the type and to write it down seems to create only little overhead. In contrast, to reconstruct the type from a defect report is a rather involved and time consuming task (a task that was necessary in our post hoc analysis). The immediate availability of the type of the requirements defect means that this useful information can already been taken into account during the requirements engineering process, for example in review meetings.

Analyse requirements defects in order to screen the requirements engineering process. Without an analysis of the requirements defects, information on the requirements defects lies dormant in the data base of defect reports. Information such as the information gathered in Tables 1, 2 and 3 is, however, useful to review decisions that have been made regarding the requirements engineering process. This information is useful continuously during the project, and it is useful in order to give recommendations for follow-up projects.

5   Threats to Validity

In this section, we analyse threats to validity defined in Neuendorf [5] and Wohlin [11].

5.1   Construct Validity

Experimenter Expectancies [11]. Expectations of an outcome may inadvertently cause the raters to view data in a different way. This threat applies to the classification of the defects, as one of the raters was aware of the results reported in the related work. However, the other analyst was not familiar with those results. The reliability analysis in Sect. 3 suggests that the classification was not biased.

Semantic Validity. This threat arises if the analytical categories of texts do not correspond to the meaning these texts have for particular readers. In this analysis the classes are clearly defined by IEEE 830 [3] so this threat is minimised. For the definition of the defect source we named the source in a most unambiguous way, gave an explanation of the source and several brief examples to minimise this threat.

5.2   External Validity

Sampling Validity [5]. This threat arises if the sample is not representative for requirements defects. In this study we analysed all requirements defects detected during the project's elapsed runtime written down either in review reports or in the fault data base. There is the risk that not all defects were tracked this way. However, as it is not allowed in the project to change requirements without a tracking number to a change request this risk is low. Another risk is that the project is not yet finished. However, as the product will go into production in six months and the product has passed thorough testing both at Bosch and at the customer we expect that all critical defects are already uncovered. Still the results may not be transferable to other projects. In this project special care was taken to ensure testable and modifiable requirements. Therefore we assume that the results presented in Sect. 3 may differ with that respect from other projects.

Interaction of Selection and Treatment [11]. This threat arises if the raters in this study (see Sect. 3) are not representative for Bosch engineers. The classification was done by a student and a PhD student at Bosch, and supervised by a requirements engineer at Bosch. The requirements engineer also classified a small sample. The reliability analysis in Sect. 3 suggests that the classification is sufficiently independent of the raters with respect to the IEEE classes.

5.3   Conclusion Validity

Low Statistical Significance [11]. This threat is concerned with statistical tests of low power. The stability analysis conducted for the IEEE 830 uses a small sample of only 16 reports. This stability analysis should give a picture of the stability of the classification. For cases where the analysis were unsure of the classification a requirements engineer from the project was consulted.

There were only 79 reports of requirements defects that slipped the requirements review at the end of the requirements development phase, thus the number of data points in data set 2 is fairly low, especially for the calculation of the average times in Table 3. This cannot be helped, as we took all defect data from the project, so we could not increase the selection.

6   Related Work

The work most closely related to ours is perhaps the work by Ott in [6] which also describes an empirical analysis on requirements defects (there, at Daimler AG). The work in [6] refers to requirements on a higher level than the system requirements to which our work refers. The requirements in [6] would be considered customer requirements at Bosch. Another difference lies in the granularity of the analysis. The work in [6] uses a classification on the same level of abstraction as our classification based on the IEEE 830 standard. The work in [6] does not refine the analysis in the way we do by considering the defect sources (*parameter*, *variant*, etc.). The classes in [6] cannot be mapped 1-1 to the classes in our work. But still, one can observe that in the distribution of requirements defects according to the work in [6] and in our work are compatible.

The work by Lauesen and Vinter in [4] describes the analysis of requirements defects in two comparatively small requirement specifications for a noise source location system (107 and 94 requirements, compared to over 1600 requirements in our work). There, about 60 % of the requirements defects related to unstated demands (i.e., to incompleteness), which is high in comparison to the corresponding number in our analysis (26 %).

The idea to refine the classification based on the IEEE 830 standard by considering defect sources is inspired by the Orthogonal Defect Classification (ODC) used by Chillarege *et al.* in [1]. More precisely, our notion of defect source is comparable to the notion of *defect type* in [1]. Instead of using the notion of *defect trigger* in [1], we use the development phase in which the requirements defect was detected (design review, system test, etc.).

Their defect categorisation is based on two groups: the defect type, which is a defect description implied by the eventual correction (e.g. assignment, function, algorithm, documentation), and the defect trigger, which describes the condition the defect surfaced under (e.g. concurrency, timing, boundary conditions). We use the basic ideas of ODC for a deeper analysis of our requirements defects by using the defective part of the requirement is similar to the defect type in ODC.

In contrast with our work on requirements defects, the work by Walia *et al.* in [10] considers the *requirements error* (i.e., the (human) error done while working on requirements; in contrast, the requirements defect is the manifestation of a requirements error in the requirements specification). The work in [10] uses a classroom experiment in order to classify requirements errors according to, e.g., human failure, process, or documentation error. Our initial attempts to analyse requirements errors for the DC-to-DC project using the classification of [10] were not successful (due to the lack of stability, i.e., the analysis results were not robust under the change of analyst). We leave the analysis of requirements errors in an industrial project to future work.

7   Conclusion and Future Work

We have analysed the set of 588 requirements defects reported in the DC-to-DC project at Bosch with over 1600 system requirements during a lifetime of 4.5 years. We have formulated the insights gained from the results of the analysis and we have used them to review decisions regarding the requirements engineering process at the beginning of the DC-to-DC project and to give recommendations for new decisions.

We have refined the initial classification of requirements defects, which is based in the IEEE 830 standard using the notion of *defect sources*. The resulting classification turned out to be useful tool for the analysis of requirements defects in the DC-to-DC project. It is an interesting topic of future work to evaluate whether this classification is more universally applicable or whether it can be used as the basis of a universally applicable classification of requirements defects.

Acknowledgements. We thank Hermann Kaindl for useful discussions that substantially helped to improve the presentation of this paper.

References

1. Chillarege, R., Bhandari, I.S., Chaar, J.K., Halliday, M.J., Moebus, D.S., Ray, B.K., Wong, M.: Orthogonal defect classification - a concept for in-process measurements. IEEE Trans. Softw. Eng. **18**(11), 943–956 (1992)
2. Emam, K.E.: Benchmarking kappa: interrater agreement in software process assessments. Empirical Softw. Eng. **4**(2), 113–133 (1999)
3. IEEE Computer Society: Software Engineering Standards Committee and IEEE-SA Standards Board. IEEE Recommended Practice for Software Requirements Specifications. Institute of Electrical and Electronics Engineers (1998)
4. Lauesen, S., Vinter, O., Defects, P.R.: An experiment in process improvement. Requirements Eng. **6**(1), 37–50 (2001)
5. Neuendorf, K.A.: Content Analysis Guidebook. Sage Publications, Thousand Oaks (2002)
6. Ott, D.: Defects in natural language requirement specifications at Mercedes-Benz: an investigation using a combination of legacy data and expert opinion. In: 2012 20th IEEE International Requirements Engineering Conference (RE), Chicago, IL, USA, 24–28 September 2012, pp. 291–296 (2012)
7. Post, A., Hoenicke, J., Podelski, A.: rt-Inconsistency: a new property for real-time requirements. In: Giannakopoulou, D., Orejas, F. (eds.) FASE 2011. LNCS, vol. 6603, pp. 34–49. Springer, Heidelberg (2011)

8. Post, A., Hoenicke, J., Podelski, A.: Vacuous real-time requirements. In: RE 2011, 19th IEEE International Requirements Engineering Conference, Trento, Italy, 29 August 2011–2 September 2011, pp. 153–162 (2011)
9. Post, A., Menzel, I., Podelski, A.: Applying restricted english grammar on automotive requirements—does it work? a case study. In: Berry, D. (ed.) REFSQ 2011. LNCS, vol. 6606, pp. 166–180. Springer, Heidelberg (2011)
10. Walia, G.S., Carver, J.C.: A systematic literature review to identify and classify software requirement errors. Inf. Softw. Technol. **51**(7), 1087–1109 (2009)
11. Wohlin, C., Runeson, P., Höst, M., Ohlsson, M.C., Regnell, B.: Experimentation in Software Engineering. Springer, Heidelberg (2012)

Take Care of Your Modes! An Investigation of Defects in Automotive Requirements

Andreas Vogelsang[1]([✉]), Henning Femmer[1], and Christian Winkler[2]

[1] Technische Universität München, Munich, Germany
{vogelsan,femmer}@in.tum.de
[2] MAN Truck & Bus AG,
Engineering E/E System Vehicle Dynamic Functions (EEV), Munich, Germany
christian.winkler.b@man.eu

Abstract. [**Context & motivation**] Requirements for automotive software systems are predominately documented in natural language and often serve as a basis for the following development process. Therefore, requirements artifact quality is important. Requirements often contain references to specific states of a system, which we call modes (e.g., "While the system is running, ..."). [**Problem**] However, these references are often implicit and therefore, we suspect them as possible source for misunderstandings and ambiguities. [**Principal idea**] In this paper, we explore the relation between quality defects of natural language requirements and the description of modes within them. For this purpose, we investigate review findings of industrial requirements specifications and assess how many findings contain issues addressing a mode and which defect types are most affected by mode-related findings. [**Contribution**] Our preliminary results show that 46 % of all considered review findings contain issues addressing a mode. Defect types in which modes played a major role were *completeness* and *unambiguity*. Based on these results, we argue that explicitly specifying modes prior to requirements formulation may increase the artifact quality of natural language requirements specifications.

Keywords: Requirements modeling · Feature specifications · Natural language requirements · Automotive software · Industry

1 Introduction

The behavior of automotive (software) systems often depends on information that represents states of the system or its surrounding environment. States may influence the activation/deactivation of vehicle features (e.g., `low battery`), determine a specific feature behavior (e.g., `ACC in follow-up`), or describe feature interaction (e.g., `feature X failed ⇒ feature Y degraded` [2]). We call these states of operation *modes*. We know from previous studies [6] that modes can be classified into three categories: They may describe states of the surrounding environment (e.g., `high temperature`), of the system itself (e.g., `ignition on`), or of a system feature (e.g., `ACC active`). We also know that

© Springer International Publishing Switzerland 2016
M. Daneva and O. Pastor (Eds.): REFSQ 2016, LNCS 9619, pp. 161–167, 2016.
DOI: 10.1007/978-3-319-30282-9_11

modes play an especially important role for the specification of *multifunctional systems*, which are characterized by a variety of different functions integrated into one system [1].

However, natural language is still the most common way to describe requirements, which often contain implicit descriptions of modes. For example, the requirement "The air conditioning must maintain the desired temperature if the engine is running." refers to a mode of the engine, namely `engine running`. In the past, we focused on researching practical applications of mode models. One of the benefits that we (together with our partners in industrial practice) assume is that explicit management of modes has the potential to improve the quality of natural language requirements specifications.

In this paper, we present an empirical investigation of defects in natural language requirements specifications of industrial automotive features. The goal of this study is to assess the relation between quality defects of natural language requirements and the description of modes within them. The results of the study show that 46 % of all considered defects address modes. The defect types in which modes played a major role were *completeness* and *unambiguity*.

Our results indicate that explicitly specifying modes may increase completeness and unambiguity in natural language requirements specifications.

2   Study Design

2.1   Goal and Research Questions

The goal of this study is to understand the relation between quality defects of natural language requirements and implicit descriptions of modes within them. To accomplish the stated goal, we aim at finding out how many review findings address system modes and which defect types are most affected by mode-related review findings. From this goal definition, we derive our research questions:

RQ1: How many defects in NL requirements specifications mention modes? With this RQ, we want to assess the extent of modes as a source for defects in NL requirements specifications. The answer to this question indicates the relevance of considering modes for NL artifact quality.

RQ2: Which types of requirements defects are issued by mode-related findings? With this RQ, we want to understand how implicit descriptions of modes impact the artifact quality of NL requirements. The answer to this question lists the expected quality defects within NL requirements containing modes.

RQ3: Which types of problems categorize the mode-related findings? With this RQ, we want to identify and articulate problems that cause the quality defects issued in mode-related findings. The identified problems define requirements for approaches that try to increase the artifact quality.

2.2 Case and Subject Description

To answer the research questions, we investigated reviews of requirement specifications for vehicle functions at our partner MAN Truck & Bus AG. MAN applies a rigorous reviewing process to assure a high quality in their development artifacts. Natural language requirements specifications for vehicle functions are subject to an extensive manual review after every major change. In this process, a specification is reviewed independently by at least three experts followed by a review meeting, in which a moderator, the responsible requirements engineer, and the reviewers discuss the findings and decide how to address them. There are no guidelines how to review a specification. In particular, there is no specific focus on modes. Findings and decisions are documented in a review protocol.

For our study, we inspected two of these review protocols that originated from the review process of two vehicle functions, one from the *driver assistance* and one from the *cabin & lights* domain. The reviews contained 134 findings for an overall of 41 requirements contained in the specifications.

2.3 Data Collection and Analysis

In the data collection process, we prepared and classified the data (see Fig. 1):

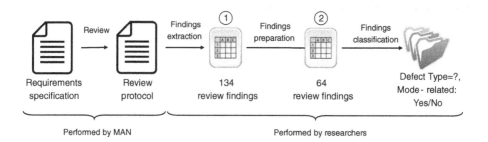

Fig. 1. Data collection process

Findings Preparation: In the review process of MAN, review findings are classified as *major defect, minor defect, spelling mistake, question,* or *process improvement.* We reduced the initial set of 134 review findings (see ① in Fig. 1) by removing findings marked as *process improvement* because we are only interested in issues related to artifact quality, and we removed findings marked as *spelling mistake.* Furthermore, we removed findings that were marked as *rejected* in the review meeting because we are interested in issues that actually caused efforts to fix them. As a final preparation step, we reduced the data set by removing *duplicate* findings, i.e., issues that were mentioned by more than one reviewer. We removed these to ensure that the same finding is not counted multiple times. After this findings preparation, we ended up with an overall of 64 findings, which served as the basis for our classification (see ② in Fig. 1).

Findings Classification: We classified each finding according to the following classification schemes:

1. **Defect type:** We used the defect type taxonomy of IEEE standard 29148 [3] to assign a defect type to each review finding (*complete, unambiguous, singular,* ... ; see [3] for details).
2. **Mode-related:** We used the definition of mode from [6] to decide whether or not a review finding mentions an issue related to a mode (*yes/no*).

To answer RQ1, we compared the number of all findings with the number of findings that we classified as mode-related. To answer RQ2, we ranked the defect types according to the number of mode-related findings in that defect type. To answer RQ3, we walked through the mode-related findings several times and annotated a keyword to each finding that describes the problem issued in the finding with respect to its content. As a result of this inductive categorization process, a set of problem classes emerged.

3   Study Results

Figure 2 shows the distribution of review findings with respect to defect types. An additional column is attached to each defect type that shows the number of mode-related findings with that defect type.

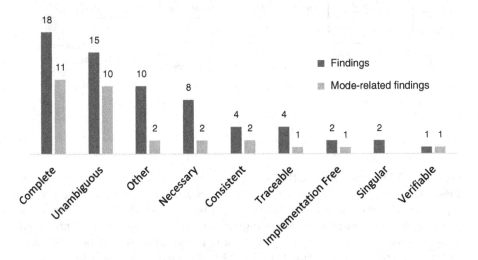

Fig. 2. Number of findings and mode-related findings per defect type.

RQ1: How many defects in NL requirements specifications mention modes? In summary, 30 of the 64 review findings that we inspected addressed issues related to a mode. That accounts for over 46 % of all considered findings.

RQ2: Which types of requirements defects are issued by mode-related findings? As shown in Fig. 2, the largest number of mode-related findings reside in the defect types *complete* and *unambiguous*. In both classes, more than 60 % of the findings are mode-related, which is the highest ratio of all defect types.[1] To illustrate typical findings of these defect types, we give two examples:

1. Defect type = unambiguous: *What does "active" in this case mean? That a warning is active or that the possibility to warn is active. Where is the definition of "active", "activation", etc.?*
2. Defect type = complete: *Missing requirement: During initialization of the vehicle, the optical icons must be activated.*

In the first example, the reviewer criticizes the ambiguous use of the mode `active`. She provides two possible interpretations of the term. In the second example, the reviewer points to a missing requirement that covers desired behavior in a special situation (mode) of the system, namely the `initialization` mode. The defect type *other*, which is the third most frequent defect type, summarizes all findings that did not fit in any of the defect type categories. Most of the findings in that category address the wording of a requirement.

RQ3: Which types of problems categorize the mode-related findings? Our open categorization process resulted in 6 categories, which characterize different problems that are issued in the mode-related findings. These categories are summarized in Table 1.

Table 1. Problem categories. In brackets, the number of findings in that category.

Category	Problem description
P1 (8)	A specific mode/situation is not considered in the function
P2 (8)	A precise mode definition is missing
P3 (5)	The reaction of a function to a mode switch is unclear
P4 (4)	It is unclear how modes are logically connected in a function
P5 (2)	The mode definition must change according to the context
P6 (2)	The validity of a mode is doubted

4   Discussion

We performed this study as a pre-study to assess the feasibility of the study design and explore whether the results are encouraging. Based on the reported results, we evaluate both intents positively. To strengthen and generalize the results, we plan to apply the study to a larger set of requirements specifications.

From the results gained so far, we infer that requirements specification in natural language suffer from a missing precise definition and specification of a set of modes. When specific terms used as modes are not precisely defined,

---

[1] *Verifiable* is neglected due to the small sample size.

a reviewer, and consequently also a developer, may not exactly know what is meant by that term (*ambiguity*). Furthermore, a precise definition of modes, and especially, the values a mode might have, can point to situations that a requirements engineer did not consider (*completeness*). The problem categories identified in RQ3 can be used as criteria to evaluate approaches that focus on explicitly documenting modes. For example, the mode modeling approach we presented in [6] supports problem categories P1, P2, and P6, but not P5.

5   Threats to Validity

A major threat to the internal validity of the results is that the classification scheme we used to classify the review findings may be blurry. A possible consequence could be that the results are not reliable and also subject to researcher bias. We tried to mitigate this threat by two measures. First, we used an established classification scheme from a standard (ISO 29148 [3]) for the classification of defect types and a definition of modes that we discussed and validated with developers in a previous study [6]. Second, we performed the classification independently by two researchers. We achieved an inter-rater agreement in terms of Kohen's Kappa of 0.68 (*substantial agreement* [4]) for the classification of the defect type and 0.42 (*moderate agreement* [4]) for the relation to a mode.

Although we selected the two inspected functions randomly and did not pick specific functions that appeared particularly defect-prone, or mode-related, our results may not be generalizable due to the small sample size. However, as a first indication, when we presented the results to practitioners involved in the vehicle functions, they stated that the presented results are plausible.

6   Conclusions

In this paper, we presented an investigation of defects documented in review protocols of natural language requirements specifications for automotive systems. This investigation revealed that over 46 % of the considered review findings addressed issues related to states of a system or its surrounding, which we call modes. Moreover, our analysis revealed that mode-related findings are predominantly represented in the defect types *unambiguous* and *complete*.

If we can reproduce and confirm the results on a larger set of review findings, we take this as a motivation to promote the explicit modeling of modes as an important means to increase the quality of NL requirements specification. Our idea is to capture modes that are relevant for more than one feature in a *mode model* [6]. Such a model provides precise and validated definitions of modes and captures them in a structured way. A requirements engineer who uses such a model, for example as a checklist, to formulate requirements may produce requirements, which are less ambiguous (due to the fixed definition of modes). Additionally, an extensive list of modes may inspire a requirements engineer to imagine different situations in which specific requirements apply. Thus, the requirements engineer may produce requirements specifications that are more complete. The evaluation of this hypothesis is subject to future research.

Existing approaches for state-based modeling of single features (e.g., [2,5]) emphasize the benefits of requirements specifications structured by modes and also its relation to feature interaction. We advance this idea and propose creating a common model of system modes that applies to every feature of a multifunctional system. In a recent study [6], we provided first evidence that it is possible to elicit such a model for realistic systems and that they are still manageable with respect to their size. In that study, the elicited mode model for an entire system consisted of 75 modes. In a future study, we plan to evaluate whether these elicited modes cover the modes that were issued in the review findings.

References

1. Broy, M.: Multifunctional software systems: structured modeling and specification of functional requirements. Sci. Comput. Program. **75**(12), 1193–1214 (2010)
2. Dietrich, D., Atlee, J.M.: A mode-based pattern for feature requirements, and a generic feature interface. In: Proceedings of the 21st IEEE International Requirements Engineering Conference (RE 2013) (2013)
3. ISO/IEC/IEEE: Systems and software engineering - Life cycle processes - Requirements engineering. ISO/IEC/IEEE 29148: 2011(E), International Organization for Standardization, Geneva, Switzerland (2011)
4. Landis, J.R., Koch, G.G.: The measurement of observer agreement for categorical data. Biometrics **33**(1), 159–174 (1977)
5. Vogelsang, A.: An exploratory study on improving automotive function specifications. In: Proceedings of the 2nd International Workshop on Conducting Empirical Studies in Industry (CESI 2014) (2014)
6. Vogelsang, A., Femmer, H., Winkler, C.: Systematic elicitation of mode models for multifunctional systems. In: Proceedings of the 23rd IEEE International Requirements Engineering Conference (RE 2015) (2015)

Empirical Studies in Requirements Engineering

Gamified Requirements Engineering: Model and Experimentation

Philipp Lombriser, Fabiano Dalpiaz$^{(\boxtimes)}$, Garm Lucassen,
and Sjaak Brinkkemper

Department of Information and Computing Sciences, Utrecht University,
Princetonplein 5, De Uithof, 3584 CC Utrecht, The Netherlands
{p.lombriser,f.dalpiaz,g.lucassen,s.brinkkemper}@uu.nl

Abstract. [**Context & Motivation**] Engaging stakeholders in requirements engineering (RE) influences the quality of the requirements and ultimately of the system to-be. Unfortunately, stakeholder engagement is often insufficient, leading to too few, low-quality requirements. [**Question/problem**] We aim to evaluate the effectiveness of gamification to improve stakeholder engagement and ultimately performance in RE. We focus on agile requirements that are expressed as user stories and acceptance tests. [**Principal ideas/results**] We develop the gamified requirements engineering model (GREM) that relates gamification, stakeholder engagement, and RE performance. To evaluate GREM, we build an online gamified platform for requirements elicitation, and we report on a rigorous controlled experiment where two independent teams elicited requirements for the same system with and without gamification. The findings show that the performance of the treatment group is significantly higher, and their requirements are more numerous, have higher quality, and are more creative. [**Contribution**] The GREM model paves the way for further work in gamified RE. Our evaluation provides promising initial empirical insights, and leads us to the hypothesis that competitive game elements are advantageous for RE elicitation, while social game elements are favorable for RE phases where cooperation is demanded.

Keywords: Gamification · Requirements elicitation · Empirical study · Agile requirements · Gamified Requirements Engineering Model

1 Introduction

Despite the crucial role of requirements engineering (RE) in software development [30], many IT projects still fail to deliver on time, within cost, or expected scope [5]. Reasons for project failures include incorrect or unsatisfied requirements, often caused by poor collaboration and communication. Furthermore, the lack of stakeholder participation in RE workshops and review meetings are additional impediments to the completion of software projects [3,18].

In this paper, we aim to improve the quality and increase the creativity of requirements by enhancing active participation of stakeholders in requirements

© Springer International Publishing Switzerland 2016
M. Daneva and O. Pastor (Eds.): REFSQ 2016, LNCS 9619, pp. 171–187, 2016.
DOI: 10.1007/978-3-319-30282-9_12

elicitation workshops, especially when online digital platforms are used. We suggest gamification as a possible way to achieve this end.

The literature on gamification and RE is limited to two main studies [12,31] that develop software tools to increase stakeholder engagement and evaluate it via a single case study. The former study [12] proposes the *iThink* tool that is designed to stimulate parallel thinking and increase group discussion. The latter study [31] introduces the *REfine* platform that aims at enlarging participation in RE by involving a crowd of both internal and external stakeholders [32]. In both works, the conducted case study showed that stakeholders felt more motivated and that participation rate increased in the requirements elicitation process.

Despite their novelty, these works have limitations. The researchers only evaluated their tool in the context of a case study, making it difficult to generalize the results and draw conclusions about causality. The impact of alternative causes, such as usability, design, and stakeholders' background were omitted.

We address these limitations by evaluating the gamification of RE in a controlled experimental setting that enables better determining patterns of cause and effect. Gamification is applied in the context of agile RE to the elicitation of user stories enriched with acceptance tests that are expressed as real-life examples. We make the following contributions:

– We propose a Gamified Requirements Engineering Model (GREM) to evaluate the impact of gamification on engagement and performance in requirements elicitation.
– We develop a gamified online platform for requirements elicitation that supports expressing requirements as user stories and acceptance tests.
– We evaluate the effectiveness of the platform through a controlled experiment with two equal balanced groups of stakeholders, and we conduct quantitative analyses on the results.
– Based on the outcomes of the evaluation, we propose a mapping between the different game elements and the RE phases they support best.

The rest of the paper is structured as follows. Section 2 reviews related work on agile RE and gamification. Section 3 presents the conceptual framework for our research. Section 4 describes our proposed gamified platform. Section 5 reports on the design and administration of the experiment, and Sect. 6 discusses the results. We analyze threats to validity in Sect. 7, and we conclude in Sect. 8.

2 Background

After reviewing scenario-based RE in the context of agile software development in Sect. 2.1, we introduce the principles behind gamification and its potential impact on motivation and engagement in Sect. 2.2.

2.1 Scenario-Based RE in Agile Development

In RE, a scenario is "an ordered set of interactions between partners, usually between a system and a set of actors external to the system" [14]. Scenarios can take many forms and provide various types of information on different levels of abstraction. The specification spectrum can vary between informal descriptions to more formal representation. They can be expressed in natural language, diagrams, pictures, wireframes, mockups, storyboards, prototypes, customer journeys, and many other formats [34]. The selection of the appropriate scenario technique depends on many factors including acceptance, notation skills, specification level, type of system, complexity, consistency, and unambiguity [30].

User Stories. After evaluating different techniques, we decided to select user stories as a requirements documentation technique because of their simplicity, comprehensibility, and their popularity in agile development [23]. They are easy to learn and can be also applied by stakeholders without any notation or modeling skills. Furthermore, user stories stimulate collaboration and facilitate planning, estimation, and prioritization. Cohn [6] suggests to use the following tripartite structure when documenting user stories:

As a [role], I want to [goal], so that [benefit]

The *role* defines who will directly benefit from the feature, the *goal* specifies which feature the system should exhibit, and the *benefit* is the value that will be obtained by implementing the user story. An example of user story is the following: "As an Administrator, I want to be notified of incorrect login attempts, so that I can more easily detect attackers".

Personas are often used to facilitate the discovery of user stories: a persona is a fictional character that represents roles and characteristics of end users [6]. Stakeholders can be assigned specific personas to obtain requirements from the perspective of specific user types.

Acceptance Tests. Acceptance criteria complement user stories with conditions that determine when a story is fulfilled [6]. They specify how the system should behave to meet user expectations. We choose to use Dan North's template [25] for expressing acceptance tests:

Given [context], when [event], then [outcome]

In summary, our baseline for representing requirements consists of: (i) *personas* to distinguish between different types of users, (ii) *user stories* to explain what the users want to achieve through the system, and (iii) *acceptance tests* to determine the correctness criteria for the system to satisfy a user story.

Quality of User Stories. INVEST is an acronym that characterizes six core attributes to evaluate the quality of a user story [35]. According to INVEST, good user stories should be *Independent* from each other, *Negotiable* as opposed to a specific contract, *Valuable* for the stakeholder, *Estimable* to a good approximation, *Small* so as to fit within an iteration, and *Testable*.

The extrinsic value of a user story, however, can be better made explicitly visible using the Kano model [17], which can be utilized to determine how satisfied or dissatisfied end users will be with the presence or absence of certain system features. Although initially developed for marketing, the Kano model can be effectively utilized in agile methodologies for prioritizing product backlog. The priority is determined by answering *functional* (what if a feature is included?) and *dysfunctional* (what if a feature is excluded?) questions [7]. The model characterizes features according to the customer value their implementation leads to:

- *Must-be:* implementation is taken for granted but exclusion from implementation leads to dissatisfaction;
- *One-dimensional:* satisfaction if implemented and dissatisfaction if excluded;
- *Attractive:* satisfaction if implemented but no dissatisfaction if excluded;
- *Indifferent:* neither satisfaction or dissatisfaction;
- *Reverse:* implementation leads to dissatisfaction.

2.2   Gamification

The principles behind gamification have existed for decades, but the term itself became mainstream only in 2010 with its initial definition of "the application of game design elements in non-gaming contexts" [11]. A principal reason why gamification has become so popular in recent years is that games have a strong "pull" factor [20]. Games affect positive emotions, relieve stress, create stronger social relationships, give a sense of accomplishment, and improve cognitive skills [15]. With gamification, the advantages of games are applied to existing business contexts in order to increase success metrics [37].

Game Elements. The classic triad of game elements in gamification consists of *points*, *badges*, and *leaderboards* (PBL) [37]. Many platforms use these elements because of their effectiveness and implementability. Points are tangible and measurable evidence of accomplishment; badges are a visual representation of achievements; and leaderboards allow players to compare themselves against each other. Next to PBL, a variety of game elements exist, including *levels, storytelling, chance, goals, feedback, rewards, progress, challenge, avatar,* and *status*. They allow for a compelling user experience and leverage motivation [37].

To understand the effects of gamification on player's behavior, a closer look at the theories of motivation and engagement is due.

Motivation. People have needs that motivate them to take action to satisfy their desires. The Maslow pyramid is one of the earliest theories describing people's needs [24]. Based on various research studies, Reiss identified 16 basic desires that guide human behavior [28]. The Self-Determination Theory (SDT) is concerned with people's inherent tendencies to be self-determined and self-motivated, without external interference [10]. SDT distinguishes between *intrinsic* and *extrinsic* motivation. People are intrinsically motivated when they do something because they simply enjoy the activity, whereas extrinsically motivated people do something for external rewards or to avoid negative consequences. "Flow" is also considered to be a motivating force for excellence. Individuals experiencing flow are more motivated to carry out further activities [8]. Optimal flow can be obtained with progression stairs, whereas engagement loops are responsible to keep players motivated by providing constant feedback [37].

Engagement. User engagement in information science covers the study of people's experience with technology [26]. The term is an abstract concept and closely related to theories of *flow*, *aesthetic* and *play*. User engagement is defined as "the emotional, cognitive and behavioral connection that exists, at any point in time and possibly over time, between a user and a resource" [2]. Therefore, engaged people not only better accomplish their personal goals, but are also physically, cognitively, and emotionally closer connected to their endeavors [26].

3   The Gamified Requirements Engineering Model

We devise a conceptual model that aims to explain the effect of gamification on stakeholder engagement and RE performance. The gamified requirements engineering model (GREM) integrates the theories of *gamification* and *engagement* presented in Sect. 2.2 in the context of *performance* in RE. The relationships between these three concepts are shown in the conceptual model of Fig. 1. The model consists of three main abstract variables: the independent variable *gamification* and the dependent variables *stakeholder engagement* and *performance*. Furthermore, two control variables mitigate threats to internal validity: *motivation* and *stakeholder expertise*. For stakeholder engagement three sub-dimensions are defined: emotions, cognition and behavior [2]. Performance is sub-divided into productivity, quality and creativity, which are perceived as supportive concepts for measuring the output in requirements elicitation [19].

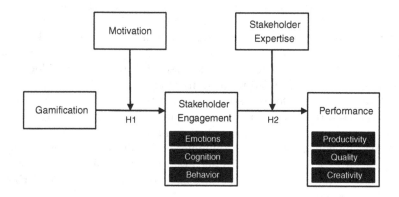

Fig. 1. The gamified requirements engineering model (GREM)

We operationalize each of the concepts of the model as follows:

- Gamification is measured with a dichotomous variable by dividing the sample into two equal balanced groups.
- Motivation is measured with the Reiss profile test [28], a rich and extensively tested tool to assess human strivings [16].
- Emotions are measured with the Positive and Negative Affect Schedule (PANAS) [36]. Since gamification is expected to provoke positive emotions, we only consider Positive Affect (PA), thereby excluding negative affective states such as distressed, upset, guilty, hostile and scared.
- Cognition is reported through the Flow Short Scale (FSS), which consists of 10 items to measure the components of flow experiences using a 7-point scale [29].
- Behavior is observed through background analytics provided by the platform that is used to express requirements.
- Stakeholder expertise is measured with a pretest questionnaire on experience in IT, RE and user stories.
- Productivity is calculated with the number of user requirements produced.
- Requirements quality is assessed with INVEST and the Kano model.
- Creativity of user stories is determined with expert opinions on a 5-point Likert scale (1 = definitely not novel, 5 = definitely novel).

Based on this conceptual model, the following two hypotheses are defined:

H1 If a diversified gamification RE platform is deployed in alignment with motivation, then stakeholder engagement is significantly increased.
H2 If stakeholders are more engaged in requirements elicitation with respect to their expertise, then the overall performance of the process and outcomes is significantly increased.

4   A Gamified Requirements Elicitation Platform

To test the effect of gamification on engagement and on performance in RE, we designed and developed an online gamified platform for eliciting requirements through user stories and acceptance tests. Our platform is developed on top of Wordpress[1]. User stories are specified by adapting blog entries to the user story template, while acceptance tests are expressed as comments to blog entries. Furthermore, a chat is included to facilitate stakeholder collaboration.

We developed the platform in such a way that the gamification elements could be enabled or disabled easily, making it possible to design specific experiments between a control group (no gamification) and a treatment group (with gamification). We embedded support for a number of gamification elements using the *Captain Up* API[2], which enables turning a website into a game experience. Basic game elements that come out of the box include points, badges, leaderboards, levels, challenges and activity feeds.

---

[1] http://www.wordpress.com.
[2] https://captainup.com/.

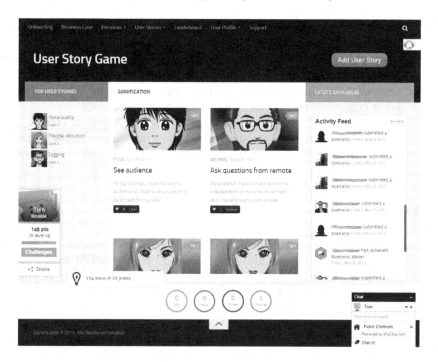

Fig. 2. A screenshot of our requirements elicitation platform showing two user stories

Using this plugin, we assign points and badges based on the actions that the user is performing on the website, such as writing user stories or acceptance tests, visiting specific pages, and sending chat messages. The number of points that are awarded is calculated based on the estimated achievement time for the different tasks that lead to points and badges.

For instance, submitting a user story is rewarded with *30 points* and adding an acceptance test with *10 points*, based on our estimation that writing a good-quality user story would take about three minutes, while creating a single acceptance test for a specified story would take approximately one minute. After writing 3 user stories a '*User Story Writer*' badge plus *90 bonus points* are credited to the user's account. Based on collected points, players can level up and compare their rank on a highscore list. The primary goal of the gamification API is to allow players to pursue mastery with a progression stair and keep them actively engaged with a positive reinforcement cycle [37]. To give points a specific, tangible meaning, a prize is awarded to the winner of the game. The player with the most points and likes receives a gift card with a value of €25. A screenshot of the platform's front-end is shown in Fig. 2.

In addition, we include further game elements that we implemented to enhance user experience and stimulate intrinsic motivation. We created a video introduction of the business case that makes use of *video animation*; the case is explained by a fictional character called Tom. Moreover, we devised a *storyline* that guides the player into the platform's basic actions, such as learning about the business case, creating a user story, specifying an acceptance test, etc.

Facial animation is used to make our personas more vivid. Talking characters are responsible to make their background stories more memorable. The primary goal of facial animation is to develop stakeholder trust in the personas by increasing empathy and provoking a fun and novel experience.

A complete list of game elements and mechanics is captured in Table 1. The purpose of this broad selection is to affect a variety of human needs. For example, while leaderboards satisfy people with desire for status and power, storytelling is more suitable for people with a demand for curiosity [27].

5   Experiment

We investigate the effect of gamification on stakeholder engagement and performance in a controlled experimental setting based on the GREM model introduced in Sect. 3. The intervention on the treatment group consists of the 17 game elements that were included in our online platform presented in Sect. 4. These game elements were disabled for the platform that was used by the control group. Our aim is to measure the response of the gamification intervention by means of an ex-post test. All details on the experiment can be found online [21].

The experiment was conducted at MaibornWolff[3], an IT consultancy company in Munich (Germany) that employs over 160 people and was founded in 1989. Our experiment involved 12 potential stakeholders. Participants were divided into two equal balanced groups with consideration to gender, motivation and expertise. The grouping used their Reiss profile test results and an experience pre-test on IT, RE, and user stories.

Before the experiment, all participants were simultaneously briefed and provided with a real business case. The company is currently lacking an efficient *video conferencing system* (VCS) for corporate team meetings. Stakeholders were asked to gather user requirements that could serve as a checklist to compare different existing VCS solutions. Both groups were given a time range of two hours to fill an initial VCS backlog with user stories together as a team.

To avoid interferences between the experimental groups, participants were told that they are working on two different cases. Furthermore, the impression was given that the aim of the experiment was to test remote requirements engineering and that communication is only allowed within the team via the integrated chat feature. The investigation of gamification was never mentioned to the participating subjects (neither in the control nor in the treatment group).

5.1   Results

The operation of the experiment went smoothly with an issue facing the treatment group. One participant from the control group dropped out after 10 min,

---

[3] http://www.maibornwolff.de/en.

Table 1. Summary of game elements and mechanics that we implemented

Game element	Affected motivation [27,28]
Points: the basis means to reward users for their activities	Order, Status, Saving
Badges: visualizations of achievements to give a surprise effect	Power, Order, Saving
Leaderboard: a ranking of the players	Power, Order, Status
Levels: phases of difficulty in a game to enable progression	Order, Independence Status
Challenges: steps towards a goal, which are rewarded with badges and points	Curiosity, Independence, Power
Activity feed: a stream of recent actions of the community	Power, Order, Status
Avatar: graphical representation of the current player	Power, Independence, Status
Onboarding: the process of getting familiar with the platform	Curiosity, Independence, Tranquility
Game master: the moderator of the game	Curiosity, Social Contact, Status
Storytelling: a background narrative to arouse positive emotions	Curiosity, Independence, Tranquility
Video: media to explain user stories and the business case	Curiosity, Order, Tranquility
Facial animation: animated characters to introduce personas	Curiosity, Order, Tranquility
Progress bar: a bar showing the player's current state in a process	Order, Tranquility
Quiz: a test to let players check their new acquired knowledge	Curiosity, Independence, Order
Timer: a clock that shows remaining time and that puts pressure	Order, Tranquility
Liking: a feature for users to support certain content	Power, Status, Vengeance
Prize: physical award given to the winner of the game	Power, Independence, Status

leaving the group with 5 stakeholders. The data from this participant is omitted from the analysis.

The following sections present the aggregated findings from the experiment, which were statistically analyzed in SPSS. Quality was rated by 5 Scrum experts, while creativity was assessed by 13 potential end users. While reading the results, bear in mind the limited size of our experiment, which threatens the generality of the results (see also Sect. 7).

Performance. We report on the results about the performance dependent variable in Fig. 1, which are measured in terms of productivity, quality and creativity.

Productivity. The average number of provided user stories within the treatment group was much higher than those of the control group. A significant difference was also identified in the total number of submitted acceptance tests between the treatment group and the control group. The total number of produced user stories and acceptance tests per group can be found in Fig. 3, whereas Table 2 reports the statistical results.

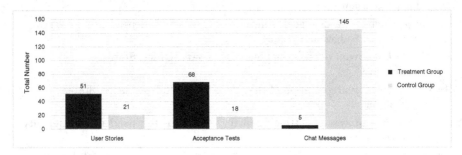

Fig. 3. Total number of produced user stories, acceptance tests and chat messages

Table 2. Independent t-test results for performance: : M = mean, SD = standard deviation, t = t-value, p = p-value

	Treatment group		Control group			
	M	SD	M	SD	t	p
User stories (Productivity)	10.000	2.345	3.500	2.258	4.673	.001
Acceptance tests (Productivity)	13.400	5.727	3.000	3.847	3.597	.006
Independent	4.022	.950	3.436	1.302	3.025	.003
Negotiable	3.985	1.099	3.891	1.048	.543	.558
Valuable	3.933	1.052	4.055	1.061	−.718	.473
Estimable	3.504	1.177	2.418	1.213	5.714	<.001
Small	3.244	1.187	2.364	1.007	4.837	<.001
Testable	4.193	1.040	3.418	1.370	3,772	<.001
Creativity	3.044	1.0850	2.236	.922	4.853	<.001

Quality. For the quality aspect, the requirements were stratified sampled and evaluated by 5 certified Scrum experts (between 1 and 9 years of experience) with the INVEST model [35].

User stories gathered by the treatment group were more independent (I), allowed for better estimations (E), were smaller (S), and better testable (T) than those of the control group. Negotiable (N) and valuable (V) did not report

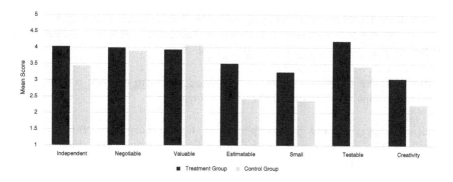

Fig. 4. INVEST and creativity scores that were rated by Scrum experts

any significant differences between the two groups. The mean score for each characteristic is presented in Table 2 and visualized in Fig. 4.

To determine the extrinsic value of user stories, the Kano questionnaire [17] was answered by 13 employees adopting the role of future end users and disjoint from the participants in the experimental groups. The results from Fig. 5 indicate that nearly half of the requirements within the treatment group were categorized as attractive requirements. Must-be requirements account for one third, and indifferent requirements for approximately a quarter of all user stories.

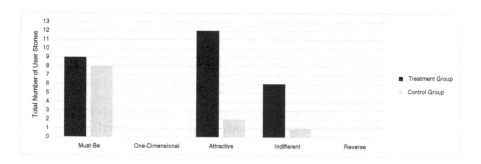

Fig. 5. Total number of user stories per Kano category classified by 13 future end users

Most of the requirements in the control group were prioritized as must-be requirements, followed by a few attractive and indifferent requirements. No requirements were classified as one-dimensional or reverse quality.

Creativity. Creativity was rated by the 5 Scrum experts and was significantly higher in the treatment group compared as well. The average creativity score per group is shown in Fig. 4. The statistical results from SPSS are listed in Table 2.

Creativity strongly correlated with the Kano categories. Higher creative requirements were classified as attractive or indifferent, whereas requirements with low creativity score were classified as must-be $[r(36) = .632, p < .001]$.

Stakeholder Engagement. As per our GREM conceptual model in Fig. 1, we measure stakeholder engagement in terms of emotions, cognition, and behavior. All the statistical results are reported in Table 3.

Emotions. Users interacting with the gamified platform did not report higher positive emotions (PA) than did the control group.

Cognition. The treatment group experienced slightly more flow compared to the control group, according to the Flow Short Scale. However, this difference was not statistically significant.

Behavior. Participants interacting with the gamified platform caused more page visits than did the control group as shown in Table 3. In sharp contrast, the control group wrote more text messages compared to the treatment group. The total number of written messages is shown in Fig. 3 and reported in Table 3.

Table 3. Independent t-test results for stakeholder engagement

	Treatment group		Control group			
	M	SD	M	SD	t	p
Emotions	36.800	4.025	37.000	4.000	−.082	.936
Cognition	50.400	7.635	43.333	5.645	1.767	.111
Page visits (Behavior)	161.000	40.367	88.833	38.338	3.036	.014
Chat messages (Behavior)	1.000	1.732	24.167	19.995	−2.560	.031

6   Discussion

Our experiment shows that a gameful experience in requirements elicitation can be used to effectively influence user behavior and to increase performance. The obtained results enable an evaluation of the hypotheses H1 and H2:

- **We retain the null hypothesis for H1.** *Emotions* and *cognition* did not exhibit statistical differences between the two experimental conditions, whereas *behavior* did. Stakeholders exposed to gamification were active with requirements production, whereas the control group was intensively collaborating during the operational phase. Therefore, it is not possible to reject the null hypothesis for H1, for stakeholder engagement was high in both groups.
- **We reject the null hypothesis for H2.** Findings from both experimental groups reported significant variations in all sub-dimensions of the performance concept. The treatment group did not only *produce* more user requirements, but their *quality* and *creativity* was higher as well. Performance was indirectly impacted by gamification, which caused a change in the behavioral dimension. Consequently, our second hypothesis provides evidence to be true and therefore, we reject the null hypothesis for H2.

Furthermore, we draw some conclusions on the role of gamification in RE.

Productivity, Quality, and Creativity *may be* **Increased by Gamification.**
The treatment group not only *produced more* unique requirements, but their *quality and creativity* were significantly *higher*. Their stories were more independent and written in smaller chunks, and the resulting product backlog allowed for better estimations and testing. Most stories were attractive requirements, which have great impact on *customer satisfaction* [17]. Moreover, they outperformed the control group in creativity: most of their requirements were *more novel*.

Competitive Gamification *may* **Reduce Stakeholder Communication.**
On the other side, the control group was very *communicative* during the execution phase of the experiment. The recorded data indicate a continuous discussion from the very beginning until the end of the experiment. This group apparently approached the task more as a team, while interpersonal communication between the other group subjects was barely present. Nonetheless, from the intensive discussion observed in the chat, we are able to deduce that this group was causing *mutual obstruction*. As a result, not only was *creativity* of their user stories *lower*, but also intrinsic and extrinsic *quality suffered* as well.

No Differences Concerning Emotions and Cognition Were Identified.
We presume that an *optimal flow* was not present in our game design, because players were not challenged enough throughout the game [8]. A second possible explanation is that the achievement system was too *extrinsically rewarding*, which might have caused an emotional and cognitive decrease [9]. A further conjecture might be that the control group was engaged by a social dimension. While the treatment group was primarily progressing in a virtual game and enhancing their competences, the control group was *socially engaged* in the requirements elicitation process [10].

Collaboration in Elicitation *may* **Have Negative Consequences.**
Although positive collaboration is deemed as a key success factor for RE [18], our case has shown that it may also have negative consequences during elicitation. The chat discussion in the control group has probably absorbed people's attention and blocked productivity, in line with the cognitive theory of idea generation [33].

7   Validity Evaluation

We discuss the main threats to internal and external validity, and explain how we dealt with them in our research.

7.1   Internal Validity

It refers to the causal conclusion between two variables [4]. Despite our efforts to precisely characterize gamification and its effect on motivation and performance, we cannot claim the GREM model to be comprehensive. However, the use of a control group helps eliminate many potential causal relationships [38].

By choosing a wide set of game mechanics and game elements, in order to support participants with different personalities, we collect limited evidence on the impact size of individual elements. We measured this impact by posing a set of questions regarding the enjoyment of individual elements in the posttest.

To mitigate this risk of poor wording and bad instrumentation, we decided to use standardized questionnaires with high validity and reliability, such as the Short Scale Flow [29] and the Positive and Negative Affect Schedule [36].

Concerning the selection of subjects, we could not perform a random selection, but rather had to use a convenience sampling technique. The experiment was announced on the corporate intranet where people could voluntarily enroll. However, these people already might were intrinsically motivated, which could significantly influence the statistical results. We did ensure, however, that both groups had similar characteristics and professional work experience.

In previous studies on gamification in RE [12], the researchers concluded that the graphical user interface had an impact on user satisfaction. To avoid the same problem, we employed the same aesthetic theme for both prototypes.

7.2   External Validity

This type of threat measures the extent to which the obtained results are valid outside the actual context in which the experiment was run. Concerning the experimental condition, the sample size is relatively small to make significant conclusions [13]. Due to the fact that this research project was conducted within a single software engineering company, we were bound to the available resources. On the other hand, it could get confusing to manage user stories on an online platform when too many stakeholders are interacting at the same time. To mitigate this threat, we strove to make the experimental environment as realistic as possible by providing them with a real company internal business case.

The experiment lasted two hours, due to practical constraints. Thus, we cannot draw conclusions on the long-term effect of gamification. Extrinsic rewards were effective in the short-term, but their long-term effect is unknown.

To mitigate the threat of interference between the two groups, we told the groups they would be working on two separate and independent cases, and we did not mention gamification as the treatment we were measuring (see Sect. 5).

8   Conclusion

We have shown how gamification can positively influence the elicitation process in agile RE. We did so by conducting a thorough *controlled experiment* where the treatment group was given the gamification intervention in the form of game elements added to the elicitation platform. To the best of our knowledge, this is the first controlled experiment that studies gamification in RE.

The success of gamification heavily depends on the choice of game mechanics and game elements, as they can affect different psychological needs. Our experiment shows that an individual leaderboard and the opportunity to win a prize incentivizes competition in a positive manner. Stakeholder rivalries increased requirements production, resulting in higher quality and more creative ideas.

We found that simulating competition with gamification can help gather basic and novel requirements, and contributes greatly to creativity. However, individual leaderboards or activity feeds might not always be the right choice. In later development stages, that focus on the creation of a shared conceptualization [1], more cooperative game elements could be more adequate for the analysis, specification and validation of requirements. Social game elements, such as team leaderboards or team challenges, can stimulate cooperation and collaboration [37]. Thus, we build a new hypothesis to validate in future studies:

H3 While requirements elicitation is positively supported by competitive game elements, cooperative game elements are more suitable for requirements analysis, specification and validation.

Future Research. More experiments are required to generalize the results and the applicability of GREM. First of all, the experiment should be executed again, but with the removal of the chat function. This would prevent the control group from being socially engaged and presumably decrease production blocking [33].

It would be valuable to conduct trials with different sample sizes and game elements. Game mechanics and elements should be tested in isolation and in partial combinations to measure their influence on motivation and behavior.

The experiment can also be repeated using different quality frameworks for user stories. For example, it would be interesting to use the Quality User Story (QUS) framework [22] that defines quality in terms of syntactic, semantic, and pragmatic attributes that go well beyond the simple INVEST mnemonic.

To generalize our claims beyond agile RE, experiments are needed with alternative notations to represent requirements. A particularly interesting facet is to explore gamification for the elicitation of non-functional requirements, either in general or looking at specific aspects such as security. Furthermore, we have not tested the long-term trends with respect to stakeholder engagement.

The GREM model contains no elements that are apply uniquely to the RE field, as it stems from theories from management science, psychology, etc. An interesting direction is to explore GREM beyond software engineering as a general model that relates gamification to performance through engagement.

Acknowledgments. We thank everyone at MaibornWolff for hosting our research; in particular, we are grateful to Franziska Metzger for her support throughout the project and to all the participants in the experiment.

References

1. Abdullah, N.N.B., Honiden, S., Sharp, H., Nuseibeh, B., Notkin, D.: Communication patterns of agile requirements engineerings. In: Proceedings of the 1st Workshop on Agile Requirements Engineering (AREW), pp. 1:1–1:4 (2011)
2. Attfield, S., Kazai, G., Lalmas, M., Piwowarski, B.: Towards a science of user engagement (position paper). In: Proceedings of the Workshop on User Modelling for Web Applications (IWUM) (2011)
3. Bano, M., Zowghi, D.: A systematic review on the relationship between user involvement and system success. Inf. Softw. Technol. **58**, 148–169 (2015)
4. Bhattacherjee, A.: Social Science Research: Principles, Methods, and Practices (2012)
5. Charette, R.N.: Why software fails [software failure]. IEEE Spectr. **42**(9), 42–49 (2005)
6. Cohn, M.: User Stories Applied: For Agile Software Development. Addison-Wesley, Redwood City (2004)
7. Cohn, M.: Agile Estimating and Planning. Pearson Education, Upper Saddle River (2005)
8. Csikszentmihalyi, M.: Flow: The Psychology of Optimal Experience, vol. 41. Harper Perennial, New York (1991)
9. Deci, E.L., Koestner, R., Ryan, R.M.: A meta-analytic review of experiments examining the effects of extrinsic rewards on intrinsic motivation. Psychol. Bull. **125**(6), 627–668 (1999)
10. Deci, E.L., Ryan, R.M.: Self-Determination. Wiley Online Library (2010)
11. Deterding, S., Dixon, D., Khaled, R., Nacke, L.: From game design elements to gamefulness: defining gamification. In: Proceedings of the International Academic MindTrek Conference, pp. 9–15. ACM (2011)
12. Fernandes, J., Duarte, D., Ribeiro, C., Farinha, C., Pereira, J.M., da Silva, M.M.: iThink: a game-based approach towards improving collaboration and participation in requirement elicitation. Procedia Comput. Sci. **15**, 66–77 (2012)
13. Fisher, R.A.: Statistical Methods for Research Workers. No. 5. Genesis Publishing Pvt Ltd., Delhi (1936)
14. Glinz, M.: Improving the quality of requirements with scenarios. In: Proceedings of the World Congress on Software Quality (WCSQ), pp. 55–60 (2000)
15. Granic, I., Lobel, A., Engels, R.: The benefits of playing video games. Am. Psychol. Assoc. **69**, 66–78 (2013)
16. Havercamp, S.M., Steven Reiss, S.: A comprehensive assessment of human strivings: test-retest reliability and validity of the reiss profile. J. Pers. Assess. **81**(2), 123–132 (2003)
17. Kano, N., Seraku, N., Takahashi, F., Tsuji, S.: Attractive quality and must-be quality. J. Jpn. Soc. Qual. Control **14**(2), 147–156 (1984)
18. Kappelman, L.A., McKeeman, R., Zhang, L.: Early warning signs of IT project failure: the dominant dozen. Inf. Syst. Manage. **23**(4), 31–36 (2006)
19. Koopmans, L., Bernaards, C.M., Hildebrandt, V.H., Schaufeli, W.B., de Vet Henrica, C.W., van der Beek, A.J.: Conceptual frameworks of individual work performance: a systematic review. J. Occup. Environ. Med. **53**(8), 856–866 (2011)
20. Lazzaro, N.: Why we play games: four keys to more emotion without story. In: Proceedings of the Game Developers Conference (GDC) (2004)
21. Lombriser, P.: Engaging Stakeholders in Scenario-Based Requirements Engineering with Gamification. M.Sc. thesis, Utrecht University (2015). http://dspace.library.uu.nl/handle/1874/317766

22. Lucassen, G., Dalpiaz, F., van der Werf, J.M., Brinkkemper, S.: Forging high-quality user stories: towards a discipline for agile requirements. In: Proceedings of the International Requirements Engineering Conference (RE), pp. 126–135. IEEE (2015)

23. Lucassen, G., Dalpiaz, F., van der Werf, J.M., Brinkkemper, S.: The use and effectiveness of user stories in practice. In: Proceedings of the International Working Conference on Requirements Engineering: Foundation for Software Quality (REFSQ) (2016)

24. Maslow, A.H.: A theory of human motivation. Psychol. Rev. **50**(4), 370–396 (1943)

25. North, D.: Introducing behaviour driven development. Better Softw. Mag. (2006)

26. O'Brien, H.L., Toms, E.G.: What is user engagement? a conceptual framework for defining user engagement with technology. J. Am. Soc. Inform. Sci. Technol. **59**(6), 938–955 (2008)

27. Radoff, J., Kidhardt, E.: Game On: Energize Your Business with Social Media Games. Wiley, New York (2011)

28. Reiss, S.: Who Am I?: 16 Basic Desires that Motivate Our Actions Define Our Persona. Penguin, New York (2002)

29. Rheinberg, F., Vollmeyer, R., Engeser, S.: Die Erfassung des Flow-Erlebens. Hogrefe, Göttingen (2003)

30. Rupp, C., Simon, M., Hocker, F.: Requirements-Engineering und -Management, 5th edn. Hanser Fachbuchverlag, Nürnberg (2009)

31. Snijders, R., Dalpiaz, F., Brinkkemper, S., Hosseini, M., Ali, R., Özüm, A.: REfine: a gamified platform for participatory requirements engineering. In: Proceedings of the International Workshop on Crowd-Based Requirements Engineering (CrowdRE) (2015)

32. Snijders, R., Dalpiaz, F., Hosseini, M., Shahri, A., Ali, R.: Crowd-centric requirements engineering. In: Proceedings of the International Workshop on Crowdsourcing and Gamification in the Cloud (CGCloud 2014) (2014)

33. Stroebe, W., Nijstad, B.A.: Warum brainstorming in gruppen kreativität vermindert. Psychologische Rundsch. **55**(1), 2–10 (2004)

34. Sutcliffe, A.: Scenario-based requirements engineering. Requirements Eng. **3**(1), 48–65 (1998)

35. Wake, B.: Invest in Good Stories, and SMART Tasks (2003). http://xp123.com/articles/invest-in-good-stories-and-smart-tasks. Accessed 20 Jan 2015

36. Watson, D., Clark, L.A., Tellegen, A.: Development and validation of brief measures of positive and negative affect: the PANAS scales. J. Pers. Soc. Psychol. **54**(6), 1063 (1988)

37. Werbach, K., Hunter, D.: For the Win: How Game Thinking Can Revolutionize Your Business. Wharton Digital Press, Philadelphia (2012)

38. Wohlin, C., Runeson, P., Höst, M., Ohlsson, M.C., Regnell, B., Wesslén, A.: Experimentation in Software Engineering. Springer, Heidelberg (2012)

Documenting Relations Between Requirements and Design Decisions: A Case Study on Design Session Transcripts

Tom-Michael Hesse[✉] and Barbara Paech

Institute of Computer Science, Heidelberg University,
Im Neuenheimer Feld 326, 69120 Heidelberg, Germany
{hesse,paech}@informatik.uni-heidelberg.de

Abstract. Context/Motivation: Developers make many important decisions as they address given requirements during system design. Each decision is explained and justified by decision-related knowledge. Typically, this knowledge is neither captured in a structured way, nor linked to the respective requirements in detail. Then, it is not obvious, how design decisions realize the given requirements and whether they further refine or shape them. Thus, the relations and alignment of requirements and design cannot be assessed properly. **Problem/Question:** While there are several studies on decision-making in general, there does not exist a study uncovering how decision-related knowledge emerges based on requirements. Such a study is important to understand the intertwined relations of requirements and design decisions as well as how requirement descriptions could be enhanced with feedback from design decision-making. **Principal Idea/Results:** We applied a flexible documentation approach for decision-related knowledge on discussion transcripts of two design sessions with professional designers. We analyzed the discussions for decision-related knowledge and documented it together with its relations to the given requirements. Several complex and incrementally growing knowledge structures for decisions were found to emerge in relation to the given requirements. Also, we uncovered that decision-related knowledge contained uncertainties about requirements and further refined them. **Contribution:** Our study uncovers detailed relations between requirements and design decisions and thereby improves the understanding of their mutual impact on each other. We also derive recommendations for the cooperation between requirements engineers and designers in practice. In addition, we demonstrate that our documentation approach for decision-related knowledge provides a comprehensive view on decisions and their relations to requirements.

Keywords: Decision documentation · Decision-making · Design decisions · Requirements traceability · Case study

1 Introduction

During software design many decisions are made. On the one hand, such design decisions significantly shape the structure of the developed system [11] with

© Springer International Publishing Switzerland 2016
M. Daneva and O. Pastor (Eds.): REFSQ 2016, LNCS 9619, pp. 188–204, 2016.
DOI: 10.1007/978-3-319-30282-9_13

respect to the given requirements. On the other hand, design decisions also impact these requirements [16], as developers face uncertainties and need to clarify them. In addition, design decisions can potentially restrict or extend the given requirements for the system. Thus, knowledge about design decisions is crucial to assess the intertwined relations between requirements and design [8]. Typically, this decision-related knowledge is complex. For instance, it may consist of multiple issues and goals, alternatives for solving the decision problem, additional context information or rationales justifying the choice. We will refer to this knowledge as *decision knowledge* and call its belonging entities decision knowledge *elements*. All of these elements can be related to requirements and, therefore, can be important drivers of the system's design.

Whereas several studies exist on decision-making in design (cf. [5,22,25]), currently no study explicitly addresses relations between requirements and decision knowledge elements in detail. Such a study is hindered by the fact that comprehensive decision knowledge is often not accessible due to missing documentation. Even if decisions are documented, detailed knowledge structures are mostly not covered. Then, also relations to requirements are only captured coarse-grained for entire decisions. However, as requirements might be the origin or driver of particular decision knowledge elements [8], a fine-grained decision documentation of realistic design discussions is needed as a foundation for this study.

In this paper, we investigate the design discussion transcripts of professional software designers to identify any contained decision knowledge elements with their relations to requirements. Therefore, we have applied our incremental documentation approach for decision knowledge [8] on these transcripts. Then, the resulting knowledge structures and relations were analyzed. Our *overall goal* is *to better understand how given requirements are exploited by designers in their design decision knowledge.* The contribution of our study to this goal is to analyze the relations between requirements and decision knowledge elements stated by designers in their decisions. We identified and examined emerged structures of decision knowledge elements and their detailed interaction with requirements. This helps to understand how requirements and design decisions influence each other. Based on these findings, software designers can be supported in identifying and documenting the relevant decisions with respect to requirements. In addition, our findings provide insights on how requirements could be enhanced with feedback from the design process, for instance by clarifying potential uncertainties with the stakeholders. Moreover, we demonstrate the capability of our documentation approach to create a comprehensive view on decision knowledge and its relation to requirements for design decisions.

The remainder of this paper is structured as follows. In Sect. 2, we briefly describe our decision documentation approach and introduce the investigated design discussion transcripts with related studies. Section 3 presents our approach for coding and analyzing the transcripts with our research questions and the resulting coding table. In Sect. 4, we describe our findings. Then, these results and the threats to validity are discussed in Sect. 5. Finally, we summarize our findings and present ideas for future work in Sect. 6.

2   Background and Related Work

In this section, we introduce our approach for *decision documentation.* Then, we briefly describe the *investigated design discussions* with the addressed requirements and present *related studies* for the transcripts and our research method.

Decision Documentation. As already defined, *decision knowledge* is concerned with all information developers need to understand a given decision problem, its context and justifications for the decision. A decision problem at least comprises a set of alternatives, which can be compared by different criteria [15]. The context of decisions might consist of constraints brought up by requirements or assumptions on the environment of the developed system. So, the context might constitute or influence criteria within the decision problem. Justifications for the decision are typically given in form of arguments supporting or challenging alternatives. As we have pointed out in [17], different models address the documentation of decision knowledge during requirements engineering and software design. However, these models either represent the entire decision in a summarized way (e.g., in pre-defined textual templates) or they only focus on parts of decision knowledge. Then, not all structures and relations within decision knowledge can be captured. In addition, the existing approaches do not support an incremental documentation of decision knowledge.

Due to these shortcomings, we decided to apply our own decision documentation model as presented in [8]. Our model offers a variety of different knowledge elements and is depicted in Fig. 1.

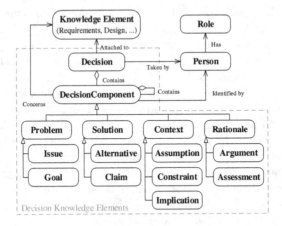

Fig. 1. Decision documentation model according to [8]

All knowledge elements concerned with particular aspects of decision knowledge are called *decision knowledge elements.* The basic element is *Decision,* which contains all related decision knowledge elements as *DecisionComponents.* Decision knowledge elements can be added incrementally over time by different *Persons.* Decisions and DecisionComponents can be linked to other knowledge elements, for instance to requirements or design artifacts. Moreover, different kinds of DecisionComponents are distinguished to describe the decision's *Problem* and *Solution*, its *Context* and *Rationale*. Problem elements contain details on the necessity to make a decision, for instance as *Issues* or *Goals* to be addressed by a decision. Solution elements contain options for the decision, like a *Claim* on how to solve a problem or different *Alternatives*. Context elements represent information on the environment of the decision and its knowledge elements. Such information can be given by *Assumptions* influencing the decision, *Constraints* restricting the decision, or *Implications* resulting from different alternatives. Rationale elements contain reasons related to other decision knowledge elements, such as *Arguments* for or against an alternative or their justification by an *Assessment* of criteria.

Investigated Data. The investigated data are transcripts of three design sessions, which were initially distributed as material for the international workshop "Studying Professional Software Design" in 2010 [9]. In all sessions, the teams received a textual description of their task. They were given one hour and fifty minutes to create a high-level system design for a traffic simulation system. The task description contained a set of briefly described requirements for the simulation system. An overview of these requirements is given in Table 1. The requirements cover different aspects of the system model, such as the representation of intersections, lights, traffic sensors and traffic simulation. We will refer to these aspects as the *System* category. In addition, the interaction of the users with the system is described. For instance, the users shall control the traffic simulation or traffic density. We will refer to this as the *Interaction* category.

The designers were instructed to use a whiteboard for any drawings or notes, but no other instructions were given. Each session was held by two professional software designers and recorded on video as well as transcribed by the workshop organizers. We have investigated two transcripts with designers from Adobe and Amberpoint. The third transcript was not investigated, as the respective session was shorter than the others and deviated in conditions.

Related Studies. In several studies on design decision-making (cf. [5,22,25]) complex decisions from real-world projects were investigated. These studies focus on the process of decision-making and the applied decision-making strategies, but they did not consider the related requirements extensively. Ko and Chilana [13] investigate decisions in issue reports of different large open-source projects. Although they evaluate design decisions with more fine-grained knowledge structures, they assess requirements only in a limited way by software qualities.

Further related studies originate from approaches concerned with design decision documentation or requirements traceability using decision knowledge. Most approaches on design decision documentation (cf. [14,23,24]) only present small examples of how they can be applied. So, they do not offer realistic and complex data in their case studies. Some approaches on requirements traceability, for instance as described by Cleland-Huang et al. [4], use decisions to create trace links between requirements and other artifacts, like design diagrams or code.

Table 1. Summary of requirements given to the designers

No.	Content of requirement
Functional requirements	
R-I	Enable students to create a visual map with at least six intersections and roads of varying length as simulation area
R-II	Enable students to describe the behavior and timing of traffic lights; the system shall allow for left-hand green arrow lights
R-II.a	Combination of traffic lights, which result in crashes, are not allowed
R-II.b	Every intersection on the map is a 4-way intersection and has traffic lights
R-II.c	Enable students to choose for each intersection to have sensors, which trigger the traffic lights
R-III	Enable students to simulate traffic flows on the map in real-time; the system shall depict the traffic flows and traffic light states
R-IV	Enable students to change the density of traffic entering the simulation
Non-functional requirements	
R-V	The system shall be easy to use
R-VI	The system shall motivate the students to explore the simulation
R-VII	The system design shall be elegant
R-VIII	The system design shall be clear

Thus, they do not represent fine-grained structures of decision knowledge for their trace links.

Several studies have been executed based on the introduced design session transcripts. They can be found in special issues of *Design Studies* in 2010 and *Software* in 2012 as well as in [18]. For instance, the studies of Jackson [10] and Shaw [20] analyze the design structures and the explored design space. The studies of Tang et al. [21] and Baker and van der Hoek [1] investigate the decision-making process. Mostly, the applied research method in these studies is similar to our study, as the transcripts were analyzed by coding relevant text parts according to given coding schemes. Only the study of Ball et al. [2] explicitly considers relations between requirements and decision knowledge. The given requirements are grouped according to their level of complexity and examined for relations to different design strategies. However, no study is investigating in detail how particular decision knowledge elements are related to requirements.

3   Research Method

In this section, we present our research method. First, we introduce our *research questions* for the study and then define the *coding table* for the text analysis of the transcripts. Finally, we briefly describe the *coding process*.

Research Questions. According to our overall goal (cf. Section 1), we aim to investigate relations between requirements and design decisions at a fine-grained level. Consequently, the first research question *RQ1* is: *Which relationships exist between requirements and decision knowledge elements?* Such fine-grained relations are likely to influence the evolution of decision knowledge structures over time. For instance, constraints based on specific requirements might restrict solution alternatives, so that new implications for the decision arise. This leads to *RQ2*: *How do fine-grained knowledge structures emerge based on the given requirements?* As pointed out by Chen et al. [3], requirements with significant influence on a system's design often are difficult to define and tend to be vaguely described. They report, that designers then make assumptions about the missing details. Thus, we address uncertainties about requirements in *RQ3*: *How do decision knowledge elements address uncertainty about requirements?* Among other reasons, these uncertainties might impact the given requirements by triggering their extension or other refinements. Therefore, we also investigate the impact of decision knowledge elements on requirements by *RQ4*: *How do decision knowledge elements impact and refine the given requirements?*

Coding Table and Coding Process. Based on the leaf entities and relations in our documentation approach, we derived a coding table to identify the different decision knowledge elements and their relations to requirements within the transcripts. All codes are given in Table 2. A general code *Context* was added to capture context knowledge, which could not be categorized in detail. As an argument may support or challenge other knowledge elements, two different codes

Table 2. Codes for transcript analysis

RQ	Code	Description
1	DKE.*concerns*(R-x)	Reference to a requirement; code was set according to keywords, like "traffic lights", "sensor" or "rate of traffic"
2	*Issue/Goal*	Concrete open question/Abstract, more general aim
2	*Alternative/Claim*	Solution proposal: can be assessed by criteria/is based on personal experience, informal knowledge
2	*Context/Assumption/ Constraint/Implication*	General information/Uncertain or approximated information/Limitation or restriction/Consequence
2	*pro-Argument/contra- Argument/Assessment*	Information supports/challenges/assesses another knowledge element
2	DKE.(Decision—DKE)	Element contained in decision or another element
3	*Uncertain*(Description)	Developers explicitly express uncertain or vague information about the given requirements
4	*Impact*(Description)	Developers explicitly express extensions to or limitations of given requirements

DKE: ID of decision knowledge element, R-x: requirement number

Table 3. Transcript excerpt with coding example

Transcript	Yes, so it's got an infinite number of roads and intersections you can lay out. ID: 6
Code RQ1	6.*concerns*(R-I)
Code RQ2	*Assumption.*(Decision "Intersections implied by road crossings")
Code RQ3	-
Code RQ4	*Impact*(it's got an infinite number of roads and intersections)

were created for arguments. For each identified decision knowledge element a unique running ID and a name were created. Elements with a late position in the transcript got a higher ID. The ID as well as the numbers of the requirements presented in Table 1 were used to express relations. We used 41 decisions of the design space described by Shaw [20] as a high-level structure, with 20 decisions belonging to the Adobe transcript and 21 to the one for Amberpoint. All identified decision knowledge elements were either contained in such a decision or in another decision knowledge element.

The first author coded both transcripts completely. The first 10 % of the data was also coded by the second author and both codings were compared. The authors discussed any deviations and further refined the coding table and the criteria for setting a code. Then, the first author coded the remaining data. A coding example is given in Table 3.

4 Results

In this section, we present the results of our coding. The percentages of all decision knowledge elements per transcript are depicted in Fig. 2. In total we found 182 decision knowledge elements with 55 relations to requirements in the Adobe transcript and 198 decision knowledge elements with 65 relations to requirements in the Amberpoint transcript. For the Adobe transcript, higher percentages of *Issues*, *Claims* and *Implications* were found than for the one of Amberpoint. In contrast, the Amberpoint team made more *Arguments* explicit in their discussions. Only one explicit *Assessment* of different alternatives was found in the Adobe transcript. It should be noted that both teams followed different solution approaches, as described by Shaw [20]. This difference is illustrated by the 5 decisions with the most decision knowledge elements for each team, as shown in Table 4. Whereas the Adobe team focused on the system's functionality and technical architecture using a Model-View-Controller-approach, the Amberpoint team was mostly concerned with designing the user interface and interaction behavior of the system.

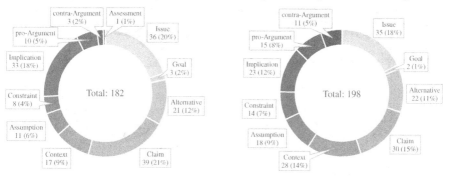

Fig. 2. Percentages of decision knowledge elements for each transcript

Table 4. Decisions with most decision knowledge elements (DKE) for each transcript

Adobe decisions	#DKE	Amberpoint decisions	#DKE
Set of objects – traversed by a controller at each clock tick	25	Discrete cars – Cars with state, route, destination	26
Intersections – Have roads (with lights and cars)	22	Intersections – Signals and sensors in approaches	23
High-level organization – Network	17	Connection of roads to intersections – Lights and sensors in approaches	20
Place in hierarchy – Traffic signals belong to roads	16	Traffic model – Master traffic object, discrete cars	20
Layout of visual map – Intersections implied by road crossings	12	System concept – User interface	16

Results for RQ1: Relations between Requirements and Decision Knowledge Elements. The detailed percentages of relations to requirements for each kind of decision knowledge element are presented in Fig. 3.

The Adobe team addressed all functional requirements in their decision knowledge, but they did not explicitly refer to any non-functional requirement. In contrast, for the Amberpoint transcript no relations to requirement II.b "Only 4-way intersections" could be identified, but the non-functional requirement V "Usability" was addressed. However, a pattern for both teams is that non-functional requirements were mostly not referenced in the investigated design decisions. When comparing both teams, several percentages for relations to requirements and decision knowledge elements are similar. Looking at the requirements addressed by the teams and the relationships of these requirements to decision elements, we found differences between the teams. This is depicted in Fig. 4.

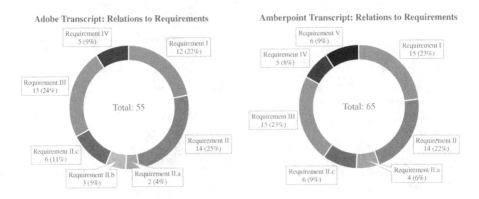

Fig. 3. Percentages of relations to requirements for each transcript

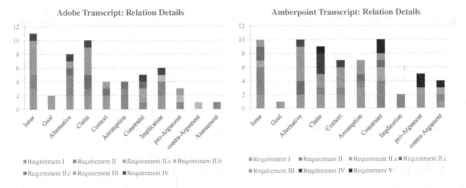

Fig. 4. Detailed percentages of relations to requirements by decision knowledge element

For instance, for the Adobe team we found three references of requirement II within *Alternatives*, but no *Assumptions* related to requirement I. In contrast, the Amberpoint transcript contained no references to requirement II for *Alternatives*, but several *Assumptions* were related to requirement I. Looking at the relationships to requirements altogether, we found for both teams that requirements were mostly related to *Issues*, *Alternatives* and *Claims*. In contrast, links between requirements and context elements seem to be specific for each team. Looking at the relationships aggregated for entire decisions, we also observed differences, as shown in Table 5. For instance, many references to requirements were found for the decision on the place for traffic lights in the system's hierarchy made by the Adobe team. However, the Amberpoint team did not consider any requirement explicitly for the same decision. In general, this indicates that references on requirements in the investigated design decisions depend not only on the actual content of the requirements, but also on the preferences and priorities of the team.

Results for RQ2: Emerged Decision Knowledge Structures. We identified complex structures of decision knowledge elements in the transcripts,

Table 5. Major deviations for the number of relations to requirements per decision

Decision	#Relations for Adobe	#Relations for Amberpoint	Δ
Road system – Connection of roads to intersections	3	13	**10**
Traffic lights – Place in hierarchy	10	0	**10**
Simulator	7	0	**7**
Road system – Intersections	3	9	**6**
System concept	2	8	**6**

which emerged based on the given requirements. During the design discussions, statements of the developers jumped between multiple decisions. However, for sequences of decision knowledge elements they typically addressed the same requirement. Different examples of resulting knowledge structures are depicted in Fig. 5. In most decisions problem (*Issues, Goals*) or solution elements (*Alternatives, Claims*) initially addressed requirements. Over time, they were accompanied by context knowledge. This reflects the further exploration of the decision and its environment by the designers. An example is shown in part (a) of Fig. 5. More complex knowledge structures addressed multiple requirements within one decision due to context elements related to different requirements. A potential cause could be that designers aim to satisfy multiple requirements within one decision. Then, they start to make trade-offs between alternatives by adapting and extending the alternatives over time. An example is given as part (b) in Fig. 5. Typically, *Solutions* were not formally assessed according to given criteria, as only one *Assessment* was found. Instead, one or more particular *Arguments* were stated by the designers to support or challenge a *Solution*. For the Amberpoint transcript, several of these *Arguments* also were explicitly related to requirements. A reason could be that often designers prefer sufficient solutions over optimal to reduce their effort [25]. Then, only the most important arguments are considered. An example for this structure is depicted as part (c) in Fig. 5.

Results for RQ3: Uncertainty about Requirements in Decision Knowledge Elements. In total, we identified 21 different uncertainties by the code *Uncertain*. We sorted them according to the affected category of requirements. The teams explicitly stated these uncertainties in their decision knowledge elements. An overview is given in Table 6.

Typically, uncertainties were addressed in *Assumptions* and *Issues*. We identified multiple uncertainties the designers had about the user's interaction with the simulation system. In addition, both teams discussed uncertainties about the capabilities and limitations of different entities implied by the requirements, such as intersections, lights and sensors. Moreover, the Amberpoint team explicitly stated several uncertainties about how parts of the simulation functionality should be addressed in their decisions. Overall, in the Amberpoint transcript we

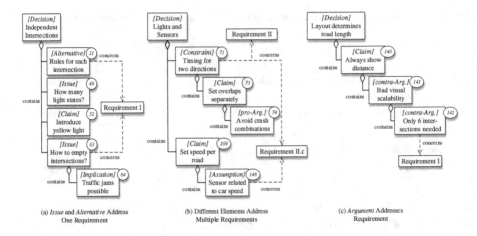

Fig. 5. Excerpts of emerged knowledge structures (with element IDs in circles)

Table 6. Uncertainty about the given requirements in decision knowledge elements

Category	Example of uncertainty
Interaction – Simulation	"[...] I don't know if there'd be two modes: an editing mode and a simulation mode." *[Assumption]*
Interaction – Traffic density	"[...] I'd go back to the customer and try and figure out, how did they collect this [traffic] data [...]" *[Assumption]*
System – Intersections	"But we are assuming straight lines." *[Assumption]*
System – Lights	"The left-hand turns are protected, but does it have only left-hand [turns]?" *[Issue]*
System – Sensors	"[...] If you have [a] sensor, what does that mean?" *[Issue]*
System – Simulation	"How do you assess the success of the timing?" *[Issue]*

identified 15 explicitly addressed uncertainties about requirements in decision knowledge elements and 6 in the Adobe transcript.

Results for RQ4: Impact of Decision Knowledge Elements on Requirements. In total, we identified 15 decision knowledge elements to impact the given requirements by the code *Impact*. Four elements were found in the Adobe transcript and 11 were contained in the Amberpoint transcript. An overview is given in Table 7.

Eight out of 15 decision knowledge elements impacting the requirements were context elements. This indicates, that information from the decision context could be a trigger to refine and adapt the given requirements. Adaptions to requirements were made either by extension or restriction. Both teams discussed

Table 7. Impact of decision knowledge elements on the given requirements

Category	Example of impact
Interaction – Simulation configuration	"[...] where you put these roads determines the maximum number of cars [...]" *[Implication]*
Interaction – Simulation usage	"[...] it could be you can draw while you're simulating." *[Claim]*
Interaction – User groups	"[...] the end users seem to be the students, and the professor." *[Assumption]*
System – Intersection structure	"[...] it's got an infinite number of roads and intersections [...]" *[Assumption]*
System – Simulation analysis	"[...] then you have an analytics piece looking in and assessing questions [...]" *[Issue]*

extensions to the given requirements in decision knowledge elements of different kinds. For instance, the Amberpoint team explicitly addressed professors as a potential user group for the system within an *Assumption*. However, this was not requested by the requirements in the prompt. In contrast, restrictions to the given requirements typically were expressed in *Solution* and *Implication* elements. For instance, the Adobe team reasoned that the road layout determines the maximum number of cars possible for the roads. This describes a potential limit of requirement IV, which requests the designers to let the users control the traffic density without limitations resulting from the physical capacity of the road.

5   Discussion

In the following paragraphs, the presented results are discussed with respect the given research questions. In addition, we describe how we have addressed potential threats to validity for our study. Our documentation approach for decision knowledge enables to uncover knowledge structures in given design decisions. The discovered differences between both transcripts were not expected. It should be noted that our study is not representative, as we have investigated the transcripts of two specific design sessions only. However, we gathered valuable insights that should be further investigated in replicated and large-scale studies.

Summary of Results for Our Research Questions. The results for our research questions show a diverse picture of the relations between requirements and decision knowledge for the two given design session transcripts. On the one hand, for both teams many similar percentages of requirement relations and decision knowledge elements in total were found. Both teams mainly focused on the given functional requirements in their design decisions. Also the decision knowledge structures showed similarities, and both teams explicitly considered uncertainties and refinements of requirements in their decision knowledge elements. On the other hand, relations between requirements and particular decision as well as kinds of decision knowledge elements strongly differ. In addition, the teams chose different solution approaches within their design and expressed different amounts of requirement uncertainties and impacts in their decision knowledge elements. They also stated these uncertainties and impacts in different kinds of knowledge elements. Overall, the coarse-grained decision knowledge structures and relations to requirements appear to be similar for both teams, whereas the more fine-grained decision knowledge elements with their particular relation to requirements deviate.

Recommendations Derived from the Results. Our findings show that for the investigated design discussions many relations were found between the given functional requirements and decision knowledge elements.

Our study also confirms the well-known fact that designers should more explicitly consider the non-functional requirements for their design within their decisions, as non-functional requirements were mostly not related to decision knowledge elements. In addition, we found relations to requirements to depend more on the preferences and priorities of the team, than on the actual content of the requirements. These two insights represent patterns for decision knowledge structures, which are likely to decrease the quality of design decisions. Therefore, these patterns should be avoided by designers.

Moreover, relations between requirements and decision knowledge elements should be made explicit, so that both requirements engineers and designers can assess the importance of particular requirements for the design. For instance, relations to requirements in problem and solution elements might indicate the significance of those requirements for the design outcomes. This would be in line with the characteristics described by Chen et al. [3] for architecturally significant requirements. Thus, designers could use these relations to recognize architecturally significant requirements more easily.

Next, requirements engineers would benefit if designers clearly stated how they want to address uncertainties about requirements. Our findings show that different kinds of decision knowledge elements, like *Assumptions* or *Issues*, were expressed due to such uncertainties. If designers explicitly noted these uncertainties and marked them as a prerequisite for a decision, valuable feedback for the requirements engineering process could be derived. For instance, such uncertainties and their impact on the design could be discussed with stakeholders to avoid a misalignment between requirements and design.

Moreover, other approaches could be extended with our insights. Goal modeling techniques, like i* or GQM, are concerned with the exploration of different alternatives for implementing given requirements [12]. These approaches could be extended to explicitly cover decisions with their relations to requirements and design artifacts. For instance, description templates for goals could be extended with a decision section, representing design decisions made to achieve a goal.

Overall, we advocate to integrate developers more closely into the requirements engineering process. Requirements engineers and developers should enter a dialogue, which could be guided by documented decisions. Then, follow-up questions on requirements by developers during the implementation can be addressed by requirements engineers.

Insights for Our Documentation Approach. From the results for RQ1 and RQ2 we conclude that our documentation approach for decision knowledge proved to be capable of capturing decision knowledge structures and their relations to requirements in a comprehensive and fine-grained way. In addition, the results for RQ3 and RQ4 indicate that our documentation approach helps to identify the mutual impact of requirements and design on each other. However, such detailed documentation is not realistic for all design decisions under real-world settings due to the required analysis effort and the differing importance of decisions. Thus, it is important to support developers, so that they can document relevant decisions with less effort. We propose to support requirements engineers and designers by semi-automatically documenting specific decisions for given requirements, such as decisions concerned with security [6]. In addition, developers could be supported by code annotations for decision knowledge to integrate decision documentation with implementation [7].

Threats to Validity. According to Runeson et al. [19], we discuss four different types of threats to validity for our study.

Internal validity is concerned with the correlation between the investigated factors and other factors [19]. First, the decision knowledge expressed by the designers might have been influenced by missing further instructions on documentation or design reasoning. Thus, the designers might have worked less structured and did not articulate all decision-related thoughts. However, this corresponds to work conditions in practice. If the designers had been asked to apply specific methods or structured processes, our results for the design decisions would depend on those methods or processes. Second, relations to requirements might have been impacted by the rather short design prompt. This might have caused additional uncertainties, which were not related to the content of a requirement, but to its description in the prompt. We addressed this threat by deriving core keywords for the content of each requirement, and used these keywords for coding relations to requirements.

External validity is concerned with the degree to which the results of our study can be generalized [19]. We only investigated transcripts of two design sessions. Therefore, our findings depend on the designers of the two investigated teams and might not be generalized for or comparable to other teams. We could have included the third transcript of the UCI design workshop in our analysis, but this would have resulted in more threats to internal validity due to the deviations in the session's settings. In addition, the involved designers were professionals from industry and had key roles in their respective companies. In consequence, the investigated data and our results are likely to represent typical design sessions and their decision knowledge.

Construct validity is concerned with any gaps between intended and actual observations of the researchers [19]. Our coding table could have identified something else than decision knowledge elements. We mitigated this threat by testing and refining the codes in previous coding experiments. Also the fit with regard to the decisions identified by Shaw [20] was very good. With our coding, we have covered 18 out of 20 decisions for the Adobe transcript, and 20 out of 21 decisions for the Amberpoint transcript. In addition, in another project we have investigated comments in issue reports within the Firefox project for decision-related knowledge. There, we applied the coding table presented in this paper successfully. As the transcripts of design discussions and discussions within issue comments are similar in structure and content, we reached a good fit of our documentation approach with the contents given in the transcripts. Moreover, our documentation approach is based on other fundamental approaches for documenting decision knowledge, as described in [8].

Reliability validity is concerned with the degree to which data and analyses of a study are dependent on specific researchers [19]. Only one coder coded all data from the transcripts, so that the codes set by this coder might not be reliable. We addressed this threat with checks and code alignments, as a second coder also coded data samples from the transcripts. Small parts of the design discussions were inaudible in the videos and, therefore, were marked and left out in the transcripts. Thus, relevant decision knowledge might have been missed in our analysis. We mitigated this threat by checking the surrounding text of any inaudible passage for hints on the missing content.

6   Conclusion and Future Work

In this paper, we have presented a study on discussion transcripts of two design sessions with professional software designers. We have investigated the transcripts for any contained decision knowledge and its relations to the given requirements. Therefore, we have coded the transcript texts according to a defined coding scheme. Designers addressed the given functional requirements in their design decisions, so that complex structures of decision knowledge emerged. Moreover, decision knowledge elements also contained uncertainty about the given requirements and impacted them with extensions or restrictions. This shows the mutual impact of requirements and decision knowledge elements on each other. It also points out that designers might benefit from making relations between requirements and decision knowledge elements explicit. Then, these knowledge elements could provide valuable feedback for the requirements engineering process and help to clarify and further improve the requirements.

As future work, it should be further investigated how designers can be supported in making the most important decision knowledge elements explicit. This requires research in two directions. First, the current study should be repeated in larger scale. Additional design sessions could be analyzed to further refine our findings. Second, the results of this study could be used to improve the tool support for our decision documentation approach. For instance, the tool for code annotations could ask developers for relations to and uncertainties about the requirements when they are documenting decision knowledge elements.

Acknowledgment. This work was partially supported by the DFG (German Research Foundation) under the Priority Programme SPP1593: Design For Future — Managed Software Evolution. Results described in this paper are based upon videos and transcripts initially distributed for the 2010 international workshop "Studying Professional Software Design", as partially supported by NSF grant CCF-0845840.

References

1. Baker, A., van der Hoek, A.: Ideas, subjects, and cycles as lenses for understanding the software design process. Des. Stud. **31**(6), 590–613 (2010)
2. Ball, L.J., Onarheim, B., Christensen, B.T.: Design requirements, epistemic uncertainty and solution development strategies in software design. Des. Stud. **31**(6), 567–589 (2010)
3. Chen, L., Babar, M.A., Nuseibeh, B.: Characterizing architecturally significant requirements. IEEE Softw. **30**(2), 38–45 (2013)
4. Cleland-Huang, J., Mirakhorli, M., Czauderna, A., Wieloch, M.: Decision-centric traceability of architectural concerns. In: International Workshop on Traceability in Emerging Forms of Software Engineering, pp. 5–11. IEEE (2013)
5. Falessi, D., Cantone, G., Kazman, R., Kruchten, P.: Decision-making techniques for software architecture design. ACM Comput. Surv. **43**(4), 1–28 (2011)
6. Hesse, T.M., Gaertner, S., Roehm, T., Paech, B., Schneider, K., Bruegge, B.: Semi-automatic security requirements engineering and evolution using decision documentation, heuristics, and user monitoring. In: First International Workshop on Evolving Security and Privacy Requirements Engineering (ESPRE) at RE2014, pp. 1–6. IEEE (2014)
7. Hesse, T.M., Kuehlwein, A., Paech, B., Roehm, T., Bruegge, B.: Documenting implementation decisions with code annotations. In: 27th International Conference on Software Engineering and Knowledge Engineering, pp. 152–157. KSI Research Inc (2015)
8. Hesse, T.M., Paech, B.: Supporting the collaborative development of requirements and architecture documentation. In: 3rd Internatioal Workshop on the Twin Peaks of Requirements and Architecture (TwinPeaks) at RE2013, pp. 22–26. IEEE (2013)
9. van der Hoek, A., Petre, M., Baker, A.: Workshop "Studying Professional Software Design" at University of California, Irvine (2010). http://www.ics.uci.edu/design-workshop/. Accessed in October 2015
10. Jackson, M.: Representing structure in a software system design. Des. Stud. **31**(6), 545–566 (2010)
11. Jansen, A., Bosch, J.: Software architecture as a set of architectural design decisions. In: 5th Working IEEE/IFIP Conference on Software Architecture (WICSA), pp. 109–120. IEEE (2005)
12. Kavakli, E., Loucopoulos, P.: Information modeling methods and methodologies: advanced topics of database research. In: Krogstie, J., Halpin, T., Siau, K. (eds.) Goal Modeling in Requirements Engineering: Analysis and Critique of Current Methods, pp. 102–124. Idea Group Publishing, UK (2005)
13. Ko, A.J., Chilana, P.K.: Design, discussion, and dissent in open bug reports. In: Proceedings of the 2011 iConference, pp. 106–113 (2011)
14. Kruchten, P., Lago, P., van Vliet, H.: Building up and reasoning about architectural knowledge. In: Hofmeister, C., Crnković, I., Reussner, R. (eds.) QoSA 2006. LNCS, vol. 4214, pp. 43–58. Springer, Heidelberg (2006)

15. Ngo, T., Ruhe, G.: Decision support in requirements engineering. In: Aurum, A., Wohlin, C. (eds.) Engineering and Managing Software Requirements, pp. 267–286. Springer, Heidelberg (2005)
16. Nuseibeh, B.: Weaving together requirements and architectures. Computer **34**(3), 115–119 (2001)
17. Paech, B., Delater, A., Hesse, T.M.: Integrating project and system knowledge management. In: Ruhe, G., Wohlin, C. (eds.) Software Project Management in a Changing World, pp. 157–192. Springer, Heidelberg (2014)
18. Petre, M., van der Hoek, A.: Software Designers in Action: A Human-Centric Look at Design Work. CRC Press, Saarbrucken (2013)
19. Runeson, P., Höst, M., Rainer, A., Regnell, B.: Case Study Research in Software Engineering. Guidelines and Examples. Wiley, Hoboken (2012)
20. Shaw, M.: The role of design spaces. Software **29**(1), 46–50 (2012)
21. Tang, A., Aleti, A., Burge, J., van Vliet, H.: What makes software design effective? Des. Stud. **31**(6), 614–640 (2010)
22. Tang, A., Babar, M.A., Gorton, I., Han, J.: A survey of architecture design rationale. J. Syst. Softw. **79**(12), 1792–1804 (2006)
23. Tang, A., Jin, Y., Han, J.: A rationale-based architecture model for design traceability and reasoning. J. Syst. Softw. **80**(6), 918–934 (2007)
24. Tyree, J., Akerman, A.: Architecture decisions: demystifying architecture. Software **22**(2), 19–27 (2005)
25. Zannier, C., Chiasson, M., Maurer, F.: A model of design decision making based on empirical results of interviews with software designers. Inf. Softw. Technol. **49**(6), 637–653 (2007)

The Use and Effectiveness of User Stories in Practice

Garm Lucassen, Fabiano Dalpiaz$^{(\boxtimes)}$, Jan Martijn E.M. van der Werf, and Sjaak Brinkkemper

Utrecht University, Utrecht, The Netherlands
{g.lucassen,f.dalpiaz,j.m.e.m.vanderwerf,s.brinkkemper}@uu.nl

Abstract. [**Context and motivation**] User stories are an increasingly popular textual notation to capture requirements in agile software development. [**Question/Problem**] To date there is no scientific evidence on the effectiveness of user stories. The goal of this paper is to explore how practicioners perceive this artifact in the context of requirements engineering. [**Principal ideas/results**] We explore perceived effectiveness of user stories by reporting on a survey with 182 responses from practitioners and 21 follow-up semi-structured interviews. The data shows that practitioners agree that using user stories, a user story template and quality guidelines such as the INVEST mnemonic improve their productivity and the quality of their work deliverables. [**Contribution**] By combining the survey data with 21 semi-structured follow-up interviews, we present 12 findings on the usage and perception of user stories by practitioners that employ user stories in their everyday work environment.

1 Introduction

User stories [6] are a popular method for representing requirements using a simple template such as *"As a ⟨role⟩, I want ⟨goal⟩, [so that ⟨benefit⟩]"*. Their adoption is growing [14], and is massive especially in the context of agile software development [29]. Despite their popularity, the requirements engineering (RE) community has devoted limited attention to user stories both in terms of improving their quality [21] and of empirical studies on their use and effectiveness.

The purpose of this study is to go beyond anecdotal knowledge and gather scientifically rigorous data on the use and perception of user stories in industry. This includes data on the development methods they are used in, the templates for structuring user stories, and the existing quality guidelines. Additionally, we explore whether practitioners perceive an added value from the use of user stories: Do they increase productivity? Do they ameliorate work deliverable quality?

Earlier studies have shown that RE practices play a central role in agile development [11,29] albeit on a small scale and in a local context. Ramesh, Cao and Baskerville pinpointed agile RE practices and challenges by studying 16 organizations [26] but they have not studied the role of user stories in detail.

© Springer International Publishing Switzerland 2016
M. Daneva and O. Pastor (Eds.): REFSQ 2016, LNCS 9619, pp. 205–222, 2016.
DOI: 10.1007/978-3-319-30282-9_14

Other works studied the effectiveness of RE practice and artifacts through experiments [7–9,24] as well as the use and perception of practitioners [1,12].

This paper describes our conducted empirical research, which includes an online survey followed by semi-structured interviews with a subset of the survey respondents. Key findings of our analysis include the strong link between Scrum and user stories, the widespread adoption of the user story template proposed by Connextra, the perception that user stories help practitioners define the *right* requirements, the crucial role of explaining *why* a requirement is expressed, and a positive evaluation of quality frameworks by respondents that use one.

The remainder of this paper is structured as follows. Section 2 presents our research questions and describes the design of our empirical study. Section 3 analyzes the survey and interview results concerning the *use* of user stories in practice, while Sect. 4 reports on the *perceived effectiveness*. Section 5 discusses validity threats to our research, while Sect. 6 reports on related literature. We discuss our results and conclude in Sect. 7.

2   Study Design

The goal of this study is to understand how practitioners use and perceive user stories, which prompts us to formulate two research questions:

RQ_1: How do Practitioners use User Stories? We investigate the context of user stories by looking at how practitioners approach working with user stories. What software development methods are appropriate for using user stories? Which templates and quality guidelines are popular among practitioners?

RQ_2: How do Practitioners Perceive the Effectiveness of User Stories? In this study, we decompose effectiveness into productivity and quality of work deliverables; although many more aspects exist, these are two basic performance indicators for software development processes. We examine whether practitioners agree that user stories increase their work productivity and/or the quality of their work deliverables. Additionally, we investigate whether practitioners find that utilizing a template and/or a quality framework further improves these aspects.

To answer these research questions, we split our study design in two stages: (1) we conduct an online survey that we distribute worldwide among software professionals to collect quantitative information from practitioners on the use of user stories and their added value for RE, and (2) we perform follow-up interviews to gather clarification of the answers of a selected sample of survey respondents, improving our understanding of the survey findings.

The authors distributed the survey over a variety of channels including the professional network of the authors and online communities such as requirements engineering and software engineering mailing lists, Twitter, Hacker News and Reddit Agile. Over a span of two weeks, from July 7 2015 until July 21 2015, the survey obtained 197 responses. 49 survey respondents were invited to participate in a follow-up interview, 21 of which accepted and contributed with more in-depth, qualitative data on the subject.

We analyzed the survey responses using SPSS, Excel and R; we transcribed the follow-up interviews and categorized them using the qualitative data analysis tool Nvivo.

2.1 Research Protocol

The goal of the survey is to gather quantitative data on how practitioners use and perceive user stories. To achieve this goal, we formulated 21 questions that are available in our online appendix [20]. After a short introduction on our research, the survey asked five questions on the respondent's demographics and organizational context, followed by six questions on their usage of and experience with user stories, templates and quality guidelines. Next, respondents were asked to indicate whether they agree or disagree with the following six Likert-Type statements, which we reference by their number throughout the paper:

S_1 Using user stories increases my productivity
S_2 Using user stories increases the quality of my work deliverables
S_3 Using a template for my user stories further increases my productivity
S_4 Using a template for my user stories further increases the quality of my work deliverables
S_5 Using a quality framework for my user stories further increases my productivity
S_6 Using a quality framework for my user stories further increases the quality of my work deliverables

Finally, the respondents could optionally provide their contact details and comment on the research and the survey. The survey has been reviewed by two academics who are not part of the authors and was piloted with three practitioners: a developer, a designer and a project manager. Based on the pilot, we revised the survey by adding six questions, removing one question, changing the order of existing questions and making three questions optional.

The goal of the follow-up interviews is to capture the respondent's rationale behind the answers they provided in the survey. The interview protocol consists of 16 questions (see [20]). After the preliminaries, the interviewee was asked to explain the role of user stories in their organization and their general perspective on user stories. Next, the respondent was asked to explain the difference between a poor and good user story in his opinion and to clarify their answers to the Likert-type statements S_1–S_6.

2.2 Survey Respondents

Because we posted links to the survey on public venues, it is practically impossible to measure how many individuals we reached. The survey website page garnered 598 unique page views. Google Analytics defines this as *"Unique Pageviews is the number of sessions during which the specified page was viewed at least once"*. These page views led to 197 submitted responses; 6 of them were duplicates, while others contained impossible or invalid answers such as unclear experience or respondents claiming to be working with user stories since before the year of their introduction. In total, we retained 182 valid responses.

2.3 Follow-Up Interview Respondents

Out of the 119 respondents (65 %) who supplied their email address at the end of the survey, the authors identified 49 respondents that could potentially provide *opinionated* answers during a follow-up interview. We invited all respondents that either (i) provided very positive or very negative answers, (ii) gave varied answers to the Likert-type questions, or (iii) added a comment at the end of the survey. In total, 21 respondents participated, leading to a response rate of 43 %.

This group of respondents is quite diverse and its composition differs from that of the survey's respondents. Notable differences are that more practitioners participated that work in consultancy (9/21) and/or have the role of requirements engineer/business analyst (6/21). The average interviewee has 6 years of experience with user stories. Respondents originated from 7 different countries; 11 from the Netherlands, 5 from the United States of America, the remaining 5 were all from different countries: Argentina, Brazil, Canada, Portugal and the United Kingdom.

3 User Story Usage

This section reports on data collected related to RQ_1 on the use of user stories by practitioners. We examine and report on the first part of the survey results and highlight specific findings from the follow-up interviews. Our twelve key findings are marked within the text as F_1–F_{12}.

3.1 Respondent Context

As recommended by Cohn [6], user stories are primarily used in combination with Agile methods. Scrum in particular is used by the majority of respondents. We asked respondents to indicate both which software development methods they used in general, and in which methods they employed user stories. The majority indicate they work with Scrum (94 %), but Kanban (40 %) and waterfall (29 %) are popular as well. XP (13 %), V-Model (7 %), Spiral (3 %) and 14 other methods (9 %) are considerably less common. Responses to this question accentuate the tight coupling of user stories with Agile methods: 99 % of respondents that work with Scrum employ user stories - all respondents but two (F_1). As one follow-up interviewee noted: *"For me, user stories and Scrum are interconnected"*. Indeed, 17 out of 21 interviewees mention Scrum without it being a subject of discussion. Kanban and XP have a tight coupling as well: 79 % and 83 % of the respondents that use these software development methods do employ user stories. However, none of the interviewees mention either method during the interview. Users of waterfall and the V-model do not employ user stories often: 21 % and 31 % of them do so.

On average, respondents had 4 years of experience with user stories; 57 of them (31 %) had more than 5 years of experience. On average, the organizations of the respondents were working with user stories for slightly longer, 4.4 years; 64 (35 %) organizations were working with user stories for more than 5 years. Respondent roles include product manager (29 %), developer (21 %), requirements engineer (18 %), software architect/CTO (8 %), project manager (8 %) and other (16 %). Respondents work for fairly uniform organization types: software product (51 %), consultancy (20 %), custom software (19 %) and other (10 %). The organization sizes, however, are quite diverse: 1–9 (12 %), 10–49 (20 %), 50–249 (27 %), 250–499 (8 %) and 500+ (33 %).

Additionally, we asked respondents to self-assess their skill level. The average years of experience per skill level are as follows: Beginner - 1.91 (n = 34), Intermediate - 3.05 (n = 77), Advanced - 4.76 (n = 49), and Expert - 8.95 (n = 22). Surprisingly, the aggregate of our respondents did not fall victim to the Dunning-Kruger effect; a cognitive bias which causes individuals with low skill to overestimate their ability and performance in comparison to their highly skilled peers - and vice versa [15].

3.2 The Role of User Stories

After introductions, the first question of each follow-up interview was to describe the role of user stories in the interviewee's organization. In our 21 interviews, we collected as many different accounts of the role of user stories in their organization. The interviewees explanations range from very close to the approach described Cohn's book [6] to adaptations that are rather far from agile software development. The majority of interviewees, however, are somewhere in between because they have adapted user story theory to their own situational context. Nevertheless, all approaches have one crucial aspect in common: the user story is the most granular representation of a requirement that developers use to build new features.

3.3 Template

The use of a template when writing user stories can be considered standard industry practice - only 27 respondents (15 %) indicate they do not use a template. The most popular template is the 'original' one [6]. 59 % of respondents utilize the Connextra template (F_2): "As a ⟨role⟩, I want ⟨goal⟩, [so that ⟨benefit⟩]". An additional 10 % of respondents use the identical template, but without the "[so that ⟨benefit⟩]" clause. The remaining 32 respondents (18 %) are spread between 15 approaches, none of which have a significant share. One of these template omits the role, including only the what and the why.

In the follow-up interview, respondents were asked to explain whether they have a specific reason for using the template they use. Out of the 19 interviewees that use a template just one decided to study and select the most appropriate template for his situation. The remaining interviewees were taught or heard of a specific template at some point and never encountered the need to change to another template. This is likely a factor in explaining the prevalence of the Connextra template.

3.4 Quality Guidelines

The use of quality guidelines is commonplace among practitioners. The most well-known framework is INVEST [28], which posits that a good user story has the following characteristics: Independent, Negotiable, Valuable, Estimatable, Small and Testable. 33 % of respondents indicate they follow self-defined quality guidelines when writing user stories, while 23.5 % use the standardized INVEST approach. 39.5 % of respondents do not validate their user stories with any form of quality guidelines. The remainder use alternatives, or indicate that it depends on the situation (4 %).

When asked to explain what their self-defined quality guidelines entail, all 10 interviewees admit they do not have a well-defined, structured list of concerns they consult when writing user stories. Instead, they rely on the experience of the user story writer and multiple rounds of peer review to ensure the quality of their user stories. Interviewees that do not use quality guidelines, indicate this is not a conscious decision but rather that they are not aware of quality guidelines like INVEST (F_3).

4 Perception of User Story Effectiveness

This section investigates RQ_2: how practitioners perceive the effectiveness of user stories. We examine the second part of the survey to report on how practitioners perceive the impact of user stories, templates and quality guidelines in terms of their productivity and work deliverable quality.

As expected, the collected data is not normally distributed, making parametric statistics that rely on testing means inappropriate for our Likert-type questions [5]. Instead, we treat the answers as ordinal data. To report on central tendency and variability of ordinal data, Boone and Boone [4] recommend using the median or mode and frequencies. To confirm that the variability is from independent populations, Boone and Boone recommend using the statistical χ-square test for independence. Throughout the remainder of this section, applying this test enables us to determine whether a specific variable influences the outcome of the Likert-type questions.

4.1 User Stories in Isolation

Both the median and mode of the Likert-style questions indicate that practitioners *agree* that representing requirements as user stories and following a template increase their work productivity and deliverable quality. For quality guidelines, both median and mode are *neutral* for gained productivity and quality. For more insights regarding practitioners' opinion on user stories we examine the frequency distributions in Fig. 1. In the subsequent subsections, we analyze

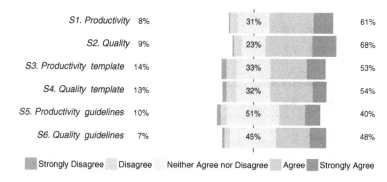

Fig. 1. Perception of user story effectiveness. The shown percentages (left-to-right) refer to Strongly Disagree + Disagree, Neither Agree nor Disagree and Agree + Strongly Agree, respectively. The same format is used in the following charts

specific slices of the data using frequency distributions and the χ-square test for independence.

Examining the frequency distribution of our respondents' answers one observation stands out: only a fraction of respondents perceive user stories, templates and quality guidelines to be detrimental to their work productivity and deliverable quality (the percentages on the left of Fig. 1 are all between 7% and 14%). Even when we consider neutral answers as negative, the majority of respondents agree or strongly agree that user stories and templates improve work productivity ($\mathbf{S_1}$: 61%, $\mathbf{S_3}$: 53%) and quality ($\mathbf{S_2}$: 68%, $\mathbf{S_4}$: 54%). Respondents are ambivalent about quality guidelines: 51% and 45% indicate they neither agree nor disagree that quality guidelines improve work productivity $\mathbf{S_5}$ or quality $\mathbf{S_6}$. During the follow-up interviews, respondents were asked to clarify their answers. From their comments on user stories in general, we present the following common sentiments to show how the interviewees perceive user stories.

The Right Software ($\mathbf{F_4}$): 10 interviewees mention that user stories are an enabler for developing the *right* software. In their experience, the technical quality of software does not improve by using user stories and neither do they directly impact the speed of software development. In fact, user stories require more work upfront because the stakeholders have to decompose a requirement into small, comprehensible chunks. This decomposition, however, forces all stakeholders to think and talk about the details of a requirement. This builds a common understanding within the team of what the end-user expects of the software. Thanks to the identification of the *right* requirements, developers are enabled to create the *right* software. According to the literature, this may prevent defects which cost 10–200 times as much to correct later in the software development lifecycle [3,22]. One interviewee reported that user stories force developers to meet the customer numerous times, resulting in code that is very close to customer expectations. This improves productivity, despite the significant amount of time that is devoted to interacting with the customer.

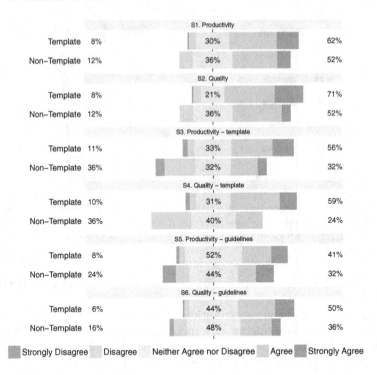

Fig. 2. Perception of respondents that use a template and those that do not.

"User Stories Optimize for Happiness" [2] **(F_5):** 5 interviewees do not view productivity or quality gains as essential contributions of user stories. Other aspects of agile development methods have a bigger impact on these concerns. The real advantage of user stories is that stakeholders enjoy working with user stories, fostering a pleasant work environment.

4.2 The Role of Using a Template

The first data slice we examine concerns respondents that follow a template for user stories (n = 155) versus those who do not (n = 27). The frequency distributions in Fig. 2 show that respondents using a template more often agree that user stories improve work deliverable quality (71 % vs. 52 %). However, because the two populations are not independent in a statistically significant manner (α = .187), we cannot claim that respondents who use a template are more positive towards user stories.

For the statements on the impact of templates on work productivity (S_3) and quality (S_4), the populations are statistically independent with α's of .02 and .00. Indeed, the difference is striking on both the negative (11 % and 9 % vs. 33 % and 37 %) and positive (57 % and 60 % vs. 30 % and 22 %) sides of the distribution. These results indicate that respondents that use templates agree considerably more often that using a template contributes to productivity and work deliverable quality. The question is, however, if this difference is an objective judgment or is rather due to the fact that the respondents are persuaded by the choice of using a template. During the follow-up interviews, we asked respondents to clarify why or how they believe that templates contribute to work productivity and quality. They shared the following comments:

A Template, not *the* Template (F_6): 12 interviewees mention the beneficial impact of a standard structure for defining user stories. Recall, however, that in Sect. 2.3 all interviewees but one did not have an explicit motivation for using the template they use. 3 respondents remark that it does not matter which particular template is used. The use of *a template*, any template is what makes the difference. A single, agreed upon template ensures that everyone within a team works in the same way. When a team can rely upon a standardized structure, their alignment improves overall work productivity and quality. This quote by one respondent effectively illustrates why: *"It's not the template that improves quality, it's what we're doing - we're sharing requirements and a template makes that easy to do and more likely that we'll do it"*.

The why is Essential (F_7): While the most popular template for user stories considers the *"[so that ⟨benefit⟩]"* or *why* section as optional, our respondents emphasize the importance of this part for reaping the full rewards of user stories. They attribute a variety of benefits to the inclusion of the purpose of a user story, which lead to work productivity and quality improvements. Adding the *why* part: (1) alleviates confusion among stakeholders, (2) reduces the amount of discussion necessary and (3) provides developers with autonomy in their work. This is, however, easier said than done. The *why* is difficult to find, as the following quote demonstrates: *"Typically, the why question is correctly answered if after the initial answer, you ask 'why?' again for three more times"*.

A developer with a negative opinion of user stories shared that in his experience business people will abuse a template to formulate the same old requirement in a different format. He complained that user stories become *"a blanket way to generally describe what the solution is the company has already defined for you"*, which conflicts with the principle that requirements should be problem-oriented [21, 32].

4.3   The Impact of Using Quality Guidelines

The second data slice looks at the perceptions of respondents that follow self-defined quality guidelines (n = 60), INVEST (n = 43) or none (n = 72)[1]. Examining the frequency distributions in Fig. 3, we see that respondents that follow quality guidelines are more positive than those that do not (F_8). The χ-square tests for independence of S_1, S_4, S_5 and S_6 are statistically significant; meaning that we can claim that respondents using quality guidelines more often agree that user stories and quality guidelines improve productivity, and templates and quality guidelines further improve work deliverable quality.

---

[1] Note that 7 responses are excluded. These respondents gave unique 'other' answers, whose samples are too small for statistical analysis.

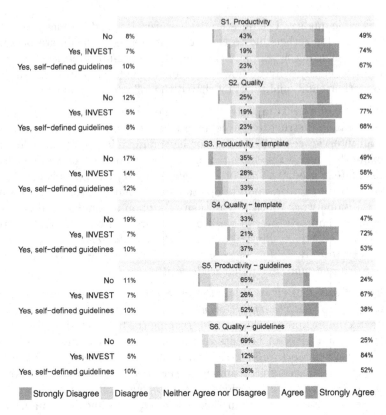

Fig. 3. Perception of respondents that use INVEST, self-defined quality guidelines or none.

The positive attitude of respondents that apply INVEST is remarkable. During the interviews, these respondents were capable of effectively arguing both for and against any productivity and quality gains. Their ideas can be summarized as follows:

INVEST is not a Checklist (F_9): 3 interviewees mention that although the INVEST mnemonic can be used as a checklist, interviewees do not use it as such. Instead, the six characteristics of a good user story are internalized by the team and whenever a user story violates INVEST, a team member brings this up for discussion.

INVEST is Useful for Inexperienced Teams (F_{10}): 2 interviewees indicate they primarily use INVEST as a training tool for inexperienced teams. INVEST's comprehensiveness is an effective starting-point for getting product owners started and the development team to understand how to judge user stories. After two or three months, however, stakeholders have sufficient experience with writing and interpreting user stories that the necessity of INVEST diminishes.

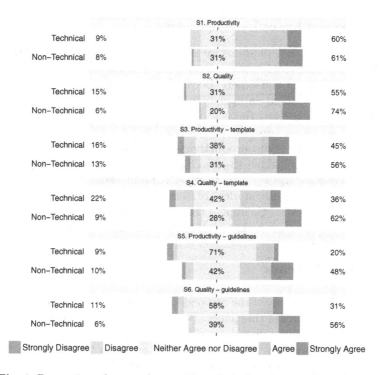

Fig. 4. Perception of respondents with technical and non technical roles.

4.4   Technical Vs. Non Technical Roles

To analyze the difference in perception between technical (n = 55) and non-technical stakeholders (n = 127) we categorize respondents by their role. Because the majority of respondents chose from the pre-defined list of roles, we could easily do this by designating roles containing the term 'software' as technical and those without that term as non-technical. The former primarily consists of developers, software architects and CTOs, while the latter includes everything else such as consultants, product managers and the occasional agile coach.

Approximately 60 % of both stakeholder types agree with S_1 that user stories improve productivity, while for the other 5 statements non-technical stakeholders are considerably more positive (Fig. 4). The average positivity difference between technical and non-technical stakeholders is 22 %. For S_4 ($\Delta = 26\,\%$), S_5 ($\Delta = 28\,\%$) and S_6 ($\Delta = 25\,\%$) the populations are independent with statistical significance (α's of .02, .001 and .003) (F_{11}). During follow-up interviews technical respondents were ambivalent about the impact of user stories on their work productivity and quality. In their experience, software development is not necessarily significantly quicker nor do they encounter less bugs.

4.5 Influence of Expertise Judgement

For one of the contextual questions we asked respondents to self-assess their user story skill level. They could choose from 5 levels of expertise: novice, beginner, intermediate, advanced and expert. Because only 2 people chose novice, for this analysis we counted them as beginners. Studying the frequency distributions in Fig. 5, a pattern catches the eye: as respondents gain more expertise they select *neither agree nor disagree* less frequently, instead opting to agree that work deliverable quality and productivity improves thanks to user stories (S_1 and S_2) and quality guidelines (S_5 and S_6) (F_{12}). This difference is particularly striking when comparing beginners to experts. From a statistical perspective, the answers to S_1 and S_2 on user stories are from independent populations for all four expertise levels. This statistic implies that the difference in their answers cannot be attributed to chance, but that each population has a different perception.

5 Validity Threats

External Validity: Many of the respondents to the survey came from the direct networks of the authors of this paper. Because our research group is focused on the software industry, 93 respondents (51 %) are employed by a product software company. Furthermore, 98 respondents (54 %) are from the Netherlands. Both have the potential to introduce a bias, which would impact the validity of the results. Examining their frequency distributions [20], we see that the percentage differences in the two comparisons are relatively small. Indeed, the χ-square tests for both threats results in significance values between .36 and .78, which is far above the significance threshold of .05. This means that both population pairs are not significantly different and these threats to validity do not hold.

In terms of its composition, the interviewee population is not representative of the survey respondents. In particular, the number of vocally negative interviewees is underrepresented. Although all negative survey respondents were invited for a follow-up interview, there is likely a self-selection process at play. To mitigate this issue, we positively discriminated remarks from negative respondents for inclusion resulting in the abuse paragraph in Sect. 4.2.

Internal Validity: One of the pre-requisites for participating in the survey was that the respondent expresses requirements as user stories. This decision introduces a selection bias for the respondent population. Potential respondents that decided not to employ user stories or stopped employing user stories are excluded from expressing their views. Thus, our results are generalizable only to user story practitioners.

The follow-up interviews were semi-structured. When an interviewee gave a long answer, the interviewer would summarize the answer and confirm with the interviewee if it was correct. In a small number of cases an experimenter bias occurred, including additional information in the summarization, followed by a potential acquiescence bias - better known as yea-saying. When detected during categorization of the transcriptions, these statements have been ignored.

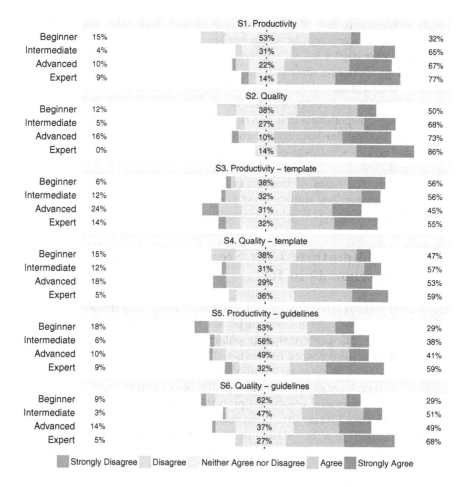

Fig. 5. Attitude differences per expertise level of respondents.

Construct Validity: The survey purposefully did not clearly define what we mean by *productivity* and *work deliverable quality*. Although metrics for quality and productivity in RE exist (e.g., [19]), these metrics were not appropriate for this survey because of our focus on practitioners' *perception*, and there is no general agreement yet on which specific factors do determine these qualities in RE. Additionally, a key phrase in S_{3-6} was *further* as in "using a template for my user stories *further* increases my productivity". However, it is impossible to confirm that all respondents fully understood the nuance that they were supposed to evaluate *'using a template'* disjoint from the user story concept itself. Although a significant threat to validity, we have reason to believe this does not invalidate the results. When the researcher put extra emphasis on this distinction during the follow-up interviews, none of the respondents indicated they misunderstood the question. Nevertheless, we cannot claim that the

Likert-type questions are 100% mutually exclusive and exhaustive. Readers should view the survey results as an exploratory evaluation of practitioner's perception of user stories.

The survey contained questions on the subjective terms *expertise*, *quality guidelines*, *role*, *software development method* and *template*. To ensure a uniform interpretation and response, each question was accompanied by standard answers. Because respondents first had to read these, all free-form 'other' answers are expressed in a similar form to the examples. In the case of *quality guidelines*, an additional link to a webpage explaining the INVEST framework was included for additional context.

Furthermore, the focus of this study was the *card* aspect of user stories. We purposefully put less emphasis on the *conversation* and *confirmation* as explained by Ron Jeffries [13], which we will study in greater detail in the future.

6   Related Literature: User Stories, and Perception and Experiments in RE

Between 2003 and 2013, the adoption of user stories has grown tremendously [14]. In agile software development user stories are the predominant method to capture requirements [29]. Despite their popularity, research efforts concerning user stories are limited. Recent work has revisited user stories from a conceptual perspective. Wautelet et al. propose a unified model for user stories with associated semantics based on a review of 85 user story templates and accompanying example stories [30]. Gomez and colleagues propose a method for identifying dependencies between User Stories [10]. In an earlier paper, we presented a conceptual model that characterizes the structure of a valid user story and decomposes its parts linguistically. This conceptual model is the foundation upon which we built the Quality User Story Framework that proposes quality criteria that a user story should adhere to [21].

Liskin et al. investigate the expected implementation duration of user story as a characteristic of granularity. They find that in practitioners' experience combining the effort estimation of two small, clear-cut user stories produces more accurate results than when estimating a single, larger, more opaque user story [18]. Multiple authors have linked user stories with goals. Lin et al. [17] propose a mixed top-down and bottom-up method where an initial top-down analysis of the high-level goals is complemented by a bottom-up approach that derives more refined goals by analyzing user stories. A similar attempt has been implemented in the US2StarTool [23], which derives skeletons of i^* goal models starting from user stories. The key difference is that these models represent user stories as social dependencies from the role of the user stories to the system actor.

The number of papers that examine how practitioners use and perceive requirements engineering methods and artifacts is limited. Rouibah and Al-Rafee conducted a similar study to ours, investigating the "awareness", "use" and "perceived value generated" of 19 RE techniques based on survey responses by 87 practitioners from Kuwait [27]. Their findings include that the most used requirements elicitation techniques are interviews and surveys, but that the highest perceived value comes from decision trees, goal-oriented elicitation and prototyping. Other studies that study perception and use in the context of RE have a different focus. Hofmann and Lehner report on the self-perceived quality of RE service and RE products within RE teams without distinguishing between RE methods [12]. Abrahão et al. present a method to evaluate requirements modeling methods by gauging end-user perceptions, an adaptation of the Method Evaluation Model, and apply it to a Rational Unified Process extension that provides specific techniques for specifying functional requirements [1].

Nevertheless, the effectiveness of an RE method or technique is a frequent subject of academic literature. In fact, up to four different systematic reviews are available for some subdomains of RE. For example, Dieste and Juristo conducted a systematic review on the effectiveness of requirements elicitation techniques and found sufficient evidence to formulate five usage guidelines [9]. One example: unstructured interviews output more complete information than introspective techniques such as protocol analysis. Condori-Ferandez et al. did a systematic mapping study on empirical evaluation studies of software requirements specification techniques and found that most papers report on experiments that took place in academic environments [7]. The number of experiments conducted with actual practitioners is low. For example, Cruz-Lemus et al. conducted an experiment with practitioners to assess how composite states impact the understandability of UML statecharts [8]. They find the results are slightly more outspoken with a population of practitioners than a population of students. Penzenstadler, Eckhardt and Fernández even conducted two replication studies to validate their earlier evaluation of an artifact-based RE approach and tool [24]. These studies confirm that their simpler artifact model improves the quality of the created artifacts and ease of use.

7 Discussion and Conclusion

This paper has explored how practitioners that already employ user stories use and perceive them. Both the data from our survey with 182 valid responses and comments by follow-up interviewees indicate that software professionals are predominantly positive about *user stories* as well as the associated constructs *templates* and *quality guidelines*. Very few practitioners are downright negative about user stories. Our key findings on user stories are that:

F_1 Most of the user story adopters (94 %) use them in combination with Scrum.
F_2 The most prevalent user story template is the 'original' one proposed by Connextra.
F_3 Self-defined quality guidelines are unstructured and not using any quality guidelines is not a conscious decision.
F_4 The simple structure of user stories enables developing the *right* software, for it facilitates creating a common understanding concerning the requirement.

F₅ Stakeholders enjoy working with user stories, as they foster a pleasant workplace.

F₆ Using *a template* benefits RE, not *the template* that the team chooses.

F₇ Specifying the *why* part of a user story is essential for requirements quality.

F₈ Practitioners who use the INVEST quality guidelines are significantly more positive about the impact of user stories on productivity and the impact of templates on work deliverable quality.

F₉ INVEST is not a checklist, but a work guideline each team member should adopt.

F₁₀ INVEST is particularly useful for inexperienced teams. The necessity of INVEST diminishes for experienced teams.

F₁₁ Technical stakeholders are less positive about the effectiveness of templates and quality guidelines than non-technical stakeholders.

F₁₂ Practitioners with more expertise with user stories perceive them more positively.

We discuss F_4, F_7, and F_8 in more detail. Throughout the interviews, respondents repeatedly mention that user stories help them create the right software. By requiring all stakeholders to think and talk about the details of a requirement, user stories build a common understanding of what the end-user expects of the software within a team. This identification of the right requirements enables development of the right software. This prevents expensive rework, improving productivity and work deliverable quality. Based on this finding, we hypothesize that using user stories reduces software development costs. An associated finding is the importance of the *why* part of a user story to deliver a common understanding and to support development of the right software. This confirms the fundamental theories in RE on the importance of the 'why' for software (process) analysis [16,25,31].

There also appears to be a correlation between relying on quality guidelines and the perception of user stories. Respondents that use INVEST are particularly positive in comparison to those that do not apply quality guidelines at all. A clear indication that having a structured list of characteristics of a good user story is beneficial. Recall, however, that our interviewees' self-defined quality guidelines are unstructured, informal approaches and that they are unaware of structured approaches like INVEST. Because of this, we call for an increase in the diffusion of knowledge concerning quality guidelines in order to further improve the positive perception of user stories.

This evaluation of practitioner's use and perception of user stories opens avenues for future research. To test whether adopting user stories reduces software development costs, we are planning to conduct a series of experiments. To improve the diffusion of structured quality guidelines like INVEST or the QUS Framework [21] we need to conduct a more thorough evaluation of their impact on software development. In particular, studies that take into account the opinion of practitioners that chose not to employ user stories or stopped employing user stories would fill a gap created by this work. Furthermore, despite user stories' increasing popularity, little to no advanced methods and tools originating from academia support them. As adoption of user stories increases, the importance of and opportunities for designing advanced methods and tools for user stories intensifies. We call for academia to focus more resources on user stories and its related concepts.

Acknowledgements. The authors would like to thank all survey respondents for participating in our research, the three respondents to the pilot survey as well as Leo Pruijt and Erik Jagroep for reviewing drafts of this paper.

References

1. Abrahão, S., Insfran, E., Carsí, J.A., Genero, M.: Evaluating requirements modeling methods based on user perceptions: a family of experiments. Inf. Sci. **181**(16), 3356–3378 (2011)
2. Bedell, K.: Opinions on Opinionated Software. Linux J. **2006**(147), 1, July 2006. http://dl.acm.org/citation.cfm?id=1145562.1145563
3. Boehm, B.W.: Understanding and controlling software costs. J. Parametrics **8**(1), 32–68 (1988)
4. Boone, H.N., Boone, D.A.: Analyzing likert data. J. Extension **50**(2), 1–5 (2012)
5. Clason, D.L., Dormody, T.J.: Analyzing data measured by individual likert-type items. J. Agric. Educ. **35**(4), 31–35 (1994)
6. Cohn, M.: User stories applied: for agile software development. Addison Wesley, Redwood City (2004)
7. Condori-Fernandez, N., Daneva, M., Sikkel, K., Wieringa, R., Dieste, O., Pastor, O.: A systematic mapping study on empirical evaluation of software requirements specifications techniques. In: Proceedings of the ESEM, pp. 502–505. IEEE Computer Society (2009)
8. Cruz-Lemus, J.A., Genero, M., Morasca, S., Piattini, M.: Using practitioners for assessing the understandability of UML statechart diagrams with composite states. In: Hainaut, J.-L., et al. (eds.) ER Workshops 2007. LNCS, vol. 4802, pp. 213–222. Springer, Heidelberg (2007)
9. Dieste, O., Juristo, N.: Systematic review and aggregation of empirical studies on elicitation techniques. IEEE Trans. Softw. Eng. **37**(2), 283–304 (2011)
10. Gomez, A., Rueda, G., Alarcón, P.P.: A systematic and lightweight method to identify dependencies between user stories. In: Sillitti, A., Martin, A., Wang, X., Whitworth, E. (eds.) XP 2010. LNBIP, vol. 48, pp. 190–195. Springer, Heidelberg (2010)
11. Hoda, R., Kruchten, P., Noble, J., Marshall, S.: Agility in context. In: Proceedings of OOPSLA, pp. 74–88. ACM (2010)
12. Hofmann, H., Lehner, F.: Requirements engineering as a success factor in software projects. IEEE Softw. **18**(4), 58–66 (2001)
13. Jeffries, R.: Essential XP: Card, Conversation, and Confirmation, August 2001
14. Kassab, M.: The changing landscape of requirements engineering practices over the past decade. In: Proceedings of EmpiRE, pp. 1–8. IEEE (2015)
15. Kruger, J., Dunning, D.: Unskilled and unaware of it: how difficulties in recognizing one's own incompetence lead to inflated self-assessments. J. Pers. Soc. Psychol. **77**(6), 1121–1134 (1999)
16. Lee, J., Lai, K.Y.: What's in design rationale? Hum. Comput. Interact. **6**(3), 251–280 (1991)

17. Lin, J., Yu, H., Shen, Z., Miao, C.: Using goal net to model user stories in agile software development. In: Proceedings of the SNPD, pp. 1–6. IEEE (2014)

18. Liskin, O., Pham, R., Kiesling, S., Schneider, K.: Why we need a granularity concept for user stories. In: Cantone, G., Marchesi, M. (eds.) XP 2014. LNBIP, vol. 179, pp. 110–125. Springer, Heidelberg (2014)

19. Lombriser, P., Dalpiaz, F., Lucassen, G., Brinkkemper, S.: Gamified requirements engineering: model and experimentation. In: Proceedings of the REFSQ (2016)

20. Lucassen, G.: Materials of survey and interviews on user story practice (2015). http://www.staff.science.uu.nl/~lucas001/user_story_materials.zip

21. Lucassen, G., Dalpiaz, F., van der Werf, J.M., Brinkkemper, S.: Forging high-quality user stories: towards a discipline for agile requirements. In: Proceedings of the RE, pp. 126–135. IEEE (2015)

22. McConnell, S.: An ounce of prevention. IEEE Softw. 18(3), 5–7 (2001)

23. Mesquita, R., Jaqueira, A., Agra, C., Lucena, M., Alencar, F.: US2StarTool: generating i* models from user stories. In: Proceedings of the iStar (2015)

24. Penzenstadler, B., Eckhardt, J., Mendez Fernandez, D.: Two replication studies for evaluating artefact models in re: results and lessons learnt. In: Proceedings of the RESER, pp. 66–75 (2013)

25. Potts, C., Bruns, G.: Recording the reasons for design decisions. In: Proceedings of the ICSE, pp. 418–427. IEEE Computer Society (1988)

26. Ramesh, B., Cao, L., Baskerville, R.: Agile requirements engineering practices and challenges: an empirical study. Inf. Syst. J. 20(5), 449–480 (2010)

27. Rouibah, K., Al-Rafee, S.: Requirement engineering elicitation methods: a kuwaiti empirical study about familiarity, usage and perceived value. Inf. Manage. Comput. Secur. 17(3), 192–217 (2009)

28. Wake, B.: INVEST in Good Stories, and SMART Tasks (2003). http://xp123.com/articles/invest-in-good-stories-and-smart-tasks/. Accessed, 18 February 2015

29. Wang, X., Zhao, L., Wang, Y., Sun, J.: The role of requirements engineering practices in agile development: an empirical study. In: Zowghi, D., Jin, Z. (eds.) APRES 2014. CCIS, vol. 432, pp. 195–209. Springer, Heidelberg (2014)

30. Wautelet, Y., Heng, S., Kolp, M., Mirbel, I.: Unifying and extending user story models. In: Jarke, M., Mylopoulos, J., Quix, C., Rolland, C., Manolopoulos, Y., Mouratidis, H., Horkoff, J. (eds.) CAiSE 2014. LNCS, vol. 8484, pp. 211–225. Springer, Heidelberg (2014)

31. Yu, E.S.K., Mylopoulos, J.: Understanding "Why" in software process modelling, analysis, and design. In: Proceedings of the ICSE, pp. 159–168. IEEE (1994)

32. Zave, P., Jackson, M.: Four dark corners of requirements engineering. ACM Trans. Softw. Eng. Methodol. 6(1), 1–30 (1997)

Requirements Engineering
Foundations

Foundations for Transparency Requirements Engineering

Mahmood Hosseini$^{(\boxtimes)}$, Alimohammad Shahri, Keith Phalp, and Raian Ali

Bournemouth University, Poole, UK
{mhosseini,ashahri,kphalp,rali}@bournemouth.ac.uk

Abstract. [**Context & motivation**] Transparency is becoming an essential requirement for business information systems. Transparency is advocated to inspire trust,. increase accountability and reduce corruption. However, it may also lead to negative side effects such as information overload, bias and unnecessary pressure on stakeholders. [**Question/problem**] Despite its distinct characteristics and importance, transparency is still a limitedly explored concept in software engineering and information systems literature, and is often fragmented across adjacent concepts such as privacy, secrecy and regulatory requirements. This limits its representation level and impedes its management. [**Principal ideas/results**] In this paper, we propose four facets for transparency and illustrate their usefulness in guiding transparency requirements engineering. [**Contribution**] These facets help clarify the concept of transparency and provide foundations for its management in information systems engineering as a distinct notion. Initiatives like the open data movement add to the timeliness and potential impact of our contribution.

Keywords: Transparency requirements · Stakeholder transparency · Meaningful transparency · Useful transparency · Information quality

1 Introduction

Transparency can be defined as the open flow of information [6] and the release of information by institutions that is relevant to evaluating these institutions [3]. The positive connotation associated with transparency implies that it is a desirable quality for information. However, transparency has been shown to be an undesirable information quality in certain cases. For example, it is indicated that increased transparency in the relationship between buyers and suppliers may bring about some negative effects such as unwanted exposure of information to competitors [9]. As a result, it is necessary to take precautionary steps towards providing transparency in order to minimise such adverse effects.

In the domain of information systems, transparency is currently an underresearched topic. There is a lack of conceptual models and rigorous methods for engineering transparency as a requirement. Transparency is often studied as an element of other requirements concepts, such as privacy, security and regulatory

© Springer International Publishing Switzerland 2016
M. Daneva and O. Pastor (Eds.): REFSQ 2016, LNCS 9619, pp. 225–231, 2016.
DOI: 10.1007/978-3-319-30282-9_15

requirements. However, in order to better manage transparency requirements of stakeholders, there is a need to study it as a first-class requirement concept.

In this paper, we propose four facets to serve the engineering of transparency requirements in a business information system. These facets relate to the stakeholders in the process and the information flow amongst them, the meaningfulness of the information made transparent, the usefulness of such information for a particular audience, and the quality of the disclosed information. These facets are meant to provide a baseline to measure and manage transparency as a first-class requirements engineering concept. We deduce our facets upon a thorough analysis of a wide range of studies on transparency in multiple disciplines including politics, human relations and psychology. The timeliness of our contribution stems from global trends, e.g., open government, to make *quality* information available in a *meaningful* and *useful* style to the *right audience*.

2   Motivation

A software system is transparent if it makes the information it deals with transparent along with its internal functioning process [13]. In requirements engineering, transparency is generally viewed as a non-functional requirement (NFR) because it is orthogonal to software functionality since it can be viewed as a quality issue, and because software can work with or without it [13]. Furthermore, it is advocated that transparency has to be managed in the context of requirements specification [13]. In one of the early works on transparency as an NFR [2], it is argued that transparency requirements can be managed using the NFR Framework and i^* modelling. The work concludes that i^* modelling is not the final answer to transparency, and certain augmentations may be needed for managing transparency requirements more efficiently.

Furthermore, the concept of transparency ladder is introduced [13] which contains the following five non-functional requirements of accessibility, usability, informativeness, understandability, and auditability, which must be achieved in order to reach transparency. This ladder, however, tends to refer to information quality attributes [10] that must be fulfilled, rather than steps to achieving transparency. Using the NFR Framework, a software transparency softgoal interdependency graph (SIG) is also proposed [13].

3   Four Facets of Transparency

Based on an extensive literature study on transparency, we identified four facets of transparency, as depicted in Fig. 1, which can help requirements engineers in the identification, analysis and specification of transparency requirements. Furthermore, these facets facilitate the modelling of transparency requirements, which can be used for conceptualisation and automated analysis of transparency.

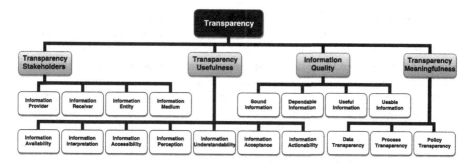

Fig. 1. The four facets of transparency

3.1 Transparency Stakeholders

In order to understand transparency requirements, one essential prerequisite is to identify all the relevant actors in an information exchange. Amongst other things, the identification of these actors makes it possible to understand where the information originates, which actors provide the information, which actors receive it, and which channels are used to relay information.

An initial model of information exchange consists of two entities, **information provider** or source and **information receiver** [16]. The source disseminates the information to the receiver, and the receiver provides feedback based on that information to the source. This model is useful for modelling information exchange, but for the study of transparency two key elements are missing.

The first one is the **information medium** which relays the information. The consideration of an information medium as a technical actor is essential because it is where information can be stored and managed, and is therefore prone to information leakage and unwanted transparency. The example of Ashley Madison website is one of the many examples depicting the significance of information exchange media in a transparency model of information exchange.

The second missing element is **information entity**, i.e., the entity whose information is being exchanged. More often than not, information providers provide information which involves other entities, e.g., another person or organisation. It is therefore essential to consider them in a transparency model of information exchange.

Furthermore, the nature of exchanged information must be considered in a transparency model of information exchange. Not all the information in this model relates to transparency, i.e., information may or may not be related to transparency. These are the concepts which should be considered in a transparency model of information exchange [7,8].

3.2 Transparency Meaningfulness

Transparency requirements can be divided into three main categories [1], which represent how meaningful the provided transparency is. These categories are meant to deal with primarily three questions and provide answers to them:

- **Data transparency**, *or questions relating to data, content, and information:*
  These questions primarily answer <u>what</u> information is needed and <u>who</u> are
  the stakeholders in the context of transparency. For example, in an online
  mail service platform, data transparency reveals whether secure mails are
  encrypted, or whether attachments are scanned for viruses or not.
- **Process transparency**, *or questions relating to processes, behaviours and
  interactions:* These questions primarily answer <u>how</u> something is performed
  in the context of transparency. For example, in an online mail service platform, process transparency reveals how secure mails are encrypted, or how
  attachments are scanned for viruses.
- **Policy transparency**, *or questions relating to intentions, policies and decision making:* These questions primarily answer <u>why</u> an action is performed in
  the context of transparency. For example, in an online mail service platform,
  policy transparency reveals why despite the impact on the delivery speed of
  the mail, encryption is needed for delivering secure mail, or why virus scanning
  is necessary for attachments.

In [1], it is pointed out that process transparency usually requires data transparency, and policy transparency usually requires data and process transparency.
For example, revealing why encryption is required for the delivery of secure mail
reveals the fact that secure mails are encrypted, and may also reveal some information about the process of mail encryption.

3.3 Transparency Usefulness

Useful transparency can only be achieved when it enables stakeholders to make
decisions based on the provided information and act upon them. For example,
in the sociological and psychological sense, transparency is defined as gaining
information and knowledge about the environment in order to prepare actions
and decisions [4]. However, there are many steps between information availability
and information actionability to be catered for. These steps are as follows:

- **Information availability** means that the information provider must disclose
  information for the use of the information receivers.
- **Information interpretation** refers to the interpretation of available information by information providers in a way that can be understood easily by
  information receivers.
- **Information accessibility** refers to the degree to which information can
  be easily located by information receivers, and is sometimes referred to as
  information visibility [12].
- **Information perception** refers to information receivers' perception of the
  transparency provided by the information. It acts at the cognitive level of
  stakeholders and is therefore difficult to assess [17].
- **Information understandability** means that for achieving useful transparency, the perceived information should also be understood and comprehended by information receivers. Therefore, understandability is sometimes
  considered as one of the two crucial dimensions of transparency [6].

- **Information acceptance** implies either information receivers' perception of information matches their beliefs, in which case the new information confirms it, or that their perception of information does not match their beliefs, but the new information changes those beliefs nonetheless.
- **Information actionability**, also referred to as informed decision making, emphasises that transparency becomes useful when the provided information to information receivers enables them to act upon it, make informed decisions, and therefore make use of the information [11].

There is a substantial difference between meaningful transparency and useful transparency. Meaningful transparency argues that stakeholders must know the actions and reasons behind the provided information, (e.g., as expressed by [5]), while useful transparency discusses that information provision should lead to stakeholders' actionability and help their decision-making, or facilitate change in their perception of the information provider (e.g., as expressed by [15]).

3.4   Information Quality in Transparency

Information quality in transparency is a crucial facet, as without it, transparency can hardly be reached. The literature on transparency does discuss the importance of information quality and provides some facets for it [5,14]. However, the inter-dependencies between these information quality dimensions and other facets of transparency have not been investigated, e.g., information believability, as an information quality dimension, has a clear link with information acceptance as a step in transparency usefulness. Furthermore, there is currently a lack of research on how these information quality dimensions should be fulfilled and by which stakeholders, and how their fulfilment can be assured. In the following, we briefly discuss four categories of information quality which can be used in transparency and the dimensions associated with them [10]:

- **Sound information** represents the quality of the information supplied by the information provider, and consists of the following information quality dimensions: *free-of-error, concise representation, completeness,* and *consistent representation.*
- **Dependable information** represents the quality of the service in providing information by the information provider, and consists of the following information quality dimensions: *timeliness* and *security.*
- **Useful information** represents the meeting/exceeding of the information receiver's expectations in the supplied information quality, and consists of the following information quality dimensions: *appropriate amount, relevancy, understandability, interpretability,* and *objectivity.*
- **Usable information** represents the meeting/exceeding of the information receiver's expectations in information provision service, and consists of the following information quality dimensions: *believability, accessibility, ease of manipulation, reputation,* and *value-added.*

4 Conclusion

In this paper, four facets for engineering transparency as a first-class requirement were discussed. These facets are meant to provide a foundation for transparency as an emerging software requirement in business information systems. They cover the level of stakeholders' engagement in transparency, the level of meaningfulness of the information provided to stakeholders, the steps to take in order to achieve useful transparency, and the information quality for transparency. As part of the future research, the authors will provide reference models based on these facets, and will build a modelling language based on these reference models.

Acknowledgements. The research is supported by an FP7 Marie Curie CIG grant (the SOCIAD project).

References

1. Bannister, F., Connolly, R.: The trouble with transparency: a critical review of openness in e-government. Policy Internet **3**(1), 1–30 (2011)
2. Cappelli, C., do Prado Leite, J.C.S., Oliveira, A.d.P.A.: Exploring business process transparency concepts. In: 15th RE Conference, pp. 389–390 (2007)
3. Florini, A., Birdsall, N., Flynn, S., Haufler, V., Lipton, D., Morrow, D., Sharma, S.: Does the invisible hand need a transparent glove? the politics of transparency. In: World Banks Annual Conference on Development Economics, pp. 163–184 (2000)
4. Frentrup, M., Theuvsen, L.: Transparency in supply chains: is trust a limiting factor. In: Fritz, M., Rickert, U., Schiefer, G. (eds.) Trust and Risk in Business Networks, pp. 65–74. ILB-Press, Bonn (2006)
5. Griffith, J.C.: Beyond transparency: New standards for legislative information systems. Citeseer (2006)
6. Holzner, B., Holzner, L.: Transparency in Global Change: The Vanguard of the Open Society. University of Pittsburgh Press, Pittsburgh (2006)
7. Hosseini, M., Shahri, A., Phalp, K., Ali, R.: Towards engineering transparency as a requirement in socio-technical systems. In: 23rd RE Conference (2015)
8. Hosseini, M., Shahri, A., Phalp, K., Ali, R.: Transparency as a requirement. In: 21st REFSQ Conference - Poster and Demo Track (2015)
9. Hultman, J., Axelsson, B.: Towards a typology of transparency for marketing management research. Ind. Mark. Manage. **36**(5), 627–635 (2007)
10. Kahn, B.K., Strong, D.M., Wang, R.Y.: Information quality benchmarks: product and service performance. Commun. ACM **45**(4), 184–192 (2002)
11. McManus, T., Holtzman, Y., Lazarus, H., Anderberg, J., Simon, C.: Corporate information transparency: the synthesis of internal and external information streams. J. Manage. Dev. **25**(10), 1029–1031 (2006)
12. Michener, G., Bersch, K.: Conceptualizing the quality of transparency. In: 1st Global Conference on Transparency (2011)
13. do Prado Leite, J.C.S., Cappelli, C.: Software transparency. Bus. Inf. Syst. Eng. **2**(3), 127–139 (2010)
14. Rawlins, B.: Give the emperor a mirror: toward developing a stakeholder measurement of organizational transparency. J. Public Relat. Res. **21**(1), 71–99 (2008)

15. Scauer, F.: Transparency in three dimensions. Univ. Ill. Law Rev. **2011**, 1339 (2011)
16. Stuart, H.C., Dabbish, L., Kiesler, S., Kinnaird, P., Kang, R.: Social transparency in networked information exchange: a theoretical framework. In: Proceedings of the ACM CSCW Conference, pp. 451–460 (2012)
17. Tagiuri, R., Kogan, N., Bruner, J.S.: The transparency of interpersonal choice. Sociometry **18**, 368–379 (1955)

What Is Essential? – A Pilot Survey on Views About the Requirements Metamodel of reqT.org

Björn Regnell[(✉)]

Department of Computer Science, Lund University, Lund, Sweden
bjorn.regnell@cs.lth.se

Abstract. [**Context & motivation**] This research preview paper presents ongoing work on the metamodel of a free software requirements modeling tool called reqT that is developed in an educational context. The work aims to make an initial validation of a survey instrument that elicits views on the metamodel of the reqT tool, which aims to engage computer science students in Requirements Engineering (RE) through an open source DSL embedded in the Scala programming language. [**Question**] The research question is: Which RE concepts are essential to include in the metamodel for a requirements engineering tool in an educational context? [**Principal ideas**] A survey instrument is developed, with a list of 92 concepts (49 entities, 15 relations and 28 attributes) and a set of questions for each concept, to elicit the respondents' views on the usage and interpretation of each concept. [**Contribution**] The survey is initially validated in a pilot study involving 14 Swedish RE scholars as subjects. The survey results indicate that the survey is feasible. The analysis of the responses suggest that many of the concepts in the metamodel are used frequently by the respondents and there is a large degree of agreement among the respondents about the meaning of the concepts. The results are encouraging for future work on empirical validation of the relevance of the reqT metamodel.

Keywords: Requirements engineering · Metamodel · CASE tool · Engineering education · Embedded domain-specific language · Empirical software engineering

1 Introduction

There are many challenges in teaching Requirements Engineering (RE) [4,6], including advancing students' requirements modelling skills that can be used effectively in an unstructured, non-ideal, real-world situation [1]. When teaching RE modelling we may ask ourselves: What are the *essential* RE concepts that we should include in a taught metamodel for requirements? This paper investigates this questions in conjunction with the on-going work of developing a metamodel for reqT.org, an open source requirements engineering tool used in RE education [7]. A survey instrument is presented aiming to elicit the frequency of RE term usage and the degree of interpretation agreement. The responses from 14 Swedish

© Springer International Publishing Switzerland 2016
M. Daneva and O. Pastor (Eds.): REFSQ 2016, LNCS 9619, pp. 232–239, 2016.
DOI: 10.1007/978-3-319-30282-9_16

RE scholars are analysed and discussed and conclusions suggest that a large subset of the concepts of the current reqT metamodel can be seen as "essential" in that a majority of the subjects use them while agreeing with the concepts' definitions. The presented work represents an initial validation of the survey instrument. Further work involving more subjects is needed to draw conclusions with more certainty.

2 Background

There are nowadays numerous commercial RE tools available, but many are expensive, complex and not sufficiently open [2]. A major aim of the reqT open source project is to provide a small but scalable, semi-formal and free software package for an educational setting [7] that can inspire code-loving computer science students to learn more about requirements modeling. The tool development started in 2011 at Lund University, where reqT is used in RE teaching at MSc level in student role-playing projects.[1]

A critical issue is how to choose the essential RE concepts that allows for sufficient expressiveness, while not overloading the metamodel with esoteric concepts just for the sake of completeness.

The reqT metamodel includes three types of concepts: entities, attributes and relations. Entities and attributes are nodes in a graph data structure, while relations are edges that can connect entities with sub-graphs. Thus a tree-like structure can be created of arbitrary depth spanning the graph that models some chunk of requirements.

The code below shows a toy example of an orthogonal variability model [5] expressed in the reqT Scala-embedded DSL [7] illustrating a small part of its metamodel. Other parts of the metamodel contains concepts that enable e.g. goal modelling, use case modelling, and user story modelling, see further Appendix A.

```
Model(
  Component("appearance") has (
    VariationPoint("color") has (
      Min(0), Max(2), Variant("blue"), Variant("red"), Variant("green")),
    VariationPoint("shape") has (
      Min(1), Max(1), Variant("round"), Variant("square")),
    VariationPoint("payment") has (
      Min(1), Max(2), Variant("cash"), Variant("credit")),
    VariationPoint("payment") requires Variant("cash"),
    Variant("round") excludes Variant("red"),
    Variant("green") requires Variant("square")),
  Component("appearance") requires VariationPoint("shape"),
  App("free") has Component("appearance"),
  App("free") binds (VariationPoint("shape") binds Variant("round")),
  App("premium") has Component("appearance"),
  App("premium") binds (
    VariationPoint("color") binds (Variant("red"), Variant("green")),
    VariationPoint("shape") binds (Variant("round"), Variant("square")),
    VariationPoint("payment") binds Variant("cash")))
```

---

[1] The Lund Univ. MSc-level RE course can be found at: http://cs.lth.se/education.

Entities in the above code listing are in bold, attributes in italics and relations start with a lower case letter. In the reqT editor, entities, attributes, and relations are syntax-coloured in blue, green and red respectively. A reqT model written in the above syntax is actually valid Scala code that, when executed, generates a data structure that can be traversed and manipulated using Scala scripts. Visualisations can be generated by export to GraphViz. Export is also available to HTML and spreadsheet formats.

3   Methodology and Data Collection

In order to validate RE scholar's opinions of the metamodel, a survey instrument was developed including the 49 entities, 15 relations and 28 attributes. All concepts and definitions are listed in Appendix A.[2] The concepts were gathered from various sources including the IREB Glossary[3], Wikipedia, agile development, variability [5] and goal modelling, and the text book [3] used in an RE course at Lund Univ (See footnote 1).

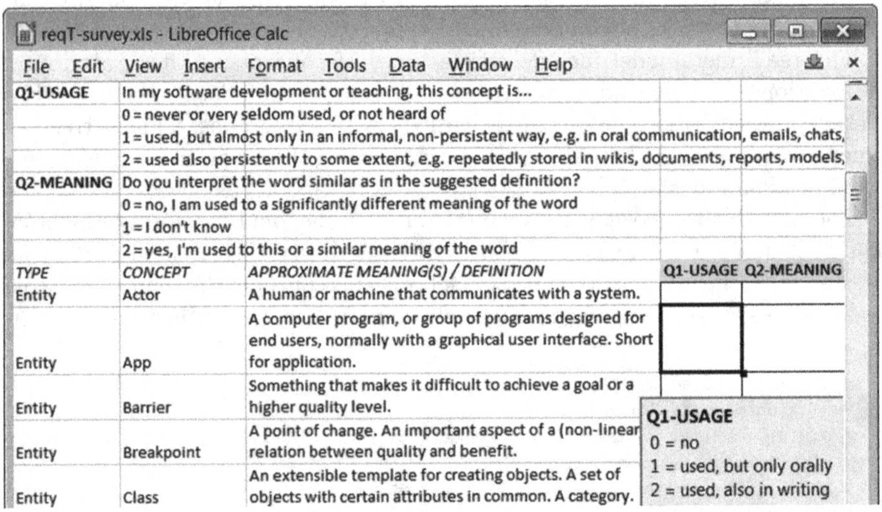

Fig. 1. A screen dump of a part of the survey instrument.

The data collection was made during a Swedish national network meeting with academic RE scholars in spring 2015. The survey was filled in during the meeting using the participants' own laptops in a spreadsheet shown in Fig. 1. The subjects were given around 20 min to complete the survey. Most of the subjects handed in the survey via email directly after the session, while a few finished it after the meeting.

---

[2] The survey is available at https://github.com/reqT/reqT/tree/3.0.x/survey.

[3] https://www.ireb.org/en/cpre/cpre-glossary/.

4   Data Analysis

Subject Background. The background questions in the survey regards the role of the subject, as shown in Table 1. The analyzed[4] total number of subjects is 14, of which 10 are teachers, 10 are developers and 13 are researchers. The response rate was 100 % after a reminder was emailed to one missing subject.

Frequency Analysis. The degree of "essentiality" is characterized as the number of subjects that has responded that they (1) use the concept at least in an informal, non-persistent way, *and* that they (2) use the concept in a similar meaning as in the definition in Appendix A. Figure 1 shows the definitions of the three-level ordinal scales of Questions $Q1_{usage}$ and $Q2_{meaning}$ respectively. Table 2 shows the results of the frequency counts. If an "essentiality threshold" is chosen at $N/2$ then only the 9 concepts from row $n = 7$ and below in Table 2 are considered "non-essential", hence showing that more than 90 % of the meta-model concepts have a majority of the subjects that use them and agree upon their definitions. Each concept has at least one subject that uses it and agrees with its definition.

The following 19 concepts were reported "missing": S01: *or*, S02: *bug, threshold*, S04: *role, problem, motivates, and, or, pattern, submodel*, S06: *plug-in, informalism*, S07: *full sentence*, S09: *satisfaction, satisfies, customer*, S11: *system-of-interest, verification, validation*, S13: *context*. Thus, the concept 'or' was the only concept that had consensus among several subjects (S01, S04) as considered "missing".

The anonymised data and analysis scripts (developed using Scala and Apache POI) are available at: https://github.com/bjornregnell/reqT-survey.

Table 1. Background of subjects, $N = 15$. The subjects were given anonymous ids S01–S15.

Background question	Subject responding YES
Do you teach software engineering and/or requirements engineering? YES/NO	S01 S03 S04 S05 S07 S08 S09 S11 S12 S14
Do you develop software by writing code and/or creating system models? YES/NO	S01 S02 S03 S07 S08 S09 S10 S11 S13 S14
Do you do academic research in software and/or requirements engineering? YES/NO	S01 S03 S04 S05 S06 S07 S08 S09 S10 S11 S12 S13 S14

---

[4] One subject answered NO on all background questions and was therefore excluded.

Table 2. Frequency analysis, where n is the number of subjects that for the respective concept answered $(Q1_{usage} >= 1)$ *and* $(Q2_{meaning} = 2)$. In total there are 92 concepts (49 entities, 15 relations and 28 attributes). The higher up in the table, the more "essential". For $n = 0, 2, 3, 5$ the were no concepts with answers by that number of subjects.

n	Entities	Attributes	Relations
14	Class, Component, UseCase, Variant	Comment, Example, Max, Min, Title	implements, verifies
13	Configuration, Data, Design, Event, Quality, Scenario, Stakeholder, System, Term	Code, Constraints, Cost, FileName, Probability, Profit, Spec, Why	excludes, interactsWith, is, relatesTo, requires
12	Actor, Domain, Feature, Function, Interface, Module, Relationship, Release, Req, Risk, Service, State, Task, Test	Benefit, Capacity, Frequency, Input, Order, Output, Prio, Text, Value	has, impacts
11	Idea, Label, Member, Meta, MockUp, Section, User	Image	precedes, superOf
10	Goal, Story	Expectation	
9	App, Issue, Target, WorkPackage	Damage	binds, helps
8	Item, Product, Resource, VariationPoint		deprecates
7	Breakpoint, Screen	Status	
6	Barrier	Deprecated	hurts
4	Ticket		
1	Epic	Gist	

5   Discussion and Conclusion

The presented survey is a pilot investigation with two main contributions: (1) the survey instrument together with the data collection and analysis approach, which are shown to be feasible in the presented context, and (2) the pilot study results: for more than 90 % of the 92 reqT metamodel concepts a majority of the 14 participating RE scholars claim to use them and agree upon their definitions. Only 1 concept was considered missing by more than one subject, while in total 19 additional concepts were reported missing by some subject.

Limitations. It can be questioned if "essentiallity" of a set of RE concepts can be characterized by how many RE scholars that use them and agree upon their definition, but it can also be argued that concept usage in an educational context is interesting to investigate when developing a metamodel for an academic RE tool. A major threat to external validity is the limited number of subjects. Due to few subjects and the high degree of homogeneity among subjects with respect to background, it is difficult to analyse and draw conclusions e.g. about potential differences in opinions between e.g. teachers and developers. Some subjects needed more time and completed their survey offline, which may give a variation in how carefully the responses were considered.

Further Work. When developing a metamodel it is interesting not just to ask if the concepts to include are essential, but also to pose the question if the set of concepts is complete. If some essential concept is missing from some stakeholder's viewpoint, then the metamodel is not sufficient. With more subjects participating in the presented RE metamodel survey, the analysis of answers to further questions on alternative terms and missing concepts will be enabled and beneficial to the further development of a comprehensive and complete, but not overloaded, RE metamodel.

Acknowledgments. Thanks to Tobias Kaufmann and Klaus Pohl for contributions to the variability model in Sect. 2. This work is partly funded by VINNOVA within the EASE project.

Appendix A: Definitions of Metamodel Concepts of reqT v3.0

Entity	Definition
Actor	A human or machine that communicates with a system.
App	A computer program, or group of programs designed for end users, normally with a graphical user interface. Short for application.
Barrier	Something that makes it difficult to achieve a goal or a higher quality level.
Breakpoint	A point of change. An important aspect of a (non-linear) relation between quality and benefit.
Class	An extensible template for creating objects. A set of objects with certain attributes in common. A category.
Component	A composable part of a system. A reusable, interchangeable system unit or functionality.
Configuration	A specific combination of variants.
Data	Information stored in a system.
Design	A specific realization or high-level implementation description (of a system part).
Domain	The application area of a product with its surrounding entities.
Epic	A large user story or a collection of stories.
Event	Something that can happen in the domain and/or in the system.
Feature	A releasable characteristic of a product. A (high-level, coherent) bundle of requirements.
Function	A description of how input data is mapped to output data. A capability of a system to do something specific.
Goal	An intention of a stakeholder or desired system property.
Idea	A concept or thought (potentially interesting).
Interface	A defined way to interact with a system.
Issue	Something needed to be fixed.
Item	An article in a collection, enumeration, or series.
Label	A descriptive name used to identify something.
Member	An entity that is part of another entity, eg. a field in a in a class.
Meta	A prefix used on a concept to mean beyond or about its own concept, e.g. metadata is data about data.
MockUp	A prototype with limited functionality used to demonstrate a design idea.
Module	A collection of coherent functions and interfaces.
Product	Something offered to a market.
Quality	A distinguishing characteristic or degree of goodness.
Relationship	A specific way that entities are connected.
Release	A specific version of a system offered at a specific time to end users.
Req	Something needed or wanted. An abstract term denoting any type of information relevant to the (specification of) intentions behind system development. Short for requirement.
Resource	A capability of, or support for development.
Risk	Something negative that may happen.
Scenario	A (vivid) description of a (possible future) system usage.
Screen	A design of (a part of) a user interface.
Section	A part of a (requirements) document.
Service	Actions performed by systems and/or humans to provide results to stakeholders.
Stakeholder	Someone with a stake in the system development or usage.
State	A mode or condition of something in the domain and/or in the system. A configuration of data.
Story	A short description of what a user does or needs. Short for user story.
System	A set of interacting software and/or hardware components.
Target	A desired quality level or goal .
Task	A piece of work (that users do, maybe supported by a system).
Term	A word or group of words having a particular meaning.
Test	A procedure to check if requirements are met.
Ticket	(Development) work awaiting to be completed.
UseCase	A list of steps defining interactions between actors and a system to achieve a goal.
User	A human interacting with a system.
Variant	An object or system property that can be chosen from a set of options.
VariationPoint	An opportunity of choice among variants.
WorkPackage	A collection of (development) work tasks.

Attribute	Definition
Benefit	A characterisation of a good or helpful result or effect (e.g. of a feature).
Capacity	The largest amount that can be held or contained (e.g. by a resource).
Code	A collection of (textual) computer instructions in some programming language, e.g. Scala. Short for source code.
Comment	A note that explains or discusses some entity.
Constraints	A collection of propositions that restrict the possible values of a set of variables.
Cost	The expenditure of something, such as time or effort, necessary for the implementation of an entity.
Damage	A characterisation of the negative consequences if some entity (e.g. a risk) occurs.
Deprecated	A description of why an entity should be avoided, often because it is superseded by another entity, as indicated by a 'deprecates' relation.
Example	A note that illustrates some entity by a typical instance.
Expectation	The required output of a test in order to be counted as passed.
FileName	The name of a storage of serialized, persistent data.
Frequency	The rate of occurrence of some entity.
Gist	A short and simple description of an entity, e.g. a function or a test.
Image	(The name of) a picture of an entity.
Input	Data consumed by an entity,
Max	The maximum estimated or assigned (relative) value.
Min	The minimum estimated or assigned (relative) value.
Order	The ordinal number of an entity (1st, 2nd, ...).
Output	Data produced by an entity, e.g. a function or a test.
Prio	The level of importance of an entity. Short for priority.
Probability	The likelihood that something (e.g. a risk) occurs.
Profit	The gain or return of some entity, e.g. in monetary terms.
Spec	A (detailed) definition of an entity. Short for specification
Status	A level of refinement of an entity (e.g. a feature) in the development process.
Text	A sequence of words (in natural language).
Title	A general or descriptive heading.
Value	An amount. An estimate of worth.
Why	A description of intention. Rationale.

Relation	Definition
binds	Ties a value to an option. A configuration binds a variation point.
deprecates	Makes outdated. An entity deprecates (supersedes) another entity.
excludes	Prevents a combination. An entity excludes another entity.
has	Expresses containment, substructure. An entity contains another entity.
helps	Positive influence. A goal helps to fulfil another goal.
hurts	Negative influence. A goal hinders another goal.
impacts	Some influence. A new feature impacts an existing component.
implements	Realisation of. A module implements a feature.
interactsWith	Communication. A user interacts with an interface.
is	Sub-typing, specialization, part of another, more general entity.
precedes	Temporal ordering. A feature precedes (is implemented before) another feature.
relatesTo	General relation. An entity is related to another entity.
requires	Requested combination. An entity is required (or wished) by another entity.
superOf	Super-typing, generalization, includes another, more specific entity.
verifies	Gives evidence of correctness. A test verifies the implementation of a feature.

References

1. Callele, D., Makaroff, D.: Teaching requirements engineering to an unsuspecting audience. In: Proceedings of the 37th SIGCSE Technical Symposium on Computer Science Education, SIGCSE 2006, pp. 433–437 (2006)
2. Carrillo de Gea, J., Nicolas, J., Aleman, J., Toval, A., Ebert, C., Vizcaino, A.: Requirements engineering tools. IEEE Softw. **28**(4), 86–91 (2011)
3. Lauesen, S.: Software Requirements - Styles and Techniques. Addison-Wesley, Reading (2002)
4. Memon, R.N., Ahmad, R., Salim, S.S.: Problems in requirements engineering education: a survey. In: Proceedings of the 8th International Conference on Frontiers of Information Technology, FIT 2010, pp. 5:1–5:6. ACM (2010)
5. Metzger, A., Pohl, K.: Variability management in software product line engineering. In: 29th International Conference on Software Engineering, pp. 186–187. IEEE (2007)
6. Regev, G., Gause, D.C., Wegmann, A.: Experiential learning approach for requirements engineering education. Requirements Eng. **14**(4), 269–287 (2009)
7. Regnell, B.: reqT.org – towards a semi-formal, open and scalable requirements modeling tool. In: Doerr, J., Opdahl, A.L. (eds.) REFSQ 2013. LNCS, vol. 7830, pp. 112–118. Springer, Heidelberg (2013)

Human Factors in Requirements Engineering

People's Capabilities are a Blind Spot in RE Research and Practice

Kim Lauenroth[1]([⊠]) and Erik Kamsties[2]

[1] adesso AG, Stockholmer Allee 20, 44269 Dortmund, Germany
kim.lauenroth@adesso.de
[2] University of Applied Science and Arts Dortmund, Emil-Figge-Strasse 42,
44227 Dortmund, Germany
erik.kamsties@fh-dortmund.de

Abstract. [**Context and motivation**] Requirements engineering (RE) has a history of nearly 40 years and has developed several methods, techniques, and tools to support RE activities in various project situations. [**Question/problem**] This paper argues that RE research and practice is people agnostic and therefore has a blind spot: it ignores the capabilities of the people involved in RE. [**Principal ideas/results**] This paper presents several arguments from the related work that show that people's capabilities may have a significant impact on their performance of RE related activities. [**Contribution**] Based on the presented arguments, this paper formulates the hypothesis that people's capabilities have a higher impact on RE performance than the project situation and the methods applied. Based on this hypothesis, this paper presents possible further research activities.

1 Introduction

Requirements engineering is close to its 40th birthday. The first publications on this topic go back to 1976 [BT76] and 1977 [Ros77]. RE research has produced a solid body of knowledge over the years. Several papers have been published that review the history of RE research and present future challenges of requirements engineering research and practice [vL00, JLL+11]. However, a recent literature review by Lenberg et al. [LFW15] has shown that the capabilities of people (e.g. cognitive abilities, education, and experience) involved in software engineering (SE) are not considered systematically in SE research.

Lenberg et al. argue in particular that *is important to clearly define a specific area concerned with more realistic notions of human nature in order to better understand and improve software development processes and practices.* They define this field as *behavioral software engineering* and presented a systematic literature review that has identified 250 publications related to this new field (e.g. psychology of programming [Saj08]). They divided SE into several subdisciplines according to SWEBOK and for software requirements, they did not find a single publication concerned with people's capabilities.

© Springer International Publishing Switzerland 2016
M. Daneva and O. Pastor (Eds.): REFSQ 2016, LNCS 9619, pp. 243–248, 2016.
DOI: 10.1007/978-3-319-30282-9_17

The literature on software estimation already has recognized the importance of people's skills since the effort adjustment factors for people's skills considerably larger and have a higher range than the factors related to technical topics. For example, the impact of the requirements analyst capability on the overall project effort ranges from 1.46 (very low skill) to 0.71 (very high skill) (cf., e.g. [Boe81,McC06]). Other disciplines already have developed dedicated fields that deal with people's capabilities. A prominent example is engineering psychology, a field of applied psychology that deals with human behavior and capability, applied to the design and operation of systems [Sta96].

We take the results from Lenberg and use these as an impulse to look at RE research from a behavioral perspective. In the remainder of this paper, we will provide arguments that support the importance of incorporating people's capabilities in RE research and practice and discuss possible further research activities in RE.

2   Research from Psychology

In this section, we will present exemplary research from psychology, that we consider as related to RE - of course not meant to be complete.

2.1   Human Memory

Psychological research provided several results on the human memory. For example, Miller argued that the typical working memory size is about $7 +/- 2$ information units [Mil56]. Engle [Eng02] shows that there are individual differences in the working memory capacity. If the working memory is stressed during a particular task (e.g. because a person has to keep several information units in the working memory), the performance of the current task is decreased and the probability of mistakes is increased (cf., e.g., [BH74]). The ability to remember certain information may depend on the domain or the experience, Chase and Simon [CS73] showed that playing strength of chess players has an impact on chess-related memory tasks. Finally, the working memory should not be considered as perfectly reliable storage for information. Roediger and McDermott [RM95] showed that memory performance can be influenced negatively, depending on the given task.

We consider working with requirements as a task, that heavily depends on the human memory. For example, requirements stated in an interview have to be remembered to document them later, or creating traceability between two requirements in a document requires to remember the specific requirement that has to be traced to the currently specified requirement. Although RE work is often tool-driven, memory performance should have an impact on RE related tasks.

2.2   Problem Solving and Creativity

Simon and Hayes [SH76] have shown that the wording of instructions can have an impact on the problem solving capabilities of a person: The identical problem presented by different instructions could slow down the problem solving or even prevent a person from finding a solution.

Batey and Furnham [BF06] presented a literature survey that showed that there are various indications for a relationship between creativity, intelligence and personality. Kaufman et al. [K+15] showed that creative performance in the fields of art and science correlates with certain personality factors, i.e., certain personality traits (e.g. openness to new experiences) predicts creative achievements.

RE is about problem solving [Mai13] and therefore a creative task. The problem solving/creative capabilities of people involved in RE should have an impact on the outcome of the RE activities.

2.3   Human Perception

Psychological research provided several results on the human perception. For example, priming is a so called implicit memory effect in which a stimulus (e.g. reading or hearing a word) influence the response to another stimulus. Kahnemann illustrates the effect of priming with a very simple example [Kah11]: *If you have recently seen or heard the word EAT, you are temporarily more likely to complete the word fragment SO_P as SOUP than as SOAP. The opposite would happen, of course, if you had just seen WASH.* The priming effect is not limited to completing word fragments, it especially extends to the human perception [MB07].

Chabris and Simons [SC99] presented an experiment that shows that our attention with respect to unexpected events and information is very limited, especially when we are working on demanding cognitive tasks[1]. RE is obviously a task that highly relies on the perception of the people involved, specifying a requirement requires that the you recognize it first. The presented results indicate that RE work can be influenced by the effects described above.

3   The POSM-Hypothesis

We have presented exemplary arguments from psychology, that cognitive capabilities of people may by affected by different factors (e.g., the priming effect) and that these capabilities of people may have an effect on requirements engineering performance as well (e.g., capacity of the short term memory).

The important question from our point of view is, how big is this effect compared to other factors, such as the methods applied or the characteristics of the project (e.g. type of system, domain of the project). Our interpretation of the presented literature and our experience from industry indicates that

---

[1] This experiment has become known as the monkey business illusion and is available on YouTube: https://www.youtube.com/watch?v=IGQmdoK_ZfY.

1. RE methods and the project characteristics can have an impact on people's capabilities.
2. the individual capabilities of people can have an impact on requirements engineering performance.

We therefore formulate the following hypothesis: *The individual capabilities of people involved in RE have a higher impact on RE performance than the situation of the given project and the RE methods applied (short: People over Situation and Method (POSM)-Hypothesis).*

4   Testing the POSM-Hypothesis

The POSM-hypothesis makes a strong assumption related to the effect of individual capabilities on RE performance. Testing the POSM-hypothesis is a long-term project that requires significant effort and attention. In the following, we describe our approach for testing of the POSM-hypothesis.

4.1   Operationalization of RE Performance

In order to study the impact of people, situation, and methods, we need a measure for RE performance. That is, a instrument that allows us to quantify the success of a particular RE process. El Emam and Madhavji published a kind of blueprint of how to develop such an instrument [EEM95]. They breakdown RE success into product quality and service quality and empirically validated this instrument. The authors conducted a field study with practitioners. Gorschek and Davis developed a taxonomy for measuring RE success [GD08], which identifies different levels of RE success. Recent work provides lists dependent variables, e.g. [F+14].

Depending on the subject of investigation, RE performance can be operationalized to a more handy instrument. For RE experiments related to the human memory (see Sect. 2.1) for instance, the ability to remember requirements is relevant. Dependent variables can be adapted from psychology. Regarding human perception (see Sect. 2.3), the ability to recognize requirements is relevant. This can be accomplished by evaluating the sensitivity and the specificity of a classificator.

4.2   Relationship Between Peoples' Capabilities and RE Methods

In the first step, we plan to investigate on the first part of the POSM-Hypothesis: the relationship between people's capabilities, RE methods, and their effect on RE performance. If we can show that the effectiveness of RE Methods is independent from people's capabilities, we have found a strong indicator that the POSM-Hypothesis does not hold.

We plan to start our investigation in the field of memory performance and RE documentation structure, since memory performance and requirements documentation are well understood aspects. We indent to investigate, for example, on the relationship between RE experience, documentation structure, and memory performance. We plan to develop a series of experiments that compare the ability to remember requirements correctly depending on the provided requirements documentation structure and on the experience of the people performing the memory task. We intend to distinguish two dimensions of experience. The first dimension is experience in the field of RE, the second dimension is the experience in the subject matter of the specified system.

4.3 Further Steps

In case we find evidence that people's capabilities have a stronger impact on RE performance than the RE methods applied, we plan to start investigating on the second part of the POSM-Hypthesis: the relationship between people's capabilities, project situations, and their effect on RE performance. Possible research directions for experiments are, e.g., the impact of stress (e.g., tight deadlines). If we again find evidence that people's capabilities have a stronger impact on RE performance, we intend to approach the full POSM-Hypothesis and develop experiments that test the combined hypothesis.

5 Summary and Conclusion

We have argued that people's capabilities are a very important factor in RE and presented the POSM-Hypothesis to document this believe. In our future work, we plan to investigate on this hypothesis as described in this paper. In this regard, the concept of people's capabilities needs further refinement. We identified three ingredients, but it can be safely assumed that there are more. Niknafs and Berry for example have shown the impact of domain experience on idea generation during requirements elicitation [NB12].

We further plan to work on the ethical dimension of the POSM-Hypthosis. The presented research focuses on individual differences of people and the results could have an impact on the values that guide software project work (e.g., prefer people with certain cognitive capabilities). We are convinced that working on the POSM-Hypothesis will lead to a better theoretical understanding of RE methods and to a better application of RE methods in industry.

References

[BF06] Batey, M., Furnham, A.: Creativity, intelligence, and personality: a critical review of the scattered literature. Genet. Soc. Gen. Psychol. Monogr. **132**(4), 355–429 (2006)

[BH74] Baddeley, A., Hitch, G.: Working memory. In: Bower, G. (ed.) The Psychology of Learning and Motivation: Advances in Research and Theory, vol. 8, pp. 47–89. Academic Press, New York (1974)

[Boe81] Boehm, B.W.: Software Engineering Economics. Prentice-Hall, Upper Saddle Rive (1981)

[BT76] Bell, T.E., Thayer, T.A.: Software requirements: are they really a problem? In: Proceedings of ICSE 1976, Los Alamitos, CA, USA, pp. 61–68. IEEE Computer Society Press (1976)

[CS73] Chase, W.G., Simon, H.A.: Perception in chess. Cogn. Psychol. 4(1), 55–81 (1973)

[EEM95] El Emam, K., Madhavji, N.H.: Measuring the success of requirements engineering processes. In: Proceedings of the 2nd IEEE International Symposium on RE, pp. 204–211. IEEE (1995)

[Eng02] Engle, R.W.: Working memory capacity as executive attention. Curr. Dir. Psychol. Sci. 11(1), 19–23 (2002)

[F+14] Fernández, D.M., et al.: In quest for requirements engineering oracles, dependent variables and measurements for (good) RE. In: Proceedings of the 18th International Conference on Evaluation and Assessment in Software Engineering, p. 3. ACM (2014)

[GD08] Gorschek, T., Davis, A.M.: Requirements engineering: in search of the dependent variables. Inf. Softw. Technol. 50(1), 67–75 (2008)

[JLL+11] Jarke, M., Loucopoulos, P., Lyytinen, K., Mylopoulos, J., Robinson, W.: The brave new world of design requirements. Inf. Syst. 36(7), 992–1008 (2011)

[K+15] Kaufman, S.B., et al.: Openness to experience and intellect differentially predict creative achievement in the arts and sciences. J. Pers. (2015)

[Kah11] Kahnemann, D.: Thinking - Fast and Slow. Pengiun Books, London (2011)

[LFW15] Lenberg, P., Feldt, R., Wallgren, L.G.: Behavioral software engineering: a definition and systematic literature review. J. Syst. Softw. 107, 15–37 (2015)

[Mai13] Maiden, N.: So, what is requirements work? IEEE Softw. 30(2), 14–15 (2013)

[MB07] Mayr, S., Buchner, A.: Negative priming as a memory phenomenon: a review of 20 years of negative priming research. Zeitschrift für Psychologie/J. Psychol. 215(1), 35 (2007)

[McC06] McConnell, S.: Software Estimation: Demystifying the Black Art: The Black Art Demystified. Microsoft Press, Redmond (2006)

[Mil56] Miller, G.A.: The magical number seven, plus or minus two: some limits on our capacity for processing information. Psychol. Rev. 63(2), 81 (1956)

[NB12] Niknafs, A., Berry, D.M.: The impact of domain knowledge on the effectiveness of requirements idea generation during requirements elicitation. In: Requirements Engineering Conference (RE), 2012 20th IEEE International, pp. 181–190, Sept 2012

[RM95] Roediger, H.L., McDermott, K.B.: Creating false memories: remembering words not presented in lists. J. Exp. Psychol. Learn. Mem. Cogn. 21(4), 803 (1995)

[Ros77] Ross, D.T.: Guest editorial - reflections on requirements. IEEE Trans. Softw. Eng. 3(1), 2–5 (1977)

[Saj08] Sajaniemi, J.: Psychology of programming: looking into programmers' heads. The Problems of Professionals, p. 3 (2008)

[SC99] Simons, D.J., Chabris, C.F.: Gorillas in our midst: sustained inattentional blindness for dynamic events. Percept. London 28(9), 1059–1074 (1999)

[SH76] Simon, H.A., Hayes, J.R.: The understanding process: problem isomorphs. Cogn. Psychol. 8(2), 165–190 (1976)

[Sta96] Stanton, N.: Engineering psychology: another science of common sense? Psychologist 9(7), 300–303 (1996)

[vL00] van Lamsweerde, A.: Requirements engineering in the year 00: a research perspective. In: Proceedings of ICSE 2000, pp. 5–19. ACM, New York (2000)

Customer Involvement in Continuous Deployment: A Systematic Literature Review

Sezin Gizem Yaman[1(✉)], Tanja Sauvola[2], Leah Riungu-Kalliosaari[1],
Laura Hokkanen[3], Pasi Kuvaja[2], Markku Oivo[2], and Tomi Männistö[1]

[1] Department of Computer Science, University of Helsinki, Helsinki, Finland
{sezin.yaman,riungu,tomi.mannisto}@cs.helsinki.fi
[2] Department of Information Processing Science,
University of Oulu, Oulu, Finland
{tanja.sauvola,pasi.kuvaja,markku.oivo}@oulu.fi
[3] Department of Pervasive Computing,
Tampere University of Technology, Tampere, Finland
laura.hokkanen@tut.fi

Abstract. [**Context and motivation**] In order to build successful software products and services, customer involvement and an understanding of customers' requirements and behaviours during the development process are essential. [**Question/Problem**] Although continuous deployment is gaining attention in the software industry as an approach for continuously learning from customers, there is no common overview of the topic yet. [**Principal ideas/results**] To provide a common overview, we conduct a secondary study that explores the state of reported evidence on customer input during continuous deployment in software engineering, including the potential benefits, challenges, methods and tools of the field. [**Contribution**] We report on a systematic literature review covering 25 primary studies. Our analysis of these studies reveals that although customer involvement in continuous deployment is highly relevant in the software industry today, it has been relatively unexplored in academic research. The field is seen as beneficial, but there are a number of challenges related to it, such as misperceptions among customers. In addition to providing a comprehensive overview of the research field, we clarify the gaps in knowledge that need to be studied further.

Keywords: Customer involvement · Customer feedback · User involvement · User feedback · Continuous deployment · Continuous delivery · Software development

1 Introduction

In today's highly competitive and quickly changing markets, the software intensive industry is evolving towards a value-driven and adaptive real-time business paradigm [1]. Customer involvement in the software development process and an understanding of customers' requirements and behaviours are essential when building successful software products and services. Customer involvement provides an opportunity to enhance product performance based on a better understanding of customers' needs and results in reduced research and development (R&D) costs [2]. In many cases,

© Springer International Publishing Switzerland 2016
M. Daneva and O. Pastor (Eds.): REFSQ 2016, LNCS 9619, pp. 249–265, 2016.
DOI: 10.1007/978-3-319-30282-9_18

customers can be seen as one of the key resources for product development, as they often gain deep knowledge and experience by using the product or service. However, customers' requirements might change very rapidly, and they are often difficult to identify. This may lead to a situation where R&D spends time and effort on developing product functionalities that do not add value for customers.

Requirements Engineering (RE) is one of the most crucial processes in software development aiming at maximizing the value of a release of software while accommodating a collaborative approach throughout the product development where multiple stakeholder perspectives are involved [3, 4]. Likewise, allowing for more flexible ways of working with an emphasis on customer collaboration, responding to change and speed of development, agile methods help companies to address many of the problems associated with traditional software development [5]. Recent studies show that even though the ways to learn about customers are increasing, software companies often find it challenging to obtain timely and accurate feedback from customers to support R&D decision-making processes continuously [6, 7]. In agile methodologies and new approaches such as continuous deployment (CD) and rapid feature validation, the customer is seen as a way to improve decision-making and R&D efficiency. Olsson et al. [8] defined CD as 'the ability to deliver software functionality frequently to the customer and subsequently, the ability to continuously learn from real-time customer usage of software'. CD-related research is also emerging in literature in the field of software engineering [9]. However, there is no common understanding of customer involvement practices in CD that would guide both researchers and practitioners.

Customer involvement is an abstract concept that refers to the ways in which the customer plays a role in the software development process and the extent of the customer's participation [2]. In general, customer involvement is studied widely in areas such as participatory design, user-centric design, usability engineering and requirements engineering [10]. In this paper, customer involvement refers to the process by which end users or customers actively or unintentionally become part of any stage of the software development life cycle. The terms 'user(s)' and 'customer(s)' are used interchangeably depending on the context. Likewise, we consider CD and continuous delivery to be synonyms.

Although CD is gaining attention in the software industry, there is no systematic literature review that provides an overview of the topic within the software engineering field. Thus, we conducted a systematic literature review (SLR) of customer involvement in CD, where the first four authors of this paper conducted the research and rest of the authors reviewed the work. The need for this SLR emerged in the context of a large Finnish research program[1] that aimed to enhance Finnish ICT companies' ability to deliver value in real-time. The main objective of this study is to discover current research on customer involvement in CD, provide a structured body of knowledge on the research area and clarify the underlying factors related to customer input during CD. We take established RE activities into account throughout the paper to see how customer involvement in CD is in line with them. Our objectives for the study are expressed in the form of research questions, which are presented in Sect. 2.1.

---

[1] Need for Speed; http://www.n4s.fi/en/.

The rest of the paper is structured as follows. In Sect. 2, we describe our research questions and research methodology. In Sect. 3, we present the results of our literature review together with discussion. Next, in Sect. 4, we address limitations and threats to our study and the countermeasures that were taken to minimise their effects. Finally, in Sect. 5, we conclude the study and provide recommendations for future works.

2 Research Method

In this study, we followed the guidelines for SLRs established by Kitchenham and Charters [11].

An SLR consists of three phases: planning, conducting and reporting. Our systematic literature review started with the planning phase, during which the need for the study was confirmed and the research protocol, which specified the research goals, research questions and review methods, was defined. A pilot search was also conducted during the planning phase in order to better define the search strings. During the conducting phase, search queries were performed and primary studies were selected and analysed based on the classification scheme. In this paper, primary studies refer to original papers that constitute this SLR.

2.1 Research Questions

The goal of this SLR is to discover existing research on customer involvement in CD. This leads to the following research questions:

Table 1. Research questions

Research Question	Aim
RQ1: What is the current state-of-the-art related to understanding customer involvement in CD? RQ1.1 Which research methods are used? RQ1.2 Which kinds of contribution have been made? RQ1.3 Which kinds of research have been done? RQ1.4 Which publication mediums have been used? RQ1.5 What are the levels of rigor and relevance in the studies?	To provide an overview of the studies on customer involvement in continuous deployment in the context of software intensive products and services To categorize available research according to research method, contribution, type, medium and to assess the quality of the studies by examining two perspectives: scientific rigor and industrial relevance
RQ2: What are the current and/or potential methods and tools for obtaining and managing customer data in a continuous process? RQ2.1 What are the current and/or potential methods and tools? RQ2.2 How the data has been utilised?	To identify the reported methods and tools for collecting and managing customer-related data in CD To identify the reported ways in which collected data was applied to support relevant functions in different contexts
RQ3: What are the current and/or potential benefits of involving the customer in CD?	To identify the reported benefits which are experienced with customer involvement in CD
RQ4: What are the current and/or potential challenges of involving the customer in CD?	To identify the reported challenges which are experienced with customer involvement in CD

2.2   Search

The search terms were identified based on the research questions presented in Table 1. Afterwards, the search terms were reviewed using the guidelines created by Kitchenham and Charters [11] for populations and interventions. Our study focuses on literature that discusses customer (population) involvement in software development practices that intend to use CD (intervention). To increase publication coverage and ensure that we did not miss any relevant primary studies, we decided to keep the search terms broad. For this reason, we employed three different search strings for each selected database and aggregated the results based on the research questions. Each string identified keywords related to common populations and interventions as well as keywords that searched the query for a specific purpose. In Query 1, we used terms related to population, including terms associated with customer satisfaction, collaborative service design and improvement. For example the term "service design" was used because it is a methodological approach for customer involvement during the software development process. In addition to the terms related to intervention in Query 2, we searched the query for software development. Lastly, we used more specific terms about continuous software development together with terms related to intervention and population in Query 3. The following search strings were piloted:

- **Query1**: ("continuous deployment" OR "continuous delivery" OR "continuous improvement") AND ("customer involvement" OR "customer feedback" OR "user involvement" OR "user feedback" OR "customer satisfaction" OR "customer focus" OR "service design" OR "co-creation" OR "co-design")
- **Query2**: ("continuous deployment" OR "continuous delivery" OR "continuous improvement") AND ("software development")
- **Query3**: ("continuous software development" OR "continuous customer feedback" OR "continuous customer involvement" OR "continuous user feedback" OR "continuous user involvement")

The search was performed from April to July 2014, after the researchers reviewed several experimental searches. Additionally, an update search was performed from January to March 2015, and the results were aggregated with those of the first search. As databases, we used ACM, IEEE Xplore, ISI Web of Science, ScienceDirect, SCOPUS and Proquest. The search was performed for all fields related to information technology, including titles, abstracts and keywords. After combining all the results together and excluding the duplicates, 2429 papers had been obtained.

2.3   Study Selection

The primary study selection process started with 2429 papers uploaded to RefWorks[2], where duplicates were automatically identified and removed. Four researchers performed a three-round screening process based on the selection criteria. The criteria for selecting the primary studies determined which studies were included or excluded in each round of the selection process. We carefully enhanced the criteria for each round so

---

[2] https://www.refworks.com/.

the risk of missing a relevant paper was minimised. General inclusion and exclusion criteria are listed below, and the enhanced criteria for each round can be seen in Table 2.

- **General inclusion criteria:** Include the paper if it is: (a conference paper, journal article, technical report, PhD thesis, tutorial, magazine article, opinion paper, chapter in a compilation book, e.g. conference proceedings) AND (discusses continuous customer involvement).
- **General exclusion criteria:** Exclude the paper if it is: not written in English, a summary, an extended abstract, a master's thesis or a whole book.

Table 2. Inclusion and exclusion criteria per round

	Include the paper if it	Exclude the paper if it
Round 1 Read only the title, check the paper type, mark your selection	Fulfils the general inclusion criteria	Fulfils the general exclusion criteria
Round 2 Read only the abstract and mark your selection	Fulfils inclusion criteria from the previous round AND is from (software engineering or business studies)	Fulfils exclusion criteria from the previous round AND is clearly not from (software engineering or business studies)
Round 3 Read the introduction, results and conclusion (do light reading if needed)	Fulfils inclusion criteria from the previous round OR is discussing customer input during a software development process that can be related to the practice of CD	Fulfils exclusion criteria from the previous round AND (does not have any customer elements OR has customer elements but they are not continuous OR they are not involved in a software development process that can be related to the practice of CD)

Four researchers individually marked the papers to be *included, excluded* or *could not be decided* based on each round's criteria, each paper was marked by two researchers. If both researchers marked the same paper as included or excluded, there was no conflict. If the researchers' marks were different, or if both researchers could not decide whether a paper should be included or excluded, then the paper was discussed during the conflict meetings conducted at the end of each round. In the conflict meetings, if the conflict could not be resolved by all four researchers, the paper was included in this round to be evaluated in more depth in the next round. At the end of the third round of the screening process, the researchers read all of the primary study candidates and performed a quality assessment. New papers were added to the primary study collection by performing backward snowball sampling [12] and tracking key researchers' work in the field. The paper selection process resulted in 25 primary studies, as can be seen in Fig. 1.

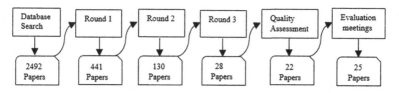

Fig. 1. Primary study selection process and number of papers

2.4   Quality Assessment and Data Extraction

In this SLR, we conducted the quality assessment and data extraction processes in parallel. The data extraction process began after the primary studies were uploaded to the QSR NVivo[3] tool. We divided the papers into three groups and randomly assigned them to three researchers, who are the first three authors of this paper. Each researcher went through her assigned portion and coded the parts of the papers that provided answers to the research questions. A spreadsheet was used to evaluate the rigor and relevance of each study as well as other data, as proposed by Ivarsson and Gorschek [13] (see Table 3). Two perspectives, scientific rigor and industrial relevance, were considered. Scientific rigor was evaluated with three aspects: (1) context: to what degree the context is described well; (2) study design: to what degree the study design is described appropriately so that it guarantees the quality of the study; (3) validity: to what extend the validity of the study is considered and evaluated. Rigor was evaluated by using a three-point scale: strong description (1), medium description (0.5) and weak description (0). Furthermore, industrial relevance was evaluated according to subject, context, scale and research method by using two values: 1, if the aspect contributed to industrial relevance and 0 otherwise. After that, the rigor and relevance ranks for each study were summed up (e.g. if a study has strongest rigor in all 3 categories, the sum is 3; if has strongest relevance in all 4 categories, then the sum is 4). Both the quality assessment and data extraction processes were iterative, and after each the researchers held an evaluation meeting and reviewed all the papers.

Table 3. Data extraction sheet items

Data item	Description	Value
General		
ID	Unique ID number for the primary study	integer
Title	Name of the study	string
Publication year	Calendar year	integer
Research method	Method used to conduct the research, adapted by [14]	case study, action research, survey, literature review, opinion paper, experience report, not stated
Contribution	Type of contribution of the study, adapted by [15]	model, theory, framework, guidelines, lessons learned, advice, tool, not stated
Research type	Type of the research, adapted by [16][a]	empirical, theoretical, both, not clear
Medium	Channel used to publish the study	conference, journal, workshop, magazine, tutorial, book chapter
Rigor	*Scientific rigor, adapted by [13]*	
Context	If the context is described well	0 for weak, 0.5 for medium, 1 strong
Study design	If the study was designed well	0 for weak, 0.5 for medium, 1 strong
Validity	If the validity was discussed	0 for weak, 0.5 for medium, 1 strong
Relevance	*Industrial relevance, adapted by [13]*	

(Continued)

---

[3] http://www.qsrinternational.com/.

Table 3. (*Continued*)

Data item	Description	Value
Subjects	If subjects of the study are associated with customer involvement in a real-world context that could be related to the CD	0 for no, 1 for yes
Context	If the study is performed in a representative setting	0 for no, 1 for yes
Scale	If the scale of the applications used in the evaluation or conclusion is realistic, i.e. the applications are industrial-scale	0 for no, 1 for yes
Research method	If the research method used in the study contributes to an investigation of real situations	0 for no, 1 for yes

[a]Due to low maturity in the envisioned field of investigation, this categorization is chosen in order to see the general picture of types of the research.

2.5 Data Analysis

The extracted data was analysed, tabulated and visualised using different strategies. RQ1, where the state-of-the-art was examined, was answered using descriptive statistics based on the data extraction sheet. Following Cruzes and Dybå's recommendations [17], RQ2, RQ3 and RQ4 were examined by a thematic analysis based on the data extracted by NVivo software. We followed the approach where one researcher identified recurring themes from the extracted data. Afterwards, other researchers reviewed the themes and reconstructed the categories. The final categories can be seen in Sect. 3.

3 Results and Discussion

From the initial set of 2429 studies, 25 studies were identified as contributing to the topic of customer involvement in CD and were analysed. Due to the space limitations, detailed list of primary studies can be found online[4] and the shortened list can be seen in Table 4. The results are structured according to the research questions presented in Sect. 2.1, followed by an overall discussion of the results.

3.1 State-of-the-Art

Figure 2 shows that the case study was the most popular research method among the primary studies. Figure 3 shows that over half of the research (19 papers) described the lessons learned as a result of research done, provided guidelines and advice. Less than half (12 papers) of the papers presented more concrete approaches, such as a model, a tool or framework. It should be noted that some studies contributed in multiple ways. As shown in Fig. 4, the majority of primary studies, 14 papers, provided empirical contributions, and only 6 papers provided theoretical contributions. Regarding publication channels, the majority (20 papers) of primary studies were published in peer-reviewed venues (including conference proceedings, journals and workshops).

---

[4] http://www.cs.helsinki.fi/group/ese/customer_involvement_slr/primary_studies.pdf.

Table 4. Primary studies

ID	First Author, Year	Title of the Primary Study
P1	Arias, G., 2012	The 7 key factors to get successful results in the IT Development projects
P2	Chen, C.C., 2011	Discriminative effect of user influence and user responsibility on information system development processes and project management
P3	Claps, G.G., 2015	On the journey to continuous deployment: technical and social challenges along the way
P4	Fabijan, A., 2015	Customer feedback and data collection techniques in software R&D: a literature review
P5	Fagerholm, F., 2014	Building blocks for continuous experimentation
P6	Ferreira, C., 2008	Agile systems development and stakeholder satisfaction: a South African empirical study
P7	Grisham, P.S., 2005	Customer relationships and extreme programming
P8	Hess, J., 2013	Involving users in the wild—participatory product development in and with online communities
P9	Jakobi, T., 2013	Always beta: cooperative design in the smart home
P10	Krusche, S., 2014	Introduction of continuous delivery in multi-customer project courses
P11	Krusche, S., 2014	User feedback in mobile development
P12	Labib, C., 2009	Early development of graphical user interface (GUI) in agile methodologies (extended)
P13	Lee, C., 2013	Learning from a design experience: continuous user involvement in development of aging-in-place solution for older adults
P14	Maalej, W., 2009	When users become collaborators: towards continuous and context-aware user input
P15	Mehlenbacher, B., 1993	Software usability: choosing appropriate methods for evaluating online systems and documentation
P16	Meijer, E., 2014	The responsive enterprise: embracing the hacker way
P17	Muthitacharoen, A. M., 2009	Examining user involvement in continuous software development: (a case of error reporting system)
P18	Ogonowski, C., 2013	Designing for the living room: long-term user involvement in a living lab
P19	Olsson, H.H., 2012	Climbing the "stairway to heaven"–a multiple-case study exploring barriers in the transition from agile development towards continuous deployment of software
P20	Olsson, H.H., 2013	Towards R&D as innovation experiment systems: a framework for moving beyond agile software development
P21	Pagano, D., 2013	User involvement in software evolution practice: a case study
P22	Poppendieck, M., 2012	Lean software development: a tutorial
P23	Schneider, K., 2010	Feedback in context: supporting the evolution of IT-ecosystems
P24	Torrecilla-Salinas, C.J., 2015	Estimating, planning and managing agile web development projects under a value-based perspective
P25	Wilcox, E., 2007	Agile development meets strategic design in the enterprise

Figure 5 provides an overview of the distribution of articles among the publication mediums. Although some studies were published between 1993 and 2012, most of the studies were published between 2013 and 2015, as can be seen in Fig. 6.

Figure 7 represents the number of studies in rigor and relevance scales, based on the evaluation process described in Sect. 2.4. In general, the majority (92 %) of the studies demonstrate strong industrial relevance (relevance >=2). Regarding scientific rigor, only 56 % of the papers have a rigor higher than 2. As a result, the primary studies regarding customer involvement in CD have strong industrial relevance and relatively

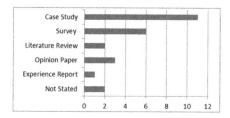

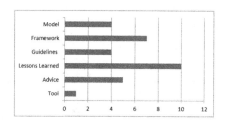

Fig. 2. State-of-the-art – research method, adapted by [14]

Fig. 3. State-of-the-art – research contributions, adapted by [15]

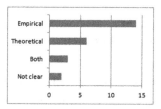

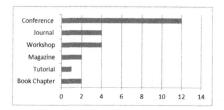

Fig. 4. State-of-the-art – research type, adapted by [16]

Fig. 5. State-of-the-art – publication medium

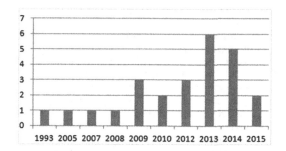

Fig. 6. State-of-the-art – publication years

low scientific rigor. This might be due to the fact that although there is industrial demand for the research topic, it is still new.

3.2 Data Collection Methods and Tools

Several methods and tools were introduced and/or used to collect customer data during CD practices, as categorised in Table 5.

Based on the categories identified above, we think that the methods and tools can be applied at different stages of software development; for example, face-to-face communication can be employed during the requirements elicitation process. Therefore, no one method or tool is better than the other. Instead, using them in combination can provide different data that improve the CD process. However, in CD process, the customer feedback collection from the deployed software should happen even near real-time or as early as possible to support design decisions on real customer usage. For

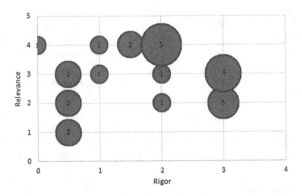

Fig. 7. Rigor and relevance overview, adapted by [13]

Table 5. Current and/or potential data collection methods and tools

Category	Description	Primary Studies
Face-to-face communication	Activities such as customer meetings, face-to-face conversations, reviews, walkthroughs, discussions, interviews, customer questionnaires, customer surveys (in person), videotaped sessions and observations are carried out when the user and developers are physically present to gather user data	P1, P2, P4, P7, P8, P9, P10, P13, P14, P15, P18, P23
Visual representations	Creations or displays are used by the user and development team to communicate about different aspects of products or services. These displays can include mock-ups, prototypes, pilots, wireframes, visual annotations and screenshots	P2, P4, P5, P10, P11, P12, P13, P14, P15, P18, P24
User activities	User activities are activities and techniques that are planned and carried out with two aims: (a) to provide training to the user or (b) to obtain feedback about different aspects of the product or the service from the user. These activities include user training, planning games, blitz planning, planning poker, the whole team, customer boot camp, workshops, focus groups, the Wizard of Oz technique, theatre sessions, software cinema, user partnering, diary studies and online meetings	P1, P2, P4, P7, P8, P13, P14, P15, P18, P24
Experiments and tests	Experiments and tests, such as continuous experimentation and A/B tests are designed to test different hypotheses with certain groups of customers to obtain real-time feedback. This feedback can be used to improve future experiments, design new experiments and/or aid decision-making	P3, P4, P5, P14, P15, P16, P17, P18, P20
Applications and application distribution platforms	Software solutions that either run independently, such as a feedback application, or are integrated in a large system, such as plugins, are used to obtain feedback from the user. Application distribution platforms are also be used to gather feedback	P5, P8, P10, P14, P18, P21, P23
Co-development with the user	Placing the user in different roles, such as lead user, lead customer, co-creator, co-developer and key user, is a way to gather users' input about the development process	P1, P8, P14, P18, P19, P20

(Continued)

Table 5. (*Continued*)

Category	Description	Primary Studies
Log data	Log data is data that has been collected from different actions by the user or the system, such as user clicks, system logs, and usage diaries	P4, P9, P10, P13, P18, P20
User communities	User communities are groups of people that are usually connected by an online platform for collaboration to generate and share ideas related to a similar product or service. If the product or service satisfies the overall user community, it can cause the user to provide efficient input about development activities. These communities are open source communities, open design spaces, innovation communities and communities for co-design	P8, P14, P17, P18, P21, P25
Bug reports	Bug reports are crash, fault or error reports sent to developers demonstrating the system or product's failure to perform as expected under specified conditions	P4, P10, P17, P18, P21
Living labs	Living labs are characterised by user-centric environments for open innovation in which early and continuous user involvement is supported. Likewise, developers are also be involved in-situ, meaning that they are next to the user and receive direct feedback in an action-centric real-world environment	P8, P9, P14, P18
Communication tools and services	Communication tools and services include various means of communication that gather feedback from the user, such as email, phones, wikis, forums, audio or video	P8, P10, P18, P21
Social media	Data sources such as Twitter, Instagram and Facebook are used to be in touch with the customer	P4, P8, P18, P21
Online data sources	Online ads, online surveys, in-product surveys and web polls are used to receive user feedback	P4, P8, P17, P18
Integrated feedback mechanisms	Integrated feedback mechanisms are channels set up within the system or server to support automatic transmission of feedback from the user	P10, P21
Developers as customers	Developers sometimes assume the role of a product owner or a customer. This helps them look at the development process from a different perspective	P4, P22

example, experiments and tests are designed to test different hypotheses with certain groups of customers to obtain real-time feedback (even without users not knowing about it). In addition, customer involvement and feedback collection are important not only in the requirements elicitation process but also other stages of the development life cycle. For instance, mock-ups or prototypes can be used to validate the customer requirements and in-product surveys can reveal necessities for software evolution. Face-to-face communication, visual representations and user activities were the most popular ways of collecting customer data, perhaps because they entail high degrees of interaction with the customer, making the customer feel more involved in the process. It is also meaningful for the customer to be involved in different roles (e.g. as lead customer, co-creator, etc.) as this enables them to experience the impact of their involvement.

3.3 Data Utilisation

We investigated the ways in which collected customer information was/can be applied in the real-world settings to support relevant functions. These applications can be seen in Table 6.

Table 6. Current and/or potential data utilisation methods and ideas

Category	Description	Primary Studies
Decision-making	Customer input is used for decision-making, including deciding if a feedback requires a fix or if it is a request for a feature and planning and prioritising tasks	P2, P4, P5, P6, P8, P13, P14, P16, P17, P18, P20, P21, P22, P25
Learning about the user	User input is used to better understand the user through, for example, user satisfaction and learning usage/behaviour patterns, such as which features are used more often than others and which mistakes are made often	P4, P5, P8, P14, P17, P18, P19, P20, P21, P22, P23, P25
Improvement	The service or the product is improved (functionality and quality) in the long term based on the collected data. New functionalities are added to the existing product based on customer input	P4, P5, P6, P10, P17, P18, P20, P22, P23
Assessing the service or the product	Software companies use the collected data to assess a service or product based on, for example, acceptance of the product and product–market fit	P4, P5, P8, P18, P20, P21, P23
Fast reaction	Developers quickly react to user input, for instance, to fix major bugs, learn more about the problems and obtain support from user communities	P4, P6, P10, P17, P18, P25

We notice that the most frequently reported way of using the customer data is to use it to support decision-making. Customer input should assist both business and technical decision-making, for instance for roadmapping and requirement prioritization processes, and guide all R&D efforts. User communities can also help with the decision-making process offering their wisdom [18]. The collected data can be also used to learn more about the users. For instance, usage patterns can be discovered to track success or failures made with a product [P25]. Similarly, A/B testing can tell about which version release is preferable by the users [P20] and the user feedback can throw light on user satisfaction [P8]. Based on what is learnt, system or product can be improved both in functionality and quality. Also, developers can react to the collected data fast, especially when critical problems need to be fixed.

3.4 Benefits

The benefits of continuously involving the customer in the development process were frequently addressed by the primary studies, as can be seen in Table 7.

Based on the frequencies of the primary studies in each category we see that involving the customer in CD practices seems to be beneficial. Building a reliable relationship with the customer eases communication and motivates them to be part of the development process. As RE research already addresses, the requirement elicitation process can be operated directly through input from first-hand users. Besides, CD enables shorter user

Table 7. Current and/or potential benefits of involving the customer in CD

Benefit	Description	Primary Studies
Continuous learning and improvement	Customer data is used to eliminate any work that does not bring value to the customer or improve the system or product (e.g. software quality improvement, higher user satisfaction). Thus, the decision-making process is based on sound evidence rather than guesswork	P2, P4, P5, P6, P7, P8, P13, P16, P18, P19, P20, P21, P22, P23, P25
First-hand user needs	Gathering first-hand user needs and direct feedback helps developers reduce the gap between user expectations and implementation. It also helps developers validate their understandings of the user requirements	P2, P6, P7, P9, P10, P11, P13, P18, P19, P20, P24
Shorter feedback loop, faster reaction	A shorter feedback cycle makes it possible to quickly learn from the user and increase the speed of decision-making, such as by taking corrective actions during product development	P3, P4, P6, P10, P12, P16, P17, P19, P20, P22, P25
Advertisement and time to market	Customer input is useful in advertising and marketing strategies for the products or services. As the feedback is received from the market, a product–market fit can be reached sooner	P3, P5, P8, P13, P16, P18, P19, P21, P22, P24
User motivation	Cooperation between the user and developers motivates the user to co-develop and participate more actively in the development process. Also, user motivation is driven by the likely benefit of providing input. Similarly, giving the customer some control over decision-making increases overall satisfaction	P13, P2, P6, P8, P10, P20, P17, P23, P7, P18
Communication and trust	Building long-term relationships and trust with customers helps to improve communication. In some cases, receiving useful feedback might be possible only after the long-term establishment of trust	P6, P7, P9, P10, P13, P18, P25
New products and features	Input from the customer shapes the product roadmap and helps developers create new, innovative features and improvements	P5, P13, P18, P20, P21
User experience and usability	Involving the customer in the development process makes the user more experienced with the product or the service. It also provides ease for usability testing	P5, P9, P11, P18

feedback loops, which enables faster reactions when decisions must be made. Customer input can also be used as a means for innovation [P20]. The collected data is used to continuously learn more about the customer, which can be used to update the product roadmap and improve the product. The time to market can be optimised through early customer involvement, which is especially crucial for start-ups, for which budget is a primary concern [P5]. Through continuous involvement in development activities, the customer will be more experienced and provide efficient feedback and usability data.

3.5   Challenges

The current and/or potential challenges of involving the customer in CD are outlined in Table 8.

According to the reported challenges, we draw the inference that establishing a trustworthy relationship with customers and communicating with the right channels are often found as challenging. For instance, through face-to-face interactions, customer input can be received directly. However, it is not always feasible due to, for instance,

Table 8. Current and/or potential challenges of involving the customer in CD

Challenge	Description	Primary Studies
Customer perception and behaviour	Customers' perceptions of their involvement in development are challenging. They might feel disturbed or interrupted from their on-going work (e.g. by product surveys or pop-up windows), and they might give negative or insufficient feedback. The customer can also be unsure about what they want and how to express it	P2, P4, P7, P8, P9, P14, P17, P18, P20, P23
Communication	Communication with the customer portrays difficulties, such as establishing trust before collaboration and choosing the right form of communication strategy. Also, managing the process, such as by dealing with conflicts, with different stakeholders is challenging	P1, P2, P8, P9, P10, P14, P18, P21, P24
Data management	The customer-related data collection process and analysis of the data reveal several challenges. For example, the internal verification loop of the collected data has to be short and systematic, and feedback should be coming from the right channel. Similarly, the data analysis process requires high effort to, for example, work with data with noise in it, eliminate human factors such as subjectivity or prioritise tasks	P3, P8, P14, P19, P21, P23
Setting the scenes	Preparing and receiving the customer input is time-consuming. For example, creating detailed feedback might be challenging due to a lack of time, and organising workshops, questionnaires, interviews, site visits or personal interactions might be expensive and laborious. Also, different data collection techniques bring different difficulties; for example, a theatre session requires sophisticated technology at a special location. Sometimes it might be necessary to educate the customer about a common, helpful way of providing feedback	P4, P17, P18, P21, P23
Transparency	Transparency in data, process and feedback affect users' intention to provide input. Limited or no transparency demotivates users to provide feedback. However, too much transparency causes customers to interfere with developers' work. Also, due to high visibility, failures might be too visible to customers	P3, P7, P17, P18, P19
Updates, new features and products	Customers might not realise or welcome changes	P3, P7, P18, P19
Customer profile	The needs of different user groups might diverge and change in different contexts. Establishing a customer sample group where all possible types of users are represented is challenging. Also, the customer's level of competence, experience, knowledge and/or reliability influences the success of customer involvement	P7, P18, P23
Experiments and A/B testing	The customer might not want to be a part of an experiment or they might not welcome partially developed functionality. Moreover, conducting several experiments in parallel and interpreting the results are challenging. Determining where to start to experiment with the customer is another challenge	P4, P5, P20
Sales and suppliers	Sometimes direct user data might not be accessible due to intermediaries, such as when a company does not sell products directly to end users. From the suppliers' point of view, they might not be interested in collecting customer feedback after selling a product or a service	P5, P19, P23

time constraints or intermediaries in the supply chain. In addition, conflicts can occur during the communication with the customer, especially when there are many stakeholders involved. On the other hand, the customers might feel disturbed by being involved in a development activity or they might not welcome any changes, such as being involved in experiments and receiving new feature updates. There is also a risk of diminishing customers' commitment if they feel that the provided feedback is not useful. Also, misinterpreting the roles and development activities might be a challenge. For example, the customer might perceive the developers as a help desk service [P9] or they might neglect context information when providing feedback [P14]. Likewise, the life cycle of customer data—collection, analysis and return to the customer if needed—poses a number of difficulties. Maalej et al. [P14] states that user input and feedback mechanisms in software systems usually follow an ad-hoc approach, if they exist at all. A systematic mechanism should provide a short internal verification loop for the collected data and ensure that data is distributed to the right parties for the analysis [P3], [P21] Unfortunately, user data might be also received from the wrong channels, lack important information or include irrelevant information [P14], [P21]. Moreover, especially when manual data analysis is required, human factors, such as analysts' subjectivity, can be a concern [P14]. Data analysis and decision-making based on the collected data can require much effort due to these difficulties. Lastly, preparing the necessary infrastructure for both continuous (e.g. establishing an integrated feedback mechanism) or event-based (e.g. conducting a theatre session) customer data collection tools and methods can be expensive and time-consuming.

In summary, we remark that the existing studies illustrate that the customer can be involved in different stages of software development: pre-deployment (e.g. requirements elicitation), during deployment and after deployment (e.g. software evolution). Many benefits and a number of current or potential challenges of customer involvement in CD were addressed in the primary studies. Various methods and tools that can be used to involve customers revealed that customers can intentionally and actively participate in development activities such as user studies, and that they can passively participate in development, such as when user clicks are counted. One fundamental finding was that the communication and relationship with the customer shapes the customer's involvement. While short-term user involvement is sometimes needed, such as for questionnaires, long-term user involvement can be also necessary, such as for living labs. The primary studies indicate that collected customer data with CD can be utilised in different ways. However, there is need for new empirical studies in real-life contexts so that data utilisation methods become more factual rather than being hypothetical.

4 Limitations

Researcher bias might be a threat during the primary study selection rounds, data extraction and analysis. Threats to the identification of primary studies were mitigated with up-front definitions of the inclusion/exclusion criteria. In addition, the research protocol was reviewed and refined by external supervisors. However, the scope of this study covers not only customer input in CD but also the concepts or techniques for involving the customer in a software development process that can be related to CD. For this reason, the researchers had to make judgments about the papers that did not discuss direct implementation of CD. In order to mitigate this limitation, every paper had to be reviewed by at least two researchers, who had to reach a consensus. Furthermore, a number of discussion meetings were held to examine the data analysis steps. There might be difficulties regarding the generalisation of this study's results. Due to the novelty of the field, the existing knowledge could lead to more generalisable results when the field is strengthened by further research.

5   Conclusions and Future Work

The objective of this systematic literature review was to summarise the state-of-the-art on customer involvement in CD, including its benefits, challenges, methods and tools. Based on 25 primary studies, we remark that customer involvement in CD is gaining attention within the software industry. We found that the scientific rigor of the studies was lower than their industrial relevance, which could indicate that the field has the potential for future discoveries. In general, customer input enhances CD activities and benefits both developers and end users. For instance, instant feedback, continuous learning, shorter time to market and improved customer satisfaction are some of the perceived benefits. We identified a number of challenges that could block customer input during development activities, such as customer misperception, customers' unwillingness to receive continuous updates, forming the right feedback methods, determining from whom and in which format the feedback should be collected. A variety of methods and tools can be used to collect and manage customer data, and the collected customer data can be utilised in several ways.

Despite the industrial demand, we identified a gap between the advantages of involving the customer in CD and the real-world utilisation of existing knowledge. The benefits of customer input in CD and the methods and tools that were used are well addressed in the primary studies, but there is less evidence on their implications. How customer involvement should be coordinated and managed still needs to be determined. However it is clear that customer involvement in CD needs an innovative and experimental organisational culture where fail fast, fail often[5] is seen as an opportunity to learn and make corrective actions. Besides, RE research can enlighten CD studies with it is established body of knowledge. Correspondingly, the increasing demand on CD and novel approaches of costumer involvement in the field can provide new insights into RE research. For example, continuous experimentation approach can innovate requirements elicitation activities. For future work, we are interested in investigating how a customer involvement model could optimise data collection methods and tools for specific cases. Likewise, efforts should be made to negate the current challenges. Performing new case studies in collaboration with the software industry could reveal information about such countermeasures.

Acknowledgments. This work was supported by TEKEs as part of the Need for Speed project of DIGILE (Finnish Strategic Centre for Science, Technology and Innovation in the field of ICT and digital business).

---

[5] http://theleanstartup.com/principles.

References

1. Järvinen, J., Huomo, T., Mikkonen, T., Tyrväinen, P.: From agile software development to mercury business. In: Lassenius, C., Smolander, K. (eds.) ICSOB 2014. LNBIP, vol. 182, pp. 58–71. Springer, Heidelberg (2014)
2. Laage-Hellman, J., Lind, F., Perna, A.: Customer involvement in product development: an industrial network perspective. J. Bus.-to-Bus. Mark. 21(4), 257–276 (2014)
3. Wiegers, K.: Software Requirements, 2nd edn. Microsoft Press, Redmond (2003)
4. Barney, S., Aurum, A., Wohlin, C.: A product management challenge: creating software product value through requirements selection. J. Syst. Architect. 54(6), 576–593 (2008)
5. Highsmith, J.: Agile Project Management: Creating Innovative Products. Addison-Wesley Professional, New York (2009)
6. Sauvola, T., Lwakatare, L. E., Karvonen, T., Kuvaja, P., Holmstrom Olsson, H., Bosch, J.: Towards customer-centric software development, a multiple-case study. In 41st Euromicro Conference on Software Engineering and Advanced Applications (SEAA) Portugal (2015)
7. Fabijan, A., Olsson, H.H., Bosch, J.: Customer feedback and data collection techniques in software R&D: a literature review. In: Fernandes, J.M., Machado, R.J., Wnuk, K. (eds.) ICSOB 2015. LNBIP, vol. 210, pp. 139–153. Springer, Heidelberg (2015)
8. Olsson, H.H., Alahyari, H., Bosch, J.: Climbing the "stairway to heaven"–a multiple-case study exploring barriers in the transition from agile development towards continuous deployment of software. In: 38th Conference on Software Engineering and Advanced Applications (SEAA), pp. 392–399. IEEE (2012)
9. Mäntylä, M.V., Adams, B., Khomh, F., Engström, E., Petersen, K.: On rapid releases and software testing: a case study and a semi-systematic literature review. Empirical Softw. Eng. 20(5), 1384–1425 (2014)
10. Abelein, U., Peach, B.: Understanding the influence of user participation and involvement on system success - a systematic mapping study. Empirical Softw. Eng. 20, 28–81 (2013)
11. Kitchenham, B., Charters, S.: Guidelines for performing systematic literature reviews in software engineering. EBSE Technical report (2007)
12. Wohlin, C.: Guidelines for snowballing in systematic literature studies and a replication in software engineering. In: Proceedings of the 18th International Conference on Evaluation and Assessment in Software Engineering, New York (2014)
13. Ivarsson, M., Gorschek, T.: A method for evaluating rigor and industrial relevance of technology evaluations. Empirical Softw. Eng. 16(3), 365–395 (2011)
14. Unterkalmsteiner, M., Gorschek, T., Cheng, C.K., Permadi, R.B., Feldt, R.: Evaluation and measurement of software process improvement—a systematic literature review. IEEE Trans. Software Eng. 38(2), 398–424 (2012)
15. Paternoster, N., Giardino, C., Unterkalmsteiner, M., Gorschek, T., Abrahamsson, P.: Software development in startup companies: a systematic mapping study. Inf. Softw. Technol. 56(10), 1200–1218 (2012)
16. Kitchenham, B.: What's up with software metrics?–A preliminary mapping study. J. Syst. Softw. 83(1), 37–51 (2010)
17. Cruzes, D.S., Dybå, T.: Recommended steps for thematic synthesis in software engineering. In: 2011 International Symposium on Empirical Software Engineering and Measurement (ESEM), pp. 275–284. IEEE (2011)
18. Hess, J., Wan, L., Ley, B., Wulf, V.: In-situ everywhere: a qualitative feedback infrastructure for cross platform home-IT. In: Proceedings of the 10th European Conference on Interactive TV and Video, pp. 75–78. ACM (2012)

Research Methodology in Requirements Engineering

Common Threats and Mitigation Strategies in Requirements Engineering Experiments with Student Participants

Marian Daun[✉], Andrea Salmon, Torsten Bandyszak,
and Thorsten Weyer

paluno – The Ruhr Institute for Software Technology,
University of Duisburg-Essen, Essen, Germany
{marian.daun, andrea.salmon, torsten.bandyszak,
thorsten.weyer}@paluno.uni-due.de

Abstract. **[Context and motivation]** Experiments are an important means to evaluate research results in the field of requirements engineering. Researchers often conduct such experiments with student participants. **[Question/problem]** The use of student participants evokes a multitude of potential threats to validity, which must be properly addressed by the chosen experiment design. In practice, attention is mostly given to threats to the generalizability of the findings. However, current experiment reports often lack a proper discussion of further threats, for example, which are caused by the recruitment of student participants. **[Principle ideas/results]** To provide mitigation strategies for student specific threats to validity, these threats must be known. We analyzed student experiments from published experiment reports to identify student specific threats and to analyze adequate mitigation strategies. **[Contribution]** This paper contributes a detailed analysis of the threats to validity to be considered in student experiments, and possible mitigation strategies to avoid these threats. In addition, we report on an experiment conducted in a university requirements engineering course, where we considered student specific threats and applied the proposed mitigation strategies.

Keywords: Student experiments · Threats to validity · Mitigation strategies · Experience report

1 Introduction

Empirical research in requirements engineering often uses students as experimental subjects. From a researcher's perspective, students are in many cases available in a sufficient number to reach statistical significance. Especially, the recruitment of students within a course setup appears to be easy. In addition, conducting student experiments within a proper setting of a university course is often valued since the participation in the experiment can additionally benefit the student's learning success (cf. [1–3]). While, in particular in requirements engineering, the research focus is strongly placed on providing solutions for real industrial needs, student experiments are still a necessary means to evaluate solution approaches (cf. [4]). Industry investigations

© Springer International Publishing Switzerland 2016
M. Daneva and O. Pastor (Eds.): REFSQ 2016, LNCS 9619, pp. 269–285, 2016.
DOI: 10.1007/978-3-319-30282-9_19

(e.g., industry surveys, cases studies) often fall short in comparing new solution approaches with common approaches, e.g., because the practitioners are well trained with the common approach and the new approach will be treated unfairly (see [5]). Therefore, it is suggested to use a mixture of different evaluation methods (cf. [6]). Particularly, controlled experiments are often valued, since they provide quantitative evidence about a measurable effect. Hence, industrial action research can be combined with controlled experiments using student participants.

However, the use of student participants may cause several threats to validity, for example, because empirical findings from student experiments might not be generalizable to industry professionals. Moreover, students are often additionally motivated to participate, for instance, through better grades for good experiment performance. Such motivation factors constitute a severe threat to validity as no longer the experiment material, but the students themselves are under investigation (cf. [7]).

At the current time some work has been done regarding the use of students in experimental software engineering. However, there is a lack of guidance in the state of the art w.r.t. identifying and mitigating threats to validity specific to student experiments. To close this gap in the state of the art, this paper provides a detailed discussion of threats to validity specific to student participation. Beside the classification of the different threats, we report on mitigation strategies to avoid or lower the identified threats. In addition, this paper reports on an experiment we conducted as part of a master-level university requirements engineering course. The design of this experiment addresses the threats arising from student participants, applies the proposed mitigation strategies, and is also designed to fit teaching purposes in requirements engineering education. In doing so, we provide an example experiment conducted with student participants that (i) mitigates threats to validity from student participation, (ii) gives an idea on how to conduct student experiments in accordance with ethical considerations regarding the teachers perspective, and (iii) shows significant and useful results, which as discussions with industry professionals revealed, are also generalizable.

The remainder of this paper is structured as follows: Sect. 2 gives an overview of the current state of the art concerning student experiments in software engineering literature. Section 3 details our findings regarding the threats to validity specific for student experiments and possible mitigation strategies in experiments with student participants. Section 4 reports the example experiment, and in doing so, our approach to integrate empirical experiments into university requirements engineering teaching. Finally, Sect. 5 concludes the paper.

2 Student Experiments in Literature

General research about experiments in software engineering such as [7–9], or [10] deals with generic issues about how to conduct experiments in an educational setting. These approaches place particular emphasis on ethical issues of student recruitment and threats induced by a certain recruitment approach. According to [9] student recruitment approaches can be separated into the following three categories:

1. The experiment is a mandatory part of the course, either conducted during teaching or as an exercise.
2. The students participate voluntarily in the experiment, but the experiment is still relevant for the exam. In this case, two subclasses are to be distinguished:
   (a) The experimental substance is relevant for the exam.
   (b) Participation in the experiment is honored with a bonus, for example, extra credit towards the final grade.
3. The experiment is not conducted within a course. In this case, it is to be distinguished between the following cases:
   (a) Students are paid for participation in the experiment.
   (b) Students participate on a purely voluntary basis.

Another research field deals with the threat of generalizability of student experiments. Research was conducted based on the question whether student participants are comparable to industry participants, and whether student results from an experiment are generalizable to real-world situations and problems. *Höst et al.* [11] show that there are only minor differences between software engineering students and professionals regarding their ability to conduct relatively small tasks of judgment. Thus, Höst *et al.* conclude that students may therefore be used as participants. The investigation of *Svahnberg et al.* [12] shows that students have a realistic perception of industrial practices in the context of requirements selection. Thus, it is concluded that students are appropriate subjects in empirical studies in this area. *Runeson* [13] investigated the differences between freshman students, graduates and professionals participating in empirical investigations. The results show that freshman students differ significantly from graduates regarding their performance. The differences between graduates and industrial professionals were smaller. *Tichy* [14] also concludes that computer science graduate students are so close to professional status that the differences between students and professionals are only marginal.

Student experiments are mainly used for "theory testing" in the sense of [15]. Generalizability can therefore be considered as a less important threat (cf. [15]), particularly, if the experiment is integrated in a broader evaluation strategy. However, further threats to validity in student experiments can be identified, which are often insufficiently addressed in current experiment reports (cf. [8]). While there exists some research on mitigation strategies for threats to validity in experimental setups in general (e.g., [16]), there is less work that deals with mitigation strategies for threats to validity caused by the use of student participants.

Two major sources for mitigation strategies for threats to validity of student experiments can be found. On the one hand, general approaches dealing with the avoidance of threats to validity (e.g., [9, 15, 17, 18], or [19]) partly describe threats resulting from student participants. On the other hand, literature that reports on specific student experiments has to be considered as well. It is to note that many publications on student experiments provide insufficient data to make statements about all induced threats to validity, the population, or on how students were recruited (cf. [8]). We analyzed experiment reports focusing on student participants and detail their recruitment strategy. As starting point we repeated the study of *Sjøberg et al.* [8] for a timeframe from 2010 to 2015. In total, we reviewed 2884 publications from 6 software engineering top venues and identified 159 experiment reports using student participants (5.5 % of all publications covered). In addition, we conducted a snow-ball search to identify further experiment reports in other venues. The identified experiment reports provide valuable hints regarding threats to validity and mitigation strategies in student experiments. For instance regarding the impact of the recruitment strategy, *Nugroho* [20] reports on the results of mandatory student experiments. Reports on voluntary student experiments where no bonuses are given but the experiment material is relevant for the exam are, for example, provided by *Espana et al.* [21] and *Genereo et al.* [22]. In contrast, *Karoulis et al.* [23] and *Genero et al.* [24] report on experiments that are voluntary in nature, but with bonuses to the student exam results to ensure student motivation. An example for paid experiments outside of a course is given by *Arisholm et al.* [25].

Related works on combining empirical research and university teaching exist. Most of them identify course setups which aid the students' learning experience and make use of the application of empirical methods in the course (e.g., [1–3]). In addition, guidelines on how to use empirical methods in general are available. For example, *Runeson* and *Höst* [26] present guidelines for conducting and reporting case study research. Regarding the alignment of university teaching and empirical research, *Carver et al.* [27] elaborate on guidelines with a particular interest in designing ethically correct student experiments with respect to external validity.

In summary, although some threats to validity particular to student experiments are well understood, the relevant literature does not provide a comprehensive analysis of these threats. To this aim, Sect. 3 summarizes our findings regarding threats to validity in student experiments and mitigation strategies, based on related approaches concerning experiment design, experiment reports, as well as on our experiences in empirical research with students as participants. In addition, we believe that the description of an example experiment which explicitly considers such threats to validity, and reporting the applied mitigation strategies can aid researchers and teachers in conducting student experiments in their courses (see Sect. 4).

3   Threats to Validity in Student Experiments and Corresponding Mitigation Strategies

As we already introduced, student experiments induce several threats to validity that differ from the threats to validity in non-student experiments with industry professionals. Based on an analysis of related work (cf. Sect. 2) and our findings from addressing the issues related to student participation in our example experiment (cf. Sect. 4), this section discusses threats particular to student participants in detail.

We use the classification proposed in *Wohlin et al.* [15] to separate between the different types and effects of threats to validity. As we assume that student experiments will most likely be conducted for theory testing, we will present the several types of threats to validity in decreasing order of importance according to [15]. For the purpose of theory testing, internal validity is threatened the most, followed by construct validity, conclusion validity, and external validity.

In the following subsections, we elaborate on respective threats in more detail. As can be seen, while some specific effects and threats do not differ from industry experiments, others are even of less relevance or severance in student experiments.

3.1 Internal Validity in Experiments with Student Participants

Internal validity is concerned with effects threatening the causal relationship between treatment and outcome of the experiment [15]. Student experiments conducted in a course setup suffer from several threats to internal validity, resulting from the fact that many influences (e.g., other courses, student self-selection to tutorial classes) are either unknown or not under the control of the researchers. Table 1 lists all threats to internal validity specific to student experiments, and appropriate mitigation strategies.

Threats to internal validity are likely to occur in student experiments. Since internal validity is of vital importance for theory testing experiments, particular emphasis must be paid to avoid these threats. As shown in Table 1, threats to internal validity stemming from student use can be mitigated by carefully selecting an appropriate experiment design. However, not all experiment designs are able to avoid such threats from student participation. For example, an experiment relying on multiple measurements/treatments throughout the whole semester will suffer from threats to history, maturation, testing, or interactions with selections. Hence, we suggest conducting an experiment at a single point in time, using randomization broadly, and using treatment and control groups. In many cases the use of a within-subject design where each participant acts as treatment and control will be preferable. As every participant uses the same methods and the same experiment material, within-subject designs allow for fair educational treatment of participants.

3.2 Construct Validity in Experiments with Student Participants

Threats to construct validity refer to the relation between the observed experiment results and the theory behind the experiment, and can be separated into design threats to construct validity and social threats to construct validity [15]. As shown in Table 2, we assume that design threats to construct validity in student experiments will most likely not differ from non-student experiments. Furthermore, design threats to construct validity due to participant heterogeneity will most likely be even less severe in student experiments, since the recruited students' experience will typically be rather homogeneous.

In contrast, social threats to construct validity might be more severe in student experiments than in non-student experiments. By providing information before the experiment, as it is common in teaching environments, the students might get to know the hypothesis and thereby try to adapt their output. In addition, researchers often motivate student participation by rating their experiment results. This is often done to induce stress situations. Such actions will typically improve the experiment results and thereby corrupt the construct validity.

Table 1. Internal validity

Threats in Student Experiments	Possible Mitigation Strategies
History: During the semester, the course's teaching material advances and thereby the students gain knowledge. Hence, students may perform differently, which may distort results in case multiple measurements are taken over time. (cf. [11])	In non-student experiments, randomization could be used to avoid these threats. However, if the material used in student experiments is related to the teaching material this is not possible since the instruction material cannot be presented in different orders for different groups of students.
Maturation: Students may also improve between two points in time because of other courses not under control of the researchers. This might have a significant impact, especially on comparing treatments at the start and at the end of the course. (cf. [21])	
Instrumentation: Experiments conducted over multiple semesters may suffer from changing instructors. (cf. [9])	Threats caused by different experiment instructors and resulting effects are hard to control, and cannot be avoided in experiment design.
The same is valid for large courses in which multiple tutorial sessions are offered. In addition, it is very unlikely that all tutorials will evolve identically (e.g., due to different students actively participating in the tutorials).	Subject selection to treatment and control group must not be based on the tutorial session membership. We suggest using randomization as an effective mitigation (cf. [23]).
Questions and other experiment material from industry may be inappropriately transferred to the students' knowledge and experience level. (cf. [21])	To assure the material has been correctly transferred from practice to an educational setting, the use of pretests seems beneficial (cf. [20], [21]).
Statistical Regression: Groups of selected student subjects may only consist of either good or bad students. Especially students self-selection may increase this threat (cf. [21])	Students should not be selected based on specific properties. Especially the use of entry barriers will exclude bad students and should be considered as threat. We suggest the recruitment of entire student populations (e.g., by conducting mandatory experiments within a course, cf. [20]).
Selection: This threat may occur when students are invited personally by the researchers, or when students are motivated by gaining extra points to be admitted to the final exam (bad students will typically have a greater need for such extra points).	
Student selection must be considered as opportunity sampling in any case.	Replication of experiments with different populations (e.g., in other courses, or at other universities) can reduce this threat. (cf. [24])
Mortality: A course may lose students throughout the semester, thereby the sizes and compositions of treatment and control groups may be decreasing differently. (cf. [9])	Randomization can aid the equal distribution of this effect among treatment and control groups. (cf. [28])
Further Effects: In general, any experiment design may require having multiple or repeated measurements over time. Hence, resulting testing effects do not differ from respective threats in non-student experiments with industry professionals (cf. [9]). Neither do threats caused by ambiguity about the direction of causal influence, since causal relationships are specific for the research questions that are studied.	

Single Group Threats

(*Continued*)

Table 1. (*Continued*)

	Threats in Student Experiments	Possible Mitigation Strategies
Multiple Group Threats	***Interactions with Selection:*** Assignment of students to treatment and control groups based on different tutorial sessions might induce interaction effects. For example, due to time constraints of the students, first semester students might gather in one tutorial session, while another session is in the majority visited by third semester students.	Subject selection to treatment and control group must not be based on the tutorial session membership. We assume randomization as an effective mitigation (cf. [23]).
	In an educational environment, it cannot be avoided that students of different treatment and control groups interact with each other. Even if treatment and control groups were assigned on the basis of different tutorial sessions, interaction effects outside the class are not under control of the researchers.	To avoid such interaction threats we assume that limiting the experiment time is appropriate. For example, try to conduct an experiment in one single day, or in even less time (e.g., within an hour). In addition, the researcher can ensure isolation of treatment and control group (cf. [23]).
Social Threats	***Diffusion or Imitation of Treatments:*** The control group might make use of an already taught method which should only be used by the treatment group.	Avoid upfront briefing and keep the teaching material made available before experiment execution to a minimum.
	Compensatory Equalization of Treatments: Students of the control group might work harder on their results to measure up to the treatment group.	Do not give bonuses based on the students' performance. Use a within-subject design or avoid that the control group gets to know the treatment group's result (e.g., [23]).
	Compensatory Rivalry: Any kind of motivation (e.g., a bonus to the final grade) will lead to students performing better than under non-rewarding conditions. In particular, this affects the control group: students might fear that students of the treatment group will receive higher grades.	Do not give bonuses based on the student's performance in the experiment. (cf. [21], [24])
	Resentful Demoralization: Students might be demoralized because of worse experiment outcomes and may give up in fear of bad grading.	

3.3 Conclusion Validity in Experiments with Student Participants

Threats to conclusion validity deal with the risk of drawing the wrong conclusions. This might be due to low statistical power, using statistical methods not applicable to the data, or the use of less reliable measures. We assume that the threats to conclusion validity in student experiments do not differ from other experiments (cf. Table 3). Since student experiments are commonly conducted because of a high number of available students, especially statistical power and significance of results can be assumed to be high. In addition, students in a course tend to be highly homogeneous. Therefore, we assume high conclusion validity of student experiments in most cases.

3.4 External Validity in Experiments with Student Participants

Finally, threats to external validity (see Table 4) undermine the generalizability of experiment results. As mentioned above, external validity is commonly seen as the least important validity for theory testing experiments. In conclusion, the evaluation

Table 2. Construct validity

Threats in Student Experiments	Possible Mitigation Strategies
Design Threats	
Confounding Constructs and Levels of Constructs: This threat seems to be less important in student experiments. Though the experience levels might also differ for students, it can be assumed that students' experience in general will be more homogeneous than in industrial experiments.	
Further Effects: Threats to validity resulting from inadequate preoperational explication of constructs, mono-operation and mono-method bias, interaction of different treatments, interaction of testing and treatment, as well as restricted generalizability across constructs do not differ from respective threats to validity in non-student experiments. These effects strongly depend on the topic of the concrete study, i.e., the theory behind the experiment, and its design (cf. [13], example mitigations can also be found in [23]).	
Social Threats	
Hypothesis Guessing: Due to the courses teaching material, students might guess the hypothesis of the experiment and base their behavior in the experiment on this hypothesis; either to impress the instructor, to perform outstandingly for achieving bonuses to their grades, or to undermine the study of unpopular instructors.	To avoid this threat, it is of importance to minimize upfront briefing related to the experiment. In course setups, the teaching material that is provided before the experiment is conducted should also not exceed the necessary limit. (cf. [28])
Evaluation Apprehension: Students might draw the conclusion they are being evaluated by the outcome of the experiment (which might be true in case special "motivations" are given to the students).	Conduct mandatory student experiments within a course, especially without bonuses given as motivation (cf. [21], [24]).
Further Effects: Threats to validity regarding *experimenter expectancies* do not show any difference compared to non-student experiments.	

Table 3. Conclusion validity

Threats in Student Experiments	Possible Mitigation Strategies
Low Statistical Power: This threat seems to be less important in student experiments. Most of the times researchers use students because such experiments can more easily achieve a sufficient number of participants.	
Reliability of Measures: Students may not understand the material in the intended way, for instance due to ambiguous phrases leading to differing measures.	Particular emphasis must be given to the verbalization of questions and experiment material in student experiments. To assure that the material has been correctly transferred from practice to an educational setting, the use of pretests and expert reviews seems beneficial (cf. [20], [21]).
Random Irrelevancies in Experimental Setting: In general, there is no significant difference to non-student experiments. However, spatial conditions will be more likely under control of the researcher in educational environments than in industrial environments, so that this threat is expected to be less severe in student experiments.	
Random Heterogeneity in Subjects: This threat seems to be less important in student experiments. Student experiments in a course will make use of a highly homogeneous set of participants. (cf. [22], [29])	
Further Effects: Threats to validity that are caused by *violated assumptions of statistical tests, fishing and the error rate*, as well as *reliability of treatment implementation* do not differ from respective threats in non-student experiments. (cf. [28])	

of generalizability to the problem domain or to real industry applications is often suggested to be performed by other empirical methods in addition to the use of controlled experiments (cf. [6]). For example, expert opinion mining, action research, or case studies seem appropriate for this task.

The threats to external validity as presented in Table 4 pose some rather fundamental issues related to student experiments, which heavily depend on the concrete study, and may not be easily mitigated in experiment design. Hence, it needs to be discussed whether the use of students instead of industry experts and professionals is in general appropriate, and whether the use of simplified experiment material can still be used to generalize to real industrial problems and solutions.

Table 4. External validity

Threats in Student Experiments	Possible Mitigation Strategies
Interaction of Selection and Treatment: Student populations might not be representative for industrial populations. (cf. [9], [30])	Use additional empirical methods such as pilot testing, expert opinion mining, action research, or case studies to evaluate generalizability (cf. [6]).
Interaction of Setting and Treatment: Simplified experiment material, which is particularly designed to fit the students' knowledge and experience, might not be representative for real-world settings. (cf. [20], [29])	
Further Effects: Threats to validity from an interaction of history and treatment do not differ from non-student experiments. These effects can happen in any kind of experiment, depending on the individual time the experiment is conducted (cf. [13]).	

Using Students as Experiment Participants. As outlined in Sect. 2, many empirical studies have been conducted with students instead of professional software developers. Beside this common practice, investigations showed that there are only minor differences between professional software developers and (graduate) software engineering students, which is why students may be used instead of professionals in experiments under certain conditions (see Sect. 2).

Using Simplified Experiment Material. Beside the use of students the use of simplified experiment material might also result in a threat to external validity. While this threat is common for most experimental setups, it is increased in student experiments as the experiment material must be transferred to the level of students' knowledge and experience in order to ensure adequate instrumentation. Otherwise, the use of real material as experiment material can easily result in threats to internal validity (cf. Sect. 3.1) due to lack of understanding by the student participants. Simplified experiment material is not only commonly used in student experiments (e.g., [20], or [29]), it is furthermore often a necessary precondition to ensure internal and construct validity, which are of particular importance in theory testing experiments.

4 Example Experiment in a Requirements Engineering Course

In this section, we will provide details on an example student experiment. The example experiment shows how the proposed mitigation strategies can be implemented in the setting of a requirements engineering course. Furthermore, we will detail the integration of the experiment into the teaching material. The example experiment shows a possibility to conduct experiments with student participants, which are in accordance with ethical considerations from a teacher's point of view (cf. [27]). To this end, we will introduce the requirements engineering course, discuss the research question of the student experiment, and discuss the study design with respect to the threats to validity from Sect. 3.

4.1 The Master-Level Requirements Engineering Course

Our main goal was to integrate a controlled experiment regarding requirements engineering research into a master-level requirements engineering course in such a way that the experiment benefits the students learning experience. In the following we will provide some details on the requirements engineering course.

Participants: The course is part of two master degree programs: M. Sc. in applied computer science with particular emphasis on systems engineering, and M. Sc. in business information systems. In addition, undergraduate students, which are provisionally accepted into the Masters' program, may also participate.

Technicalities: The course is for elective credit. In recent years between 40 and 50 students took the course each year. The course comprises 15 weeks in the summer-term, each week one lecture and one tutorial session are offered, each of which lasts 90 min. Successful participation in the course is valued with six graded credit points (ECTS, European Credit Transfer and Accumulation System). The grade is determined solely by the student's performance on the final exam at the end of the semester. Attendance at lectures and tutorial sessions is voluntary. However, in order to be admitted to the exam, successful completion of the tutorial is mandatory. The tutorial is completed successfully once the students solved several modeling tasks regarding a case example. Note that performance in the tutorial itself is not graded. Students work in teams of four to six and the task is discussed for each group's case example during the tutorial session. For more detailed information on the course setup please refer to [31]. We introduced a mandatory experiment in the 2014 edition of the requirements engineering course. The experiment was designed as an online-questionnaire, and had to be completed by each student on her own outside the tutorial session. The experiment was discussed afterwards in the tutorial session.

Course Substance: The course aims at teaching advanced methods and techniques pertaining to the documentation and analysis of requirements. The course places particular emphasis on model-based approaches, and builds upon foundations instructed in a companion undergraduate course that teaches the basic concepts of requirements engineering. The course aims at teaching four topics of major importance in requirements engineering: goal-oriented requirements engineering, scenario-based requirements engineering, essential systems analysis, and validation activities. The course makes use of industrial case examples from the embedded systems industry to provide insights into realistic problem situations.

4.2   Purpose of the Experiment

In the past years, no practical insight was given into requirements validation. As the relation between documented requirements and constantly changing stakeholder intentions is of particular importance, we identified this as a shortcoming of our course design. Hence, we conducted mandatory student experiments in 2014 and 2015 as introduction to requirements validation to address this issue. Subsequently, we will briefly outline the research question of the experiment.

In the area of manual reviews lots of research has been done to evaluate the effectiveness of review approaches (e.g., [32–37]). In consequence, reviews using perspective-based reading seem to be effective. When applying perspective-based reviews to model-based development it is to question which notation format aids the review from a certain perspective best. In this area of requirements engineering we proposed a new validation approach using dedicated review models. These automatically generated review models aid the manual review of embedded systems' functional design by visualizing inconsistencies between the functional design artifacts and the behavioral requirements. Inconsistencies may occur due to later changes in the functional design, which are then not reflected in the original behavioral requirements. It is essential to ensure the correctness of both types of artifacts w.r.t. the current stakeholder intentions, which can only be carried out in manual reviews. More detailed information on the approach can be found in [38], a detailed report on the concrete experimental setup and its outcome can be found in [39].

4.3   Experimental Setting and Student Tasks

In the experiment, students were asked to review certain artifacts from a requirements engineering perspective. In particular, the experiment aimed at determining the use of dedicated review models as review artifacts compared to the use of the original functional design as a review artifact. Each participant was asked to review a set of artifacts according to two different review styles. One review style was to review the functional design as review artifact directly; the other review style was to review the functional design by investigating the dedicated review model as review artifact. For both cases the task was to check the information contained in the review artifact against textually documented stakeholder intentions. As we used a within-subject design the order of the tasks was randomized.

After experiment completion, an intensive debriefing was done within a tutorial session. In this session, the issues of reviews, changing stakeholder intentions, and individual effects of model cognition were discussed. In addition, simplifications due to the experimental setup were outlined and insight into real-world situations was provided. Of course, the research question, the results of the student experiment, and the matter of experiments in software and requirements engineering were part of the discussions as well.

Table 5. Mitigation strategies applied and threats to validity addressed

Mitigation Strategy and Implementation	Addressed Threat Effects
Multi Group Design. To avoid the multitude of single group threats to internal validity we used a multiple group setup with treatment and control groups.	*Internal Validity* • All Single Group Threats
Single Point of Measurement. To allow for a within-subject design and the broader use of randomizations, we limited the experiment to a single measurement taken in a limited time frame. The study was conducted as an online experiment. The experiment was designed to take about 20 to 30 minutes, and the participants were given a time frame of five days for participation. This was done to minimize interaction effects, and to ensure that participants will not lose motivation during the experiment. It must be noted that, of course, by giving a time frame of five days and allowing participation from home, we minimized interaction effects in class during participation, but had no control over interaction effects between students.	*Internal Validity* • History • Maturation • Interactions with Selection
Within-Subject Design and Randomization. We used a within-subject design with randomization of group assignments and treatments. In doing so, we reduced effects from interactions among subjects. In addition, the within-subject design aids in avoiding threats from compensatory equalization of treatments.	*Internal Validity* • Instrumentation • Interactions with Selection • Compensatory Equalization of Treatments
Give No Bonuses and Use Mandatory Participation. To avoid social threats to internal validity we decided to conduct the experiment as a mandatory part within the master-level requirements engineering course, and explicitly decided to give no bonuses or credits as motivation. It is to mention that the experiment was closely integrated into the course's teaching material; otherwise mandatory participation can easily contradict ethical guidelines. This also aids in avoiding threats from evaluation apprehension. In total, we had 45 participants. Note that the results of four participants were not considered, as for these participants, it was obvious that they answered the questions by clicking through, which resulted in certain answering patterns and in extremely fast completion time. Based on our experience of mandatory but anonymous student participation, we assume that exclusion of less than 10% of the participants is acceptable. We believe that a serious participation of 90% of the students does not justify the use of bonus systems, which would result in severe threats to internal and to construct validity.	*Internal Validity* • Statistical Regression • Selection • Compensatory Equalization of Treatments • Compensatory Rivalry • Resentful Demoralization *Construct Validity* • Evaluation Apprehension

(*Continued*)

Table 5. (*Continued*)

Mitigation Strategy and Implementation	Addressed Threat Effects
Expert Reviews. We used expert reviews of the experiment material in order to avoid threats from unreliable measures. We involved industry professionals to ensure that the transformation of industrial examples into experiment material did not corrupt the original intention of industrial problems and examples.	*Conclusion Validity* • Reliability of Measures *External Validity* • Interaction of Setting and Treatment
Conduct Additional Investigations. To ensure external validity we used additional empirical methods involving industry professionals. In particular, we conducted case studies and expert investigations. These activities are described in [40].	*External Validity* • Interaction of Selection and Treatment • Interaction of Setting and Treatment
Minimize Upfront Teaching. We gave a minimum of instruction related to the experiment beforehand, and we did not give a detailed upfront briefing, to lower threats from hypothesis guessing. In order to lower effects from diffusion or imitation of treatments we used the experiment as an introduction to a new topic of the course material. Thereby, we also avoided providing too many details by the instruction material of the course.	*Internal Validity* • Diffusion or Imitation of Treatments *Construct Validity* • Hypothesis Guessing
Conduct a Pretest. We used a pretest with different participants to validate students' ability of understanding the material in the intended way. Please note that it would affect threats to internal validity resulting from testing and interactions with selection if the students participating in the pretest were chosen from the same course in which the major experiment shall be conducted.	*Internal Validity* • Instrumentation *Conclusion Validity* • Reliability of Measures

The experiment material was derived from real industrial examples and was reviewed by our industrial partners. On the one hand, this action was taken to ensure a proper level of external validity, but on the other hand this aimed also at industry-orientation of the teaching material.

4.4 Discussion of the Remaining Threats to Validity

As we used a within-subject design there is a risk that learning effects impact the results. To evaluate these effects, we compared the dependent variables across the different orders in which participants conducted the experiment. Since the values are equally distributed across all orders, and differences are far from approaching significance, we did not recognize any effects on the results.

A severe threat to validity is the use of an online experiment to determine efficiency, as there is no knowledge about the actual time consumption for each decision taken. We measured the time consumption for each page of the questionnaire (i.e. for the review of one review artifact), but these values can easily be corrupted (e.g., by a participant taking a break during answering one page). In addition, as can be seen in

Table 5, threats due to interaction effects resulting from the time frame of five days must be considered. While we avoided interaction among students in class (i.e. during the experiment conduction), we had no control over private interactions.

To validate the assumption that conclusion validity is higher in experiments with student participants, we measured several covariates. For example, highest educational achievement, degree program, semester, age, gender, as well as participants self-rated experience in six categories related to conducting reviews in general, and the used modeling notations in particular. It turned out that the students within the master-level requirements engineering course were homogeneous regarding their knowledge and experience level. To evaluate the assumption that sufficient statistical power in experiments with student participants can be easily achieved, we conducted post-hoc power analysis for all hypotheses, which showed high effect sizes and high power for each.

5   Conclusion

In this paper we report on specific threats to validity in controlled experiments with student participants and on mitigation strategies for these threats. Based on related work in these areas, as well as on the experience we gained from our own empirical research, this paper analyzed and discussed respective threats and potential mitigation strategies in detail. As a result, we can conclude that, in a proper empirical setting, students can compensate for the lack of professional software engineers in controlled experiments when these evaluations are combined with other industry evaluations as suggested by [6].

In addition, we described parts of an experiment that made use of student participants and was embedded into a university requirements engineering course. We have shown how to address threats to validity that are specific to experiments with students as subjects. The experiment design addressed, in particular, these threats to validity and considered related mitigations taken from the literature. As a result, we can conclude that experiments with student participants can be conducted such a way that student specific threats to validity are mitigated and the experiment benefits the students learning experience as well.

In future work, it will be of particular interest whether experiments with undergraduate student as subjects solely have a limited generalizability, or if other threats to validity are more severe as well. In addition, there is a need to investigate how student experiments consisting of multiple measurements and pairwise matched cases can be properly conducted under consideration of the existing threats to validity.

Acknowledgements. This research was partly funded by the *German Federal Ministry of Education and Research* under grant no. 01IS12005C and grant no. 01IS15058C. Thanks to our industrial partners for their support in creating the experiment material used. In particular we thank Peter Heidl, Jens Höfflinger and John MacGregor (Bosch), Frank Houdek (Daimler), and Stefan Beck and Arnaud Boyer (Airbus).

References

1. Port, D., Klappholz, D.: Empirical research in the software engineering classroom. In: Proceedings of the 17th IEEE Conference on Software Engineering Education and Training, pp. 132–137 (2004)
2. Boehm, B., Koolmanojwong, S.: Combining software engineering education and empirical research via instrumented real-client team project courses. In: Proceedings of the 17th IEEE Conference on Software Engineering Education and Training, pp. 209–211 (2014)
3. Höst, M.: Introducing empirical software engineering methods in education. In: Proceedings of the 15th IEEE Conference on Software Engineering Education and Training, pp. 170–179 (2002)
4. Siegmund, J., Siegmund, N., Apel, S.: Views on internal and external validity in empirical software engineering. In: Proceedings of the 37th IEEE/ACM International Conference on Software Engineering, ICSE 2015, pp. 9–19. IEEE, Florence, Italy, 16–24 May 2015. ISBN 978-1-4799-1934-5
5. Salman, I., Misirli, A.T., Juzgado, N.J.: Are students representatives of professionals in software engineering experiments? In: Proceedings of the 37th IEEE/ACM International Conference on Software Engineering, ICSE 2015, pp. 666–676. IEEE, Florence, Italy, 16–24 May 2015. ISBN 978-1-4799-1934-5
6. Wieringa, R.: Empirical research methods for technology validation: scaling up to practice. J. Syst. Softw. **95**, 19–31 (2014)
7. Carver, J., Jaccheri, L., Morasca, S., Shull, F.: Issues in using students in empirical studies in software engineering education. In: Proceedings of Software Metrics Symposium, pp. 239–249 (2003)
8. Sjøberg, D., Hannay, J., Hansen, O., Kampenes, V., Karahasanovic, A., Liborg, N., Rekdal, A.: A survey of controlled experiments in software engineering. IEEE Trans. Softw. Eng. **31**, 733–753 (2005)
9. Sjøberg, D., Anda, B., Arisholm, E., Dybå, T., Jørgensen, M., Karahasanovic, A., Koren, E., Vokác, M.: Conducting realistic experiments in software engineering. In: Proceedings of the International Symposium on Empirical Software Engineering, pp. 17–26 (2002)
10. Berry, D., Tichy, W.: Response to 'comments on formal methods application: an empirical tale of software development'. IEEE Trans. Softw. Eng. **29**(6), 572–575 (2003)
11. Höst, M., Regnell, B., Wohlin, C.: Using students as subjects - a comparative study of students and professionals in lead time impact assessment. J. Empirical Softw. Eng. **5**, 201–214 (2000)
12. Svahnberg, M., Aurum, A., Wohlin, C.: Using students as subjects – an empirical evaluation. In: Proceedings of the International Symposium on Empirical Software Engineering and Measurement, pp. 288–290 (2008)
13. Runeson, P.: Using students as experiment subjects - an analysis on graduate and freshmen PSP student data. In: Proceedings of the International Conference on Evaluation and Assessment in Software Engineering, pp. 95–102 (2003)
14. Tichy, W.: Hints for reviewing empirical work in software engineering. J. Empirical Softw. Eng. **5**, 309–312 (2000)
15. Wohlin, C., Runeson, P., Höst, M., Ohlsson, M., Regnell, B., Wesslén, A.: Experimentation in Software Engineering. An Introduction. Kluwer Academic Publishers, Boston (2000)
16. Neto, A., Conte, T.: A conceptual model to address threats to validity in controlled experiments. In: Proceedings of the 17th International Conference on Evaluation and Assessment in Software Engineering, pp. 82–85 (2013)
17. Robson, C.: Real World Research, 3rd edn. Wiley, Hoboken (2011)

18. Campbell, D., Stanley, J.: Experimental and Quasi-Experimental Designs for Research. Houghton Mifflin Company, Boston (1963)
19. Cook, T., Campbell, D.: Quasi-Experimentation - Design and Analysis Issues for Field Settings. Houghton Mifflin Company, Boston (1979)
20. Nugroho, A.: Level of detail in UML models and its impact on model comprehension: a controlled experiment. J. Inf. Softw. Technol. **51**, 1670–1685 (2009)
21. Espana, S., Condori-Fernandez, N., Gonzalez, A., Pastor, O.: Evaluating the completeness and granularity of functional requirements specifications: a controlled experiment. In: Proceedings of the International Conference on Requirements Engineering, pp. 161–170 (2009)
22. Genero, M., Manso, E., Visaggio, A., Canfora, G., Piattini, M.: Building measure-based prediction models for UML class diagram maintainability. J. Empirical Softw. Eng. **12**, 517–549 (2007)
23. Karoulis, A., Stamelos, I., Anglis, L., Pombortsis, A.: Formally assessing an instructional tool: a controlled experiment in software engineering. IEEE Trans. Educ. **48**, 133–139 (2005)
24. Genero, M., Cruz-Lemus, J., Caivano, D., Abrahao, S., Insfran, E., Carsi, J.: Assessing the influence of stereotypes on the comprehension of UML sequence diagrams: a controlled experiment. In: Czarnecki, K., Ober, I., Bruel, J.-M., Uhl, A., Völter, M. (eds.) MODELS 2008. LNCS, vol. 5301, pp. 280–294. Springer, Heidelberg (2008)
25. Arisholm, E., Sjoberg, D., Jorgensen, M.: Assessing the changeability of two object-oriented design alternatives - a controlled experiment. J. Empirical Softw. Eng. **6**, 231–277 (2001)
26. Runeson, P., Höst, M.: Guidlines for conducting and reporting case study research in software engineering. J. Empirical Softw. Eng. **14**, 131–164 (2009)
27. Carver, J., Jaccheri, L., Morasca, S., Shull, F.: A checklist for integrating student empirical studies with research and teaching goals. J. Empirical Softw. Eng. **15**, 35–59 (2009)
28. Ricca, F., Di Pinta, M., Torchiano, M., Tonella, P., Ceccato, M.: The role of experience and ability in comprehension tasks supported by UML stereotypes. In: Proceedings of the International Conference on Software Engineering, ICSE (2007)
29. Aceituna, D., Gursimran, W., Do, H., Lee, S.: Model-based requirements verification method: conclusions from two controlled experiments. J. Inf. Softw. Technol. **56**, 321–334 (2014)
30. Berander, P.: Using students as subjects in requirements prioritization. In: Proceedings of the International Symposium on Empirical Software Engineering ISESE 2004, pp. 167–176 (2004)
31. Daun, M., Salmon, A., Tenbergen, B., Weyer, T., Pohl, K.: Industrial case studies in graduate requirements engineering courses: the impact on student motivation. In: Proceedings of the IEEE Conference on Software Engineering Education and Training, pp. 3–12 (2014)
32. Miller, J., Wood, M., Roper, M.: Further experiences with scenarios and checklists. J. Empirical Softw. Eng. **3**, 37–64 (1998)
33. Basili, V., Green, S., Laitenberger, O.L.F., Shull, F., Sorumgard, S., Zelkowski, M.: The empirical investigation of perspective-based reading. J. Empirical Softw. Eng. **1**, 133–164 (1996)
34. Porter, A., Votta, L., Basili, V.: Comparing detection methods for software requirement inspection: a replicated experiment. IEEE Trans. Softw. Eng. **21**, 563–575 (1994)
35. Laitenberger, O.L.F., Emam, K., Harbich, T.: An internally replicated quasi-experimental comparison of checklist and perspective-based reading of code documents. IEEE Trans. Softw. Eng. **27**, 387–421 (2001)

36. Berling, T., Runeson, P.: Evaluation of a perspective based review method applied in an industrial setting. IEEE Proc. Softw. **150**, 177–184 (2003)
37. Sabaliauskaite, G., Kusumoto, S., Inoue, K.: Assessing defect detection performance of interacting teams in object-oriented design inspection. J. Inf. Softw. Technol. **46**, 875–886 (2004)
38. Daun, M., Weyer, T., Pohl, K.: Detecting and correcting outdated requirements in function-centered engineering of embedded systems. In: Fricker, S.A., Schneider, K. (eds.) REFSQ 2015. LNCS, vol. 9013, pp. 65–80. Springer, Heidelberg (2015)
39. Daun, M., Salmon, A., Weyer, T., Pohl, K.: The impact of students' skills and experiences on empirical results: a controlled experiment with undergraduate and graduate students. In: Proceedings of the 19th International Conference on Evaluation and Assessment in Software Engineering, pp. 29:1–29:6 (2015)
40. Daun, M., Höfflinger, J., Weyer, T.: Function-centered engineering of embedded systems: evaluating industry needs and possible solutions. In: Proceedings of the International Conference on Evaluation and Assessment of Novel Approaches to Software Engineering (2014)

Lean Development in Design Science Research: Deliberating Principles, Prospects and Pitfalls

Umar Ruhi[1] and Okhaide Akhigbe[2(✉)]

[1] Telfer School of Management, University of Ottawa, Ottawa, Canada
umar.ruhi@uottawa.ca
[2] School of Computer Science and Electrical Engineering,
University of Ottawa, Ottawa, Canada
okhaide@uottawa.ca

Abstract. **[Context and motivation:]** As a relevant and viable research methodology that addresses the development and empirical investigation of new artifacts, design science research (DSR) has gained traction in the requirements and software engineering research community over the past decade. **[Question/Problem:]** In this paper, we deliberate the synergies between the lean mindset and DSR, and explore the application of lean development approaches in the planning and execution of software and requirements engineering research projects. **[Principal idea:]** The widespread adoption of lean approaches in many business and technology practices today provides the impetus to explore their application in the context of software and requirements engineering empirical research. Toward this, we offer a review of key principles underlying the lean mindset and provide an overview of the typical processes followed in DSR research projects. Subsequently, we reflect the potential for lean development approaches to facilitate DSR projects. **[Contribution:]** We propose a conceptual framework that integrates lean principles with DSR phases and outputs, and we aim to inspire future discussion on the application of the lean mindset in the planning and execution of empirical research projects.

Keywords: Design Science Research · Lean development · Lean mindset · Requirements engineering · Research methodology · Research strategy · Software engineering

1 Introduction

The widespread application of software today facilitates addressing practical and real problems organizations and their consumers encounter on a daily basis. Organizations are now more knowledgeable of customers' needs while customers' demands for prompt and quality products and services are at an all-time high. Contemporary requirements and software engineering as well as information system (IS) research focuses on addressing this concerns. They seek to find better ways of developing, operating, and maintaining software and IS towards improving the effectiveness and efficiency of interactions between organizations and their consumers towards meeting respective

© Springer International Publishing Switzerland 2016
M. Daneva and O. Pastor (Eds.): REFSQ 2016, LNCS 9619, pp. 286–300, 2016.
DOI: 10.1007/978-3-319-30282-9_20

business needs [1, 13, 17]. Interestingly, business needs continues to evolve. This evolution is prompted by new customer demands and preferences, new laws and policies, stricter regulations and new or existing competition. These scenarios therefore demand that organizations continue to innovate towards having a competitive edge with respect to understanding and addressing requirements as well as dealing with the vast amount of information they encounter daily. This is in addition to satisfying their primal concern of creating value for their respective stakeholders while minimizing waste.

Now value has been described to be created as a result of the interaction of people, technology and shared information in addressing different problems [23]. It includes the various software and systems created to facilitate this interaction. So also is the research processes involved in their creation. Among the different research approaches used in requirements and software engineering to create such software and IS that offer value, is design science research (DSR). Rather than follow a descriptive or prescriptive approach to problem solving common to research, the DSR methodology attempts to create innovative things; artifacts, that solve human problems in a formalized manner [28]. In its application, DSR proposes that knowledge and understanding of a problem domain and its solution are achieved in building and applying the designed artifact [13]. This indicates a close relationship between design and research. The problem domain reveals two kinds of problems that DSR address, practical and knowledge problems. While practical problems requires a change in the world so it better agree with some stakeholders' goal, knowledge problems requires a change in our knowledge about the world the problems exist [30]. To solve practical problems, DSR's objective is to come up with technology-based solutions relevant to the organization's problems; changes that meet their goal. To solve knowledge problems, propositions claimed to be true to the respective laws in the problem environment are sought towards arriving at an effective artifact that meet the goals of stakeholders. Solving a practical problem utilizes criteria specific to the organization whose problem the DSR project seeks to address while solving a knowledge problem considers organization independent criteria [13, 30].

This DSR approach towards problem solving while rigorous tends to focus on the *output* of the research, the artifact which addresses the organization' or stakeholder's problem. It does not focus on the expected *outcome*, the value obtained. From the perspective of the stakeholder, value is expressed in terms of the outcome rather than the output. This outcome takes into consideration conditions of practice, variables that exist in created outputs which can impact their behavior, avenues to address waste [31]. With DSR as a pragmatic approach therefore, the need to factor in value, in the DSR process is required. To address this concern, a *lean mindset* to DSR which puts the emphasis on the expected outcome of value creation is needed. A *lean mindset* will motivate the research process to build upon a core principle in lean development; *continuous delivery* of the solution to solve stakeholders' problems. Also knows as *design thinking,* this approach takes into consideration the constantly changing environments the stakeholders' problems exist. It employs a combination of discovery and development of a solution in iteration towards achieving outcomes [12, 27]. With this, working collaboratively with the stakeholder, the learning obtained in iteration is employed towards arriving at the appropriate solution. Instead of considering the artifacts to be created as a series of requirements to be built, they are considered as a set of hypothesis about the problem to be validated. This results in a focus on artifacts that work and not on aesthetics which consumes resources. The DSR process can then include early and ongoing elicitation, specification and validation of stakeholders' requirements allowing for earlier agreement or refinements or prioritized artifacts.

The objective of this paper therefore is to add to the existing conversation on value in requirements and software research projects brought about by lean [3, 5] and agile [18, 19] methods. We aim to inspire a discussion on the application of a lean mindset and lean development approaches in the planning and execution of DSR projects towards this regard. To enable rapid and flexible cycles of requirements elicitation, specification and validation, lean design approaches can help DSR projects through their emphasis on clear articulation of goals and regular interaction with stakeholders'. We believe that lean development practices can benefit DSR by virtue of their highly iterative, continuous feedback driven processes. The paper is organized as follows. First we provide information on DSR, describe its process and outputs in Sect. 2. In Sect. 3, the lean approach is described; here we address lean development principles, the lean loop, lean iteration patterns and the lean canvass. Section 4 presents our proposition on how lean principles can help in DSR and Sect. 5 introduces the integrated framework, while Sect. 6 provides a caveat on research rigor. Finally, we conclude in Sect. 7 with proposed directions for further conversation on the topic.

2 Design Science Research (DSR)

Having struggled for acceptance within academia because of its peculiar approach, DSR is emerging as a legitimate research paradigm today [10, 29]. Innate to DSR is its process and outputs as discussed herein.

A. *DSR Process.* The DSR process constitutes a series of rigorous activities involved in designing, evaluating and communicating artifacts used to solve organizational problems [26]. It has as its main focus; the knowledge DSR contributes [29]. The process indicates how researches using the DSR paradigm should be carried out and communicated. Activities involved in DSR process models are listed below and illustrated in Fig. 1.

    i. *Awareness of the problem:* While the source of the problem may come from multiple sources, the output of this step is a formal or informal proposal for a new research effort.

    ii. *Suggestion:* This step involves the identification of a tentative design and likely performance of a prototype based on the design.

    iii. *Development:* The tentative design is further developed and implemented at this stage with the creation of an artifact.

    iv. *Evaluation:* In this step, based on predefined criteria, the artifact is evaluated and its performance measured. Qualitative and quantitative deviations from expectations should be carefully explained.

    v. *Conclusion:* This could be the end of a design phase or the final research effort. The results of the research effort are written and communicated accordingly.

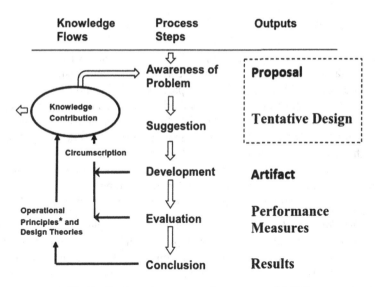

Fig. 1. Design science research process model [29]

Another commonly used DSR process models is the DSR methodology [26]. With its six process interactions and four possible entry points, it provides the context which researchers can use to describe how they systematically and rigorously carry out DSR. It also provides a template to present the outputs of the research. Readers and reviewers of DSR can use this template as a mental model with which to recognize and evaluate the research and its outputs.

B. *DSR Output.* The outputs of a DSR are the artifacts intended to solve the identified organizational problems. These artifacts which are *social-technical* in nature, attest to the peculiar nature of the contemporary environments with interfaces between objectives, people and technology. They are prescriptive knowledge designed to improve the natural world. They include *constructs, models, methods or instantiations* [10]. They also include *better theories*; social innovations and new properties of technical, social and/or informational resources [26, 29].

Constructs offer the vocabulary and symbols used to define and understand problems and solutions. They significantly impact how tasks and problems are conceived, and enable construction of models for the problem and solution domain. *Models* are designed representations of the problem and possible solutions. *Methods* are algorithms, practices and recipes for performing a task. They provide the instructions for performing goal-driven activities. *Instantiations* are physical realizations that act on the natural world. They operationalize constructs, models and methods and can embody design knowledge if more explicit descriptions are absent. *Better theories* are artifact constructions as analogous to experimental natural science, coupled with reflection and abstractions.

3   The Lean Approach

At the core of lean is the emphasis to systematically minimize waste [9, 27]. The lean approach contains a set of principles which lead to process and quality improvements. Lean development is a product development paradigm which embodies the emphasis of lean. It is a collection of rules, standards, methods, tools and underlying philosophy and culture specific to an enterprise and responsible for the comprehensive and viable design of development [7]. The lean development approach proposes a flexible, iterative and light weight development approach where the emphases of problem solving are the resultant outcomes and not the outputs [12]. This new way of thinking about product development concentrates on creating value for the customer, eliminating waste, optimizing value streams, empowering people and continuously improving [9, 12].

A. *Lean Development Principles.* Lean development principles characterize lean software development and they inform how process and quality improvements can be achieved. They call for a whole-product, complete life-cycle and cross-functional approach to development leading to the discovery and delivery of value. This is achieved by a well guided combination of design, development, deployment and validation of solution in iteration and appropriate for the individual context or situation [20, 21]. There appears not to be a consensus on what lean development principles are [8]. While some principles target lean for improved user experience [11], others target software development [27] and a lean development framework [7]. The fundamental emphases of these principles however are:

    i.   *Frontloading:* This describes efforts at the early stages of the project to think thoroughly and as far as possible concerning the intended solution. It addresses situations where an individual solution is necessary, often as observed in development rather than production.

    ii. *Standardization:* This involves the description of phases and tasks of the development processes and, standardized procedure for each phase and task. Standardization reduces methods that lead to improvisation and ineffective actions.

    iii. *Visualization:* This describes how to make information about work flow and work outcome visible, creating transparency about goals, processes and performance. It enables better identification of the current state and makes problems noticeable.

    iv. *Synchronization:* This involves creating a process with a fast, continuous and steady flow of information across all value streams. It operates as a flow and pulls system. The flow refers to scheduling the development process in uniform working phases harmonized so they have the same working content. While the pull refers to delivery of only what is internally demanded. Based on this, wastes can be identified and eliminated.

    v. *Experimentation:* This describes the build, measure, learn cycle involved in arriving at a solution to a problem and going through the cycle quickly and as frequently as necessary. It emphasizes understanding what is going on and being open to new possibilities.

vi. *Validation*: This describes how the problems and solution are made valid and to reduce uncertainty. For problems, qualitative conversations and open questions are used to discover real needs. For solutions however, qualitative and quantitative means are used.

vii. *Engage everyone*: This involves increasing motivation and qualification of everyone involved. Decision making should be moved to the lowest possible level by making the responsibility for discovering, creating and designing value that of all teams involved in the respective value stream.

B. *Lean Process.* The lean process is focused on learning while creating. To solve a problem, based on lean development principles, you build a solution, measure its effect, and learn from it to build a better solution the next time [1]. With this you can iterate quickly and decide early in the process what should receive more or less attention.

Referred to as the *Build-Measure-Learn loop* or *validated learning loop*, the lean process drives learning and contains three stages whose output serves as input for the next stage of the iteration [20, 21] as illustrated in Fig. 2 and described below. A cycle around the validated learning loop is called an experiment.

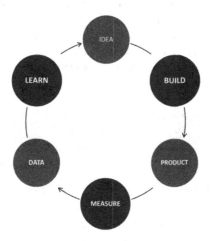

Fig. 2. The lean loop [21]

i. *Build:* In this stage, the project is framed and objectives are defined. Assumptions in the problem domain and expected solutions are used to postulate hypotheses based on the proposed solution with their expected outcomes. A minimum viable product (MVP), which suggests the smallest thing built to create the expected value, is then built to test the hypotheses and begin the process of learning.

ii. *Measure:* In this stage, the MVP is presented to the stakeholder organization and validated against qualitative and quantitative actionable metrics established in the build step.

    iii. *Learn:* The learning in this stage is based on the data obtained from the validations done in the measure step. The data is studied to see if it validates or refutes the hypothesis towards further refinements.

C. *Lean Iteration Patterns.* The proposition of the lean iteration meta-pattern is that to graduate from an idea to a desired solution, multiple iterations of connected experiments are required. Here a continuous iteration of the lean process is necessary until the desired goal is achieved. Whereas the lean experiment aids in validating or invalidating hypotheses postulated for the problem in question, the iterative nature of the lean process enables linking multiple experiments together towards achieving the desired value for the organization [21].

As illustrated in Fig. 3, an identification and understanding of the stakeholder problem facilitated by the elicitation and negotiation of requirements is first needed and then the quest for a solution. Then you iterate towards specifying a solution fit for purpose from amongst all viable possibilities. The specified solution is then validated qualitatively. The emphasis of a qualitative validation is to use a small sample size to explore how well the specified solution performs in line with the problem hypothesis. A negative performance suggests the solution will not address the problem requiring refinement or quest for another solution while a positive performance suggest it will. Based on a positive performance from the qualitative validation, the specified solution is then verified to see how well it will scale with a large sample size. At this stage, the emphasis of a quantitative validation is to test how statistically significant performance of the specified solution is in addressing the problem hypothesis.

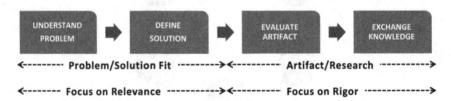

Fig. 3. The lean iteration meta-pattern [21]

D. *Lean Canvas.* To validate projects carried out using the lean approach, the lean canvas is used. The lean canvas is a one paged business model validation tool which can be used to document, measure progress and communicate learning with the respective stakeholders [21]. It provides an actionable and entrepreneur-focused business plan which emphasizes problems, solutions, key metrics and competitive advantages available.

As illustrated in Fig. 4, it addresses broad customer problems and solutions and delivers them to customer segments through a unique value proposition [22]. It emphasizes identifying the respective stakeholders and understanding their problems, the context and related ecosystems they exist. A clear and specific way to articulate the novelty of solution provider and solution as well as defined ways of communicating with identified stakeholders. Finally funding for the project, how obtained funds will

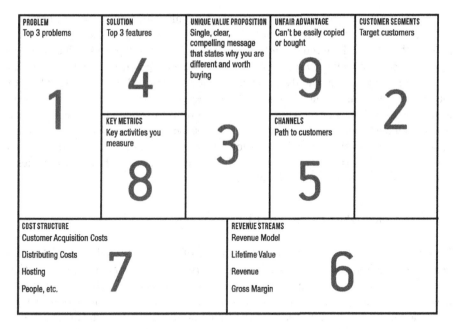

Fig. 4. The lean canvas [21]

be utilized, and metrics to indicate progress as well as how the effort put in will stand out in comparison to competition is also emphasized.

4   Why Use the Lean Approach in DSR

In DSR, the problems encountered by research teams are often messy and difficult to organize in the context of existing research theories. Problems may not be well defined on the outset, and little or no theoretical scaffolding may be available to conceptualize the research constructs or operationalize desired artifact attributes. As noted by other DSR researchers, in some circumstances it is not only difficult but often unrealistic to expect DSR projects to be grounded in established theoretical works [14, 15]. To tackle these problems, researchers need to be creative and engage in cycles of inquiry through constant experimentation. Lean principles may offer an archetype for such a course of action. Through carefully deliberated rapid iterations of the problem → solution → artifact → knowledge pattern, researchers can identify additional opportunities from the contextual environment and find alternative knowledge sources for grounding their investigation. Without the rapid iterations, these useful opportunities or knowledge sources may have remained unexplored. Lean development in DSR would allow the use of positivist research principles such as hypotheses test, rather than following a technophilic mindset. With this, a template such as the lean canvas can serve as a starting point for the research design. This will lead to more formalism in terms of best practices that can be followed in artifact creation.

Interestingly, the DSR and action research [2, 11] methods emphasizes this iterative/cyclic nature involving rapid iterations of solutions, artifacts and knowledge gained, albeit with feedback between the different stages of the research process which the lean process also recommends. Our choice for DSR however is predicated on the notion that action research is fundamentally a change-oriented approach. The build stage phase of the lean process can be said to contain the awareness of the problem, suggestion and development activities of the DSR process. The product obtained from this lean stage is akin to the artifact of the DSR process. In the same manner, the lean measure stage contains the DSR evaluation and conclusion activities with the outputted data and results synonymous. The learn stage of lean which is absent in the DSR however provides a good avenue for feedback towards enhancing DSR projects.

5   The Lean-DSR Integrated Framework

Designs are artifacts that contain great amount of knowledge embedded. They are generated in elicitation of research questions, problems or phenomena, when stakeholders goals or knowledge are specified and when results or research outputs are validated. The design process is therefore an interaction between an idea (with values imbedded in it), the characteristics of the situation in question and the expectation of stakeholders involved. With organizations and society at large being presented with uncertainties today, design is being recognized as a critical factor for success, especially in business [24, 25].

The emphasis of design is now in the quality of design and how design can be improved. The knowledge contained in designs often more visible to "experts" in the same discipline, is becoming visible and appreciated by all. This is because this knowledge is used to create artifacts to solve problems and the artifacts are evaluated to build knowledge [10, 25] making their viability visible. With a constantly evolving landscape the contemporary organizations and society present, a flexible and sound capacity for reframing design is imperative for the process of design.

A. *Application of Lean Principles in DSR.* There exist a link between principles of lean and the output, artifacts of DSR. As described in Sect. 3, lean principles inform how process and quality improvement can be achieved. In their application to DSR therefore, they can determine how value is emphasized in the DSR process and reflected in its output. As such, the *frontloading* principle can enable obtaining better *constructs* and *models* since it focuses on arriving at a solution for the problem in question. The descriptions of a uniform procedure for addressing phases and task which the *Standardization* principle emphasizes can align with creating better *models* and *methods* since these outputs need to adhere to standards. Similarly, *models* and *methods* align with the *visualizations* principle since they make information about problems, solution and respective relationships visible.

The *Synchronization* principle can enable better *constructs* and *instantiations* since it offers and ways to define and understand problems and solutions as well as their physical realization in the respective value streams. Likewise the *Experimentation* principle aligns with *methods* and *instantiations* since it presents algorithms, practices and recipes for playing out solutions to problems in the respective contexts and ways of addressing the learning that comes with it. Finally the *validation* and *engage-everyone* principle enable better *constructs, models, methods and instantiations*. They both address means of defining, understanding and representing respective solutions to problems. They also address ways these solutions are performed, how they are played-out and evaluated.

The respective lean principles and the corresponding DSR outputs they enable and align with are presented in Table 1 below.

Table 1. Lean principles and their corresponding DSR output

Lean principles	Constructs	Models	Methods	Instantiations
Frontloading	X	X		
Standardization		X	X	
Visualization		X	X	
Synchronization	X			X
Experimentation			X	X
Validation	X	X	X	X
Engage everyone	X	X	X	X

B. *Lean DSR Iteration Meta-Pattern.* The DSR iteration meta-pattern draws upon the relevance and rigor cycle described in [14]. The relevance cycle associates inputs from the specific contexts where the problems exist to DSR activities. The rigor cycle connects these DSR activities with the necessary scientific knowledge base, domain experience and expertise about the project. This implies also that the relevance cycle addresses how the solution fits within the context of the problem in question referring to the problem/solution fit of the lean iteration meta-pattern. The rigor cycle then informs how the DSR activities arrive at the solution, the artifact, drawing from necessary theories, domain experience and expertise, also referring to the product/market fit of the lean iteration meta-pattern.

Consequently as illustrated in Fig. 5, the first part of the meta-pattern constitutes an interaction with the respective stakeholder, the organization/society environment, towards identifying and understanding the respective problem and specifying a viable solution from a pool of possible solutions. This is facilitated by elicitation and negotiation of requirements as well as coming up with a hypothesis of the problem which emphasizes the required value which the solution will validate. The second part of the meta-pattern relates to drawing upon as well as extending the existing body of research, by evaluating how well the specified solution, the artifact, performs in line with the problem hypothesis and the value it produces. Subsequently, a negative performance suggests the artifact will not address the problem requiring refinement or quest for another artifact and a positive performance suggest it will.

Fig. 5. Lean-DSR iteration meta-pattern

The knowledge obtained from a successful artifact as regards the propositions claimed to be true to the respective laws in the problem environment is then exchanged with the academic community. This solution to the DSR knowledge problem [30] adds value to DSR.

C. *Lean-DSR Canvas.* To validate a DSR project using the lean approach and incorporating the Lean-DSR iteration meta-pattern therefore, a lean-DSR canvas becomes necessary. This canvas should also be actionable and can serve as a good substitute to the traditional DRS methodologies for DSR projects or lean canvas for lean projects. The proposed Lean-DSR canvas as part of the integrated framework should also enable DSR projects to be documented, measured and the learning obtained, communicated.

Building upon the DSR Knowledge Contribution Framework [10] and the Lean canvass [21, 22], we propose the following elements of the Lean-DSR canvas as illustrated in Fig. 6 and described as follows:

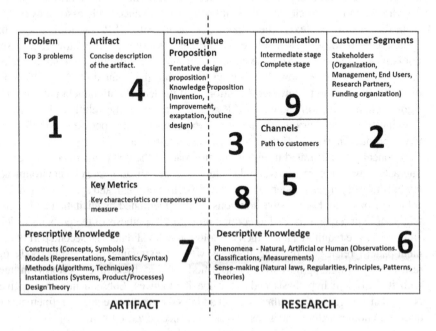

Fig. 6. Lean-DSR canvas

1. *Problem:* Articulate in clear terms, the top 3 problems the project addresses.
2. *Stakeholder Segment:* Identify the respective stakeholders involved in the research project. This includes the organization, end users, research partners, funding organizations etc.
3. *Unique value proposition:* Identify a tentative design proposition that articulates how the solution is defined. Also position the research project in terms of its knowledge proposition, if the type of knowledge it contributes is an invention, improvement, exaptation or routine design.
4. *Artifact:* Outline the simplest things that can be created to address each problem. The emphasis at the first iteration should be on a minimum viable product.
5. *Channels:* Identify effective and scalable means of communicating iterations of the solution to the organization. This is necessary for obtaining necessary feedback and refinement if necessary.
6. *Descriptive Knowledge:* Identifies descriptions of natural, artificial and human-related phenomena and knowledge of the sense-making relationships amongst these phenomena.
7. *Prescriptive Knowledge:* Identifies knowledge about artifact designed by humans to improve the natural world.
8. *Key Metrics:* Identify key activities or responses to measure, concepts to operationalize either based on the artifact and it behavior or on theory towards hypothesis development.
9. *Communication:* Identifies how the research project and its knowledge contributions should be communicated. At the intermediate stage are conferences or workshops where feedbacks are obtained for further refinement. Afterwards are journals and tutorials which provide a more formal ways of sharing the knowledge obtained.

The lean-DSR canvas can therefore be used by researchers as a starting template for research projects that emphasizes using the lean mindset. This one-paged visual research plan like its contemporaries; the Business Canvass and Lean Canvas, can walk both researchers and stakeholders through the most important aspects of the research project while enabling how best to choose and steer the research project.

6   A Caveat on Research Rigor

The most relevant problems for organizations and for society are in messy and swampy situations where research-based theories do not apply. This includes instances where the problems are new, not well defined, no theory suffices or contradictory theories exist. If practitioners remain in the high grounds where they can apply their research-based theories, their work will be non-relevant. Particularly since most of the important problems our constantly evolving societies face today are new and not well defined. To tackle these problems, professionals will need a lot of artistry; will need to apply a set of skills that go far beyond their theoretical base.

With much successful work on lean today, it makes sense to also apply it in a research context. Our recommendation therefore is more along the lines of adopting lean approach as a core project management practice aimed at producing short delivery cycles for artifact development with systematic quality checks throughout the research process. Within the context of technology projects, such practices have been shown to improve project performance and ensure value assurance [1].

By adopting a lean mindset as a project orientation for design science research projects, we aim to highlight a means to help overcome initial barriers to onboarding in a design science project, as well to alleviate intermittent research paralysis due to lack of theoretical scaffolding. And to avoid this pitfall, being mindful of rigor and validation at every step, iterations based on lean principles can be of help to researchers. A lean mindset will employ researchers to be mindful of the value of the activities that they are engaging in terms of how they contribute to the overall success of the project. Rapid advancement can also help reduce the time spent on extraneous activities that do not result in practitioner or academic contributions as these contributions could be evaluated over several cycles of activities against waste produced and value obtained. Counter-actions and improvements can then be identified with regards to value stream mapping [19].

At first sight, "following a lean approach in research" may be counterintuitive with respect to ensuring rigor in academic research. As such, it is our contention that such an approach does not necessarily undermine the rigor expected in DSR. As highlighted in the Lean-DSR proposed iteration meta-pattern, we incorporate rigor in addition to other necessary actions for control to reduce bias, in every cycle of inquiry by recording insights from previous steps, and grounding next steps in the context of available knowledge. Hence, in combination across the cycles of inquiry, the research investigation remains thorough and comprehensive. Within the milieu of lean principles, this amounts to the ensuring the whole being optimized, rather than the individual parts of the research project.

7 Future Work

Although our proposed framework has not been validated, we are aware that a real research project affords us the opportunity to test out our claims. In line with the lean mindset advocated in this paper however, communication of the proposed conceptual framework is our attempt at adapting the *build-measure-learn* activities of the lean process. Subsequently, our intention is to explore the applicability of our approach to address research projects in the requirements engineering (RE) domain. Herein, we are reminded that RE is not a phase or stage but rather activities involved in the development, elicitation, specification, analysis, and management of stakeholder requirements, which are to be met by systems [16]. We observed similarities between lean principles and RE processes such as; *frontloading* appears similar to requirements elicitation, *standardization* to requirements identification, *visualization* to requirement analysis, *synchronization* to requirements specification, *experimentation* to system modeling, *validation* to requirements validation and *engage everyone* to the requirements management process. Our focus will be on the problem domain where believe the Lean-DSR Iteration Meta-Pattern can facilitate an adaptation of requirements engineering towards structuring the problem space and deriving design decisions systematically [4]. This will further present an opportunity to address the often overlooked discussions about what value and waste mean from a research perspective.

Acknowledgements. This work was supported in part by NSERC (Discovery program) and by the University of Ottawa.

References

1. Abran, A., Moore, J.W., Bourque, P., Dupuis, R. (eds.): Guide to the Software Engineering Body of Knowledge (2004 version). IEEE Computer Society Press, Los Alamitos, CA (2004). http://www.swebok.org
2. Baskerville, R.L.: Investigating information systems with action research. Commun. AIS **2**(3es), 4 (1999)
3. Barboza, S.L., Filho, G.A.C., de Souza, R.A.C.: Towards a legal compliance verification approach on the procurement process of it solutions for the Brazilian federal public administration. In: 7th IEEE Requirements Engineering and Law Workshop (RELAW), pp. 39–40 (2014)
4. Braun, R., Benedict, M., Wendler, H., Esswein, W.: Proposal for requirements driven design science research. In: Donnellan, B., Helfert, M., Kenneally, J., VanderMeer, D., Rothenberger, M., Winter, R. (eds.) DESRIST 2015. LNCS, vol. 9073, pp. 135–151. Springer, Heidelberg (2015)
5. Cawley, O., Wang, X., Richardson, I.: Lean software development – what exactly are we talking about? In: Fitzgerald, B., Conboy, K., Power, K., Valerdi, R., Morgan, L., Stol, K.-J. (eds.) LESS 2013. LNBIP, vol. 167, pp. 16–31. Springer, Heidelberg (2013)
6. Croll, A., Yoskovitz, B.: Lean Analytics. O'Reilly Media, Inc., Sebastopol (2013)
7. Dombrowski, U., Zahn T.: Design of a lean development framework. In: IEEE International Conference on Industrial Engineering Management (IEEM), pp. 1917–1921 (2011). doi:10.1109/IEEM.2011.6118249
8. Dombrowski, U., Zahn, T., Schulze, S.: State of the Art-Lean Development (2011). http://koasas.kaist.ac.kr/handle/10203/23703
9. Ebert, C., Abrahamsson, P., Oza, N.: Lean software development. IEEE Softw. **29**(5), 22–25 (2012)
10. Gregor, S., Hevner, A.R.: Positioning and presenting design science research for maximum impact. MIS Q. **37**(2), 337–356 (2013)
11. Gorschek, T., Wohlin, C., Carre, P., Larsson, S.: A model for technology transfer in practice. IEEE Softw. **23**(6), 88–95 (2006). doi:10.1109/MS.2006.147
12. Gothelf, J., Seiden, J.: Lean UX: Applying Lean Principles to Improve User Experience. O'Reilly Media, Inc., Sebastopol (2013)
13. Hevner, A., March, S., Park, J., Ram, S.: Design science in information systems research. MIS Q. **28**(1), 75–105 (2004)
14. Hevner, A.R.: A three cycle view of design science research. Scand. J. Inf. Syst. **19**(2), 4 (2007). http://aisel.aisnet.org/sjis/vol19/iss2/4
15. Iivari, J.: A paradigmatic analysis of information systems as a design science. Scand. J. Inf. Syst. **19**(2), 5 (2007). http://aisel.aisnet.org/sjis/vol19/iss2/5
16. ISO: Systems and software engineering – life cycle processes – requirements engineering. In: ISO/IEC/IEEE 29148, pp. 1–94 (2011). doi:10.1109/IEEESTD.2011.6146379
17. Jarke, M., Loucopoulos, P., Lyytinen, K., Mylopoulos, J., Robinson, W.: The brave new world of design requirements. Inf. Syst. **6**(7), 992–1008 (2011)

18. Khurum, M., Gorschek, T., Wilson, M.: The software value map – an exhaustive collection of value aspects for the development of software intensive products. J. Softw. Evol. Proc. **25**, 711–741 (2013). doi:10.1002/smr.1560

19. Khurum, M., Petersen, K., Gorschek, T.: Extending value stream mapping through waste definition beyond customer perspective. J. Softw. Evol. Proc. **26**, 1074–1105 (2014). doi:10.1002/smr.1647

20. Klein, L.: UX for Lean Startups. O'Reilly Media, Inc., Sebastopol (2013)

21. Maurya, A.: Lean Running, Iterate from Plan A to a Plan That Works, 2nd edn. O'Reilly Media, Inc., Sebastopol (2012)

22. Maurya, A.: Why lean canvas vs business model canvas? (2012). http://leanstack.com/why-lean-canvas. Accessed 27 July 2015

23. Normann, R.: Reframing Business: When the Map Changes the Landscape. Wiley, Chichester (2001)

24. Owen, C.L.: Understanding design research toward an achievement of balance. J. Jpn. Soc. Sci. Des. **5**(2), 36–45 (1997)

25. Owen, C.L.: Design research: building the knowledge base. Des. Stud. **19**(1), 9–20 (1998). doi:10.1016/S0142-694X(97)00030-6

26. Peffers, K., Tuunanen, T., Rothenberger, M.A., Chatterjee, S.: A design science research methodology for information systems research. J. Manage. Inf. Syst. **24**(3), 45–77 (2007)

27. Poppendieck, M., Cusumano, M.A.: Lean software development: a tutorial. IEEE Softw. **29**(5), 26–32 (2012)

28. Simon, H.A.: The Sciences of the Artificial, 3rd edn. MIT Press, Cambridge (1996)

29. Vaishnavi, V., Kuechler, W.: Design Science Research in Information Systems (2004)

30. Wieringa, R.: Design science as nested problem solving. In: Proceedings of the 4th International Conference on Design Science Research in Information Systems and Technology, pp. 81–92 (2009)

31. Wieringa, R., Heerkens, H.: Design science, engineering science and requirements engineering. In: 16th IEEE International Requirements Engineering Conference (RE), pp. 310–313 (2008). doi:10.1109/RE.2008.63

How Do We Read Specifications? Experiences from an Eye Tracking Study

Maike Ahrens, Kurt Schneider^(✉), and Stephan Kiesling

Software Engineering Group, Leibniz Universität Hannover,
Welfengarten 1, 30167 Hannover, Germany
M.Ahrens@stud.uni-hannover.de,
{KS,Stephan.Kiesling}@inf.uni-hannover.de

Abstract. **[Context and motivation]** Writing good specifications is difficult and takes time. There are several guidelines such as the Volere template to assist writing a good specification. They provide a table of contents which can be used like a checklist to consider all relevant aspects. Voluminous specifications take more time to write, and also more time to read. A larger specification is not always a better one. **[Question/Problem]** A requirements engineer should be aware of how readers make use of a specification and consider their interests in writing it. In addition, some people prefer reading on a screen while others hold a preference for paper printouts. Some parts or aspects may be read differently in both representations. **[Principal ideas/results]**: We have conducted an Eye Tracking study investigating how specifications are read. We compared paper-based with on-screen presentation, and different reading perspectives such as UI designers, tester, software architects etc. We derived study goals by using GQM down to the level of quantitative and statistical eye tracking analyses. **[Contribution]**: There is a two-fold contribution: (a) Observations and findings about the way specifications are read; e.g., we had expected paper-based reading to be faster. Instead, we found similar reading patterns on paper versus on screen. (b) Insights with respect to eye tracking as a research method for requirements engineering. We discuss strengths and shortcomings, and provide lessons learned.

Keywords: Eye tracking · Requirements specification · Empirical studies · Research agenda · View-based requirements specification · Perspective-based specification

1 Introduction

A requirements specification is the point of reference for a (traditional, non-agile) software project. After requirements have been elicited, interpreted, and maybe negotiated to resolve inconsistencies, they are documented in a specification. A good specification must be comprehensible to a variety of readers: Customers, developers, and a variety of specialists. They will read, check, and use the specification throughout the project. Natural language is often the only common denominator of all these groups.

It is important to structure and phrase a specification according to the needs of its readers. This will help them to identify relevant parts and focus their attention and time

© Springer International Publishing Switzerland 2016
M. Daneva and O. Pastor (Eds.): REFSQ 2016, LNCS 9619, pp. 301–317, 2016.
DOI: 10.1007/978-3-319-30282-9_21

to the most rewarding parts of the document. Several authors have identified frequent wording problems, and heuristics to avoid them [1]. Templates such as Volere [2] or EARS were proposed to provide a useful structure and cover all important aspects. At the same time, they should exclude unnecessary information to save time and effort for both writers and readers. Since different readers will have different interests, each section of a specification may be read with different intensities.

We wanted to investigate the reading profiles of specifications that were written according to a given template. Many companies use a template such as Volere as a starting point. They adapt the template by deleting unnecessary parts and may also refine certain aspects that are of particular importance to them. Along the same lines, our template is a slightly simplified and adapted version of the Volere template which has been used for a similar type of student projects for 10 years. It has been optimized during that period to avoid trivial or repetitive entries and aspects that do not appear in this concrete environment.

Some parts of the template seem obviously important to several reader groups – such as the mission statement or target user group. We wanted to check the validity of these and similar assumptions. In particular, we were interested in the difference of reading the same specifications on paper and on screen. If those reading profiles differ significantly, one would need to consider or even recommend the intended reading style during the writing process. The investigation used a selection of two specifications following the same template. We decided to use eye tracking for the investigation for a variety of reasons which are further described in section three.

The goal of this paper, therefore, is three-fold:

- We report on our findings on how specifications are read: relative reading times and profiles for different sections; we also compare reading on paper and on screen.
- We partially replicated a study by Gross et al. [3]. This served as validation of our study approach and their findings. Deviations were considered a reason and opportunity for a more detailed investigation and discussion.
- We discuss the merits, potential and challenges of applying eye tracking to this requirements engineering topic.

2   Structure and Contents of Specifications

The Volere template mentioned above by Robertson and Robertson [2] is a widely used template for specifications of software projects. It basically prescribes four main sections: "product constraints", "functional requirements", "non-functional requirements" and "project issues". A specification should begin with the section "product constraints". This section consists of all important information regarding the whole software project. Such information is important for any person reading a specification.

Starting with the purpose of the product to build, the section should provide information and descriptions about clients, customers, stakeholders and most important: users. It also includes requirements constraints, naming conventions and definitions, and relevant facts. This information is important to create a shared context for all readers of this specification. Finally, this section should contains assumptions, which are both important for customers as well as software engineers. The section "functional requirements" is divided into two parts. The first part should discuss the scope of the product followed by the second part, the functional requirements.

Robertson and Robertson recommend dividing the most important types of non-functional requirements into different sections. These sections are "look and feel requirements", "usability requirements", "performance requirements", "operational requirements", "maintainability and portability", "security requirements", "cultural and political requirements" and "legal requirements".

Finally, the last section "project issues" provides information about remaining but necessary aspects like "open issues", "tasks", "risks", "costs" and a so-called "waiting room" gathering suspended requirements.

All specifications regarded in this paper are based on a slightly altered Volere template. Figure 1 shows the table of contents comprising all sections.

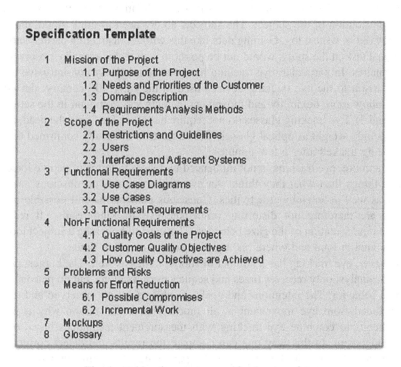

Specification Template

```
1   Mission of the Project
        1.1  Purpose of the Project
        1.2  Needs and Priorities of the Customer
        1.3  Domain Description
        1.4  Requirements Analysis Methods
2   Scope of the Project
        2.1  Restrictions and Guidelines
        2.2  Users
        2.3  Interfaces and Adjacent Systems
3   Functional Requirements
        3.1  Use Case Diagrams
        3.2  Use Cases
        3.3  Technical Requirements
4   Non-Functional Requirements
        4.1  Quality Goals of the Project
        4.2  Customer Quality Objectives
        4.3  How Quality Objectives are Achieved
5   Problems and Risks
6   Means for Effort Reduction
        6.1  Possible Compromises
        6.2  Incremental Work
7   Mockups
8   Glossary
```

Fig. 1. Table of contents: specification template

Basically, this template provides information and hints about how to be filled out by still learning students. The adaption considers the common constraints and characteristics of our projects. In the adapted version, we emphasize some subsections of the Volere template and upgraded them to full sections in our template. Our template requires functional requirements to be written as use cases.

We used this simplified version of the Volere template for the following reasons: Due to the limited size of the projects, several aspects of the full Volere template were unnecessary or always the same, due to the same environment. They were, thus, omitted. The use of this adapted version had additional advantages: all participants had worked with it before in a project course that all of them had attended successfully as a mandatory prerequisite. Thus, participants were able to judge what they considered the most important parts. In addition, this template was already used for 10 years at our university. Thus, we could make sure that the chosen specifications are of good and comparable quality.

3 Eye Tracking for Investigating RE Issues

We used eye tracking in this study for a variety of reasons. With eye tracking, one can observe, count and measure times and sequences of fixations objectively without any active contribution of the subject. The subjects do not need to think aloud, remember what they did or write a log. Gaining data like this without distracting participants from their actual task in the study, would not be possible with techniques like observation or questionnaires. In particular, eye tracking has become relatively non-intrusive by now in comparison to the eye tracking devices used in the early 20th century: devices are smaller, allow more flexibility and movement, and are less dominant in the set-up (see Figs. 2 and 3). Eye tracking glasses do not require hardware for fixing the head, and are almost as light-weight as optical glasses. The subjects in this study confirmed that they forgot being tracked after a few minutes.

Furthermore, eye tracking is not influenced by biases in terms of people looking at different things than what they think. An eye tracker records unconscious gazes and fixtures as well as intentional activities. Conscious perceptions and possible misconceptions are therefore not distorting immediate eye tracking results. It records a real-time representation of the gaze behavior. This can tell how long a subject looked at a certain area in total and where his attention was at a certain time.

However, eye tracking has a number of shortcomings as well. The biggest problem is that the analyst only receives times and sequences of fixations, but no reasons for the recorded behavior. The intentions and goals of subjects are not observed and may not be concluded from eye movement at all times. That is the reason why it is often advantageous to combine eye tracking with measurement techniques based on conscious judgement. In this way one can compare the results and detect correlation or discrepancy. Moreover when reading on paper or tracking something off-screen in general, subjects need to wear eye tracking glasses which may initially distract them. Tracking with eye tracking glasses is also relatively time-consuming. Even though recording can start right away, gaze data has to be mapped on a reference image before quantitative values are obtained. This consumes time and effort.

For our study we decided to use eye tracking because it offers a detailed quantitative way of comparing reading on paper and screen objectively. One could get concrete reading intensities and speed values which may differ from subjective judgment. Subjective ratings have the risk of being based on taught knowledge instead of individual assessment. We used eye tracking and then asked subjects to complete a questionnaire. Thus, we could detect possible inconsistencies between consciously rated relevance and measured reading time. This would have not been possible through methods like thinking aloud or pure observation. In addition, using heat maps we were able to notice reading intensity differences even within sections. These heat maps visualize how long the subject looked at certain areas by warm and cold colors, respectively. Furthermore, thinking aloud for example is nearly as time-consuming to analyze as the result data of eye tracking.

4 Related Work

Effective requirements communication is crucial for a successful software project. A specification is one of the most important documents to ensure effective transfer of requirements and supportive knowledge to developers and other project participants [4]. In our FLOW project, we developed an information flow modeling notation [5] and technique. It serves for capturing verbal and informal expressions of requirements together with more formal and documented ones [6]. For example, phone calls, meetings or video recordings of stakeholder meetings (as presented from Fricker et al. [7]) can complement regular documents. In [8], Liskin presents an approach of linking artifacts from various RE methodologies together to bridge the gap between more traditional and more flexible approaches.

In this paper, we focus on the case of traditional, specification-based requirements processes and investigate what can be done to optimize its ability to convey requirements. The structure and content of information is obviously relevant; we wanted to know how specifications are read. Eye tracking the process of browsing and reading a specification should indicate what parts are examined more carefully than others. A questionnaire can explore how this objective eye tracking data is correlated to assumptions and priorities of the readers.

Eye tracking has been used in this domain by Fraunhofer IESE [9] before, conducting a similar study to investigate information needs of different roles using requirements specifications and offering an approach to improve its usage efficiency. They performed three studies differing in the taken sample and the used measurement techniques. The first study had a similar design like the one described in this paper. The Fraunhofer IESE observed two usability experts and two software architecture experts while reading a specification comprising 273 pages in total followed by 82 pages of appendix. This specification was based on the TORE framework [10]. Depending on their role the participants had a task either to imagine designing a user interface or architecture for the described software. During this procedure they were filmed by an external camera and their gaze behavior was observed with eye tracking glasses. In addition, to find out how relevant the different parts of the specification are, they were told to think aloud and fill out a subsequent questionnaire rating the several parts.

All three studies revealed both differences between the roles but also between persons with the same role. They considered only the roles usability expert and software architect. The results indicated that usability experts strongly rely on artifacts containing information about supported stakeholders, goals, the target processes and interactions. In contrast the architects rated descriptions of goals and technical requirements as the most important parts. These studies' settings and lessons learned were used as a basis for the study described in this paper. We assigned related actual tasks to all subjects for assessing their ability in the corresponding area. We made sure no subject was involved in the creation of their respective specifications. In addition, we followed the suggestion of using questionnaires for capturing the relevance of artifacts.

5   Study Design

According to the GQM paradigm [11, 12], we started by defining our improvement goals, deriving research goals and refining them to questions and metrics. Metrics were applied to collect data during the experiment. Those measurements were then interpreted with respect to the questions and goals that had led to the metrics.

Our main operational goal was to improve both the efficiency of using software requirements specifications and the effectivity of writing them. Based on these, the measurement goal was defined as follows:

> **Research GOAL RG$_1$**
> Investigate the information needs of the specifications' readers with regard to their role and the medium of presentation.

To find out which information is relevant or irrelevant for the roles of readers and therefore being able to define view-based specifications, several *questions* were surveyed. First of all, it needs to be identified which parts of the document are more or less relevant to the considered roles which leads to the first research question.

> **Research question RQ$_1$**
> Which artifacts are most and least important to the different roles?

A fundamental assumption of this approach is that the different roles have different information needs and make different demands on the specification. To verify this assumption the next research question was defined:

> **Research question RQ$_2$**
> Is there a difference between different roles regarding their information needs?

These two questions were also considered by the study of Gross et al. [13].

We were also interested whether the presentation medium has an influence on the specification user's way of reading. In that case, specification authors would need to consider the target medium. The criteria here were user's preference, reading speed and ability for reproduction.

Research question RQ₃

Which way of representation (paper or screen) is more appropriate?

Research question RQ$_3$

Which way of representation (paper or screen) is more appropriate?

Hypotheses: During the GQM refinement process, hypotheses are stated (e.g. in Abstraction Sheets). They are used as a source of meaningful questions and metrics, and they provide a reference point to compare results to. The following hypotheses guided our selection process. Some of them are based on other studies' findings regarding the general differences between paper and screen presentation [15].

H1_1: Subjects prefer the paper version to the screen version.
H1_2: Ability of subjects to reproduce differs between paper and screen.
H1_3: Printed specifications are read faster than on-screen specifications.
H2_1: Different specification sections are rated differently for relevance.
H3_1: At least two roles have a different average relevance rating.
H3_2: Section rated more important are read more intensely.

Metrics: We determined four metrics to investigate the above-mentioned hypotheses that were related to GQM-questions:

- Relevance ratings of sections provided by subjects in questionnaire
- Total reading time (by eye tracking)
- Length of sections in [cm] (to allow normalization of reading intensity)
- Reading times per section (eye tracking).

Collecting data for metrics: With eye tracking, it was possible to gain quantitative data of the exact reading times of each part of the specification and therefore determine the reading intensity and speed. The resulting reading intensities were compared to the relevance ratings that the participants provided in a questionnaire on a scale from "very important" to "unimportant". This ordinal scale was the same as the one used in the study of Gross et al. [14].

The subjects' reading speed in each section was determined by using the reading times and length of its parts. The ability of readers to reproduce the material they had read was measured by asking six multiple choice questions about the content of the specification (e.g. "What is the preferred browser for this application? A: Chrome, Firefox, Safari, Internet Explorer B: Chrome, Firefox, Safari, Opera C: Chrome").

The questionnaire also asked whether readers preferred a presentation on paper or on screen.

The study is restricted to roles in the development process. These are UI designers, software architects, testers and developers. Each role was characterized by tasks that had to be carried out. For example, a UI designer had to build a user interface and design first drafts. In contrast, the software architect concentrated on the development of main software components, which should be outlined in class diagrams. The task of the tester was to specify test cases checking the consistency with the customer requirements. The role of a developer combined the tasks of all three, which refers to small-team developers who carry out various tasks. They had to create class diagrams, mock ups of the user interface, and test cases.

The participants were randomly assigned to one of these roles. To make sure that each of them has the necessary abilities for the requested tasks, they were asked to judge their skills and experience in terms of software projects, specifications, mockups, test cases and class diagrams in a questionnaire at the beginning. Each skill (e.g., writing test cases, building GUIs etc.) was self-assessed on a four step ordinal scale from "very good" to "bad". Thus, no participant was confronted with a task he or she was not able to cope with. Furthermore the participants were told to read two specifications created with the template described in section two. Both of them were created in university software projects. One of them described a desktop multiplayer card game in 26 pages, the other one was a translate application and comprised 18 pages. We randomized the order of specifications, and the choice of paper or screen as the medium. To get a balanced design, each role was taken by two participants and both specifications were read on screen as often as on paper. Since the sample mainly consisted of students not having a lot of experience in industrial software development, we added two experienced developers in order to compare the results.

6   Conducting the Study

As soon as the planning and preparation step was finished the study could be conducted. The sample consisted of eight students and two experienced developers. Each of them took part at an individually made appointment. One session lasted for about an hour and consisted of two parts: one part reading the first specification on screen using an external eye tracker and one part reading the second one on paper using the eye tracking glasses.

6.1   Study Set-Up

The study took place in a calm room at the university with no distractions from outside. An appointment was made individually with the subject. The mobile eye tracking glasses were placed on one side of the room where the participants could take a seat and use the desk with some paper in front of them. On a different desk, a 22 inch-monitor was placed with the on-screen eye tracker attached to it. Keyboard, mouse, and scratch paper were provided for the subjects. Figures 2 and 3 show what the sessions looked like with the external eye tracker and the eye tracking glasses.

Before starting the eye tracking phase, participants filled out a questionnaire of general questions such as their degree program and about their experience and skills. They also decided whether they preferred a presentation on screen or paper. The questionnaire was printed on paper and there was no time limit set for the participants to fill it out. Next, participants received a short written introduction about their role and task. Then the eye tracker was calibrated and the reading part started. They were not prescribed the order of section to read. They could take notes. After the reading phase, they had to answer content-related questions.

Fig. 2. Eye tracking on screen

Fig. 3. Eye tracking on paper

Participants had 20 min in which they had to read the specification and complete their task. We set this time limit for three reasons:

- We wanted to build a typical situation due to the fact that developers mostly need to work under time pressure in an industrial environment. This method was used in other environments as well [16].
- Confounding factors like fatigue and less motivation would increasingly falsify the results of the study.
- With a given time limit subjects needed to choose the most important parts instead of reading everything in detail. In the study by Gross et al., there was no explicit time limit [13]. However, reading a full specification of 273 pages within one session is imposing significant time pressure on subjects, similar to allowing 20 min for about 20 pages. The explicit necessity to make selections and read fast was a relevant aspect from reality we wanted to capture.

As soon as the time ran out, the participants were given the second questionnaire including the sections to be rated with a relevance. Again, no time limit was given for the answers and the questionnaire was handed in a printed version. Afterwards they could have a short break and the procedure was repeated with the second specification and the other eye tracker, but still having the same role with the same task.

We observed that subjects followed different approaches of handling the document. Some of them stacked parts of the specification, others read it straightforwardly. This can actually be detected as a disadvantage of digital documents because you cannot re-sort the pages that easily. Furthermore, participants who did not know the described card game in advance, slowed down when reading the introduction part. Besides that no reading problems could be noticed which leads to the assumption that the content could be well understood. Concerning the observation with the eye tracking glasses some subjects mentioned that it felt unfamiliar at first, especially for those who do not wear glasses usually, but one can forget about it fast. In the end all participants reflected that it did not distract them while reading and performing their task.

6.2 Analyzing Study Results

Collected gaze data had to be mapped to a common reference image on which the reading times of different sections of the specification were determined.

The resulting data is provided in Table 1: Artifact types stand for the sections in the template (Fig. 1). Columns represent one of the participating roles. There are two sub-columns for each role: average relevance ratings (left) and average reading intensities (right), each on a scale from 1 (very important) to 4 (unimportant). Darker shades indicate more important ratings or higher intensity readings, respectively.

Table 1. Relevance ratings and reading intensities of the considered roles

Artifact types	UI designer		Software architect		Tester		Developer	
Purpose of the project	1,5	1,09	1	1,13	1,5	1,25	1,5	1,27
Needs and Priorities of the Customer	1,5	1	1,5	1,06	1,75	1,19	1,5	1,39
Domain descriptions	2	3,08	2	1,44	2,5	1,38	2,5	2,20
Requirements Analysis Methods	2,75	2,89	3,5	2,99	3,75	2,93	3,63	3,53
Restrictions and Guidelines	1,75	1,73	2,25	1,92	2,5	1,28	1,75	1,71
Users	1,75	1,66	2,75	1,98	2	1,47	1,88	2,31
Interfaces and Adjacent Systems	2,75	1,88	1,5	1,35	3,5	1,51	1,88	2,18
Use Case Diagrams	2	2,01	2	1,41	1,5	2,45	2,38	1,74
Use Cases	1,25	2,58	2,75	3,15	1	2,29	1,38	2,64
Technical Requirements	2,75	3,62	2,25	2,64	2,5	2,23	1,88	1,81
Quality Goals	2	2,48	1,75	3,18	1,5	1,76	2,38	2,58
Customer Quality Objectives	1,75	2,45	1,75	3,24	1,5	2,04	2,25	3,10
How Quality Objectives are Achieved	2,5	3,31	1,75	2,77	2,5	2,33	2,38	3,18
Problems and risks	2,75	3,94	3,5	3,53	3,75	3,43	2,75	3,68
Possible Compromises	2,25	3,53	2,25	2,61	3,25	2,20	2,5	2,20
Incremental work	2,5	3,87	2	1,60	4	3,46	2,13	3,35
Mockups	1	2,74	3,75	3,84	2,5	3,65	1,38	2,96
Glossary	3	3,72	3	3,31	3,25	3,81	3,5	3,86
Acceptance Tests	3	3,56	2,5	3,08	3	2,86	2,38	3,54
very important	important		rather unimportant		unimportant			

We derive expected and unexpected observations from Table 1 by comparing the relevance ratings and reading intensities of respective entries. For example, Interfaces and Adjacent Systems were considered important (1.5) by Software architects, and they read it at high (1.35) intensity. This was not surprising. Testers, on the other side, considered that same Artifact type (i.e., section of the specification) much less relevant (3.5), but read it rather intensely (1.51), which we consider an unexpected finding. Vice versa, developers considered Mockups very relevant (1.38), but did not spend much time looking at (2.96), which was yet another unexpected finding. Table 1 is a summary of measured reading intensities compared to relevance ratings.

As soon as all reading times had been measured and the questionnaires completed, resulting data was entered in Excel tables and checked for plausibility and validity. This was done by analyzing the data's graphical visualization. Afterwards, the previously defined hypotheses were tested on a 5 % significance level. With regard to the comparison of the presentation medium (RQ_3), there was no significant difference between paper printouts and screen in terms of reading speed, the ability of reproduction and the reader's preference. The corresponding hypotheses could not be confirmed. Looking closer on the preferences of the participants, we observed that the experienced developers mostly voted for the digital version. The motivation for this trend could be the availability of additional specification-related functionality on screen, like version control. Of course, features like these are not possible with printed documents. With regard to research questions RQ_1 und RQ_2, the relevance ratings of the specification sections were analyzed.

6.3 Findings and Interpretation

The data revealed that UI designers rate the quality goals of the project, as well as the UI mockups significantly as (very) important. However the introduction part including the purpose of the project serves as an important source of information for software architects. Observations are taken from Table 1, as described above. Testers primarily rely on use cases and consider information about incremental work to be totally unimportant. The relevant sections for the developers are "purpose of the project", "needs and priorities of the customer", "restrictions and guidelines", "use cases", "technical requirements", "incremental work" and "mockups". In contrast, they rated the sections "requirements analysis methods" and "glossary" as unimportant.

Regarding the glossary it could be noticed that all subjects rated this part as quite irrelevant. This can be explained by the comparatively simple projects that were used in the study. That is the reason why the participants were mostly familiar with the domain notation and did not need a glossary. Hence this should not be seen as a general advice to leave it out. The reason for the small number of significant results in terms of the roles UI designer, software architect and tester in comparison to the developer is that there were only two subjects playing this role. In contrast there were four participants – two students and two experienced developers – with the developer role. Statistical significance is problematic with small numbers like this. We chose to report it anyway, as an indication of how eye tracking can be analyzed statistically.

Subsequently these relevance ratings were compared to the corresponding reading intensities. To get these values, the measured reading times were divided by the length of the section. Afterwards they were rescaled on values from 1 (high reading intensity) to 4 (low reading intensity). Looking at the relevance ratings as well as the reading intensity, discrepancy could be noticed at some parts and roles.

Especially conspicuous were differences including a relatively high relevance rating, but a low reading intensity. These occurred at the sections "use cases", "domain descriptions", "incremental work" and the section "non-functional requirements".

Looking closer at the subsections "domain descriptions" and "incremental work", it could be noticed though that these are only 2 cm to 4.5 cm long including the headline. In this range the reading intensity is thus less meaningful than in longer sections.

Regarding the use cases a similar argumentation could be found because these were presented as tables including more white space than usual text which leads to lower reading intensity. Furthermore considering the heat maps of this section as well to verify this assumption, it could be found that the participants tended to read only the headline and the described steps of the use case instead of the whole table including e.g. preconditions and system boundary. Thus it also had an effect on the low reading intensity. The only difference that could not be explained is the one including non-functional requirements. Participants having the software architect role rated these parts as important, but did not read them intensely. Reasons for this trend could be that non-functional requirements in general are important to the document user, but the given part did not satisfy their information needs.

After looking at the information needs of the several roles, it was investigated if there were any differences between the roles (RQ$_2$) that would serve as a reason for defining separated view-based requirements for each of them. Due to the small sample size there were significant differences only considering the sections interfaces and adjacent systems, incremental work and mock ups.

6.4   Replicating an Earlier Study

Comparing these results with those of the IESE studies [13] using the TORE framework, it could be detected both complying findings and divergent values. Not all of the

Table 2. Comparison of our results with similar studies [13]

TORE artifact types	SWP artifact types	TORE relevance ratings				Relevance ratings of this study	
		A$_S$	A$_E$	U$_E$	U$_T$	Software architect	UI designer
Descriptions of Stakeholders	Users	2,46	2	1	1,78	2,75	1,75
Descriptions of Stakeholder Goals	Purpose of the project	2,31	1	2	1,5	1	1,5
Domain Data	Domain description	2,69	1,5	2	2,78	2	2
Descriptions of NFRs	Non-functional Requirements	1,58	1,5	2	-	1,75	1,875
Descriptions of Technical Constraints	Technical Requirements	1,77	1	2,5	-	2,25	2,75
very important		important		rather unimportant		unimportant	

A$_S$: Architects from students sample, A$_E$: Architects from eye tracking study,
U$_E$: Usability experts from eye tracking study,
U$_T$: Usability experts from Tutorial study

data could be compared due to different templates. The matching parts are shown in Table 2 comprising the average relevance ratings of Gross et al. in the left columns and our results on the right side. The relevance ratings were mapped to numbers from very important (1) to unimportant (4).

The largest differences could be found regarding the sections "users" and "technical requirements". The reason for this gap could be that these sections were relatively short in the specifications used in this study and therefore contain less information which may lead to the lower ratings. Moreover, small differences occurring between all of the values are probably due to an unavoidable disparity of the environment.

7 Discussion: Plans Versus Situated Action

In this section, we discuss the implications and validity of our results, and discuss whether eye tracking turned out to be an appropriate technique to study the topic of reading a specification. We refer to observations, events, and unforeseen changes in our plans. Referring to Suchman's seminal book on "plans and situated action" [17], a systematic study in requirements engineering that uses a rather novel technique like eye tracking will need to combine both systematic planning, flexible reaction to unexpected situations, and valid analysis techniques.

7.1 Expectations Confirmed by the Study

A first set of findings confirmed our expectations: There was a correlation between reading times and relevance ratings. According to that sections that are considered more relevant are also read more intensely. This confirms the previously defined hypotheses and it is actually no surprise since readers tend to skim over paragraphs considered unimportant to them which leads to a low reading intensity of course.

Furthermore it could be confirmed that introductive sections like the "purpose of the project" and "needs and priorities of the customer", as well as use cases were read with the highest reading intensity by far. This trend was expected due to the high information density of these parts containing general information which should be relevant for all roles. In addition, results like UI designers relying strongly on mockups or software architects not being interested in those were also expected because they can be basically derived from their task descriptions.

7.2 Unexpected Findings

Some findings were counter-intuitive, did not comply with the study by Gross et al. [13], or our documented initial expectations: We did not expect subjects to rate sections as important, but barely read them: the software architects did that regarding the section of non-functional requirements, and further examples reported in Sect. 6.2.

We were surprised that it seemed to have no effect whether specifications are read on paper or on screen. One may think that such different ways of presenting artifacts would have an effect on aspects like reading time or the ability of reproduction.

Comparing our results with the findings of the IESE studies [9] some deviations could be found as already described above. These could mostly be attributed to the shortness of these sections in the used specifications though. This probably led to lower relevance ratings due to a smaller amount of presented information. In addition, the environment differed from the one used by Gross et al. resulting in unavoidable influences as well.

7.3   Reflection on Eye Tracking: Lessons Learned

Regarding reflections on the adequacy of eye tracking a number of observations and events caused us to reflect on the advantages and challenges associated with eye tracking in requirements engineering research:

General observations: We consider eye tracking one of several adequate methods for this type of studies in requirements engineering: eye tracking enables researchers to address subconscious aspects that could not be addressed explicitly. Where this is important, eye tracking has a clear advantage. For example, asking subjects what part of a UML diagram they were looking at for how long cannot be answered; according to Schoen [18], practitioners in action cannot remember exactly what they do. Schoen proposes to create a breakdown, interrupting the activity a practitioner is involved in; in this case, however, reading the specification would be interrupted and affected. The phenomenon under study should not be modified through the observational method.

However, eye tracking causes a lot of effort for preparing the experiment, analyzing the eye tracking glasses data and exporting its fixation times subsequently. Furthermore, we do not recommend eye tracking as a single research method due to the problem of missing intentions behind the gaze date. As described in Sect. 3, eye tracking does not provide any reasons for the detected eye movement. On the other hand, eye tracking offers quantitative gaze data that allows you to judge reading times or the received attention of an object. Particularly it cannot be replaced by any other method because none of them provide such possibilities. In addition, techniques like thinking aloud cause a greater distraction to the participants because they need to reflect their actions on top of the actual study task. They do not allow subjects to forget about the study situation. This leads to the conclusion that eye tracking is worth the effort due to the unique results you can get with it.

More specific lessons learned based on our experiences made in this study include:

We recommend larger sample sizes to get more significant results and consolidate the findings. The 20-min time limit for the reading part urged subjects to choose most important parts instead of reading the whole specification in detail. Nevertheless, we recommend allowing more time for the subjects, especially for the role of the developer due to the fact that they were quite stressed while performing their tasks. On the other hand, restricting time seemed to be a good way to perform eye tracking and conscious judgment via questionnaires together and compare the results afterwards. In general, when conducting eye tracking experiments it should be scheduled enough time for technical setup, which is easily underestimated.

Lessons from replication: we consent with the lessons learned given by Fraunhofer IESE [13] recommending to give real tasks to the subjects instead of imagining situations, taking specifications that the participants are not familiar with and choosing questionnaires as a way to observe relevance ratings.

7.4 Threats to Validity

According to Wohlin et al. [19] we distinguish four types of threats:

Conclusion validity was guaranteed by judging on a 5 % significance level and assuring that all necessary preconditions for significance tests are given. Moreover, to assure a high level of internal validity unintentional influencing factors on the results were either excluded or are the same for the compared groups of data. Examples are the different abilities of the subjects to answer questions to the specification's content in the questionnaire due to different roles. We used at least two subjects for each role to mitigate this threat. Influences occurring as a results of the order of the used eye tracker or presentation medium are mitigated in the same way. Besides, learning effects during the study were irrelevant since they applied to all measurements alike. Furthermore, possible effects due to different length of the specification were considered by using the blocking principle. The reading speed which could have been biased by the specification's length was analyzed for both documents separately. However, influences may occur based on the order of letting the participants read the specification and answer the questionnaire. That is why we recommend replicating the study using these methods unconnected and compare the results afterwards.

Construct validity was achieved by using requirements specifications of real software projects and giving real tasks to the subjects. Thus, they did not have to imagine fictitious scenarios.

External validity: The results cannot be generalized readily due to the small number of subjects. However, interesting qualitative observations can be made: Comparing results of students to those of experienced developers showed no major or significant differences; in our study, they read in a similar way. There are numerous factors influencing the process, including the structure of the template. The closer a study gets to a full-scale real-world situation, the more potential influence factors appear. Nevertheless, observations should be reported for later replication. Controlling them all is infeasible in a first study. Our results showed similar findings to the effects observed by Gross et al. [13], on longer specifications.

8 Conclusions

Eye tracking is increasingly used in software engineering. We chose Gross et al. [3] as a reference for our study. Although a full replication was not possible (we did not have their specification), we were able to repeat some of their findings. Regarding sections "users" and "technical requirements", our findings diverged from theirs. We consider this partial overlap a promising sign: Results were similar, but not identical, which is probably due to some unavoidable differences in the environment. Eye tracking seems to be a valid technique able to deliver reproducible results.

Some measures of eye tracking were objective, while others were addressed via questionnaires. Questionnaires and objective measures complement each other, since the trace of the eyes cannot tell the intentions and priorities of subjects. It was interesting to see a number of deviations between questionnaire responses and eye tracking data, such as the gap between the relevance ratings and reading intensities of the software architects concerning the section of non-functional requirements.

For improving the efficiency of using specifications based on eye tracking, it is necessary to get more significant results. This means that the study needs to be replicated with larger samples. Afterwards, the findings can be used to provide a tool in which only the relevant parts of a specification are shown to the reader role. Resources and time could be saved without compromising specification quality.

References

1. Rupp, C.: Requirements-Engineering und -Management: professionelle, iterative Anforderungsanalyse für die Praxis. Hanser, Munich (2004)
2. Robertson, S., Robertson, J.: Mastering the Requirements Process. Addison-Wesley, Boston (1999)
3. Gross, A., Dörr, J.: What do software architects expect from requirements specifications. In: First IEEE International Workshop on the Twin Peaks of Requirements and Architecture (TwinPeaks), Chicago, Illinois, USA (2012)
4. Fricker, S.: Requirements value chains: stakeholder management and requirements engineering in software ecosystems. In: Wieringa, R., Persson, A. (eds.) REFSQ 2010. LNCS, vol. 6182, pp. 60–66. Springer, Heidelberg (2010)
5. Schneider, K., Stapel, K., Knauss, E.: Beyond documents: visualizing informal communication. In: Proceedings of Third International Workshop on Requirements Engineering Visualization (REV 2008), Barcelona, Spain (2008)
6. Stapel, K., Schneider, K.: Managing knowledge on communication and information flow in global software projects. Expert Systems - Special Issue on Knowledge Engineering in Global Software Development (2012)
7. Fricker, S., Schneider, K., Fotrousi, F., Thuemmler, C.: Workshop videos for requirements communication. Requirements Engineering Journal, Springer, pp. 1–32 (2015)
8. Liskin, O.: How artifacts support and impede requirements communication. In: Fricker, S.A., Schneider, K. (eds.) REFSQ 2015. LNCS, vol. 9013, pp. 132–147. Springer, Heidelberg (2015)
9. Gross, A.: Anforderungen an die Anforderungsspezifikation aus Sicht von Architekten und Usability Experten. Softwaretechnik-Trends **32**(4), 7–8 (2012)
10. Adam, S., Riegel, N., Doerr, J.: TORE - a framework for systematic requirements development in information systems. Requirements Eng. Mag. (2014). Online Journal, No. 4
11. Basili, V.R., Caldiera, G., Rombach, H.D.: The goal question metric approach. In: Encyclopedia of Software Engineering, pp. 646–661. Wiley, Hoboken (1994)
12. van Solingen, R., Berghout, E.: The Goal/Question/Metric Method: a Practical Guide for Quality Improvement of Software Development. McGraw-Hill Publishing Company, New York (1999)
13. Gross, A., Dörr, J.: What you need is what you get! The vision of view-based requirements specifications. In: 20th IEEE International Requirements Engineering Conference, Chicago, Illinois, USA (2012)

14. Gross, A., Hess, S.: UX meets RE: Hohe User Experience durch bedarfsgerechte Anforderungsspezifikation. In: Usability Professionals 2011 - Tagungsband, German UPA e.V., pp. 24–29 (2011)
15. Dillon, A.: Reading from paper versus screens: a critical review of the empirical literature. Ergonomics **35**(10), 1297–1326 (1992)
16. Brill, O., Schneider, K., Knauss, E.: Videos vs. use cases: can videos capture more requirements under time pressure? In: Wieringa, R., Persson, A. (eds.) REFSQ 2010. LNCS, vol. 6182, pp. 30–44. Springer, Heidelberg (2010)
17. Suchman, L.A.: Plans and Situated Actions: the Problem of Human-Machine Communication. Cambridge University Press, Cambridge (1987)
18. Schön, D.A.: The Reflective Practitioner: How Professionals Think in Action. Basic Books, New York (1983)
19. Wohlin, C., Runeson, P., Höst, M., Ohlsson, M., Regnell, B., Wesslén, A.: Experimentation in Software Engineering: An Introduction. Kluwer Academic Publishers, London (2000)

Author Index

Printed in the United States
By Bookmasters